MARKET ABUSE REGULATION

MARKET ABUSE REGULATION

SECOND EDITION

Edward J Swan and John Virgo

OXFORD

UNIVERSITY PRESS

OXFORD

UNIVERSITY PRESS

Great Clarendon Street, Oxford ox2 6dp

Oxford University Press is a department of the University of Oxford.
It furthers the University's objective of excellence in research, scholarship,
and education by publishing worldwide in

Oxford New York

Auckland Cape Town Dar es Salaam Hong Kong Karachi
Kuala Lumpur Madrid Melbourne Mexico City Nairobi
New Delhi Shanghai Taipei Toronto

With offices in

Argentina Austria Brazil Chile Czech Republic France Greece
Guatemala Hungary Italy Japan Poland Portugal Singapore
South Korea Switzerland Thailand Turkey Ukraine Vietnam

Oxford is a registered trade mark of Oxford University Press
in the UK and in certain other countries

Published in the United States
by Oxford University Press Inc., New York

First published 2010

British Library Cataloguing in Publication Data
Data available

Library of Congress Cataloging in Publication Data
Data available

Typeset by Glyph International, Bangalore, India
Printed in Great Britain
on acid-free paper by
Antony Rowe, Chippenham, Wiltshire

ISBN 978-0-19-9532834

1 3 5 7 9 10 8 6 4 2

Ned Swan dedicates this edition to his wife Carole and his daughters Molly and Mary.

John Virgo dedicates this edition to his children Kate, James, Hope, Samuel and Mollie.

PREFACE

When the first edition of *Market Abuse Regulation* was published in early 2006, I felt confident that it was on the 'cutting edge' of explication of the subject. It dealt not only with the original market abuse regime of the Financial Services and Markets Act 2000 (FSMA), but also dealt with the proposed changes brought by the EU Market Abuse Directive.

However, market abuse regulation has turned out to be subject to considerable debate as a result of its interpretation by the Financial Services Authority (FSA) and the Financial Services and Markets Tribunal ('the Tribunal'). In some key cases, the Tribunal has disagreed significantly with the FSA about how the market abuse regime should be applied. As a result, the standard of proof and the scope for application of market abuse regime has changed significantly from what the FSA may have originally hoped.

Added to that has been the difficulty of controlling market misconduct (particularly insider dealing) in the London market. Despite the 'paper trail' that is created by most securities transactions, statistics reveal unusual levels of 'preannouncement' trading in something between 20 and 30 per cent of instances where shares are likely to be affected by important future announcements.

This level of apparent market misconduct has stimulated the FSA to bring administrative enforcement actions and criminal prosecutions against those alleged to have engaged in market misconduct. As a result, the market abuse regime along with other FSA rules (such as, notably, the Principles for Business) have become more important parts of the FSA's regulatory toolkit. This is likely to continue for the foreseeable future. Whether or not the FSA's regulatory remit is modified in the future, these tools will continue to play an important role in helping to preserve market confidence. As pointed out in the latter part of this edition, the EU is only one jurisdiction to employ statutes and regulations to prevent and punish market misconduct. The US is, of course, an important jurisdiction to pay attention to whenever one is dealing in essentially international markets.

As a result of all this, it was important to bring out a second edition to reflect the many changes in this area. Unfortunately, because I work in the financial services sector on a daily basis, the recent financial crisis has made it extremely difficult for me to find the time to update the book. Fortunately, Oxford University Press was kind enough to suggest John Virgo as a distinguished co-author.

John is the first person who deserves thanks for helping to complete the second edition. He worked extremely hard over a number of months to update chapters, applying his knowledge, experience and writing skills to making the book more complete and more relevant. Without John, this edition would not have been finished.

Another person who was critical to completing the second edition is Michael Blair, QC, the distinguished former General Counsel of the FSA and its predecessor, an author of *Financial Services Law* (now out in second edition, co-authored with George Walker), and a very distinguished senior member of the Bar with long experience in the financial services sector. Michael was kind enough to review the manuscript at various stages and to offer praise when he thought it was deserved, and constructive criticism where things needed to be improved.

I must also sincerely thank Sir Stephen Oliver, President of the Financial Services and Markets Tribunal, for his kind comments when the first edition was published. His positive remarks about the usefulness of a book that attempted to organize information relating to the market abuse regime was an important factor in persuading me that a new edition was a worthwhile project.

It is also the case that this second edition could not have been completed without the help of three young lawyers: Jean Flannery, Emma Channing, and Meredith Esser. They all did excellent work, and provided badly needed help at critical times.

Finally, much thanks must go the team at Oxford University Press that encouraged, persuaded and cajoled me into finally getting the manuscript finished. It was they who got John Virgo and Michael Blair to provide the assistance and critical thought necessary to complete this project. I sincerely thank Rachel Mullaly, Rebecca Howes, Kate Whetter, Clodagh McAteer, Anna Krzyzanowska and Bethan Cousins.

Ned Swan
London
September 2009

CONTENTS—SUMMARY

CONTENTS

ABOUT THE AUTHORS

Ned Swan is Counsel at Skadden, Arps, Slate, Meagher & Flom (UK) LLP, where he advises on all aspects of financial services law, regulation and litigation. He was previously a partner at two major international law firms and as Visiting Professor at University College London, he originated and taught the LLM course in Regulation of Financial Markets. Dr Swan has practised financial market law and regulation for over 30 years in London, New York and Paris advising the world's leading banks, investment firms, funds, exchanges, clearing houses, energy groups, trading companies, commodity producers, shippers, government regulatory agencies, and international organizations.

John Virgo (Barrister, called 1984) has a predominantly commercial practice with an emphasis on financial product mis-selling claims. John has conducted a number of group mis-selling actions: as lead counsel to some 400 pension mis-selling claimants; in a managed action on behalf of late joiners to Equitable Life and in a 400-strong group action in the Commercial Court on behalf of Equitable Life trapped annuitants. He also acts for the industry and was retained to defend claims for product mis-selling following the collapse of the Bahamian Imperial Consolidated Fund (*Seymour v Ockwell* [2005] PNLR 758). John frequently advises authorized firms and investors on thematic mis-selling liability issues.

John has appeared in a number of judicial review hearings relating to the jurisdiction of the Financial Ombudsman Service (*Bunney v Burns Anderson plc* [2007] 4 All ER 246 and *Brinsons and the Financial Ombudsman Service* [2007] EWHC 2534).

He is co-author of *Financial Advice and Financial Products, Law and Liability* (OUP).

John practises from Guildhall Chambers, Bristol BS1 2HG.

TABLE OF CASES

TABLE OF LEGISLATION

UNITED STATES

TABLE OF EUROPEAN LEGISLATION

TABLE OF FSA AND OTHER RULES

LIST OF ABBREVIATIONS

FSMA	Financial Services and Markets Act 2000
FSA	Financial Services Authority
the Tribunal	Financial Services and Markets Tribunal
SRO	Self-regulatory organization
FS Act	Financial Services Act 1986
CJA	Criminal Justice Act 1993
SIB	Securities and Investments Board
SFA	Securities and Futures Authority
COMC	Code of Market Conduct
MAR	Market Conduct Sourcebook
N2	30 November 2001
COB/COBS	Conduct of Business Sourcebook
RINGA	relevant information not generally available
LME	London Metal Exchange

1

EVOLVING REGULATION

A. Background

(1) Introduction

The UK Government, like most others, has long said that the principal aims of its **1.01** financial services regulation are to preserve the integrity of its financial markets and to protect consumers.[1] The UK Regulator – the Financial Services Authority (FSA) – considers these aims to embrace both 'preserving ... actual stability in the financial system and the reasonable expectation that it will remain stable'.[2] One of the principal ways that this is done is by preventing what is called 'market abuse'. 'Market abuse' can generally be described as improper market behaviour, such as:

- insider trading;
- various techniques of market manipulation, and
- any other behaviour interfering with the fair and efficient operation of financial markets.

---

[1] Financial Services and Markets Act 2000 (the 'Act' or 'the FSMA') Pt I, 'The regulatory objectives', ss 3–6. The four stated objectives of the Act are: market confidence, public awareness, the protection of consumers, and the reduction of financial crime. Also see the FSMA Explanatory Notes ('Act Notes'), Pt I.

[2] FSA, *A new regulator for a new millennium* (January 2000), Ch. 1, para. 2.

1.02 Historically, the UK Government had developed two principal tools for addressing improper market behaviour:

- criminal sanctions for insider dealing and misleading statements and practices;[3]
- supervisory and disciplinary powers exercisable over regulated firms and registered individuals employed by a variety of former self-regulatory organizations (SROs)[4] and, later, similar powers conferred on the FSA in respect of authorized firms and approved persons working within them.[5]

The FSA's powers in this regard might be considered powerful weapons against market abuse. They include the 'Principles for Businesses', which are described as 'the fundamental obligations of all firms under the regulatory system' in the FSA Handbook. These impose such general obligations such as the requirement that 'a firm must conduct its business with integrity'.[6] They apply to all firms regulated by the FSA. If the FSA decides that some firm has violated a Principle it may employ a range of sanctions up to and including the option of putting the firm out of business by withdrawing its authorization.

1.03 The above measures were considered, however, in some respects ineffective and in others incomplete. For example, the failure of a number of high-profile criminal trials exposed weaknesses in the insider trading laws and attempts to criminalize improper market behaviour as fraud were not generally successful.[7] As to this 'gap'

---

[3] Financial Services Act 1986, s 47 (now FSMA, s 397).

[4] A variety of disciplinary powers were exercisable, for example by the Life Assurance and Unit Trust Regulatory Organisation (LAUTRO); the Financial Intermediaries Managers and Brokers Regulatory Association (FIMBRA); the Personal Investment Authority (PIA) – see in particular Chapters 9 and 10 of the PIA Handbook on the intervention and disciplinary powers of that SRO.

[5] See the disciplinary and intervention powers of the FSA in Part IV of the FSMA in relation to approved persons and firms and the further disciplinary measures in Part XIV of the FSMA (superseding similar provisions in the Financial Services Act 1986.

[6] This is the first Principle for Business listed in PRIN, s 2.1 of the FSA *Handbook*. FSA *Handbook*, *High Level Standards, Principles for Businesses*, Reference Code PRIN, 2.1. NOTE: all references in this book to sections of the FSA *Handbook* will be by Reference Code and section number. For example, the section referred to in this footnote will be 'PRIN 2.1'. Where appropriate, the section number will be followed by a 'status icon' letter. These are letters which the FSA uses in its *Handbook* to indicate whether a section is 'R', rules made under the FSMA, s 138; guidance, 'G'; E, which in the FSA *Handbook* Market Code of Conduct (MAR) may be relied on to indicate whether or not conduct is market abuse; 'UK', indicating non-FSA UK legislative material; 'EU' or EU, indicating non-FSA EU legislative material. All references in this book to *Handbook* sections are, unless otherwise noted, references to editions published after 1 July 2005. However, readers should assume that all FSA is subject to continuous revision. For further information see the FSA website and/or contact the FSA.

[7] Notably the failure to sustain convictions against directors and financial advisers for improper conduct in connection with a rights issue in the *Blue Arrow* case (*R v Cohen* [1992] 142 NLJ 1267; see, further, the failure to make criminal allegations stick against Ernest Saunders in relation to suspected wrongdoing in respect of Guinness plc's take-over of Distillers plc (*Saunders v United Kingdom* [1996] 23 EHRR 313.

in protection, Melanie Johnson, economic secretary to the Treasury, commented during parliamentary consideration of the FSMA:

> We protect the financial markets in two ways. First, there are the criminal regimes for market manipulation and insider dealing. These are both serious criminal offences … Secondly, there is the regulatory regime under which various regulatory bodies can take action against regulated persons for market abuse. However, there is a gap in the protections.[8]

The gap was filled by the market abuse prohibitions now found in ss 118–132 of the FSMA and the explanatory regulations found in the FSA's *Code of Market Conduct*[9] contained within the Business Standards section of the FSA's *Handbook of Rules and Guidance*.[10] This book is principally concerned with this new 'civil offence' of market abuse.   **1.04**

(2) The broad scope of the new 'civil offence'

Since the introduction of express market abuse prohibitions in 2001, and during more recent discussions of the adoption and implementation of the EU Market Abuse Directive,[11] a great deal of concern has been expressed by different sections of the financial services industry concerning the exact descriptions of possible market abuse behaviour and problems of ambiguity relating to such descriptions in the MAR or implementing instruments of the Directive. In fact, it is not particularly useful to spend too much time worrying about such things. True, the MAR does provide some detail about what the FSA is likely to regard as market abuse. However, the sanctions specifically defined as being applicable to market abuse are in many respects no less precise than the disciplinary sanctions the FSA has at its disposal to control and punish market misbehaviour mentioned above. It is clear that complaints about the broad nature of these powers will be given short shrift by the UK Courts. In *Fleurose v The Disciplinary Appeal Tribunal of the Securities and Futures Authority Limited*[12] a complaint that charges made against a Senior Cash Arbitrage Trader employed at the time by J P Morgan Securities Ltd in the following terms were unfairly vague so as to prejudice a fair trial were rejected. The charges read: **1.05**

> The Securities and Futures Authority Limited pursuant to Rules 7-60 and 7-61 of SFA's Rules, hereby institutes disciplinary proceedings against Mr. Bertrand Fleurose

---

[8] Standing Committee A, 2 November 1999, HMSO.
[9] Referred to below as the MAR, and/or the 'Code'.
[10] Referred to below as the 'FSA *Handbook*'.
[11] Directive 2003/6/EC of the European Parliament and of the Council of 28 January 2003 on Insider Dealing and Market Manipulation (market abuse) (OJ L96, 12.4.2003) (referred to below as the 'Market Abuse Directive', or simply the 'Directive'.
[12] [2001] EWCA Civ 2015.

on the grounds that: A. He has committed that following acts of misconduct: (1) In breach of Principle 1 of the FSA's Statements of Principle, Mr. Fleurose failed to observe high standards of integrity and fair dealing in his involvement in the trading activities of the Equity Derivatives Group of J P Morgan Securities Limited on 28th November 1997. (2) In breach of Principle 3 of the FSA's Statement of Principle, Mr. Fleurose failed to observe high standards of market conduct in trading for J P Morgan Securities Limited on the London Stock Exchange on 28th November 1997.

There followed 11 pages of a document headed 'Summary of Facts' giving extensive details of the case and evidence relied upon. In relation to a complaint that such broad allegations conflicted with Mr Fleurose's Article 6 Right to a Fair Trial under the European Convention on Human Rights, the Court held:

> So far as vagueness is concerned, [Counsel for Mr Fleurose] did not and could not seek to suggest that M Fleurose did not know of what he was accused. Having received the document referred to in paragraph 8 of the judgment as the Summary of Facts, he both knew what were the specific acts alleged and what was the state of mind alleged. M Fleurose throughout the disciplinary hearing accepted that those acts coupled with that state of mind amounted to the disciplinary offence alleged. His defence was that he did not have the relevant state of mind. Like the Judge we consider that the admitted lack of specificity in the general principles, quoted in paragraph 18 of the judgment below, did not, in those circumstances, help M Fleurose to make out a case that the hearing had been unfair.[13]

1.06 Therefore, rather than being too concerned about the exact boundaries of specific descriptions of market abuse, it is far healthier for a financial market participant, and its advisers, to be constantly aware of the UK's general regulatory position that market activity must not jeopardize the fair and efficient operation of the UK financial markets. As the FSA continually emphasizes in its press releases:

> The FSA aims to promote efficient, orderly and fair markets, help retail consumers achieve a fair deal, and improve its business capability and effectiveness.[14]

1.07 How the 'civil offence' of market abuse came to be a distinct tool in the UK's regulatory armoury is discussed in the following sections.

B. The Evolution of Market Abuse Regulation

1.08 The regulation of market abuse is an increasingly complex and controversial issue in the world of financial trading. It is increasingly complex because of the proliferation of regulations in different jurisdictions that overlap in the international market. It is increasingly controversial because traders are afraid that overlapping market abuse regulations will harm market liquidity and trading profitability.

---

[13] *Ibid.*, para[16].
[14] FSA, 'Make sure contracts terms are fair, FSA tells firms', FSA *Press Release*, 19 May 2005.

In the US, 'market manipulation' and 'insider dealing' have long been subject to **1.09** both regulatory and criminal penalties. In some circles, this has been perceived as an effective method of giving US regulators the flexibility they need to deal quickly with developing market changes and/or disruptions.

Prior to the advent of the 'civil offence' of market abuse in the FSMA, the UK did **1.10** not have a specific scheme to control 'market abuse'. Aside from the criminal and regulatory sanctions mentioned above, the main protection for investors was to remember the maxim *caveat emptor*, or 'let the buyer beware'. As noted above, there were good reasons to beware. From a criminal perspective, for example, even outright fraud was extremely difficult to prove in the context of investment transactions.

In fact, it was the *laissez-faire* 'self-regulation' climate of the City of London (where **1.11** the traditionally guarantee of integrity was 'my word is my bond')[15] that kicked off the original author's long career in financial services law. As a young lawyer, struggling to build his own practice in New York in the late 1970s and early 1980s, the original author had cases involving claims of UK financial market participants against US or UK companies referred to him because redress could not be effectively sought in the UK, and no major US firm would risk taking such untried claims on a speculative basis. Naively, the author did, and established that foreign claimants could bring such litigation in the US.

Since that time, the financial services business has grown dramatically. The London **1.12** Stock Exchange's so-called 'Big Bang' of 1986 abolished the traditional regime of 'single capacity dealings', that is, where an investor had to seek advice from a 'stockbroker' who acted as intermediary between the investor and a 'stockjobber' or retailer of shares. This offered some measure of investor protection. Once 'dual capacity dealing' became the norm, firms became simultaneously brokers and dealers. The potential for conflicts of interest became acute and contributed to the implementation of the UK's Financial Services Act 1986 ('FS Act') as a necessary measure to provide protection for investors and deter abuses of the market.

The UK Government became increasingly persuaded that more formal protec- **1.13** tion of UK financial markets from 'abuse' would be a key factor in assuring their success. This climate was responsible for the creation of two specific categories of market conduct criminal offences. First, the Companies Act 1980 made insider

---

[15] Oddly enough, that phrase originally signalled a trader's willingness to flout English law. In the 18th and 19th centuries, most transactions in which the promissor agreed to deliver certain assets to the buyer in the future were forbidden by statute and unenforceable under English law. Nevertheless, City traders entered into such illegal contracts all the time. Therefore the only hope that the agreement would be kept was that the promissor intended to keep his word. No enforcement remedy was available at law.

from the Companies
Act 1985
to the Criminal
Justice Act
1993.

dealing a criminal offence for the first time. This made it a criminal offence for the possessor of non-public information which affected the price of *securities* (known as 'inside information') to deal in those securities, to encourage others to do so, or to disclose the information other than in the proper performance of his employment, office or profession. Following revisions to the Companies Act in 1985, the offence was replaced by the Companies Securities (Insider Dealing) Act 1985. In 1993 an EU Directive on Insider Dealing led to the Criminal Justice Act 1993 (CJA) and the insider dealing offences now found in Part V.

1.14   Secondly, s 47 of the FS Act made it a criminal offence for any person to knowingly make a false or misleading statement or to dishonestly conceal material facts in connection with the purchase or sale of an investment.[16]

1.15   Both the above provisions impose severe penalties (fines or imprisonment of up to seven years) but their effectiveness in regulating financial markets is limited in important ways. First, the application of the insider dealing prohibition of the CJA is limited to "price-affected securities", which has been a difficult concept to define. Second, the bringing of a criminal prosecution is a cumbersome process. It takes time, and obtaining a conviction for an offence requires proof of the *mens rea* constituting the offence established *beyond reasonable doubt*, with the defendant entitled to *legal aid* under certain circumstances. It is easy to see that with the high standards required in criminal prosecutions, criminal penalties cannot be used as flexible or efficient regulatory tools.[17]

1.16   The regulatory authorities including the Securities and Investments Board (SIB), the Securities and Futures Authority (SFA), and their successor, the FSA, relied on conduct constituting insider dealing as evidencing a lack of fitness and propriety by the perpetrator to operate in the financial services sector. This could lead to a direction disqualifying an individual from employment in investment business,[18] but such powers did not permit the quick action needed to respond to market disruptions. Also, in responding to an incident of insider dealing the FSA could seek to impose punishment for such behaviour on the basis that the registered person in question was guilty of violating more general FS Act principles such as:

- Principle 1: failure to observe high standards of integrity and fair dealing;
- Principle 2: failure to act with due skill, care and diligence;

---

[16]   This is now found in FSMA, s 397.

[17]   Criminal Justice Act 1993, s 61(2).

[18]   Financial Services Act 1986, s 59; see further: Injunction against Mr Sahib Saini, FSA Press Release, 17 March 1999, FSA/PN/027/1999; Disciplinary Action against Richard Philip King, SFA Board Notice 589, 11 June 2001. King pleaded guilty to three charges of insider dealing under Criminal Justice Act 1993, s 52.

- Principle 3: failure to observe high standards of market conduct, and
- Principle 6: conflict of interest.[19]

However, as Sir Howard Davies, then Chairman of the FSA, the UK's main finan- **1.17**
cial services regulator, reflected in 1998:[20]

> I think we have to recognise, sadly, that the City's image is not all it might be. There
> have been too many 'accidents' for that to be so… Putting all these together might
> suggest that the City was constantly riven with scandal. And of course those who
> watch these affairs closely will be aware that in this lengthy list of scandals, relatively
> few of the participants have been brought to book. There have been some prosecu-
> tions, certainly … But the record in heavily contested serious fraud trials has, frankly,
> not been good. And remarkably few prosecutions have been brought for insider trad-
> ing. There is a common perception, which is hard to dismiss, that City crime is
> simply not punished on the same basis as other forms of theft.

By that time it was recognized that the financial markets were changing and **1.18**
expanding too rapidly for financial services regulation under the FS Act to be able
to keep up. As Howard Davies said in another speech that year:

> One of the problems we have experienced with the Financial Services Act of 1986 is
> that it is not as adaptable to the new markets and products as we, or financial institu-
> tions themselves, would like it to be.

Consequently, in May 1997, the Government announced proposals to reform the **1.19**
financial services regulatory system in the UK. In July 1998, the Treasury published a paper explaining the policy of the proposed financial services reforms in
detail and including a draft of a new Financial Services and Markets Bill[21] ('the
Bill'). The Bill proposed to change UK financial services regulation by designating
the FSA as the single regulator for authorization, supervision and enforcement in
financial services business[22] and giving the FSA a range of new powers to combat
market misconduct including:

- investigation powers;
- the power to bring criminal proceedings in cases of insider dealing or with
  respect to misleading statements and practices;
- the power to impose civil fines in cases of market abuse, and
- the power to seek restitution orders in cases of market misconduct.[23]

---

[19] SFA disciplines William Dootson and Paul Sharples for dealing on the basis of inside information: 22 April 1999, SFA Board Notice 514.
[20] Securities Institute Ethics Committee: 3rd Annual Lecture, 2 November 1998, 'Are Words
Still Bonds: How Straight is the City?'
[21] HM Treasury, Financial Services and Markets Bill: *A Consultation Document*, July 1998.
[22] FSA, Financial Services and Markets Act, Explanatory Notes.
[23] FSA, *Consultation Paper 17, Financial services regulation: Enforcing the new regime*, December
1998, s 115.

1.20   With respect to that Bill, Sir Howard Davies said:

> It is clearly intended to create a one-stop arrangement for regulation and to provide both flexibility and accountability.[24]

1.21   In the Bill, the Government made it clear that its principal regulatory objective was to maintain market confidence in the financial system of the UK, which included the financial markets and exchanges, regulated activities, and any other activities connected with financial markets and exchanges.[25] The other objectives were promoting public understanding of the financial system, protection of consumers and the reduction of financial crime. As the Treasury has stated in a memorandum to the Joint Committee on Financial Services and Markets:

> The UK financial services industry is highly successful and vitally important to the UK economy. It accounts for 7% of the GDP and employs over one million people.[26]

1.22   Early on in consideration of the Bill, Davies made it clear that having the flexibility to deal with changing markets was an important element in the new Bill:

> Stephen Byers has explained the Government's aim in reforming the regulatory system. He has explained that the new legislation is designed to be flexible enough to cope with changing financial markets in the future. Indeed, when he first announced the reform, the Chancellor of the Exchequer said that he planned to devise a regulatory system for the 21st century … But flexibility means a greater degree of freedom for the Regulator to make rules, from time to time, and change them. And that puts a heavy burden of responsibility on those responsible for the details of regulation. So we decided that it was important for the FSA to publish, alongside the new draft Bill, a paper which explained how, in current circumstances, we would use the freedom we would be given, were the Bill to pass its present form. Of course, this cannot prejudge the ways in which we might change the regulation in the future.[27]

1.23   As Davies said in the same speech:

> … [T]hat points to the need to regulate financial markets in a way which attempts to raise standards within firms themselves, rather than simply imposing them through inflexible rules from the outside.[28]

---

[24] Howard Davies, Chairman, Financial Services Authority, Financial Services and Markets Bill Conference, Grosvenor House Hotel, 24 September 1998.

[25] Financial Services and Markets Bill 1999 [HC Bill 1, Session 1999–2000], Part I, s 3.

[26] Joint Committee, Second Report, Minutes of Evidence taking before the Joint Committee on Financial Services and Markets, Wednesday 19 May 1999, p. 2, para. 4.

[27] Howard Davies, speech, *Financial Services and Markets Bill Conference*, Grosvenor House Hotel, 24 September 1998, p. 1.

[28] *Ibid.*, p. 8.

Clearly, the messages which both the FSMA and the FSA are trying to get over to **1.24** the industry are that:

- confidence in financial markets is critical to the economy of the UK;
- those markets offer significant opportunities to profit and significant risks, both to individuals and to the UK economy;
- participating in those markets is a privilege, not a right;
- to earn that privilege, a participant must be willing to assume, in co-operation with other participants, certain obligations, and
- the principal obligation is for market participants to conduct their affairs so as not to compromise the fair and efficient operation of the market, or to unfairly damage the interest of the investors.[29]

Effective enforcement of this key obligation requires a regulatory system which the **1.25** Government, the regulators and market users must recognize requires enough flexibility to deal with unforeseen future events which prevents regulatory standards from being defined, in advance, with complete precision. In late 2001, the UK thus implemented new penalties for market abuse in the FSMA. Their adoption had two important general consequences. First, these penalties for market abuse apply to all regulated markets and to most trading 'related' to regulated markets. Second, they were thought to provide the UK with a new flexibility in regulating its financial markets nearly equivalent to that enjoyed by US regulators.

The FSA has not had a long history of actively enforcing the UK market abuse **1.26** regime. However, as shown in Chapter 14 below, it has become increasingly active in imposing fines for certain kinds of market abuse.

C. Implementation of the EU Directive

Another key block in the structure of UK market abuse regulation is the adoption **1.27** and implementation in the UK of the new EU Market Abuse and Insider Trading Directive. The Market Abuse Directive was passed by the European Parliament by a substantial majority on 14 March 2002.[30] The European ministers approved a 'compromise text' on 7 May 2002. The Directive was formally made a Directive of the European Parliament and Council on 28 January 2003 and entered into force in April 2003.[31] In theory, the implementation date for the Directive to be written into the national law of Member States was 12 October 2004.[32] In fact,

---

[29] MAR 1.2.3(5) (revoked 30 June 2005). References to the MAR, cited in this way, are to the pre-1 July 2005 Code.
[30] EUROPARL Daily Notebook: 14.03.2002, p. 5.
[31] Implementing Directive, 2003/124.
[32] Directive, Art. 18.

the effective date for UK regulations implementing the Market Abuse Directive was 1 July 2005. In truth, this apparent delay should be set against the backdrop of a tough regime the UK was already operating which required minor adaptations to bring it into line with the detailed requirements of the Directive.

1.28   Technical implementation of the Directive was assisted by measures decided by the European Commission, with the aid of the European Securities Commission (made up of Member State Representatives) with consideration of technical advice from CESR[33] (made up of national authorities). The Directive required each Member State to nominate one regulatory body to deal with market abuse and insider dealing.[34] In the UK, that body (or 'Authority' as it is often referred to in legislation or regulations) is the FSA. For purposes of the EC Directive, market abuse may be described as:

> Behaviour causing investors to be unreasonably disadvantaged by others through insider dealing or market manipulation.[35]

1.29   There are a number of similarities and differences between the UK market abuse regime introduced after 30 November 2001[36] and the Directive, which are discussed in more detail in the following chapters. However, the principal differences are threefold. First, in the UK regime, the standard against which market behaviour was originally based on an overarching 'regular user' test. The Directive does not replicate this approach and the 'regular user test' is now the subject of 'sunset provisions' as discussed in Chapter 3.[37] Second, the number of 'safe harbours' is significantly fewer. At present, there are only two definite safe harbours found in the Directive. One relates to share buy-backs and the second relates to price stabilization. These elements of the Directive are discussed more fully below. Third, the pre-Directive definition of market abuse included conduct which a regular user of the market would, or would be likely to, regard as behaviour which would, or would be likely to, distort the market in investments of the kind in question.[38] In essence, the pre-Directive regime dealt with three types of behaviour: insider dealing, market manipulation, and market distortion. The post-Directive regime sees market distortion, judged by the regular user of the market, as now subject to the sunset provisions discussed in Chapter 3.[39]

---

[33] Now the European Securities Authority ('ESA'); formerly the Committee of European Securities Regulators.

[34] Directive, Recital 36.

[35] Directive Proposal, pp. 2–3.

[36] The introduction date, frequently referred to as 'N2'.

[37] See paragraph 3.11.

[38] See s118(2)(c) as originally enacted and further the discussion in Chapter 3 at paragraphs 3.2 to 3.11.

[39] See paragraph 3.11.

The international control of market abuse became a particularly urgent issue for **1.30** the EU. It required adoption of common regulatory provisions by all EU Member States and cooperation between those states to prevent market abuse from being initiated in one state and impacting on others.

The Directive required adoption of regulations to control market abuse that impose **1.31** both negative and positive duties on both Member States and those involved in the financial markets. At the national level, the Directive required Member States to implement the following basic protections against market abuse:

- a requirement that any professional arranging transactions who has any reasonable suspicion that a transaction might constitute market abuse, notify the regulatory authority without delay;[40]
- regulations requiring those producing or distributing research to present it fairly and disclose any conflicts of interest;
- a requirement that issues of financial instruments inform the public of inside information as soon as possible,[41] and
- a requirement that management of issuers (and any persons closely associated with them) disclose their dealing in the issuer's shares or other financial instruments linked to the shares.[42]

On individual financial market participants, the Directive also required Member **1.32** States to impose both negative and positive duties. On the negative side, traders must be required to avoid conduct that would constitute insider dealing or market abuse. On the positive side they must be required to take steps to make the financial markets more transparent, such as:

- reporting suspicious transactions;
- maintaining lists of insiders;
- disclosing inside information, and
- disclosing insider trades in an issuer's financial instruments.

An important element of this Directive is that its provisions apply to both finan- **1.33** cial and commodity derivatives, generally. The UK Government recognized that the implementation of the Directive in the UK required substantial changes to the UK's market abuse regime. A full review and implementation of those changes was accordingly scheduled for late 2004 and early 2005.[43] To effect the implementation of the Directive in the UK (which was supposed to have been completed by 12 October 2004), the Treasury and the FSA issued a Joint Consultation Paper on

---

[40] Directive, Art. 6.9.
[41] Directive, Arts. 6.1 and 6.2.
[42] Directive, Art. 6.3.
[43] HM Treasury/FSA, *UK Implementation of the EU Market Abuse Directive (Directive 2003/6/EC), A consultation document*, June 2004 ('Joint Consultation Paper').

18 June 2004 proposing changes to UK legislation and the FSA Handbook necessary meet the requirements of the Directive. The FSA requested responses to the Consultation by 10 September 2004. They finalized the new provisions at the end of March 2005 and gave the industry three months to adjust. Despite the 12 October deadline, the UK market abuse regime implementing the Directive was not finally implemented until 1 July 2005.[44]

D. International Complications

1.34   All the above creates a complicated situation for those operating in international markets. Market participants cannot simply review UK market abuse regulation and take that as their sole guide to proper behaviour in the world's financial markets. True, the UK is an important market for international trading. But the US is also an important jurisdiction which gives its financial services regulation a very long reach. Regulations in other European jurisdictions introduced in consequence of the Directive will now both overlap, and be somewhat different from, both the previous UK and US regulations.

1.35   The impact of the overlapping nature of these different regulatory schemes needs to be considered by anyone operating in international markets. The markets affected are not discrete national venues for the purchase and sale of financial products. All important financial and commodity markets operate internationally in developing sources of supply, in creating products for sale, and in finding customers. In our electronic age, even if a particular market participant is not physically present in a particular market location his activities can have a significant impact. Market abuse regulation seeks to control not only presence but effect as well. Consequently, the developing market abuse regulations apply to traders who are located far beyond the borders of the government implementing the regulatory schemes.

1.36   Although this book will concentrate on UK regulation, it cannot ignore important international schemes that traders need to keep in mind. Therefore, some attempt will be made to outline the key issues which may make certain market abuse vulnerable to European and US regulatory action or private litigation in key jurisdictions, particularly in the US which, after all, boasts the world's largest economy. The aim of this is to make the consequences of trading in important international markets, and the risks of being charged with 'market abuse' a little less uncertain.

---

[44] FSA, *Market Watch*, Issue No. 10, July 2004, p. 3.

E. Other Uncertainties

In the UK, there are other important levels of uncertainty. The original UK mar- **1.37**
ket abuse provisions of the Act were themselves a relatively new concept when first
introduced and did not lead to an extensive record of enforcement. Now even that
early sketchy record is compounded by the introduction (on 1 July 2005) of newer
provisions and statutory amendments implementing the Market Abuse Directive.
Therefore, there is not yet available a long-established body of precedents to
inform traders about how they are expected to behave and where their behaviour
might cross the line into constituting market abuse.

F. The Approach of the Book

The complexities and uncertainties outlined above create a difficult situation for **1.38**
anyone trying to comment on market abuse at the moment. Nevertheless, this
book will try to overcome those difficulties with the following approach.

(1) UK market abuse regime

First, the UK provisions against market abuse will be the principal focus of this **1.39**
book. This will discuss not only the UK market abuse provisions which have been
in operation since N2, but also the changes to that regulatory scheme which were
brought about by the implementation of the Directive. Subject to the caveat in
paragraph 1.37 above, the fact that the UK has had a formal market abuse regime
in operation for several years will assist in describing the reach and impact of UK
regulation with some greater certainty than might otherwise be possible.

(2) The move to principles-based enforcement

Second, the reasons for, and the impact of, the FSA's announced move of its **1.40**
enforcement philosophy from rule-based to 'principles-based' enforcement will
be examined. Since the introduction of the market abuse regime, its initial impact
was probably less than market participants expected, and less than the FSA had
hoped. More recently, however, it is clear the FSA is increasingly exercising its
powers conferred by the FSMA to address market abuse and send a clear message
to the industry that it will not be tolerated. In the years following the enactment
of the market abuse provisions in the FSMA the FSA has dealt with a variety of
market abuse cases involving allegations such as misuse of information/insider
dealing and breaches of High Level Principles; and has recently increased the

number of criminal cases involving insider dealing, misleading statements and inaccurate or misleading disclosures.[45] But it is generally conceded that more needs to be done. On 1 June 2009 Margaret Cole, head of enforcement at the FSA, announced a major recruitment initiative of an additional 80 staff dedicated to investigating 'wholesale' cases. Approximately a third of the enforcement staff are now involved in insider dealing cases.[46] It has also made significant technological advances in its fight against market abuse. There is a new Digital Evidence Unit with a team of 10 specialist investigators responsible for stripping and analysing computers, BlackBerrys and other electronic devices seized from suspected insider dealers.

1.41   For a couple of reasons, the impact of the regime was not what the Government may have initially intended. First, the Government's expressed hope that the market abuse regime would constitute an administrative remedy for market misconduct which could be dealt with by the FSA through the regulatory process was unsettled by decisions of the independent Financial Services and Markets Tribunal ('the Tribunal') to the effect that the standard of proof required for the imposition of market abuse penalties should not be any different from the judicial standard that determines whether legal penalties are to be considered 'civil' or 'criminal'. The more severe the penalties which the FSA seeks to impose, the higher the standard of proof the FSA will have to meet in order to defend those penalties to the Tribunal (and, when appropriate, higher courts). It makes no difference whether the statute characterizes the market abuse regime as a civil remedy. Where the penalties sought to be imposed are sufficiently severe, the standard of proof will be the same as if the remedies were defined as criminal penalties. As shown below, the imposition of this somewhat more difficult standard has caused some important failures for the FSA in attempts to prosecute what it regarded as severe market abuse infractions. In particular, the FSA's failure to persuade the Tribunal that its imposition of penalties was justified in the highly publicized 'Plumber' case was particularly galling to the regulators.[47]

1.42   Perhaps, as a result of this and the general recognition that the standard of proof in market abuse cases is not going to be particularly easy, the FSA might be viewed initially as having decided to make enforcement easier by putting enforcement on a different base. Rather than seeking to enforce penalties based on decisions derived from more 'rule-bound' regulations such as those for market abuse, the

---

   [45] Sally Dewar, Director of FSA Markets Division, 'Market Abuse Policy and Enforcement in the UK', 22 May 2007.

   [46] *Times*, 1 June 2009.

   [47] FSMT Decision No. 031: Paul Davidson and Ashley Tatham (16 May 2006); FSMT Decision No. 40: Cost Decision of Davidson and Tatham (11 October 2006). See discussion of case in Chapter 14, Market Abuse Cases, below.

FSA determined to impose penalties for violation of much more ambiguous, broad-ranging, and therefore easier-to-prove violations of High Level Principles. This early set-back, however, has proved less important as cases have been pursued. The forensic reality of the process has demonstrated that in practice it is difficult to draw a meaningful distinction between the so-called criminal standard of proof and simply recognizing that on a sliding scale of proof the FSA and the Tribunal need to approach a serious allegation from the perspective not that the standard of proof is higher but rather that 'the inherent probability or improbability of an event is itself a matter to be taken into account when weighing the probabilities and deciding whether on the balance of probabilities the event occurred'.[48] Indeed, cases have now succeeded in establishing market abuse practices based solely on circumstantial evidence – including an insider dealing case where the FSA accepted it could not demonstrate conclusively that the individual concerned had access to inside information and relied on inferences to that effect drawn from all the background circumstances of the case.[49]

The FSA has written and spoken a great deal about its move to principles-based **1.43** enforcement. Consequently, this book will discuss how that relates to market abuse and how it will change the way in which market participants must defend their behaviour under FSA scrutiny. It remains to be seen, however, whether the FSA's expressed commitment to principles-based enforcement survives the impetus of the global crash for a return to rules-based regulation.[50]

(3) US jurisdictional reach

Third, there is included a description of the reach of US jurisdiction over UK and **1.44** European financial market activity with respect to 'market abuse' and 'insider dealing' regulations in the US. It is not a full examination of US law on these issues, but non-US traders should be aware of the extent to which their activities may cross the line into US regulatory jurisdiction, because it is nearly impossible to avoid that overlap in contemporary financial trading.

Insider dealing, market manipulation, monopolies and conspiracies in restraint of **1.45** trade have long been crimes and provided grounds for both regulatory action and private rights of action under US financial services law and regulation. In most jurisdictions outside the US, people are often surprised by the reach of US

---

[48] Lord Nicholls in *Re H* [1996] 1 All ER 1 at 16–17; accepted as the correct approach by the FSM Tribunal in the *Parker* case (*James Parker v FSA* FSMT, Case 037, 18 August 2006).
[49] *Shevlin* (an RDC decision) – FSA Final Notice to John Shevlin dated 1 July 2008.
[50] A move back to a hard-edged rules-based regime is suggested by the Turner Review – 'A regulatory response to the global banking crisis' (FSA, March 2009).

jurisdiction over these types of activities. It is worth remembering that a US Federal Court held that:

> [A]ny market that is not exclusively a foreign market is part of US commerce.[51]

1.46   It is also worth remembering that one is not immunized from US law suits or regulatory action simply by the fact that the same area is covered by UK, EU or other non-US financial services regulation. The US Supreme Court has held that where a party is subject to both:

> If compliance with US (in that case, anti-trust) law is not made impossible by British law; there is no excuse for not complying with US law.[52]

1.47   Hopefully, this will give readers an understanding of how far market abuse regulations reach, when conduct begins to cross the line from permitted into abusive market behaviour, how one must conduct trading to comply with the new anti-market abuse standards, and what enforcement actions can follow allegations of market abuse. The issues that will be discussed in the chapters of this book will include the following:

1. What are the underlying elements of the market abuse regime?
2. What is 'market abuse'?
   (a) What sort of 'behaviour' constitutes market abuse?
   (b) Must the behaviour in question actually be market abuse or is it sufficient that it is 'likely' to constitute market abuse?
3. How does 'insider dealing' constitute market abuse?
4. How does 'market manipulation' constitute market abuse?
5. Who judges whether market abuse has occurred?
   (a) Who is the 'actor' whose behaviour is judged?
   (b) Must 'intent' be proved?
   (c) What 'standard' must be met?
6. Which markets are covered?
   (a) Which investments are covered?
   (b) Where will the market abuse provisions apply?
7. What is the relationship to existing 'criminal law'?

---

[51] Judge William C. Conner, US District Judge, Southern District of New York in the *Transnor* case. *Transnor v BP North America Petroleum*, 738 F. Supp. 1472 (SDNY 1990). 'The *Transnor* case was a watershed event for energy derivatives and the CFTC's [US Commodity Futures Trading Commission — the principal US regulator for derivatives] approach to OTC ['over-the-counter' or off-exchange] derivative products, upholding on a motion for summary judgment a complaint contending that Brent oil contracts were futures contracts subject to the anti-manipulation provisions of the CEA [the US Commodity Exchange Act].' Susan C. Ervin, 'CFTC Regulation of Energy Derivatives: An Overview' (American Bar Association, Section on Business Law, Committee on Futures Regulation: 'The Aftermath of Enron: More Regulation or Continued Deregulation', 13 August 2002), p. 2.
[52] US Supreme Court in *Hertford Fire Insurance v California* 509 U.S. 764 (1993).

8. What are the penalties for market abuse?
9. What are 'defences' or 'safe harbours'?
10. What is the 'enforcement procedure'?
11. What 'appeal' processes are available?
12. What can be learned from the market abuse cases that have been brought so far?
13. What is the impact of US market abuse regulation on non-US markets?
14. What conclusions can be drawn about the complex web of market abuse regulation?

The intention of these sections is to give the reader a better understanding of what market behaviour is expected in the financial markets, what behaviour is unacceptable and how the regulators in the UK, Europe and the US intend to enforce separation of the two. **1.48**

However, the regulation of any behaviour is not an exact science with clearly defined boundaries. It can probably only be understood as a mandated direction of travel, the exact route of which will have to be modified, as a result of unforeseen events and changing conditions as the journey progresses. **1.49**

It may not be possible to know how market abuse regulation will ultimately develop. The paths and byways of market abuse regulation, as discussed in the following chapters, may be seen as diverse and complex. However, the regulators have given a clear message as to where they want to end up. Their goal is to have financial markets that are fair and efficient. **1.50**

It is certainly true that the terms 'fair' and 'efficient' are qualitative, ambiguous and resistant to precise interpretation. What they mean will undoubtedly change as time goes on, and the markets evolve. However, no market participant would claim (at least publicly) that it is beneficial to the UK to have markets that are unfair and inefficient. Therefore, in order to avoid unfairness and inefficiency a certain amount of market advantage is going to have to be forfeited to compromise, cooperation and consensus. In seeking to achieve this, the regulator has to maintain a difficult balance between encouraging opportunities for 'fair' profit and limiting opportunities for inequitable profit. This is no easy task. How the regulators intend to maintain this balance is the central subject of the following chapters. **1.51**

2

PROMOTING FAIR MARKETS

A. Introduction

The basic questions that any market participant wants answered when dealing **2.01** with market abuse regulation is: 'What do I have to do?' More specifically: 'What is required and what is forbidden?'

(1) The duties of market participants

Fair and efficient market behaviour is a clearly stated requirement under the **2.02** Market Abuse Directive:

> Practising fairness and efficiency by market participants is required in order not to create prejudice to normal market activity and market integrity.[1]

UK policy has the same requirement. In its public announcements and press **2.03** releases, the FSA often declares its principal objectives in language similar to the following:

> The FSA aims to promote efficient, orderly and fair markets, help retail consumers achieve a fair deal and improve its business capability and effectiveness.[2]

---

[1] Commission Directive 2004/72/EC of 29 April 2004 Implementing Directive 2003/6/EC of the European Parliament and of the Council as regards accepted market practices, the definition of inside information in relation to derivatives on commodities, the drawing up of lists of insiders, the notification of managers' transactions and the notification of suspicious transactions, OJ L162, 30.4.2004, Recital 1, p. 70, ('Implementing Directive 2004/72').

[2] FSA, *Make sure contracts terms are fair, FSA tells firms*, note 5, *Press Release*, 19 May 2005.

2.04   Under the financial services law of the UK, participation in the financial market whether as an intermediary or professional market participant is not a right, it is a privilege. The privilege is granted to those who agree to fulfil certain fundamental obligations to conduct their market-related business fairly and efficiently. In particular, Principle 3 of the Financial Services Authority's Principles for Businesses requires authorized firms to take reasonable care to organize and control their affairs responsibly and effectively, with adequate risk management systems. Further, Principle 8 requires a firm to manage conflicts of interest fairly, both between itself and its customers and between a customer and another client. Specifically, the Systems and Controls block of the Financial Services Authority's Handbook obliges firms to maintain and operate effective organizational and administrative arrangements with a view to taking all reasonable steps to prevent conflicts of interest from constituting or giving rise to a material risk of damage to the interests of its clients;[3] the firm must seek to identify conflicts of interest between the firm including its managers, employees and appointed representatives (or where applicable tied agents) and a client that arise or may arise in the course of its business.[4] This involves an assessment as to whether in particular the firm is likely to make a financial gain, or avoid a financial loss, at the expense of the client or has an interest in the transaction which is distinct from the client's interest.[5] In this regard, a conflict is to be recognized even where the firm may gain a benefit if there is not also a possible disadvantage to a client.[6] In addition, it must implement and maintain an effective conflicts of interest policy that is set out in writing and is appropriate to the size and organization of and nature of our business, including its scale and complexity.[7]

2.05   The obligations of market participants under the UK market abuse regime are thus one category of the range of duties owed by financial market participants. Under UK law, the hierarchy of duties owed by market participants can be described as follows:

1. His first obligation is to protect the integrity of the financial markets.
2. His second obligation is to his clients (if he acts as an intermediary).
3. His third obligation is to other interests, including those of market counterparties, and his own (or those of his shareholders).

---

[3] SYSC 10.1.7 R.
[4] SYSC 10.1.1 R.
[5] SYSC 10.1.4 R.
[6] SYSC 10.1.5 G.
[7] SYSC 10.1.10 R.

The obligation to market integrity derives from the importance of the financial **2.06** markets to both the UK and the EU. This is emphasized in the first two Recitals of the Market Abuse Directive, which say the following:[8]

(1) A genuine Single Market for financial services is crucial for economic growth and job creation in the [European] Community.
(2) An integrated and efficient financial market requires market integrity. The smooth functioning of securities markets and public confidence in markets are prerequisites for economic growth and wealth. Market abuse harms the integrity of financial markets and public confidence in securities and derivatives.

The importance of this is reinforced by the FSMA, which states its first regulatory **2.07** objective to be the maintaining of market confidence, as shown in the following quote:[9]

(2) The regulatory objectives are:
  (a) market confidence;
  (b) public awareness;
  (c) the protection of consumers; and
  (d) the reduction of financial crime.

Further, on 8 July 2009 the UK Government announced that it was proposing to add a further regulatory objective on financial stability.

The objective of maintaining market confidence is explained in FSMA, s 3 as **2.08** follows:[10]

3. – (1) The market confidence objective is: maintaining confidence in the financial system.
  (2) The financial system means the financial system operating in the United Kingdom and includes —
    (a) financial markets and exchanges;
    (b) regulated activities; and
    (c) other activities connected with financial markets and exchanges.

With respect to the UK market abuse regime under the FSMA, and the measures **2.09** now taken to implement the Directive, one hears criticism that the requirements of market abuse regulation are too complex to allow market participants to have a clear picture of what they can and cannot do. Much of the criticism is misplaced. Some of it is the result of the extension of regulation to some markets, such as those for energy and commodity derivatives, where formerly there was little such regulation. The formerly 'light-handed' or 'hands-off' regulation for financial markets and the derivatives traded on them in some jurisdictions has been replaced

---

[8] Directive, Recitals 1 and 2.
[9] FSMA, s 2(2).
[10] FSMA, s 3(2).

by the far-reaching market abuse regulations now applying. These sectors of the market have had to adjust to the new regime.

2.10 Secondly, the basic requirement of market abuse regulation is one that many market participants find difficult to accept. In essence, the new market abuse regulations mean that financial market participants have an overriding duty to ensure that the markets are run 'efficiently and fairly'. This new duty is superior to the duty that financial market participants owe to their owners, or to their market counterparties. The market abuse regulations mean that participants have a duty to run the markets not only for their own benefit, but for the benefit of other market participants and investors generally. With the wide reach of the UK market abuse regime, the EU Directive on market abuse and regulations such as those in the US, this duty now applies to all financial markets whether they are traded on-exchange, OTC or in 'grey' or 'black' form.

2.11 This creates a complicated situation for traders operating in an international market. Market participants must think carefully about how these regimes apply to them and how they will affect their business. We consider below the implementation of this duty of 'fairness'.

B. UK Regulation of Market Abuse

2.12 Of all the provisions of FSMA, the ones that caused the most comment and enquiry are the provisions against 'market abuse' in ss 118–131 of Part VIII, as interpreted by the Rules and Guidance of the FSA.

2.13 Originally, three types of behaviour were recognized as market abuse. The first was 'misuse of information'; conduct which constituted either (a) insider dealing, or (b) improper disclosure of information.[11] The second was behaviour likely to give 'false or misleading impressions' as to the supply, demand or price of a qualifying investment or relevant product.[12] The third, 'distortion', was conduct likely to distort the market in question.[13] The 'sunset provisions' (discussed in Chapter 3) now impact on this third category.

2.14 However, the repeated use of the word 'likely' in the statute created some ambiguity in the definition of market abuse behaviour. Whether someone has done some positive act or failed to fulfil some positive duty is a matter of objective inquiry. However, whether behaviour was 'likely' to bring about some unrealized result

---

[11] MAR 1.4 (revoked 30 June 2005). For detailed definition, see FSMA, s 118, discussed in Chapter 3.
[12] MAR 1.5 (revoked 30 June 2005).
[13] MAR 1.6 (revoked 30 June 2005).

requires application of fine gradations of subjective judgment in each case. This gave the FSA a much bigger, unpredictable role in deciding whether market abuse had been committed.

Pre-Directive, the judge of whether behaviour fell below an acceptable market **2.15** standard was often thought to be the 'regular user' of the market in question. This is the 'regular user test'.[14] The regular user in question was a hypothetical reasonable person, who regularly dealt on the market in question, in investments of the kind in question.

The market abuse regime in the UK did not require a finding of 'intention' to **2.16** commit market abuse.[15] This meant in theory that one could commit market abuse by 'mistake' or 'inadvertence'. For example, a market trader entering an order into the market may add an extra zero to his order. That addition could affect market prices significantly. Even if the extra zero is a mistake, the FSA could still find that the trader was guilty of market abuse because he had failed to take reasonable care to prevent the mistake. In other words, one could negligently commit market abuse.[16] In practice the mental element of the 'market abuser' is important in a number of respects. First, the FSA's enforcement policy includes consideration as to whether any conduct was 'deliberate or reckless' when deciding whether to take proceedings for market abuse.[17] Second, FSMA, s 123(2)(a) prevents the FSA imposing a penalty for market abuse where it has reasonable grounds to be satisfied that the alleged market abuser 'believed on reasonable grounds' that his behaviour did not amount to market abuse or 'requiring or encouraging'. Third, the state of mind of the alleged abuser is relevant to a number of types of behaviour outlawed by the Act, for example 'dissemination' under s 118(7) requires that the person who disseminates false information 'knew or could reasonably be expected to have known' that the information was false or misleading.

Thus, although the FSA has taken a very broad view of the scope of the application **2.17** of the market abuse regime by stating in the Code of Market Conduct (COMC) that s 118 of the Act 'does not require the person engaging in the behaviour in question to have intended to commit market abuse', in practice the purpose behind an alleged market abuser's conduct will be relevant to whether action is taken by the FSA.[18] Nonetheless, in principle, there are very few people indeed whose conduct is not theoretically reached by the market abuse regime.[19] This is

---

[14] MAR 1.2 (revoked 30 June 2005).
[15] MAR 1.2.5 (revoked 30 June 2005).
[16] MAR 1.2.6 (revoked 30 June 2005).
[17] DEPP 6.2.1G (1)(a).
[18] See MAR 1.6.5 E.
[19] FSA *Factsheet; Why market abuse could cost you money* (December 2001).

an indication that the FSA wants to give itself the flexibility to deal with any market disruption which may affect the UK.

2.18 The FSMA market abuse regime was not intended to replace existing criminal laws but to work alongside the criminal laws while covering a wider range of activities.[20] For example, the Criminal Justice Act makes 'insider dealing' an offence. Under s 52 of that Act, a person may be found guilty of insider dealing if he is an individual who has 'inside information', and deals in *securities* that are 'price affected' by the information.

2.19 Also, under FSMA, s 397 (replacing FS Act, s 47), a person is guilty of an offence who induces or discourages investment decisions by:

- knowing or recklessly misleading false or deceptive statements; or
- concealment of material facts; or
- creating a false or misleading impression of the market price or value of any investment.

2.20 Overall the FSMA market abuse regime was intended to provide the FSA with a more flexible administrative remedy for market disruption which requires a lower standard of proof to be applied than required to obtain conviction for the above offences.

2.21 Pre-Directive there were a number of defences available to charges of market abuse under the FSMA which fell into two basic categories:

(1) 'safe harbours'; and
(2) 'evidentiary defences'.

There is no point in discussing those in detail here. The Directive mandates a narrower range of defences than would be permitted by the FSMA or the regular user test. Indeed, the FSA has considerably narrowed the application of the regular user test in its implementation of the Directive.

2.22 However, one should note carefully that no defence will excuse any activity that contravenes criminal law or other applicable legal or regulatory requirements. For example, any person's obligations under the rules of prescribed markets or other relevant rules, regulations, codes of conduct or good practice continue to apply. Consequently, even if a person's behaviour does not constitute market abuse it could still breach criminal codes and other regulatory rules.

---

[20] For a more detailed description of this relationship, see Chapter 9.

C. The Origins of the Standard of Fairness

In general, the purpose of the market abuse regime is to deter 'abusive behaviour' **2.23** which could undermine confidence in UK financial markets, damaging the integrity of those markets. However, the regime is not intended to deter acceptable market practices or innovation in financial markets.[21]

This begs the question as to what is the underlying standard against which behaviour is to be judged? During the time that the first FSMA market abuse regime was in force and during the discussions of the implementation of the Directive there was a great deal of reference to the 'regular user' of the market and 'the standards that are generally accepted by users of the market'.[22] One could have gained the impression that the regular user test was a great protection for market participants in that they would be excused for any behaviour which could be shown to conform to generally accepted market practices. **2.24**

In fact, this would be a gross overstatement of the importance of the 'regular user **2.25** test'. Even under the pre-Directive FSMA regime, it was not the critical standard against which market behaviour would have been judged by the FSA. The crucial standard was whether or not one's behaviour detracted from the fair and efficient operation of the financial markets. An examination of the relevant regulations shows this to be the case.

It is true that under the FSMA, ss 118(4) and 118(8), market abuse behaviour was **2.26** to be judged by the standards of the 'regular user of the market'. However, the 'regular user' was not a real market participant but 'a 'hypothetical reasonable person, familiar with the market in question'[23] who was intended to judge behaviour according to whether it constituted:

> a failure on the part of the person or persons concerned to observe the standard of behaviour reasonably expected of a person in his or their position in relation to the market;[24]

or

> would be, or would be likely to be, regarded by a regular user of the market as behaviour that would distort, or would be likely to distort, the market in such an investment.[25]

---

[21] FSA, *Consultation Paper 10: Market Abuse* (June 1998).
[22] MAR 1.2.4 (revoked 30 June 2005).
[23] MAR 1.2.2 (revoked 30 June 2005).
[24] FSMA s 118(4)(b).
[25] FSMA s 118(8)(b).

2.27 Since the regular user was not a real trader, one had to ask what things were to constitute his reasonable expectation of behaviour in the market in question. What elements would be added to his *tabula rasa* to construct his expectation? Would it simply be a statistical report of what traders were actually doing in the market? In much of the discussion about the regular user test, there seemed to be an expectation on the part of the industry that this would be the case—that proper behaviour would be a reflection of what was generally happening in the market. A closer reading of the MAR revealed that actual market practices were not going to be the crucial standard by which the regular user would decide whether particular behaviour was market abuse. This is logical in that a community of bad practice cannot make for good practice.

2.28 In the MAR, the FSA began to fill in the regular user's blank slate. First, they pointed out that the regular user's examination of behaviour would be illuminated by 'all the relevant circumstances'. Would 'all the relevant circumstances' be drawn solely from the characteristics of the market in question? No.

2.29 Certainly among the relevant circumstances would be the characteristics of the market in question, the investments traded on that market and the users of the market (including the person in question). However, also relevant would be:

- any applicable laws, regulations, rules or codes;
- the position of the person in question and the standards reasonably expected of him in light of his experience, skill and knowledge, and
- 'the need for market users to conduct their affairs in a manner that does not compromise the fair and efficient operation of the market as a whole or unfairly damage the interests of investors'.[26]

2.30 As the FSA made clear, the generally accepted practices of a market were not of primary importance:

> The *regular user* is likely to consider it relevant, **although not determinative**, that the *behaviour* conforms with standards that are generally accepted by users of the market.[27]

2.31 As can be seen, market practices, far from being a general defence against charges of market abuse, were merely a factor 'likely' (as distinguished from required) to be considered relevant by the regular user. Market practices constitute only some of the circumstances that make up the population of 'all relevant circumstances' which the regular user was stated to be likely to consider.[28] Finally, accepted

---

[26] MAR 1.2.3 E (revoked 30 June 2005).
[27] MAR 1.2.4 E (revoked 30 June 2005).
[28] MAR 1.2.2 E (revoked 30 June 2005).

market practices expressly do not, of themselves, 'determine' whether behaviour constitutes market abuse.[29]

If market practice was not the key determinative factor of whether behaviour **2.32** was market abuse, what was? The FSA originally clarified this in what was MAR 1.2.10 G saying:

> As stated in MAR 1.2.4 E, it is likely to be relevant to consider whether to take into account the extent to which the *behaviour* conforms with standards that are generally accepted by users of the market, but again this will not in itself be determinative. Such standards will be acceptable where they promote the fair and efficient operation of the market as a whole and do not unfairly damage the interests of investors. In circumstances where there is a range of practices which are generally accepted by users of the market, each practice is to be judged objectively on its own merits.[30]

This guidance note was weightier than it initially appeared. First, it pointed out **2.33** that although the hypothetical regular user was likely to find that whether behaviour conforms to generally accepted market standards, that would not be determinative of itself. Second, that in order to be 'acceptable' (presumably as evidence of proper market behaviour) even those standards that have already achieved general acceptance by users of the market (and regardless of how long they have enjoyed such acceptance) would need to pass the muster of entirely separate criteria, that is, whether they:

- promote the fair and efficient operation of the market as a whole, and
- do not unfairly damage the interests of investors.

Third, each accepted market practice needed to be 'judged objectively on its own **2.34** merits' as to whether it met those criteria. The hypothetical regular user could not use a finding of general market approval to determine the acceptability of any particular market practice. This left open the question as to where was the regular user supposed to seek guidance to form the basis of his objective judgment as to whether a market practice promoted fair and efficient market operation while not disadvantaging investors unfairly? What moral, ethical or regulatory standard should he use? Who would choose which standard would determine the outcome of this 'objective' inquiry? As the FSA indicated in a 2002 policy statement, initially the FSA would. The FSA would decide which standards the regular user should apply and that, ultimately, was subject to review by the Financial Services and Markets Tribunal and the courts.[31]

---

[29] MAR 1.2.4 E, 1.2.8 G, 1.2.9 G, and 1.2.10 G (revoked 30 June 2005).
[30] This language revoked 30 June 2005.
[31] FSA, *Market conduct sourcebook* (specialist topics and frequently asked questions), Feedback on CP124' (Policy Statement June 2002).

2.35 Consequently, it would never have made sense to place too much reliance on seeking protection from a finding of market abuse behind accepted market practices or the phantom regular user. It was always the FSA that one would be confronting when debating the propriety of market conduct. The FSA representation that 'we are not the regular user' was never going to be of much use. The pre-Directive FSMA regime emphasis on the regular user of the market was apt to be something of a chimera.

2.36 The real standard that the market user had to meet was whether his behaviour promoted fair and efficient market operation without disadvantaging investors. That would be judged by the FSA (and possibly reviewed by the Tribunal). Conveniently, this approach is in line with the mandates of the Directive.

2.37 In many respects both the pre- and post-Directive regimes seek to give regulatory effect to the obligations firms owe to customers as fiduciaries. In *Investment Banks as Fiduciaries: Implications for Conflicts of Interest*[32] Andrew Tuch identified three categories of fiduciary relationships including[33] that of customer and financial adviser, it being a particular feature of the latter relationship that the fiduciary adviser has power to affect the customer's interests and the customer has a reasonable expectation that the fiduciary will act in his interests for the purposes of the relationship. Analogical analysis of the role of a financial adviser leads to the conclusion that the adviser does indeed owe similar fiduciary duties to clients. In *Investors Compensation Scheme v West Bromwich Building Society*[34] the trial Judge, Evans Lombe J, stated:

> where an adviser undertakes whether pursuant to contract and for consideration or otherwise to advise another as to his financial affairs it is commonplace for the court to find that the adviser has placed himself under fiduciary obligations to that other.

2.38 The issue of a financial adviser's fiduciary obligation to clients was further addressed in *Brandeis (Brokers) Ltd v Black and Others*,[35] which considered the relationship between an LME broker and a metal trader client. Having considered (in the context of an appeal against an arbitrator's award based on breach of an alleged fiduciary duty) submissions on behalf of Brandeis Brokers that it owed no fiduciary obligation to its clients, Toulson J held that the appellant firm's 'position was not materially different from that of the brokers in *Glynwill Investments NV v Thompson McKinnon Futures Ltd* (unreported, 13 February 1992) where Mr Simon Tuckey QC held the firm to be accountable as fiduciaries'. Toulson J took

---

[32] [2005] *Melbourne University Law Review* 15.
[33] See further *Hospital Products Ltd v United States Surgical Corps* (1984) 156 CLR 41 at 96, per Mason J.
[34] [1990] Lloyds Rep PN 496 at 509 citing *Woods v Martins Bank* [1959] 1 QB 55 at 72, per Salmon J.
[35] Commercial Court, 25 May 2001 (unreported).

into account the regulatory status of Brandeis Brokers to comply with the Securities and Investments Board's Principle 6 ('a firm should either avoid any conflict of interest arising or where conflicts arise should ensure fair treatment to all its customers by disclosure, internal rules of confidentiality, declining to act or otherwise'. 'A firm should not unfairly place its interests above those of its customers and where a properly informed customer would reasonably expect that the firm would place his interests above its own, the firm should live up to that expectation.')

D. The EU Market Abuse Directive

Under the Directive on market abuse, implemented in the UK in mid 2005, the central standard of 'fairness' is continued. The stated aims of the Directive are to assure market integrity and public confidence by deterring and punishing market abuse, particularly in the forms of insider dealing and market manipulation.   **2.39**

There are a number of similarities and differences between the pre-Directive UK market abuse regime discussed above and those now in place following the implementation of the Directive. However, important differences are that, unlike the pre-Directive UK regime, the standard against which market behaviour is tested does not include an overarching 'regular user' test. It remains a factor in only two of the seven possible types of market abuse—each subject to the 'sunset provisions' discussed in Chapter 3.[36]   **2.40**

As shown in following chapters, the judges of whether or not behaviour constitutes market abuse are to be the regulatory authorities of each Member State. Secondly, post-Directive the number of safe harbours is significantly more limited. One relates to share buy-backs and another relates to price stabilization. These will be discussed at greater length in the chapters following.   **2.41**

However, the general duty of fairness is not neglected. With respect to the market abuse area of 'market manipulation', the Directive gives three specific 'core' definitions but also states that market manipulation can consist of any conduct creating 'unfair trading conditions'.[37] The Directive is also intended to be implemented in conformity with: **2.42**

> the need to achieve a level playing field for all market participants …[38]

---

[36] FSMA, ss 118(4) and 118(8).
[37] Directive, Art. 1.2.
[38] Directive, Recital 43.

Those who produce research concerning financial information must assure that the information is 'fairly presented'.[39] Public institutions disseminating financially relevant statistics must disseminate them 'in a fair and transparent way'.[40]

(1) The duty of fairness under the Directive

2.43   In its initially proposed revisions to the Market Conduct Sourcebook ('MAR' or 'COMC'), undertaken to implement the Directive, the FSA gave examples of behaviour which, in the opinion of the FSA, would or would not amount to market abuse. However, they emphasized that:

> The Code does not exhaustively list of all types of *behaviour* that may or may not amount to *market abuse*.
>
> * * *
>
> Likewise, the Code does not exhaustively describe or of all the factors to be taken into account in determining whether *behaviour* amounts to *market abuse*.[41]

2.44   What other factors will be considered? The FSA deleted much of the old MAR Provision 1.2, discussed above, but the COMC now shows that the FSA will still expect market participants to conduct their affairs so as not to compromise the fair and efficient operation of the market or unreasonably disadvantage investors. Indeed, the FSA identifies, as one of its 'overriding principles':

> the need for market participants to operate fairly and efficiently without interfering in normal market activity,

in a regulatory context 'fostering innovation and the continued dynamic development of financial markets'.[42]

2.45   Does the reference to not interfering with normal market activity mean that the FSA has made any substantive change in its belief in the importance of these principles? As the quoted provisions of the MAR revisions have shown above, that does not seem to be the case. In the legislative implementation of the Directive it clearly stated that:

> The Government wishes to retain the breadth of the current Part 8 [FSMA market abuse provisions] regime.[43]

---

[39] Directive, Art. 6.5.

[40] Directive, Art. 6.8.

[41] FSA, Implementation of the Market Abuse Directive, March 2005, Appendix 1, Market Abuse Directive Instrument 2005 ('Directive Instrument'), Annex B Amendments to the Market Code Sourcebook, MAR 1.1.6 G and 1.1.7 G (in force from 1 July 2005).

[42] Directive Instrument, MAR 1 Annex 2G, 'Accepted Market Practices (AMP)', Overriding Principles.

[43] HM Treasury/FSA, UK implementation of the EU Market Abuse Directive (Directive 2003/6/EC), a consultation document, June 2004 ('Joint Consultation Paper'), s 3.13.

The FSA clarified that they had not made any significant change in their regula-   **2.46**
tory attitude in the Cost Benefit Analysis and Compatibility Statement they prepared for the implementation of the Directive. In particular, the FSA stated with
respect to the changes to the Code of Market Conduct:

> The guidance in the Code is being amended to bring it into line with the require-
> ments of the directive and the level 2 implementing measures. There have been a
> number of key changes to the current guidance, including the replacement of some
> sections that are currently designated as safe harbours with descriptions of behaviour
> that does not amount to market abuse. In revising the guidance, we have taken into
> account the directive recitals text and have endeavoured to give market participants
> clarity on whether particular behaviour is acceptable. *Accordingly, we consider that the
> changes to the code are not substantive.*[44]

In the section of the same document relating to the direct costs of changes to the   **2.47**
MAR, the FSA commented:

> Furthermore, as the changes to the guidance are largely presentational rather than
> substantive, we consider that the additional costs associated with the need to give
> guidance on the changes will be of no more than minimal significance.[45]

It remains nonetheless critically important that market participants understand   **2.48**
their fundamental obligation under the market abuse regime. Their fundamental
obligation is to ensure that their trading practices contribute to the fair and efficient operation of the UK financial markets. There is no doubt that achieving that
fair and efficient operation is the principal aim of the FSA in enforcing its market
abuse regime. This FSA expressly makes this clear in its statement of 'compatibility with the FSA's general duties' where it lists 'market confidence' as its first statutory regulatory objective and says:

> Bringing the various sections of the Handbook into line with the requirements of the
> Directive and the implementing measures will reassure market users that the FSA is
> committed to take action against those who abuse markets and thereby also deter
> those who would otherwise do so. This in turn reinforces market participants' confi-
> dence in the *fairness* of prescribed markets and avoids them incurring the cost of
> satisfying themselves that the relevant markets are indeed *clear and fair*.[46]

It is important that market participants do not become distracted by the apparent   **2.49**
detail of the description of market abuse prohibitions in the post-Directive regime.
Avoiding a finding of market abuse should not be a question of examining all of

---

[44] Joint Consultation Paper, Annex E, Cost Benefit Analysis and Compatibility Statement, s 2.2
(emphasis added). In the Directive Instrument, Overview, s 1.8, the FSA noted that the Cost Benefit
Analysis and Compatibility Statement included in the Joint Consultation Paper ('Cost Benefit
Analysis') remained valid.
[45] Joint Consultation Paper, Cost Benefit Analysis, s 3.1.
[46] Joint Consultation Paper, Cost Benefit Analysis, Compatibility with the FSA's general duties,
s 3(a) (emphasis added).

the details of MAR and plotting a careful and convoluted path between the various descriptions and explanations of the prohibitions. It should be the much more general goal of making certain that one's business practices do not interfere with the fair and efficient operation of the markets or unreasonably disadvantage investors.

(2) The role of regulatory ambiguity

2.50 There have been complaints that the market abuse regime does not provide sufficient clarity for market participants to fully understand what they may do and what is prohibited. However, it is naïve for market participants to expect that there will be no ambiguity in a market abuse regime. In order to have an effective market abuse regime, a certain flexibility is essential. A goal of the market abuse regime has always been to give the FSA that flexibility which it needs to deal rapidly and effectively with market disruptions in the rapidly changing environment of international financial markets. In order to achieve that flexibility, some open texture to the regime is necessary to cover unexpected and unforeseen developments. As the Government has stated:

> We believe that it is essential to have a comprehensive market abuse regime to enable the Financial Services Authority (FSA) to meet its regulatory objectives, in particular maintaining confidence in the UK's financial system and reducing financial crime.[47]

2.51 This is necessary because, in any regulatory environment, there are two types of behaviour which the regulator is seeking to control. The first consists of the well-known and clearly understood violations of insider dealing and market manipulation which take forms which have been seen many times in the past (such as the misuse of non-public information gained from one's employment or position; and 'corners', 'squeezes', and 'wash sales').

2.52 However, in the rapidly evolving world of financial trading there is a second, equally important category of market abuse offences which are going to be the result of previously unknown or cleverly disguised ways of rigging the markets in one's favour. Because it is not always possible for a regulator to anticipate what forms these disruptive techniques may take, a significant amount of ambiguity needs to be built into the market abuse regime to allow its prohibitions to be flexible enough to stretch to cover unforeseen situations. Indeed, the Directive expressly commands such flexibility. It says, at Article 1(2)(c):

> The definitions of market manipulation shall be adapted so as to ensure that new patterns of activity that in practice constitute market manipulation can be included.[48]

---

[47] Joint Consultation Paper, s 3.13.
[48] Directive, Art. 1.

It seems that almost every year, the financial press reports new ways of abusing the **2.53** financial markets which in some instances have led to prosecutions and calls for more effective regulation to prevent their occurrence.

In order to be happy with the state of the regulation in the UK financial markets, **2.54** it is necessary to recognize that is not possible for any regulator to fully anticipate even some of the worst and most damaging abuses in market behaviour. It is not possible for the FSA to read the minds of all its regulated entities no matter how much information it requires that they routinely disclose.

Much of the regulation is going to take place after the damage has already been **2.55** done and finally brought to light. Regulatory 'autopsies' of this kind require a regulatory system that is flexible enough to allow a regulator to punish and correct previously unforeseen market abuse techniques. To restrict that flexibility too much, by requiring the FSA to anticipate and describe every possible illegal activity, is to condemn the critical financial markets to inadequate and ineffective regulation. That cannot be a sensible long-term solution for a financial economy as vital as that of the UK. After many years of trying different regulatory techniques, the UK Government has had the foresight to recognize that a certain amount of flexibility needs to be part of an effective regulatory system. Consequently there is going to be a certain amount of necessary ambiguity in the UK regulatory regime. This serves as a warning to financial market participants that they will not be able to escape their reasonable obligations to conduct their affairs in a fair and efficient manner by cleverly ring-fencing innovative and profitable disruptive schemes beyond the reach of narrowly defined regulatory prohibitions.

Although it is helpful, from an educational point of view, for compliance officers **2.56** and company directors of market participants to carefully read the descriptions that the FSA gives of specific activities that it will or will not consider to be market abuse, they must keep in mind that the real prohibitions are much more general in their coverage than any of the specific descriptions. The fundamental duty is to conduct one's affairs in a fair and efficient manner. If one does not, it is not the specific detailed prohibitions that will be most effective in punishing the wrong-doing; it is the general prohibitions contained not only in the market abuse regime but also the general principles set out as a required basis for any market activity.

All of the above is a plea that market participants must, when considering their **2.57** position in relation to the market abuse regime, not lose sight of the of the forest for the trees. The core 'forest' consists of a market operating fairly and efficiently. The trees are specific activities which are given as examples of conduct which expressly do or do not constitute market abuse. But avoiding running into any of the trees does not get one out of the forest. It does not matter how ingenious a market participant is, he still has to make certain that his activities do not detract from the fair and efficient operation of the financial market. If he fails to comply with that duty, he is subject to sanctions drawn from a very flexible regulatory toolkit.

E. Conclusion

2.58   Market abuse regulation has two sides: negative and positive. It would be a mistake for market participants to fail to comply with both.

2.59   On the negative side, one has a duty to avoid conduct that constitutes market abuse, but on the positive side one has a duty to conduct one's affairs so that they contribute to the fair and efficient operation of the market. The licence that a market participant has to take part in the international financial markets makes that duty superior to duties he may owe to his owners, financers, affiliates or market counterparties.

2.60   Under the current market abuse regulations implemented in the UK, the EU and other major jurisdictions, that duty is inescapable.

3

DEFINING MARKET ABUSE

A. Genesis of Market Abuse

(1) Historic framework

The original UK statutory provisions against civil market abuse were contained in **3.01** FSMA, ss 118–131 of Part VIII, which replaced the FS Act after 30 November 2001 (N2). They were explained and interpreted by the Code of Market Conduct (COMC) issued by the FSA and other comments and publications by which the FSA sought to clarify its interpretation of the market abuse provisions.

(2) Pre-definitions of market abuse

The definition of 'market abuse' has undergone some changes as a result of the **3.02** implementation of the Directive. Prior to the statutory modifications required by the Directive, s 118 of the FSMA defined 'market abuse' under UK law as follows:

(1) For purposes of this Act, market abuse is behaviour (whether by one person alone or by two or more persons jointly or in concert) —
   (a) which occurs in relation to qualifying investments traded on a market to which this section applies;
   (b) which satisfies one or more of the conditions set out in sub-section (2); and
   (c) which is likely to be regarded by a regular user of that market who is aware of the behaviour as a failure on the part of the person or persons concerned to observe the standard of behaviour reasonably expected of a person in his or their position in relation to the market.

(2) The conditions are that —

    (a) the behaviour is based on information which is not generally available to those using the market but which, if available to a regular user of the market, would or would be likely to be regarded by him as relevant when deciding the terms on which transactions in investments of the kind in question should be effected;

    (b) the behaviour is likely to give a regular user of the market a false or misleading impression as to the supply of, or demand for, or as to the price or value of, investments of the kind in question;

    (c) a regular user of the market would, or would be likely to, regard the behaviour as behaviour which would, or would be likely to, distort the market in investments of the kind in question.

3.03   That was a good 'official' definition of market abuse but not an easy one for any busy market practitioner to keep in mind. In a nutshell, the pre-Directive UK view of market abuse could best be summarized as:

behaviour likely to be regarded as below the expected market standard.

A cornerstone of this definition was the 'regular user of the market' test. This was designed to import an objective element into the judgment of market behaviour, whilst retaining some subjective elements related to the markets in question.[1]

(3) The post-Directive era

3.04   Because of the implementation of the Directive in the UK, both the official definition and any general understanding of market abuse had to change. As a result of the requirements of the UK implementation of the Directive, market abuse can now probably best be summarized as any conduct that undermines the fair and efficient operation of the financial markets, or unreasonably disadvantages investors.

3.05   In the Joint Consultation Paper, the FSA and the Treasury described market abuse as follows:

Market abuse, which consists of insider dealing and market manipulation, arises in circumstances where investors have been unreasonably disadvantaged by others. It prevents full and proper market transparency and undermines market integrity and investor confidence.[2]

3.06   This is a significant shift of focus for UK regulation. Despite the fact that from the beginning of its consideration of introducing market abuse legislation, the Government has said that its priorities were: (1) the integrity of the financial markets; and (2) the protection of consumers, there is little doubt that the principal

---

[1] MAR, 1.2.21G.
[2] Joint Consultation Paper, s 2.2.

focus of the language of regulation was on the issue of the integrity of the markets.

Indeed, as noted above in the pre-Directive implementation language of FSMA, **3.07** s 118, the person against whose understanding market behaviour would be judged was not simply an 'investor' or even a 'hypothetical reasonable investor', but the 'regular user' of the market in question who regularly traded in the financial products at issue. In other words, on the face of the statute no notice was to be taken of the needs or views of new or relatively inexperienced investors. This is hardly a formula to encourage new investors in the financial markets said to be so crucial to the financial health of the UK.

However, the implementation of the Directive has now apparently changed that **3.08** focus to a concern equally divided between the integrity of the markets and fair treatment of investors generally. Although this places a greater regulatory burden on the FSA (and other European regulators subject to implementation of the Directive), this is a welcome change. As the very least it will encourage wider participation in the financial markets which should lead to an overall strengthening of the economies of the EU.

Although the UK Government has stated that its fundamental views on market **3.09** abuse regulation have not changed, the implementation of the Directive has required a number of 'presentational' changes to the FSMA, the FSA *Handbook*, including the MAR, and other regulatory instruments affected by the issues covered in the Directive including the Price Stabilising Rules, the Listing Rules and the Conduct of Business Sourcebook (COB).

Directive-driven amendments to the FSMA, s 118, changed the statutory descrip- **3.10** tion of market abuse, as of 1 July 2005, to the following:

118   Market abuse

(1) For purposes of this Act, market abuse is behaviour (whether by one person alone or by two or more persons jointly or in concert) which —
   (a) occurs in relation to qualifying investments traded or admitted to trading on [a] prescribed market or in respect of which a request for admission to trading on such a market has been made, and
   (b) falls within any one or more of the types of behaviour set out in subsections (2) to (8).
(2) The first type of behaviour is where an insider deals, or attempts to deal, in a qualifying investment or related investment on the basis of inside information relating to the qualifying investment.
(3) The second is where an insider discloses inside information to another person otherwise than in the proper course of the exercise of his employment, profession or duties.
(4) *The third is where the behaviour (not falling within subsection (2) or (3)) —*
   (a) *is based on information which is not generally available to those using the market but which, if available to a regular user of the market, would be, or would be*

likely to be, regarded by him as relevant when deciding the terms on which trans-actions in qualifying investments or related investments should be effected, and

(b) *is likely to be regarded by a regular user of the market as a failure on the part of the person concerned to observe the standard of behaviour reasonably expected of a person in his position in relation to the market.*

(5) The fourth is where the behaviour consists of effecting, or participating in effecting, transactions or orders to trade (otherwise than for legitimate reasons in conformity with accepted market practices on the relevant market) which —

    (a) give, or are likely to give, a false or misleading impression as to the supply of, or demand for, or as to the price or value of, one or more qualifying investments or related investments, or

    (b) secure the price of one or more such investments at an abnormal or artificial level.

(6) The fifth is where the behaviour consists of effecting, or participating in effecting, transactions or orders to trade which employ fictitious devices or any other form of deception or contrivance.

(7) The sixth is where the behaviour consists of disseminating, or causing the dissemination of, information by any means which gives, or is likely to give, a false or misleading impression as to a qualifying investment or related investment by a person who knew or could reasonably be expected to have known that the information was false or misleading.

(8) *The seventh is where the behaviour (not falling within subsection (5), (6) or (7)) —*

    (a) *gives or is likely to give, a regular user of the market a false or misleading impression as to the supply of, demand for or price or value of, qualifying or related investments, or*

    (b) *would be, or would be likely to be, regarded by a regular user of the market as behaviour that would distort, or would be likely to distort, the market in such an investment*

and the behaviour is likely to regarded by a regular user of the market as a failure on the part of the person concerned to observe the standard of behaviour reasonably expected of a person in his position in relation to the market.

(9) Subsections (4) and (8) and the definition of 'regular user' in section 130A(3) cease to have effect on [31 December 2009] and subsection (1)(b) is then to be read as no longer referring to those subsections.

3.11 The above subsection (9) was substituted by the Financial Services and Markets Act 2000 (Market Abuse) Regulations 2008.[3] It will thus be noted that the types of behaviour proscribed by subsections 118(4) and (8) are still expressed by reference to the 'regular user of the market' test. These so-called 'legacy offences' were subject to a 'sunset date' of 30 June 2008 unless action was initiated to retain them.[4] In February 2008 the Treasury published its consultation – *FSMA market abuse regime: a review of the sunset clauses* – and recommended an extension of the date to 31 December 2009.[5] The reasoning behind this recommendation

---

[3] SI 2008/1439, regulation 3(1) and (2).

[4] FSMA, s 118(9).

[5] See now Financial Services and Markets Act (2000) (Market Abuse) Regulations 2008, SI 2008/1439.

was in essence twofold. First, in anticipation of the 2008 European Commission's review of the Directive it was considered less disruptive to retain the legacy offences pro tem and respond to any further amendments necessary in consequence of the EC review once completed. Second, the legacy offences were in any event 'super-equivalent' and broader in scope than the Directive offences.

The Government pointed out in its Joint Consultation Paper that there is a differ- **3.12** ence between FSMA and the Directive descriptions of market abuse. The FSMA characterizes market abuse as 'behaviour'. The Directive employs more specific descriptions of activity such as 'transactions' or 'orders to trade'. Consequently, the range of activities covered by the FSMA is wider than in the Directive.[6] Also, the FSMA definition of 'behaviour' includes not only action but inaction as well.[7] For example, if a party has a duty to act, and fails to do so, he may be found guilty of market abuse even though his role was entirely passive. In addition, although the sections of the Directive itself that deal with misuse of information refer to 'inside information', the UK implementation of the Directive applies to a broader range of information including so-called 'relevant information not generally available' ('RINGA'). In particular, the behaviour caught by section 118(4) is based on RINGA, rather than inside information.[8]

However, on examination it appears that these differences may not be terribly **3.13** significant overall. The Directive states that its objective is to promote the integ-rity of an integrated and efficient financial market, and that preventing market abuse is essential to achieving that goal.[9] In order to reach this objective, the Directive describes a long list of both active *and passive* conduct which it seeks to prevent.[10] These things do not seem to be very different from the 'behaviour' which constitutes market abuse under the FSMA.

B. Defining 'Behaviour'?

The types of behaviour occurring in relation to qualifying investments (as **3.14** described in FSMA, s 118(1)) which are covered by the UK market abuse regime will include (but will not be limited to) the following:

• dealing in qualifying investments;

---

[6] Joint Consultation Paper, s 3.12.
[7] FSMA, s 130A(3); SI 2005/381.
[8] HM Treasury, *FSMA market abuse regime: a review of the sunset clauses—a consultation* (February 2008), pp. 9–14.
[9] Directive, Recital 2.
[10] Directive, Recitals 12–20.

- dealing in either commodities or investments which are the subject matter of or whose price or value is determined by reference to a qualifying investment. Those things which are the subject matter of or whose price or value is determined by reference to or qualifying investment are 'relevant products' to a qualifying investment;
- arranging deals with respect to qualifying investments;
- causing, requiring or advising others to deal in qualifying investments;
- making statements, representations or assimilating information which a regular user is likely to regard as relevant in determining the price or terms or transactions and qualifying investments;
- providing advice or otherwise conducting corporate finance activities in qualifying investments, and
- managing the qualifying investments belonging to a third party.

3.15 Market abuse can constitute either engaging in sub-standard behaviour oneself, with respect to activities such as those listed above, or requiring or encouraging sub-standard behaviour by others.[11] Behaviour can be by one person acting alone or by two or more persons acting jointly or in concert.[12] Behaviour can be either action or inaction. If one has a duty to act and fails to do so one can be guilty of market abuse. Therefore one can commit market abuse both passively as well as actively.[13]

3.16 There are two behavioural duties that one is subject to with respect to market abuse. The first category constitutes *negative* duties that require one to refrain from certain behaviour that constitutes market abuse. The second category consists of positive duties that one must fulfil if one does not wish to be found guilty of market abuse.

3.17 The negative duties consist of the duties to avoid insider dealing and market manipulation. The positive duties include duties to discharge regulatory obligations, to report suspicious transactions, keep lists of insiders and to make public announcements as soon as possible through accepted channels.

3.18 There are also positive and negative duties that apply to relevant regulators under the Directive. For example, Member States must interpret and implement the Directive in a manner consistent with effective regulation, and they must not fail to appoint a single competent authority to effectively enforce the Directive.

3.19 Behaviour is reached by the Act if it occurs in the UK in relation to 'qualifying investments' traded on a market to which the market abuse provisions apply,

---

[11] MAR, 1.1.2.
[12] FSMA, s 118(1); SI 2005/381.
[13] MAR, 1.2.6.

which includes both markets in the UK or those accessible electronically in the UK.[14]

Behaviour is also regarded as occurring 'in relation to qualifying investments', for the purposes of FSMA s 118 subsections (2) and (3), where it occurs in relation to investments which are qualifying investments, and, additionally, in relation to FSMA s 118 (4) and (8), if it occurs in relation to anything which is the subject matter of, or the price or value of which is expressed by reference to the price or value of, or any investment the subject matter of which is comprised of, qualifying investments.[15]   **3.20**

There are two types of market on which improper behaviour can occur. The first is comprised of markets in qualifying investments which are situated in the UK. The second is comprised of markets trading qualifying investments which are electronically accessible in the UK. For example, if a market exists outside the UK (perhaps on a Caribbean island) and trades shares listed admitted to listing in the UK, improper behaviour reached by the FSMA market abuse provisions can occur 'in relation' to that offshore market.   **3.21**

The legal construction of the phrase, 'in relation', must be considered when interpreting these provisions. 'Relation' is a very broad term, having been used at law to mean 'reference or application to', generally.[16] Therefore, when behaviour is 'in relation' to a qualifying investment (or market) it need not necessarily directly involve the qualifying investment. It may be sufficient for improper behaviour merely to have 'reference or application' to a qualifying investment for that behaviour to come within the market abuse prohibitions.   **3.22**

The intended scope of the phrase 'in relation' has yet to be exhaustively defined for purposes of market abuse regulation. Support for a broad definition may be gathered from a preliminary hearing of the FSMT in the *Jabré* case.[17] The case concerned share transactions on the Tokyo market which were also listed on the LSE. The Tribunal determined that the transactions in question had occurred in relation to qualifying investments 'traded' on a prescribed market. The Tribunal commented: **3.23**

> [T]he vice of insider dealing and the reason why it was prohibited was that it reduced confidence in the integrity and transparency of the market in the particular security that was being abused. The FSA had an interest in preventing market abuse that impacted on the market and its institutions because the abuse related to shares traded within the territory of its authority.

---

[14] FSMA, s 118A(2); SI 2005/381.
[15] FSMA, s 118A(3); SI 2005/381.
[16] *Oxford English Dictionary*, 2nd ed. (1991), s.v. 'relation', 4b.
[17] *Philippe Jabré v FSA*, FSMT Case 036, 2006—Decision on Market Abuse.

Further, when determining the scope of this phrase under English and international law, the FSA, the Tribunal and the courts may determine that its definition varies with the circumstances of the behaviour under scrutiny.

3.24   Section 119 of the Act required the FSA to issue a code giving appropriate guidance in determining whether or not behaviour amounts to market abuse.[18] Section 119 suggested that the code may include the following:

1. Descriptions of behaviour that, in the opinion of the FSA, amounts to market abuse.
2. Descriptions of behaviour that, in the opinion of the FSA, do not amount to market abuse.
3. The factors that, in the opinion of the FSA, are to be taken into account in determining whether or not behaviour amounts to market abuse.

3.25   This has resulted in the COMC, contained in Chapter 1 of the MAR. Constructed around the seven types of behaviour identified above, the COMC provides non-exhaustive detail of certain types of conduct that will or will not amount to market abuse, along with published particulars of factors that the FSA will take into account in deciding whether behaviour will amount to market abuse or not. COMC also sets out a number of safe harbours.

3.26   The COMC thus reflects the Directive's list of proscribed conduct which could constitute or contribute to market abuse (interestingly enough by persons, legal entities, Member States or even the EU). The latter includes:

*   insider dealing and market manipulation;[19]
*   wrongful conduct which would undermine public confidence and therefore prejudice the smooth functioning of the markets;[20]
*   financing terrorist activities;[21]
*   engaging in the preparation or execution of criminal activities which could have a significant effect on the prices of one or more financial instruments or on price formation in a regulated market;[22]
*   under some circumstances, the execution of orders to acquire or dispose of financial instruments on behalf of some one who is known to be (or reasonably should be known to be) in possession of inside information;[23]

---

[18]   FSMA, s 119(1).
[19]   Directive, Recital 12.
[20]   Directive, Recital 13.
[21]   Directive, Recital 14.
[22]   Directive, Recital 17.
[23]   Directive, Recital 18.

- 'front running', which is the practice of engaging in transactions in the market ahead of the execution of client orders to profit from price movements likely to be caused by the future placement of such client orders in the market;[24]
- failure to comply with appropriate standards when producing or disseminating research related to financial instruments, or recommending or suggesting investment strategy;[25]
- failure to make prompt and fair disclosure of relevant information to the public;[26]
- failure to ensure proper transparency (such as appropriate publication) of transactions conducted by persons discharging managerial responsibilities within issuers of financial instruments;[27]
- failure by market operators to adopt appropriate structural provisions aimed at preventing and detecting market manipulation practices;[28]
- under certain circumstances, using inside information in the context of a public takeover bid or merger;[29]
- engaging in inappropriate activities related to share buyback or stabilization programmes;[30]
- failure by a Member State to be sufficiently sensitive to the need to ensure a degree of uniformity of regulation from one Member State to another when adopting regulations and sanctions;[31]
- failure by a Member State to organize supervisory and investigatory powers so that they do not hinder cooperation between competent national authorities;[32]
- failure by the European Community to adopt measures at the community level to achieve the objectives of preventing market abuse in the form of insider dealing and market manipulation;[33]
- failure by the European Commission to provide technical guidance and implementing measures which respect the following principles:[34]
  - the need to ensure confidence in financial markets by encouraging high standards of transparency in those markets;
  - the need to provide investors with a wide range of competing investments and appropriate levels of disclosure;

---

[24] Directive, Recital 19.
[25] Directive, Recital 23.
[26] Directive, Recital 24.
[27] Directive, Recital 26.
[28] Directive, Recital 27.
[29] Directive, Recital 29.
[30] Directive, Recital 33.
[31] Directive, Recital 39.
[32] Directive, Recital 40.
[33] Directive, Recital 41.
[34] Directive, Recital 43.

– the need to ensure that independent regulatory authorities diligently enforce the rules, particularly to prevent economic crime;

– the need to encourage markets to be innovative, dynamic and efficient;

– the need to monitor financial innovation so as to ensure market integrity;

– the need to increase access to capital and reduce its cost;

– the need to balance the costs and benefits of market participation so as not to unfairly burden small and medium-sized businesses or investors;

– the need to encourage international competitiveness without discouraging the expansion of international cooperation;

– the need to achieving a level financial market playing field by consistently maintaining common EU-wide regulations;

– the need to respect national market differences that do not interfere with maintaining consistent EU-wide regulations; and

– the need to maintain consistency throughout Community legislation so that imbalances of information or lack of financial market transparency do not harm consumers and small investors.

3.27   The COMC adopts a lettering code in which provisions are annotated variously as (E), indicating an evidential presumption that the described conduct is or is not likely to constitute market abuse, (G), indicating that the text is intended to provide guidance to the user and (C), identifying a provision containing a safe harbour.

C. Scope of UK Market Abuse Regulation

3.28   It should be borne in mind that the Directive is a *minimum standard* instrument. The Directive states that:

> A common minimum set of effective tools and power for the competent authority of each Member State will guaranty supervisory effectiveness.[35]

3.29   Member States can impose stricter market abuse regulation, within certain limits,[36] if they wish. As noted above, the UK Government has decided to follow that course. Its implementation of the Directive adapts the UK's existing regime to comply with the Directive while retaining the scope of the current regime where it goes beyond the Directive. This was accomplished in a number of ways. For example, the UK retained two 'super-equivalent' market abuse definitions intended to capture behaviour not expressly described in the Directive. The first

---

[35] Directive, Recital 37.

[36] For example, Member States are required to recognize that there are certain exemptions to market abuse regulations in the areas of share buy-backs and stabilization. See discussions of these 'safe-harbours', and other defences, in Chapter 11.

is s 118(4), which catches behaviour based on RINGA rather than 'inside information'. The second is s 118(8), which catches behaviour that is likely to give a false or misleading impression.[37] As noted above, these so-called 'legacy offences' are now subject to an end date of 31 December 2009. In addition, the UK implementation has resulted in new rules extending the FSA's regulatory powers, particularly in the areas of requiring companies to disclose inside information and to maintain lists of those with access to inside information.[38]

D. Conclusions on Defining Market Abuse?

In summary, the types of behaviour which can constitute market abuse (in the UK specifically, and under the Directive generally) includes directly or indirectly: **3.30**

- using information not publicly available that is likely to have a significant effect on prices of financial instruments (or related derivatives) to the advantage of oneself or to the advantage of others;
- transactions or orders which give or are likely to give false or misleading signals about supply, demand or price of financial instruments, or which move such prices to artificial levels, or which employ any form of deception or contrivance; and
- disseminating information giving or likely to give false or misleading signals as to financial instruments.[39]

On its face, the Directive description of 'market abuse' appears to be quite simple: **3.31**

Market abuse consists of insider dealing and market manipulation.[40]

The wider descriptions of the prohibitions against market abuse are found in Articles 1–5 of the Directive. They are intended to prevent situations where some investors are unreasonably disadvantaged by others. Such inequities are thought to be most likely under two sets of circumstances. The first occurs when insiders use, or try to use, non-public information ('inside information') to gain advantage for themselves or others ('insider dealing'). Second, when someone seeks to artificially change ('distort') the price of financial instruments, or arranges financial transactions, or information, in a way which is likely to create false of misleading impressions about financial instruments ('market manipulation').   **3.32**

---

[37] HM Treasury, *A review of the sunset clauses*, p. 10.
[38] Joint Consultation Paper, Executive Summary, paras 3–5, p. 3.
[39] Directive, Art. 1.
[40] Directive, Recital 2.

3.33 Under the FSMA, s 118, seven types of behaviour are identified as market abuse.[41] However, each of these is actually a more detailed description of behaviour that constitutes a particular pattern of either 'insider dealing' or 'market manipulation'. Despite the changes to UK regulation brought about by the Directive, these two major categories, between them, encompass the full range of behaviour that constitutes illegal market abuse. Therefore the details of particular kinds of market abuse will be examined in the next two chapters under the headings of 'insider dealing' and 'market manipulation'.

---

[41] FSMA, s 118, SI 2005/381.

4

INSIDER DEALING

A. Insider Dealing under FSMA

4.01 Following implementation of the Directive, the types of behaviour that would constitute 'insider dealing' as market abuse in the UK are specifically described in FSMA, s 118, subsections (2), (3) and (4):

(2) The first type of behaviour is where an insider deals, or attempts to deal, in a qualifying investment or related instrument on the basis of inside information relating to the qualified investment.

(3) The second is where an insider discloses inside information to another person otherwise than in the proper course of the exercise of his employment, profession or duties.

(4) The third is where the behaviour (not falling within subsection (2) or (3)) —

    (a) is based on information which is not generally available to those using the market but which, if available to the regular user of the market, would be, or would be likely to be, regarded by him as relevant when deciding the terms on which transactions in qualifying instruments or related instruments should be effect, and

    (b) is likely to be regarded by a regular user of the market as a failure on the part of the person concerned to observe the standard of behaviour reasonably expected of a person in his position in relation to the market.

4.02 For purposes of assessing whether market abuse has occurred, 'insiders' are defined as follows:

118B Insiders

For the purposes of this Part an insider is any person who has information —

    (a) as a result of his membership of the administrative, management or supervisory bodies of an issuer of qualifying investments,

    (b) as a result of his holding in the capital of an issuer of prescribed investments,

    (c) as a result of having access to the information through the exercise of his employment, profession or duties,

    (d) as a result of his criminal activities, or

    (e) which he has obtained by other means and which he knows, or could reasonably be expected to know, is inside information.[1]

4.03   MAR, 1.2.8 E states that for the above purposes a person could be 'reasonably expected to know' that information in his possession is inside information where a normal and reasonable person in the position of that person would both (a) know that the person from whom he received it was an insider and (b) know that it is inside information.

4.04   Subsections (a)–(d) above are virtually the same as the Directive description of persons who possess inside information in Directive, Article 2, subsections 1(a)–(d).[2] Subsection (e) in the UK definition adds a general catch-all to cover persons who could have obtained 'inside information' by any other means, which effectively replicates Article 2 of the Directive.[3]

4.05   The Directive's 'catch-all' provisions of 'insiders' are more formally set out in Articles 3 and 4 of the Directive. Article 3 says:

> Member States shall prohibit any person subject to the prohibition laid down in Article 2 from:
> (a) disclosing inside information to any other person unless such disclosure is made in the normal course of the exercise of his employment, profession or duties;
> (b) recommending or inducing another person, on the basis of inside information, to acquire or dispose of financial instruments to which that information relates.[4]

4.06   This requires prohibition of those described in Article 2 from improperly revealing inside information to, or improperly using it on behalf of others. Article 4 extends the coverage of Articles 2 and 3 to:

> any person, other than the persons referred to in those Articles, who possesses inside information while that person knows, or ought to have know, that it is inside information.[5]

---

[1] FSMA, s 118B; SI 2005/381, the Financial Services and Markets Act 2000 (Market Abuse) Regulations 2005.

[2] Directive, Art. 2(1).

[3] Directive, Art. 2.

[4] Directive, Art. 3.

[5] Directive, Art. 4.

B. Inside Information under the Directive

Under Article 1 of the Directive, 'inside information' falls into three categories. **4.07**
First, it relates generally to 'financial instruments' and means information:

> of a precise nature which has not been made public, relating directly or indirectly, to
> one or more issuers of financial instruments *or to one or more financial instruments*
> and which, if it were made public, would be likely to have a significant effect on the
> prices of those financial instruments or on the price of related derivative financial
> instruments.[6]

No person possessing such inside information is to be permitted to take advantage **4.08**
of that information by acquiring or disposing of financial instruments related to
the information. Misuse of information covers primary as well as secondary
markets.[7] For purposes of the Directive and the FSMA, the term 'financial
instrument' covers a wide range of assets including:

- transferable securities (as defined in EC Directive 93/22/EEC of 10 May 1993
  on investment services in the securities field);
- units in collective investment undertakings;
- money-market instruments;
- financial-futures contracts, including equivalent cash-settled instruments;
- forward interest-rate agreements;
- interest-rate, currency and equity swaps;
- options to acquire or dispose of any instrument falling into these categories,
  including equivalent cash-settled instruments. This category includes in particular options on currency and interest rates;
- derivatives on commodities;
- any other instrument admitted to trading on a regulated market in a Member
  State or for which a request for admission to trading on such a market has been
  made.[8]

The second category is *a more limited category* than the first and defines 'inside **4.09**
information' that relates to derivatives on commodities. In such cases, the Directive
narrows the definition of 'inside information' to include *only*:

> information of a precise nature which has not been made public, relating, directly or
> indirectly, to one or more such derivatives and which users of markets on which such
> derivatives are traded would expect to receive in accordance with *the accepted market
> practices* on those markets.[9]

---

[6] Directive, Art. 1(1).
[7] Directive, Art. 1.
[8] Directive, Art. 1(3).
[9] Directive, Art. 1(1).

4.10   The third category has an even more limited application relating to 'persons charged with the execution of orders concerning financial instruments'. In such cases, 'inside information' has the additional meaning of:

> information conveyed by a client and related to the client's pending orders, which is of a precise nature, which relates directly or indirectly to one or more issuers of financial instruments or to one or more financial instruments or to one or more financial instruments, and which, if it were made public, would be likely to have a significant effect on the prices of those financial instruments or on the price of related derivative financial instruments.[10]

C. Inside Information under FSMA

4.11   In FSMA, s 118C, the Directive definition of 'inside information' has been adapted and expanded as follows:

> 118C Inside information
> (1) This section defines 'inside information' for the purposes of Part [VIII of the FSMA].
> (2) In relation to qualifying investments, or related investments, which are not commodity derivatives, inside information is information of a precise nature which —
>   (a) is not generally available,
>   (b) relates, directly or indirectly, to one or more issuers of the qualifying investments or to one or more of the qualifying investments, and
>   (c) would, if generally available, be likely to have a significant effect on the price of the qualifying investments or on the price of related investments.
> (3) In relation to investments which are commodity derivatives, inside information is information which —
>   (a) is not generally available,
>   (b) relates, directly or indirectly, to one or more such derivatives, and
>   (c) users of markets in which the derivatives are traded would expect to receive in accordance with accepted market practices on those markets.
> (4) In relation to a person charged with the execution of orders concerning any qualifying investments or related investments, inside information is information conveyed by a client and related to the client's pending orders which —
>   (a) is of a precise nature,
>   (b) is not generally available,
>   (c) relates, directly or indirectly, to one or more issuers of qualifying investments or one or more qualifying investments, and
>   (d) would, if generally available, be likely to have a significant effect on the price of those qualifying investments or the price of related investments.

---

[10] Directive, Art. 1(1).

(5) Information is precise if it —
  (a) indicates circumstances that exist or may reasonably be expected to come into existence or an event that has occurred or may reasonably be expected to occur, and
  (b) is specific enough to enable a conclusion to be drawn as to the possible effect of those circumstances or that event on the price of qualifying investments or related investments.

(6) Information which a reasonable investor would be likely to use as part of the basis of his investment decisions is information which, if it were generally available, would be likely to have a significant effect on the price of qualifying investments or of related investments.

(7) Users of markets on which investments in commodity derivatives are traded are to be treated as expecting to receive information relating directly or indirectly to one or more such derivatives, which is —
  (a) routinely made available to the users of those markets, or
  (b) required to be disclosed in accordance with any statutory provision, market rules, or contracts or customs on the relevant underlying commodity market or commodity derivatives market.

(8) For the purposes of this Part, information which is 'generally available' in relation to qualifying investments, commodity derivatives or other related investments means information which is generally available to users of the relevant market on which those qualifying investments, commodity derivatives or other related investments are traded.

(9) Information which can be obtained by research or analysis conducted by, or on behalf of, users of a market is to be regarded, for the purposes of this Part, as being generally available to them.[11]

D. Information Generally Available

The FSA has published the COMC, which identifies a number of factors which **4.12** the Authority will take into account in deciding whether information is generally available. These include:

- whether the information has been disclosed to a prescribed market through a Regulatory Information Service;
- whether the information has been disclosed in accordance with the rules of the relevant prescribed market;
- whether the information is contained in records open to public inspection;
- whether the information can be accessed publicly, for example via the Internet or from analysis using expertise and resources available at cost (providing this does not infringe rights or obligations of privacy, property or confidentiality).

---

[11] FSMA, s 118C; SI 2005/381.

Thus, the reports and recommendations of 'star analysts' will not usually constitute inside information. Care is nonetheless required in the dissemination of the fruits of such research. In *FSA v Casoni*[12] a research analyst for a London investment bank was found to have breached Principle 3 of the FSA's Statement of Principles for Approved Persons. In preparing a report in connection with possible coverage by the bank of an Italian company containing recommendations as to target price, he selectively disclosed details of his valuation and the target price to certain clients – all in advance of publication. This conduct attracted a penalty of £52,500 (discounted by 30 per cent for early settlement) even though the FSA accepted that Mr Casoni had no intention of manipulating the market, had not made any financial gain from the disclosure and no trading in the shares of the company took place.

E. Market Practices

4.13 Note that the practices and expectations of those using the markets in question are relevant in a number of the subsections of s 118C quoted above.

4.14 For purposes of the Directive, the term 'accepted market practices' is defined as:

practices that are reasonably expected in one or more financial markets and are accepted by the competent authority in accordance with the guidelines adopted by the Commission in accordance with the procedure laid down in Article 17(2).[13]

4.15 However, for purposes of Part VIII of the FSMA, the term 'accepted market practices' goes beyond this, and includes:

practices that are reasonably expected in the financial market or markets in question and are accepted by the Authority or, in the case of a market situated in another EEA State, the competent authority of that EEA State within the meaning of Directive 2003/6/EC of the European Parliament and of the Council of 28 January 2003 on insider dealing and market manipulation (market abuse).[14]

4.16 In the UK, the 'competent authority' is the FSA, which fulfils the Directive's requirement that:

a single administrative authority [be designated in each Member State] competent to ensure that the provisions adopted pursuant to this Directive are applied.[15]

4.17 The 'guidelines' for accepting expected market practices which the FSA will apply in assessing whether to accept a market practice in the UK markets to which it

---

[12] *FSA v Casoni* (Final Notice), 20 March 2007.
[13] Directive, Art. 1(5).
[14] FSMA, s 130A(3); SI 2005/381.
[15] Directive, Arts. 1(7) and 11.

regulates are set our in MAR 1, Annex 2. The FSA says that it will take the following *non-exhaustive* list of factors into account:

1. the level of transparency of the relevant market practice to the whole market;
2. the need to safeguard the operation of market forces and the proper interplay of the forces of supply and demand (taking into account the impact of the relevant market and practice against the main market parameters, such as the specific market conditions before carrying out the relevant market practice, the weighted average price of a single session or the daily closing price);
3. the degree to which the relevant market practice has an impact on market liquidity and efficiency;
4. the degree to which the relevant practice takes into account the trading mechanism of the relevant market and enables market participants to react properly and in a timely manner to the new market situation created by that practice;
5. the risk inherent in the relevant practice for the integrity of, directly or indirectly, related markets, whether regulated or not, in the relevant *financial instrument* within the whole Community;
6. the outcome of any investigation of the relevant market practice by any competent authority or other authority mentioned in Article 12(1) of the *Market Abuse Directive*, in particular whether the relevant market practice breached rules or regulations designed to prevent *market abuse*, or codes of conduct, be it on the market in question or on directly or indirectly related markets within the Community;
7. the structural characteristics of the relevant market including whether it is regulated or not, the types of *financial instruments* traded and the type of market participants, including the extent of retail investors' participation in the relevant market.[16]

F. Energy and Commodity-related Derivatives

With respect to energy, and other commodity-related derivatives, it is important **4.18** to note that the prohibition against insider dealing has a more restricted application. Specifically, 'inside information' with respect to derivatives on commodities is restricted to information of a precise nature, not made public, which relates (directly or indirectly) to these derivatives and 'which users of markets on which such derivatives are traded would expect to receive in accordance with accepted market practices on those markets'.[17] This is not quite a 'regular user' test, but it does include a requirement that users of particular commodity markets and accepted market practices should be taken into consideration. This restriction also recognizes that there will be different expectations and different market

---

[16] MAR 1, Annex 2, Table: Pt. 1, 2 G.
[17] Directive Art. 1(1).

practices in different markets. This is a crucial issue for energy markets where many different kinds of markets operate in different ways.[18]

G. Legacy Offences

4.19 One important distinction between the UK implementation and the Directive application of market abuse is that the UK implementation adds two categories of 'misuse of information' which are subtly different from 'insider dealing'. These are sections 118(4) and 118(8). These are known as the UK 'super-equivalent' provisions and are a carry-over from pre-Directive market abuse provisions.[19]

4.20 These sections incorporate some distinct differences from the Directive. First, insider dealing under the Directive is based on the concept of 'inside information'. However, s 118(4) is based on the use of RINGA. Consequently, this provision captures behaviour based on broader categories of information than the Directive. Second, s 118(4) does not require an 'insider'. It only requires that someone behave inappropriately in relation to RINGA. Third, the Directive usually requires some 'positive action'. However, the 'super-equivalent' provisions capture behaviour that constitutes inaction. For example, under s 118(8), failure to correct information creating a false or misleading impression can constitute market abuse.[20]

4.21 There are some types of behaviour that could be caught under the 'super-equivalent' sections that may not be obvious. For example, information about negotiations over a major contract may have to be disclosed if failing to disclose it would allow some to trade to the disadvantage of others on the basis of such information. Also, non-disclosure of major shareholdings can also result in the market being misled. It may give a false picture of the true composition of the shareholder base of the company, or may conceal an intention to accumulate a significant stake in a company.[21]

4.22 It should be noted by those who may be considering engaging in insider dealing, or believe they have been victimized by insider dealing, that this has been the variety of market abuse that has been most enthusiastically prosecuted by the FSA to date. As a review of the market abuse cases summarized in Chapter 14 of this book shows, almost all the penalties that have been imposed for market abuse have been in insider dealing cases.

---

[18] MAR, 1.3.22 G.
[19] See now Financial Services and Markets Act (2000) (Market Abuse) Regulations 2008, SI 2008/1439.
[20] Treasury, *Review of sunset clauses*, p. 10.
[21] Treasury, *Review of sunset clauses*, pp. 10–11.

The nature of insider dealing is that it leaves a relatively clear paper record of the **4.23** transactions that constituted the transactions in question. It is nearly impossible for an 'insider' to hide the evidence of improper dealing. Consequently, it is not that difficult for the FSA to assemble clear proof (especially in an administrative, regulatory case—as opposed to a criminal prosecution) that an insider has engaged in, or assisted, improper trading.

Under the new market abuse regulations, it is not a good idea to attempt insider **4.24** dealing. It seems the likelihood of being caught and punished is fairly high.

5

MARKET MANIPULATION

A. Introduction

The second general type of activity which constitutes market abuse under the **5.01** Directive is 'market manipulation'.[1] This is targeted by Article 5 of the Directive, which states:

> Member States shall prohibit any person from engaging in market manipulation.[2]

On 22 December 2003, the Commission of the European Communities pub- **5.02** lished Commission Directive 2003/124/EC Implementing the Market Abuse Directive ('Implementing Directive 2003/124').[3] Article 4 of Implementing Directive 2003/124 described the type of conduct which is prohibited as the creation of false or misleading impressions in relevant markets. That Article provided a 'non-exhaustive' list of descriptions of the kinds of 'signals, which should not necessarily be deemed in themselves to constitute market manipulation' but which

---

[1] Directive, Recital 12.
[2] Directive, Art. 5.
[3] Commission Directive 2003/124/EC of 22 December 2003 Implementing Directive 2003/6/EC of the European Parliament and of the Council as regards the definition and public disclosure of inside information and the definition of market manipulation, OJ L339/70, 24.12.2003.

should be taken into account when competent authorities review transactions or trading orders of market participants to determine whether they constitute manipulative behaviour 'related to false or misleading signals and to price securing'.[4] They included (but are not limited to):

(a) the extent to which orders to trade given or transactions undertaken represent a significant proportion of the daily volume of transactions in the relevant financial instrument on the regulated market concerned, in particular when these activities lead to a significant change in the price of the financial instrument;

(b) the extent to which orders to trade given or transactions undertaken by persons with a significant buying or selling position in a financial instrument lead to significant changes in the price of the financial instrument or related derivative or underlying asset admitted to trading on a regulated market;

(c) whether transactions undertaken lead to no change in beneficial ownership of a financial instrument admitted to trading on a regulated market;

(d) the extent to which orders to trade given or transactions undertaken include position reversals in a short period and represent a significant proportion of the daily volume of transactions in the relevant financial instrument on the regulated market concerned, and might be associated with significant changes in the price of a financial instrument admitted to trading on a regulated market;

(e) the extent to which orders to trade given or transactions undertaken are concentrated within a short time span in the trading session and lead to a price change which is subsequently reversed;

(f) the extent to which orders to trade given change the representation of the best bid or offer prices in a financial instrument admitted to trading on a regulated market, or more generally the representation of the order book available to market participants, and are removed before they are executed;

(g) the extent to which orders to trade are given or transactions are undertaken at or around a specific time when reference prices, settlement prices and valuations are calculated and lead to price changes which have an effect on such prices and valuations.

5.03   Article 5 of the Implementation Directive 2003/124 was a catch-all section which added to descriptions in Article 4 the requirement that Member States needed to be on guard against 'any other form of deception or contrivance' as a tool for market manipulation. That section gave descriptions of two other categories of things to take account of when reviewing transactions or orders.[5] They were:

(a) whether orders to trade given or transactions undertaken by persons are preceded or followed by dissemination of false or misleading information by the same persons or persons linked to them;

(b) whether orders to trade are given or transactions are undertaken by persons before or after the same persons or persons linked to them produce or disseminate research or investment recommendations which are erroneous or biased or demonstrably influenced by material interest.

---

[4] Implementing Directive 2003/124, Art. 4.
[5] Implementing Directive 2003/124, Art. 5.

In addition to the transactions or orders described above, false or misleading **5.04** impressions can also be created by the dissemination of false or misleading information through the media.[6] The following, non-exhaustive list of trade-based actions[7] can create a false impression of market activity by means of:

- 'wash sales', which are transactions in which there is no genuine change of ownership of financial instruments or real assumption of market risk;
- 'improper matched orders', which consist of transactions to buy or sell the same quantity of a relevant asset at the same price by colluding parties;
- 'painting the tape', which consists of a series of transactions for public display which give the impression of activity or price movement of a financial instrument;
- 'pumping and dumping', which consists of pushing prices to an artificially high level, followed by the massive selling of the relevant instrument for profit, and
- 'advancing the bid', which consists of increasing bids to increase prices which give a false impression of market activity or demand.

To describe them in terms that are perhaps more familiar to market participants,[8] **5.05** the non-exclusive list of 'information-related' market manipulation includes activities such as:

- 'scalping', which consists of purchasing financial instruments for one's own account before recommending them to others, causing prices to rise and then selling at a profit;
- spreading false rumours to induce buying or selling by others;
- making untrue statements of material facts, and
- non-disclosure of material facts or interests.

B. Market Manipulation under MAD

The UK implementation of the 'market manipulation' category of market abuse **5.06** was set out in subsections (5)–(8) of s 118 of the FSMA.[9] In particular:

> (5) … where the behaviour consists of effecting, or participating in effecting, transactions or orders to trade (otherwise than for legitimate reasons in conformity with accepted market practices on the relevant market) which —

---

[6] Directive, Art. 1.
[7] Implementing Directive 2003/124, Art. 4.
[8] Which is how they were described in section B of the Annex to the Proposal for a Directive of the European Parliament and of the Council on Insider Dealing and Market Manipulation (market abuse), 30 April 2001, 2001/0118 (COD).
[9] See above and SI 2005/381.

(a) give, or are likely to give, a false or misleading impression as to the supply of, or demand for, or as to the price or value of, one or more qualifying investments or related investments, or

(b) secure the price of one or more such investments at an abnormal or artificial level.

(6) … where the behaviour consists of effecting, or participating in effecting, transactions or orders to trade which employ fictitious devices or any other form of deception or contrivance.

(7) … where the behaviour consists of disseminating, or causing the dissemination of, information by any means which gives, or is likely to give, a false or misleading impression as to a qualifying investment or related investment by a person who knew or could reasonably be expected to have known that the information was false or misleading.

(8) … where the behaviour (not falling within subsection (5), (6) or (7) —

(a) gives, or is likely to give, a regular user of the market a false or misleading impression as to the supply of, demand for or price or value of, qualifying or related investments, or

(b) would be, or would be likely to be, regarded by a regular user of the market as behaviour that would distort or would be likely to distort, the market in such an investment

and the behaviour is likely to regarded by a regular user of the market as a failure on the part of the person concerned to observe the standard of behaviour reasonably expected of a person in his position in relation to the market.

Details of the FSA's regulation of such behaviour are found in MAR 1.6. The 'legacy offence' in s118(8) is subject to the 'sunset provision' discussed in Chapter 3.

(1) Manipulating transactions as market abuse

5.07 The FSA has adapted and expanded the descriptions found in Article 1.2 of the Market Abuse Directive described above in seeking to describe conduct capable of amounting to market abuse.[10] The following materials set out the FSA's approach.

Conduct which will amount to market abuse

5.08 MAR 1.6.2 E says that the following behaviour *will* amount to market abuse, for being manipulating transactions:[11]

(1) *buying and selling qualifying investments* at the close of the market with the effect of misleading investors who act on the basis of closing prices, other than for legitimate reasons;[12]

(2) wash trades — that is, a sale or purchase of a *qualifying investment* where there is no change in beneficial interest or market risk, or where the transfer of beneficial

---

[10] MAR 1.6.

[11] MAR 1.6.2 E.

[12] See, Directive, Art. 1.2(c).

interest or market risk is only between parties acting in concert or collusion, other than for legitimate reasons;

(3) painting the tape — that is, entering into a series of transactions that are shown on a public display for the purpose of giving the impression of activity or price movement in a *qualifying investment*; and

(4) entering orders into an electronic trading system, at prices which are higher than the previous bid or lower than the previous offer, and withdrawing them before they are executed, in order give a misleading impression that there is demand for or supply of the *qualifying investment* at that price.

A second category of behaviour that is, in the opinion of the FSA, market manipu‑ **5.09** lation ('manipulating transactions') is behaviour that involves 'securing the price' of a qualifying investment, as follows:[13]

(1) transactions or orders to trade by a *person,* or *persons* acting in collusion, that secure a dominant position over the supply of or demand for a *qualifying* investment and which have the effect of fixing, directly or indirectly, purchase or sale prices or creating other unfair trading conditions, other than for legitimate reasons;

(2) transactions where both buy and sell orders are orders at, or nearly at, the same time, with the same price and quantity by the same party, or different but col‑ luding parties, other than for legitimate reasons, unless the transactions are legitimate trades carried out in accordance with the rules of the relevant plat‑ form (such as crossing trades);

(3) entering small orders into an electronic trading system, at prices which are higher than the previous bid or lower than the previous offer, in order to move the price of the *qualifying investment*, other than for legitimate reasons;

(4) an abusive squeeze — that is, a situation in which a *person*:
   (a) has a significant influence over the supply of, or demand for, or delivery mechanisms for a *qualifying investment* or *related investment* or the underly‑ ing product of a derivative contract;
   (b) has a position (directly or indirectly) in an *investment* under which quanti‑ ties of the *qualifying investment, related investment,* or product in question are deliverable; and
   (c) engages in *behaviour* with the purpose of positioning at a distorted level the price at which others have to deliver, take delivery or defer delivery to satisfy their obligations in relation to a *qualifying investment* (the purpose need not be the sole purpose of entering into the transaction or transactions, but must be an actuating purpose);[14]

(5) parties, who have been allocated *qualifying investments* in a primary offering, colluding to purchase further tranches of those *qualifying investments* when trading begins, in order to force the price of the *qualifying investments* to an artificial level and generate interest from other investors, and then sell the *quali‑ fying investments*;

(6) transactions or orders to trade employed so as to create obstacles to the price falling below a certain level, in order to avoid negative consequences for the *issuer*, for example a downgrading of its credit rating; and

---

[13] MAR 1.6.4 E.
[14] See MAR 1.6.4(4) and MAR 1.6.11 E.

(7) trading on one market or trading platform with a view to improperly influencing the price of the same or a related *qualifying investment* that is traded on another *prescribed market.*

Abusive squeezes

5.10   As an example of an abusive squeeze, MAR 1.6.16 E describes a trader with a long position in bond futures who buys or borrows a large number of the bonds which are cheapest to deliver (in satisfaction of the futures contracts) and refuses to re-lend them to others in the market. His purpose is to position the price at which holders of short positions will have to acquire bonds to satisfy their obligations at a level high enough to make him a profit.[15]

5.11   The FSA says that the following factors will be taken into account when determining whether someone has engaged in an abusive squeeze:[16]

(1) the extent to which a *person* is willing to relax his control or other influence in order to help maintain an orderly market, and the price at which he is willing to do so; for example, *behaviour* is less likely to amount to an abusive squeeze if a *person* is willing to lend the investment in question;

(2) the extent to which the *person's* activity causes, or risks causing, settlement default by other market users on a multilateral basis and not just a bilateral basis. The more widespread the risk of multilateral settlement default, the more likely that an abusive squeeze has been effected;

(3) the extent to which prices under the delivery mechanisms of the market diverge from the prices for the delivery of the *investment* or its equivalent outside those mechanisms. The greater the divergence beyond that to be reasonably expected, the more likely that an abusive squeeze has been effected; and

(4) the extent to which the spot or immediate market compared to the forward market is unusually expensive or inexpensive or the extent to which borrowing rates are unusually expensive or inexpensive.

Conduct which may amount to market abuse

5.12   The FSA also gives examples of behaviour which *may* constitute market abuse in the sense of being 'manipulating transactions':[17]

(1) a trader simultaneously buys and sells the same investment, to give the appearance of transfer of title, risk or both,[18] for a price outside the normal trading range of that investment. He does this while holding an option the value of which is related to the investment. His purpose in doing this is to position the price of the investment at an artificial level which will make him a profit or avoid a loss;

---

[15] MAR 1.6.16 E.

[16] MAR 1.6.11 E.

[17] MAR 1.6.15 E.

[18] This type of transaction, whether the purchase and sale is arranged by one trader or several in collusion, is sometimes called a 'wash sale', or 'spin'.

(2) a trader buys a large number of commodity futures whose price is relevant to the settlement value of derivatives also held by the trader. His purpose is to position the price of the commodity futures at an artificial level making him a profit on his derivatives position;

(3) a trader holds a short position in an investment which is currently a component of an 'index' of investments (examples: FTSE 100, S&P, Dow Jones, etc). His position will be profitable if the price of the investment declines to a level that would cause the investment to be dropped from the index. The trader places a large 'sell' order just before the close of trading for the purpose of lowering the investment's price to a false, misleading, abnormal or artificial level which would cause the investment to be dropped from the index, earning the trader a profit on his short position;

(4) a fund manager's quarterly performance is rated on the basis of whether his portfolio's value is higher or lower at the end of the quarter. For the purpose of raising that value (and improving his performance rating) he places a large 'buy' order of relatively illiquid shares which are components of his portfolio. His purpose is to position the price of those shares at a false, misleading abnormal or artificial level.

Illegitimate trade

It should be noted that certain behaviour will be considered market abuse if it is entered into 'other than for legitimate reasons' (numbers '(1)' and '(3)' above). In the opinion of the FSA, the following factors are to be considered indications that behaviour is *not* for legitimate reasons:[19] **5.13**

(1) if the person has an actuating purpose behind the transaction to induce others to trade in, or to position or move the price of, a qualifying investment;
(2) if the person has another, illegitimate, reason behind transaction or orders to trade;[20]
(3) if the transaction was executed in a particular way with the purpose of creating a false or misleading impression.

The FSA, at MAR 1.6.9 E, gives a list of factors which, in the opinion of the FSA, should be taken into account when the FSA considers whether transactions or orders are *manipulating transactions* and, consequently, market abuse:[21] **5.14**

(1) the extent to which orders to trade given or transactions undertaken represent a significant proportion of the daily volume of transactions in the relevant *financial instrument* on the regulated market concerned, in particular when those activities lead to a significant change in the price of the *financial instrument*.

---

[19] MAR 1.6.5 E.
[20] See also, Directive, Recital 20.
[21] MAR 1.6.9 E. The FSA notes that this relates to Art. 4 of Implementing Directive 2003/124.

(2) the extent to which orders to trade given or transactions undertaken by *persons* with a significant buying or selling position in a *financial instrument* lead to significant changes in the price of the *financial instrument* or related derivative or underlying asset admitted to trading on a regulated market;

(3) whether transactions undertaken lead to no change in beneficial ownership of a *financial instrument* admitted to trading on a regulated market;

(4) the extent to which orders to trade given or transactions undertaken include position reversals in a short period and represent a significant proportion of the daily volume of transactions in the relevant *financial instrument* on the regulated market concerned, and might be associated with significant changes in the price of a *financial instrument* admitted to trading on a regulated market;

(5) the extent to which orders to trade given or transactions undertaken are concentrated within a short time span in the trading session and lead to a price change which is subsequently reversed;

(6) the extent to which orders to trade are given to change the representation of the best bid or offer prices in a *financial instrument* admitted to trading on a regulated market, or more generally the representation of the order book available to market participants, and are removed before they are executed;

(7) the extent to which orders to trade are given or transactions are undertaken at or around a specific time when reference prices, settlement prices and valuations are calculated and lead to price changes which have an effect on such prices and valuations.

Legitimate trade

5.15 One the other hand, it is the opinion of the FSA that the following factors are to be taken into account as indications that behaviour *is* for legitimate reasons:[22]

(1) if the transaction is pursuant to a prior legal or regulatory obligation owed to a third party;

(2) if the transaction is executed in a way which takes into account the need for the market as a whole to operate fairly and efficiently;

(3) the extent to which the transaction generally opens a new position, so creating an exposure to market risk, rather than closes out a position and so removes market risk; and

(4) if the transaction complied with the rules of the relevant prescribed markets about how transactions are to be executed in a proper way (for example, rules on reporting and executing cross-transactions).

5.16 The FSA gives the following guidance examples of conduct which are unlikely, *by themselves*, to be market abuse:

(1) market users trading at times and in sizes most beneficial to them whether for:
  (a) long-term investment objectives,
  (b) risk management, or
  (c) short-term speculation,

---

[22] MAR 1.6.6 E.

and seeking maximum profit for themselves. The FSA recognizes that such activities usually improves market liquidity and efficiency;[23]

(2) trading at prices outside their normal range. Such prices can result from the proper interplay of supply and demand.[24]

The FSA recognizes that, in certain market situations, it is necessary to recognize **5.17** that, to preserve an orderly market, trading restrictions that might be deemed as manipulating transactions under other circumstances should not constitute market abuse by virtue of being recognized as 'accepted market practices'. The factors that the FSA will take into consideration when deciding whether to recognize certain trading restrictions as 'accepted market practices' are discussed above. One example of procedures that they have recognized as legitimate 'accepted market practices' and, therefore, not manipulative transactions is the group of practices described in the London Metal Exchange's (LME's) paper on *Market Aberrations: The Way Forward*, which regulates the behaviour of long position holders on the LME in certain situations.[25] In the future, the FSA will undoubtedly consider whether other market situations will require the recognition of additional 'accepted market practices' and the factors entering into their consideration of such practices are described in MAR 1 Annex 2G.[26] The distinction is illustrated by the *EBG and Potts* decision[27] in which Mr Potts, the head of marketing at EBG, and EBG engaged in short selling of shares in an AIM-listed company. EBG eventually achieved short positions in the company equal to 252 per cent of the issued share capital with no prospect of settling sales. A significant number of investors were affected and the LSE intervened to suspend trading. In the FSA's view this amounted to distortion in that:

> The normal market forces of supply, including sellers taking short positions, depends upon the reasonable expectation of market users that the selling party will be in a position to settle transactions in a timely fashion. If sellers cannot settle transactions in a timely fashion, or at all, because they have short sold beyond the level for which they have a reasonable settlement plan, then this will inevitably distort the market for those shares at the point of sale because the expectation of timely delivery on the part of investors who enter into that market and contract to buy shares will not be met.[28]

---

[23] MAR 1.6.7 G.
[24] MAR 1.6.8 G.
[25] MAR 1.6.14 E.
[26] MAR 1.6.14 E.
[27] FSA (Final Notice) dated 12 November 2004.
[28] Paragraph 37 of the Decision Notice.

Stock lending

5.18 With respect to a category of trading that generated some controversy in recent years, stock lending, the FSA has decided to clarify that as *not* being 'wash trades' under MAR 1.6.2 E(2):

> For the avoidance of doubt a stock lending/borrowing or repo/reverse-repo transaction, or another transaction involving the provision of collateral, do not constitute a wash trade under *MAR* 1.6.2 E(2).[29]

Price positioning

5.19 One element that will trigger a finding of market abuse is whether the transactions were undertaken with an *actuating purpose* of 'positioning the price at a false, misleading, abnormal or artificial level'. If that is the motivation for the transaction (no matter how many other positive, wonderful, or laudable motivations may also be attached to it), that is relevant to a finding of market abuse.

5.20 As to whether a person has 'positioned the price' of a regulated investment, the FSA lists the following factors which, in the FSA's opinion, should be taken into account when considering whether 'price positioning' has occurred:

(1) the extent to which the *person* had a direct or indirect interest in the price or value of the *qualifying investment* or *related investment*;

(2) the extent to which price, rate or *option* volatility movements, and the volatility of these factors for the *investments* in question, are outside their normal intraday, daily weekly or monthly range; and

(3) whether a *person* has successively and consistently increased or decreased his bid, offer or the price he has paid for a *qualifying investment* or *related investment*.[30]

5.21 In the future, the FSA will undoubtedly consider whether other market situations will require the recognition of additional 'accepted market practices' and the factors entering into their consideration of such practices are described in MAR 1 Annex 2G.[31]

(2) *Manipulating devices as market abuse*

5.22 FSMA, s 118(6) seeks to regulate the use of fictitious devices, or other forms of deception, to influence the market's view as to the meaning or purpose of transactions or orders. Examples of such devices are found in Articles 4 and 5 of the EC's Implementing Directive A, described above. The FSA fleshes out its regulations on such devices in s 1.7 of the MAR.

---

[29] MAR 1.6.3 G.
[30] MAR 1.6.10 E.
[31] MAR 1.6.14 E.

The following are given as examples of behaviour that will amount to market **5.23**
abuse:[32]

(1) taking advantage of occasional access to the traditional or electronic media by
voicing an opinion about a *financial instrument* (or indirectly about its *issuer*)
while previously taken positions on that *financial instrument* and profiting subsequently from the impact of the opinions voiced on the price of that instrument, without having simultaneously disclosed the conflict of interest to the
public in a proper and effective way;[33]

(2) a transaction or series of transactions that are designed to conceal the ownership
of a *qualifying investment*, so that disclosure requirements are circumvented by
the holding of the *qualifying investment* in the name of a colluding party, such
that disclosures are misleading in respect of the true underlying holding. These
transactions are often structured so that market risk remains with the seller. This
does not include nominee holdings;

(3) pump and dump—that is, taking a long position in a *qualifying investment* and
then disseminating misleading positive information about the *qualifying investment* with a view to increasing its price;

(4) trash and cash—that is, taking a short position in a *qualifying investment* and
then disseminating misleading negative information about the *qualifying investment*, with a view to driving down its price.

Factors that the FSA says, in its opinion, will be taken into account in determining **5.24**
whether behaviour constitutes market abuse in being a manipulative device
include the following, non-exhaustive list:[34]

(1) if orders to trade given or transactions undertaken in *qualifying investments* by
persons are preceded or followed by dissemination of false or misleading information by the same *persons* or *persons* linked to them;

(2) if orders to trade are given or transactions are undertaken in *qualifying investments* by *persons* before or after the same *persons* or *persons* linked to them produce or disseminate research or investment recommendations which are
erroneous or biased or demonstrably influenced by material interest.[35]

(3) *Regulation of producing and disseminating investment recommendations*

As can be seen in the discussion above, the regulation of market abuse committed **5.25**
by using manipulating devices overlaps with the regulation of producing and
disseminating investment recommendations, which under the FSMA is the sixth
type of behaviour that, if improperly done, can constitute market abuse.[36]

---

[32] MAR 1.7.2 E(1). Referring to Art. 1.2 of the Directive.
[33] See also Directive, Art. 1.2.
[34] Taken from Art. 5 of the Implementing Directive 2003/124.
[35] MAR 1.7.3 E.
[36] FSMA, s 118 (7).

5.26 Article 6.5 of the Directive requires those producing or distributing research or other information recommending or suggesting investment strategy to present the information 'fairly', and to disclose any conflicts of interest. In ss 2.9–2.11 of the Joint Consultation Paper, the FSA outlined its proposal for the regulation of the production and dissemination of investment research. Their proposal stated that EU Member States are entitled (by Recital 22 of the Directive) to choose the most appropriate form of regulation to ensure compliance with the Directive's provisions—including self-regulatory mechanisms. The FSA pointed out that in some cases a self-regulatory approach is necessary because the scope of the Directive extends beyond the regulation of investment firms and banks. In particular, journalists who make investment recommendations are also covered. In the FSA's view journalists fall into a different category from independent analysts,-investment firms, banks and others whose main business is to produce investment recommendations. These, in the view of the FSA, are subject to additional obligations to make fair presentations and disclose conflicts of interest.

5.27 For example, investment firms and banks making such recommendations will be required to make quarterly disclosure of all recommendations falling into the categories of 'buy', 'hold', 'sell' (or equivalent terms) and they will be required to disclose the proportion of issuers corresponding to each of these categories to which they have supplied 'material' investment banking services during the previous 12 months.[37]

5.28 FSMA, s 118(7) deals particularly with the dissemination of investment information as market abuse. It says that market abuse can be found:

> ... [Where the behaviour] consists of disseminating, or causing the dissemination of investment information, by any means which gives or is likely to give a false or misleading impression as to a *qualifying investment* or a *related investment*, by a person who knew or could reasonable be expected to have known that the information was false or misleading.

5.29 MAR section 1.8 and the FSA *Handbook, New Conduct of Business Sourcebook* ('COBS') sections 12 and 13, among others, include special regulations dealing with 'dissemination' of investment information. In MAR section 1.8, the following examples of dissemination which *may* constitute market abuse are given:[38]

> (1) a *person* posts information on an Internet bulletin board or chat room which contains false or misleading statements about the takeover of a *company* whose *shares* are *qualifying investments* and the *person* knows that the information is false or misleading;
> (2) a *person* responsible for the content of information submitted to a *regulatory information service* submits information which is false or misleading as to

---

[37] FSA *Handbook, Conduct of Business Sourcebook* ('COB') s 7.17.11 R.
[38] MAR 1.8.6 E.

qualifying investments and that *person* is reckless as to whether the information is false or misleading.

Note that, in these examples, the classifying of certain behaviour as market abuse is not strictly 'result'-determined. Some form of 'intent' is required. In the first instance, positive knowledge of the misrepresentational character of the information is present. In the second, the person is guilty of recklessness when he submits the information in question. **5.30**

The FSA identifies the following factors to be taken into consideration when determining whether certain disseminations of information will amount to market abuse: **5.31**

in the opinion of the *FSA*, if a normal and reasonable *person* would know or should have known in all the circumstances that the information was false or misleading, that indicates that the *person* disseminating the information knew or could reasonably be expected to have known that it was false or misleading;[39]

in the opinion of the *FSA*, if the individuals responsible for dissemination of information within an organisation could only know that the information was false or misleading if they had access to other information that was being held behind a *Chinese wall* or similarly effective arrangements, that indicates that the *person* disseminating did not know and could not reasonably be expected to have known that the information was false misleading.[40]

(4) Misleading behaviour and distortion as market abuse

Market abuse in the forms of 'misleading behaviour' and 'distortion' are presently covered in s 118(8), one of the 'super-equivalent' sections of the FSMA.[41] They are subject to the 'sunset provision' discussed in Chapter 3. These types or market abuse are described as follows: **5.32**

... [W]here the behaviour (not falling within subsections [of FSMA 118] (5), (6) or (7)

    (a) is likely to give a *regular user* of the market a false or misleading impression as to the supply of, demand for or price or value of, *qualifying investments, market abuse (misleading behaviour)*; or

    (b) would be, or would be likely to be, regarded by a *regular user* of the market as behaviour that would distort, or would be likely to distort, the market in such an investment *market abuse (distortion)*

and ... is likely to be regarded by a *regular user* of the market as a failure on the part of the persons concerned to observe the standard of behaviour reasonably expected of a person in his position in relation to the market.[42]

---

[39] MAR 1.8.4 E.

[40] MAR 1.8.5 E.

[41] For further discussion of these 'super-equivalent' sections, see the preceding chapter.

[42] FSMA, s 118(8); SI 2005/381.

5.33 Under the Directive, forbidden 'market distortion' can consist of, among other things, the following inappropriate conduct.[43] The first is trade-based actions intended to create a shortage. These can consist of:

- 'cornering' a market, which is securing a dominant position in any asset or derivative or which can be exploited to manipulate its price; or
- 'abusive squeezes', which consist of having sufficient influence over the supply or demand to dictate arbitrary and abnormal prices.

5.34 The second type of market distortion is based on time-specific trade-based actions which can include:

- 'marking the close', which consists of buying or selling at close of market to alter the closing price or to manipulate transactions based on closing prices;
- trading for the purpose of interfering with spot or settlement prices of derivative contracts, and
- trading to change a spot price or to manipulate transactions indexed to a spot price.

5.35 In the MAR, the FSA gives the following examples of conduct that may amount to market abuse in that they constitute 'market misbehaviour':[44]

(1) the movement of physical *commodity* stocks, which might create a misleading impression as to the supply of, demand for, or price or value of, a *commodity* deliverable under a *commodity futures* contract, and

(2) the movement of an empty cargo ship which might create a false or misleading impression as to the supply of, or the demand for, or the price or value of a *commodity* deliverable under a *commodity futures* contract.

5.36 The FSA goes on to say that:

Behaviour that complies with the requirements imposed on long position holders in the London Metal Exchange's document 'Market Aberrations: The Way Forward' published in October 1998 will not amount to *market abuse (distortion)*.[45]

5.37 The FSA also gives in the COMC lists of factors that will be taken into account in determining whether behaviour will amount to market abuse either as misleading behaviour or distortion. The factors to be taken into account in determining whether behaviour is likely to give a regular user of the relevant market a false or misleading impression as to the supply or demand for or as to the price or value

---

[43] Implementing Directive 2003/124, Arts. 4 and 5.
[44] MAR 1.9.2 E.
[45] MAR 1.9.3 C.

of *qualifying* or *related investments* will include (but are not limited to) the following, according to the COMC:

    (1) the experience and knowledge of the users of the market in question;

    (2) the structure of the market, including its reporting, notification and transparency requirements;

    (3) the legal regulatory requirements of the market concerned;

    (4) the identity and position of the *person* responsible for the *behaviour* which has been observed (if known); and

    (5) the extent and nature of the visibility or disclosure of the person's activity.[46]

The COMC also lists the following factors which, in the opinion of the FSA, will **5.38** be taken into account when determining whether behaviour that creates a false or misleading impression as to, or distorts the market for, a qualifying investment also falls below the standard expected by the *regular user* of the market in question:

    (1) if the transaction is pursuant to a prior legal or regulatory obligation owed to a third party;

    (2) if the transaction is executed in a way which takes into account the need for the market to operate fairly and efficiently; or

    (3) the characteristics of the market in question, including the users and applicable rules and codes of conduct (including, if relevant, any statutory or regulatory obligation to disclose a holding or position, such as under section 198 of the Companies Act 1985);

    (4) the position of the person in question and the standards reasonably to be expected of him in light of his experience, skill and knowledge;

    (5) if the transaction complied with the rules of the relevant *prescribed markets* and how transactions are to be executed in a proper way (for example, rules on reporting and executing cross-transactions); and

    (6) if an *organisation* has created a false or misleading impression, it will be relevant to consider whether the individuals responsible could only know they were likely to create a false or misleading impression if they had access to other information that was being held behind a Chinese wall or similarly effective arrangements.[47]

(5) Short selling rules

The FSA has recently had to address the practice of short selling, which was **5.39** thought to be contributing to market instability. It did so by introducing two sets of Rules. The first created a disclosure obligation in relation to any 'significant' short position created or increased while the issuer was pursuing a rights issue. In particular it was provided that 'failure by a person to give adequate disclosure that he has reached or exceeded a disclosable short position where (1) that position

---

[46] MAR 1.9.4 E.

[47] MAR 1.9.5 E.

relates, directly or indirectly, to securities which are the subject of a rights issue; and (2) the disclosable short position is reached or exceeded during a rights issue period; is behaviour which, in the opinion of the FSA, is market abuse (misleading behaviour)'.[48]

5.40 Second, a further set of Rules was introduced on 19 September 2008 which effectively prohibited the active creation or increase of net short positions in publicly quoted UK banks, UK insurers or their parents.[49] Again, the FSA indicated that such conduct would be regarded as amounting to market abuse (misleading behaviour). There was an exception in the case of market makers. These provisions required daily disclosure of all net short positions in excess of 0.25 per cent of the ordinary share capital of the relevant companies held at close of market the previous day under threat that a failure so to do would amount to market abuse in the opinion of the FSA. As originally introduced the Short Selling No. 2 Rules were timed to expire on 16 January 2009. These provisions, contained in MAR 1.9.2 C, D and E, have subsequently undergone a number of modifications such that the current text now provides:

> MAR 1.9.2.D E (1) Failure by a person who has a disclosable short position in a UK financial sector company to provide adequate ongoing disclosure of their position is behaviour which, in the opinion of the FSA is market abuse (misleading behaviour).
>
> (2) In (1), 'adequate ongoing disclosure' means disclosure made on a RIS by no later than 3.30pm on the business day following the day on which the position reaches, exceeds or falls below a disclosable short position of 0.25%, 0.35%, 0.45% and 0.55% of the issued share capital of the company and each 0.1% threshold thereafter.
>
> (2A) The disclosure referred to in (1) must include the name of the person who has the position, the amount of the disclosable short position and the name of the company in relation to which it has that position.
>
> (3) For the avoidance of doubt, changes in a disclosable short position between the thresholds referred to in (2) do not need to be disclosed under this section. For example, an increase from 0.25% to 0.31% of the issued share capital of the company does not need to be disclosed.
>
> (4) For the avoidance of doubt, (1) applies during a rights issue period.

5.41 The Short Selling No. 2 Rules were introduced in the light of the demise of Lehman Brothers and the proposed take over of HBOS by Lloyds TSB following the collapse of HBOS shares.

---

[48] MAR 1.9.2A E introduced by the Short Selling Instrument 2008 (FSA 2008/30).
[49] Short Selling (No. 2) Instrument 2008 (FSA 2008/50) promulgating MAR 1.9.2 C, D and E.

C. Some Thoughts on Market Manipulation

As can be seen from the detail discussed above, market manipulation is a complex   **5.42**
category of market abuse. Its complexity makes it difficult to prove, and therefore
difficult to punish.

Unusual changes to market prices can have many causes. It is not easy to show that   **5.43**
any particular change was a result of any particular factor. However, as discussed
above, in previous chapters, the FSA has other regulatory tools at its disposal to
avoid the difficulties that proving 'market manipulation' may present. An example
is provided by the FSA's actions in the *Citigroup Global Markets Limited* (*'Citigroup'*)
matter.[50] In the *Citigroup* case, the FSA concluded that Citigroup had employed
a strategy in the European government bond markets whereby Citigroup built up
and rapidly exited those positions within a particular period of time. Despite the
fact that the FSA found that disruptions of certain market volumes and prices had
resulted, the FSA did not charge Citigroup with 'market manipulation'.

On 28 June 2005, the FSA fined Citigroup £13.9 million for breaching FSA   **5.44**
Principles 2 and 3 by not conducting its business with due skill, care and diligence
and failing to effectively control its business.

Hector Sants, then FSA Managing Director for Wholesale Business, said:

> The FSA views firms' adherence to its principles as fundamental in helping to main-
> tain efficient, orderly and fair markets. [Citigroup] planned authorised and executed
> a trading strategy without having due regard to the risks and likely consequences of
> its action for the efficient and orderly operation of the MTS platform. Furthermore
> the lack of adequate systems and controls meant that the strategy was never fully
> considered as would be expected, at an appropriate senior level within
> [Citigroup].[51]

This regulatory action should be taken as a signal to entities regulated by the FSA   **5.45**
that where the FSA can use a more flexible regulatory tool to control market
abuse, such as breach of FSA Principles, they will do so. This avoids the risk that
they may fail to establish all the elements that a specific allegation of 'market
abuse' may require.

---

[50] FSA, Final Notice to Citigroup Global Markets Limited, 28 June 2005.
[51] FSA, *Press Release*, FSA/PN/072/2005, 28 June 2005, p. 1.

6

INTERPRETATION

A. Introduction

Interpreting and understanding the statutes and other regulating provisions on market abuse requires some effort. Therefore, it may be useful to review the guidance provided on how this task should be approached. **6.01**

Part XXIX of FSMA provides help with interpretation. Section 417 gives a number of specific definitions. Sections 418 and 420–425 contain interpretative provisions relating to: **6.02**

- carrying on regulated activities in the United Kingdom;
- parent and subsidiary undertaking;
- group;
- controller;
- manager;
- insurance;
- 'investment firm';[1] and
- expressions relating to authorization elsewhere in the single market.

---

[1] Added by FSMA 2000, s 424A pursuant to the Financial Services and Markets Act 2000 (Markets in Financial Instruments) (Modification of Powers) Regulations 2006, SI 2006/2975, regs 2, 10.

In addition, s 419 gives power to the Treasury to define 'carrying on regulated activities by way of business', which it has duly done under an Order under that section (see next paragraph).

6.03   The above statutory provisions are supplemented by a large number of Statutory Instruments which provide further definitional detail[2]—such as the Financial Services and Markets Act 2000 (Regulated Activities) Order 2001;[3] the Financial Services and Markets Act 2000 (Carrying on Regulated Activities by Way of Business) Order 2001;[4] and the Financial Services and Markets Act 2000 (Financial Promotion) Order 2005.[5] This body of subordinate legislation has been the subject of frequent amendment. In the context of market abuse, the financial promotion regime is important owing to the overarching duty of firms to issue promotions which are clear, fair and not misleading. On 10 January 2008 the FSA imposed a £250,000 financial penalty on Square Mile Securities Ltd for persistently using high-pressure sales tactics and providing misleading information to sell shares to customers that they did not want or could not afford. The FSA found that:[6]

> Square Mile failed to pay due regard to the information needs of its customers and communicate clear, fair and not misleading information about the Securities by making false representations and/or providing inaccurate and incomplete information in conjunction with ambiguous personal and speculative opinions. Square Mile failed to provide full explanations about the significant risks associated with the Securities and/or made statements which otherwise obscured, diminished or unfairly distorted the risks (and other characteristics) of the Securities. As a result, there was a likelihood, or a reasonable possibility, that customers were misled and/or formed erroneous impressions about the Securities.

B.   The Code of Market Conduct

6.04   FSMA, s 119 requires the FSA to:

> issue a code containing such provisions the FSA considers will give appropriate guidance to those determining whether or not behaviour amounts to market abuse.

6.05   The COMC may, among other things, specify:

> factors that, in the opinion of the [FSA], are to be taken into account determining whether or not behaviour amounts to market abuse.[7]

---

[2] Which the FSA is empowered to make under FSMA 2000, s 419.
[3] SI 2001/544.
[4] SI 2001/1177.
[5] SI 2005/1529.
[6] *FSA v Square Mile Securities* (Final Notice), 10 January 2008 at para 2.2(3).
[7] FSMA, s 119(2)(c).

In 2005 s 119 was amended to provide for the COMC further specifying 'descriptions of behaviour that are accepted market practices in relation to one or more specified markets' and 'descriptions of behaviour that are not accepted market practices in relation to one or more specified markets'.[8]

The FSA has met its obligation under FSMA, s 119 by publishing the COMC[9] in the Market Conduct ('MAR') manual in the Business Standards 'block' of the FSA *Handbook*.[10]   **6.06**

The *Handbook* itself is divided into several broad scope 'blocks' on different topic areas. Each block contains a number of specific sourcebooks or manuals on more discrete topics. With respect to interpretation there is a 'General Provisions' manual ('GEN') in the High Level Standards block which includes information (at the 'GEN 2' section) about interpreting the *Handbook* generally. The FSA *Handbook* also includes a Glossary which defines terms. Both of these can be found on the FSA website.[11]   **6.07**

The COMC consists of MAR 1.1–MAR 1.11,[12] plus MAR 1 Annex 1 (Provisions of the Buy-back and Stabilisation Regulation relating to buy-back programmes) and MAR 1 Annex 2 (Accepted Market Practices), Annexes 3 (Specialist Topics) and 4 (Frequently asked Questions) having been revoked on 30 June 2005. The latest 'edition', in response to the implementation of the EU Market Abuse Directive, first came into effect on 1 July 2005, but one must remain aware that the COMC is subject to being continually updated and supplemented on the FSA's website.   **6.08**

The scope of application of the COMC required by FSMA, s 119 is stated in MAR 1.1.1:   **6.09**

> This chapter (which contains the COMC) applies to all persons seeking guidance on the market abuse regime.[13]

MAR 1.1.5 G states that: **6.10**

> Part VIII of the Act, and in particular s 118, specifies seven types of behaviour which can amount to market abuse. This chapter considers the general concepts relevant to market abuse, then each type of relevant market behaviour in turn and then describes

---

[8] See s 119(2)(d) and (e) inserted by the Financial Services and Markets Act 2000 (Market Abuse) Regulations 2005, SI 2005/381, reg 5, Sch 2, para 2(1) and (2).

[9] Otherwise referred to elsewhere in this work as 'COMC'.

[10] As has been seen throughout this book, footnote references to the Code of Market Conduct are written: 'MAR', followed by the section of the Code, e.g. 'MAR 1'.

[11] <www.fsa.gov.uk>.

[12] MAR 1.11 (Scope of the market abuse regime) ceased to be in force from 30 June 2005.

[13] MAR 1.1.1.

exceptions to market abuse which are of general application. In doing so, it sets out the relevant provisions of the COMC, that is:

(1) descriptions of behaviour that, in the opinion of the FSA, do or do not amount to market abuse (see section 119(2) (a) and (b) and section 122 of the Act [FSMA].[14]

(2) descriptions of behaviour that are or are not accepted market practices in relation to one or more identified markets (see section 119(2)(d) and (e) and section 122(1) of the Act (subject to the behaviour being for legitimate reasons)); and

(3) factors that, in the opinion of the FSA, are to be taken into account in determining whether or not behaviour amounts to market abuse (see section 119(2)(c) and section 122(2) of the Act).

6.11 Section 122(1) of the FSMA states that:

> If a person behaves in a way which is described (in the code in force under section 119 at the time of the behaviour) as behaviour that, in the Authority's [the FSA's] opinion, does not amount to market abuse that behaviour of his is to be taken, for the purposes of this Act, as not amounting to market abuse.

Importantly, s 122(2) then goes on to provide:

> Otherwise, the Code in force under section 119 at the time when particular behaviour occurs may be relied on so far as it indicates whether or not that behaviour should be taken to amount to market abuse.

6.12 In interpreting the Code, the FSA has provided additional help. It has published the Reader's Guide to the FSA *Handbook*, which answers a number of questions about structure and interpretation.[15] The Reader's Guide, in a section entitled 'Understanding Handbook Text: Interpretation Tips', states that:

> Perhaps the most important provision of GEN 2 is that it requires a purposive interpretation of the rules.[16]

This indicates that the interpretation of a word may differ depending on the context or purpose behind the rule.

6.13 MAR 1.1.6 points out an important limitation on the guidance provided by the COMC with respect to market abuse:

> The COMC does not exhaustively describe all types of behaviour that may or may not amount to market abuse.[17]

6.14 In other words, although the FSA wishes to provide enough guidance to allow market participants to understand the nature of market abuse, it is not going to

---

[14] MAR 1.1.5.
[15] FSA, 'Reader's Guide: an introduction to the FSA *Handbook*' (17 March 2005) ('Reader's Guide').
[16] Reader's Guide, p. 23.
[17] MAR 1.1.6.

allow the COMC to limit the FSA in punishing newly developed and/or previously unheard-of ways of abusing the financial markets. In any event what constitutes market abuse ultimately depends on the correct statutory construction of FSMA and the subordinate legislation made under the Act.

The COMC is marked by the FSA to indicate that different provisions provide **6.15** different types of guides and have different evidential weight when used in making a judgment about whether or not behaviour would be considered market abuse. The COMC flags how the market users will be judged against the standards for the prevention of market abuse mandated by the FSMA. To that end, the COMC includes text icons containing letters intended to identify the legal status of particular provisions.

There are three types of designations which are marked in the COMC by the **6.16** letters 'C', 'E', and 'G'.

(1) Conclusive provisions

MAR 1.1.4, entitled 'Using MAR 1', points out that: **6.17**

> Provisions designated with a 'C' indicate behaviour which conclusively, for purposes of the Act, does not amount to market abuse' (see s 122(1) of the Act [FSMA]).[18]

If a person confirms his behaviour to those descriptions, his behaviour will not amount to market abuse. Such descriptions are regarded as 'conclusive' by the FSA (hence the 'C') that such behaviour does not amount to market abuse.

(2) Evidential provisions

Descriptions of behaviour which carry evidential weight are indicated by 'E'. **6.18** Unlike the safe harbours, they are not conclusively determinative as to whether or not behaviour constitutes market abuse but they do carry evidential weight and may be relied upon to that extent, in judging whether or not behaviour will constitute market abuse.

According to the Reader's Guide, the letter 'E' is used to identify evidential provi- **6.19** sions with the characteristics specified in s 149 of the FSMA. The Reader's Guide states:

> An evidential provision is a rule, but it is not binding in its own right. It always relates to some other binding rule.[19] ... These paragraphs [that are labelled 'E'] of the Code

---

[18] MAR 1.1.4(2).
[19] Reader's Guide, p. 19.

of Market Conduct may be relied on so far as they indicate whether or not particular behaviour should be taken to amount to market abuse.[20]

Evidence in COMC is therefore of evidential weight for the purposes of FSMA, s 119 and is therefore good authority as to the meaning of market abuse in FSMA, s 118.[21]

6.20 When the letter E is used it is intended to identify evidential provisions as described in s 149 of the Act.[22] An evidential provision is a 'rule' but it is not binding by itself. It is always related to some other binding rule. When the provision says so, compliance with an evidential provision may be relied on as 'tending to establish compliance' with the related rule. Also, when it says so, contravention of the provision will tend to establish contravention of the related rule. Such an evidential provision should always say one of those things or both. What these provisions do is to create reasonable presumptions of compliance with or contravention of related binding rules. In particular, with respect to the COMC, such paragraphs identify:

- behaviour which, in the opinion of the FSA will amount to market abuse, and
- factors that, in the opinion of the FSA, should be taken into account in deciding whether or not behaviour constitutes market abuse.

6.21 Paragraphs of the COMC may be relied on to the extent that they identify whether or not particular behaviour should be interpreted as market abuse.[23] In this regard, s 122(2) of the Act is of crucial importance in providing that the COMC in force under s 119 at the time when particular behaviour occurs may be relied on so far as it indicates whether or not that behaviour should be taken to amount to market abuse.

(3) Guidance provisions

6.22 Sections of the COMC marked with the letter 'G' are used to indicate 'guidance' as described by the FSMA, s 157. This guidance is intended to illuminate the

---

[20] *Ibid.*

[21] It must be noted that this guide does not constitute formal guidance. 'In the event of any conflict between this guide and the Handbook, the Handbook will take precedence.' Reader's Guide, p. 2.

[22] s 149 says: '(1) if a particular rule so provides, contravention of the rule must not give rise to any of the consequences provided for by other provisions of the Act. (2) a rule that so provides must also provide — (a) that contravention may be relied on as intending to establish contravention of such other rule as may be specified; or (b) that compliance may be relied on as intending to establish compliance with such other rule as may be specified. (3) a rule may include the provision mentioned in sub-section (1) only if the Authority considers that it is appropriate for it also to include the provision required by sub-section (2).'

[23] Reader's Guide, p. 19.

operation of the FSA *Handbook*, its relation to the FSMA and other matters. The guidance will usually be contained in the *Handbook*, but in some cases, it will be published in a separate 'Guidance Note'. Therefore, it is important to keep track of new additions to the FSA's website which are relevant to the market participant in question.

Ways in which guidance may be used are to explain provisions of the rules or to indicate likely means of compliance to recommend courses of action or for other purposes. Regardless of how the guidance is used, it is not 'binding', nor does it have 'evidential' effect. To comply with relevant requirements, one need not follow the guidance. Nor will any deviation from the guidance be presumed to be a breach of the relevant rule.   **6.23**

The purpose of guidance is to shed light on regular requirements, but it is not intended to be an exhaustive description of market participants' obligations. However, it is likely that acting in accordance with guidance in the relevant circumstances will at least encourage the FSA to proceed on the basis that the person in question has complied with rules or requirements to which the guidance relates.   **6.24**

The rights of third parties will not be affected by guidance given by the FSA, nor is FSA guidance binding on courts in cases relating to regulated activity, contract actions or other actions. The FSA points out that the parties will need to seek their own legal advice.   **6.25**

The 'G' is also used to indicate FSA procedure for giving statutory notices under the FSMA, s 395, for policy statements about the FSA's enforcement powers, to indicate arrangements of the FSA under paragraph 7 of Schedule 1 to the FSMA, regarding the exercise of its non-legislative functions, and to indicate other background information which is not 'guidance'.[24]   **6.26**

C. 'Likely'

Despite all the guidance provided in various forms by the FSA on the general subject of market abuse (and this book also includes a glossary of terms), there are some specific terms that are important enough to merit a fuller explanation. It is not within the scope of this book to expand all such terms. However, one such word is the word 'likely'. It may be useful to say some more about that.   **6.27**

'Likely' frequently appears in the statutory and *Handbook* sections relating to market abuse. It is used to emphasize that in a number of cases market abuse can   **6.28**

---

[24] For information about the use of the letter 'G' in the *Handbook*, see the Reader's Guide, p. 20.

result not only from conduct that does cause a particular effect, but also from conduct 'likely' to have such an effect.[25] As can be seen from these and other sections, under the Directive and its UK implementation it is not only where the alleged conduct has an actual impact on the market that it can constitute market abuse. In addition, conduct that is only 'likely' to have an adverse effect on markets can, in some circumstances, be sufficient.

6.29   In the certain cases described under FSMA, s 118, the word 'likely' is used to indicate that market conduct 'likely' to have particular adverse effects can constitute market abuse as well as positive conduct which does cause the market effects.[26]

6.30   The use of the word 'likely' by the FSA in the COMC relates specifically to the sections on creating false and misleading impressions, or manipulating transactions (MAR 1.5 and MAR 1.6, respectively). This makes the 'likelihood' of a state of affairs resulting from certain behaviour an issue in determining culpability for market abuse.

6.31   In the past, the FSA has interpreted the meaning of the word 'likely' as used in the market abuse regime as meaning that there must be a real (non-fanciful) likelihood that the behaviour will have the abusive effect.[27] Although this specific clarification was not reproduced in the final text of the Rules it is suggested that the FSA will not be required to establish 'likelihood that abusive behaviour will have an adverse effect' as a fact on the balance of probabilities. To set the threshold that high would detract from the need to ensure effective powers to regulate the market.

6.32   Further, the FSA has reported that it observed that the courts have provided a variety of definitions of 'likely', depending on the context.[28] After reviewing the various definitions, the FSA concluded that, for its purposes, the appropriate definition of 'likely' is that there must be a real and not fanciful likelihood that the result at issue will occur. It is more than a 'bare possibility', but less than 'more likely than not'.[29] As shown above, FSMA, s 119 indicates that the FSA's opinion is the point of reference in determining whether a behaviour amounts to market abuse. Therefore, it is reasonable to rely on the FSA's opinion of the definition of the word 'likely' as it relates to market abuse.

---

[25] For examples, see FSMA, s 118, sub-ss (4), (5), (7) and (8).

[26] Directive, Art. 1 and Implementing Directive 2003/124, Arts. 1 and 2.

[27] A draft MAR 1.6.4 E(2) quoted in Consultation Paper CP59 said: 'in order to be likely, there must be a real and not fanciful likelihood that behaviour will have such an effect, even if that likelihood is less than 50%.'

[28] FSA, *Code of Market Conduct, Feedback on CP 59 and CP 76*, April 2001, p. 11, s 4.10.

[29] See, e.g., the discussion of Lord Woolf MR on likelihood and probability in *Allied Maples Group Ltd v Simmons & Simmons* [1995] 4 AER 907.

The FSA now provides less guidance on the definition of the word 'likely', but there is no reason to believe that the FSA has changed its opinion on the meaning of 'likely'. **6.33**

Referring to the distortion test under pre-Directive MAR 1.6.4, the FSA also noted that sometimes behaviour may be likely to give rise to more than one effect, including the bad effect in question. However, one would not escape a finding of market abuse because the behaviour in question had several positive effects as well as a likely abusive effect.[30] The FSA has conceded that, with respect to proceedings involving allegations of market abuse, the FSA will have the burden of proof to show that a result is 'likely'. The FSA will have to prove its case on the balance of probabilities.[31] **6.34**

D. Conclusion

The fundamental standard of behaviour is relatively simple: the duty not to compromise the fair and efficient operation of the market or to unfairly damage investors. However, the ways in which this standard will be applied and interpreted are many and flexible. For that reason, the FSA has tried to give guidance about how this may be dealt with in various circumstances. **6.35**

Further guidance will emerge from decisions of the Financial Services and Markets Tribunal. By way of example in the recent determination of a reference by Winterflood and two of its traders, Mr Sotiriou and Mr Robins, the Tribunal gave important guidance on the meaning of MAR 1.6.4E.[32] The background to the case was as follows. In June 2008, the FSA found that Winterflood and its traders had played a pivotal role in an illegal share ramping scheme relating to Fundamental-E Investments plc (FEI), an AIM-listed company. In particular, the market maker had misused rollovers and delayed rollovers thereby creating a distortion in the market for FEI shares and misleading the market for about six months in 2004. The FEI share trades executed by Winterflood had a series of unusual features which should have alerted the market maker to the clear and substantial risks of market manipulation. Rather than taking steps to ensure that the trades were genuine, Winterflood continued the highly profitable trading. Winterflood made about £900,000 from trading in FEI shares, its single most profitable stock at the time. The share ramping scheme led to the FEI share price increasing from 4p in December 2003 to a high of 12.25p in June 2004. The London Stock Exchange suspended trading in shares in FEI on 15 July 2004. **6.36**

---

[30] MAR 1.6.4(2)E (revoked 30 June 2005).
[31] *Feedback on CP 59 and CP 76*, April 2001, p. 11, s 4.11.
[32] *FSA v Winterflood and Others*, Decision 11 March 2009.

Following the resumption of trading on 23 July 2004, the price dropped back to 4p and has never recovered. As a result of their conduct, the FSA decided to impose fines of £4 million, £200,000 and £50,000 on Winterflood, Mr Sotiriou and Mr Robins respectively.

6.37 Winterflood did not challenge the findings of the FSA investigation at the Tribunal but referred the matter on a point of legal interpretation. In particular, Winterflood submitted that MAR 1.6.4E under the heading Element of the test was framed in unambiguous and unqualified terms such that the Code, it was argued, required that Winterflood had an actuating purpose of positioning prices at a distorted level which the FSA would need to prove. This argument was rejected, the Tribunal holding:[33]

> We do not consider that Winterflood's interpretation 10 of MAR 1.6.4E is correct. The first sentence of MAR 1.6.4E provides that the behaviour must be such that a regular user would, or would be likely to, regard it as behaviour which would, or would be likely to, distort the market in question. The second sentence merely describes an instance where behaviour with an actuating purpose will amount to market abuse. The second sentence does not purport to provide an exhaustive description of behaviour which will amount to market abuse or to set out an essential requirement which must be present before the requirements of section 118(2)(c) are satisfied. By referring to an instance which will amount to market abuse the Code is not to be taken as providing that other circumstances will or will not amount to market abuse. The fallacy in Winterflood's submission is that it assumes that the Authority in MAR 1.4.4E has chosen to indicate, in clear terms, that certain behaviour (here: relevant behaviour without the relevant actuating purpose) is not market abuse, then that indication may be relied upon. MAR 1.6.4E can not be read as providing that the absence of actuating purpose results in behaviour not amounting to market abuse. It simply states that certain behaviour with actuating purpose will amount to market abuse. It does not make any specific reference to behaviour occurring absent an actuating purpose and such conduct is not to be taken as excluded from market abuse by the express reference to actuating purpose in MAR 1.6.4E.

6.38 The Tribunal was clearly concerned to construe the provisions of the COMC in context and to produce consistency of interpretation. Thus, it observed:[34]

> We also note that, consistently with the conclusion set out above, MAR 1.6.11E, which sets out a list of factors to be taken into account in determining whether behaviour amounts to market abuse, does not expressly refer to actuating purpose and that there is no safe harbour in MAR 1.6 where behaviour occurs absent an actuating purpose.

---

[33] *Ibid.*, paras 43–44.
[34] *Ibid.*, para 45.

7

SCOPE OF COVERAGE

A. The Reach of the Market Abuse Regime

From the outset, the FSA took a very broad view of the coverage of the market **7.01** abuse regime. In their December 2001 'Factsheet', the Authority stated:

1. The Code [of Market Conduct] covers a range of abuses not covered by existing criminal law and it will apply to everyone who participates in, or whose conduct may have an effect on, the UK financial markets.
2. Everyone is covered, whether regulated by the FSA or not, based in the UK or overseas, and whether a professional or retail investor.[1]

This continues to represent the approach of the FSA.

B. Which Products are Covered?

Article 9 of the EU Market Abuse Directive[2] stated: **7.02**

This Directive shall apply to any financial instrument admitted to trading on a regulated market in at least one Member State, or for which a request for admission

---

[1] FSA *Factsheet*; 'Why market abuse could cost you money' (December 2001).
[2] Directive 2003/6/EC of the European Parliament and of the Council of 28 January 2003 on Insider Dealing and Market Manipulation (market abuse) (OJ L96, 12.4.2003) (referred to below as the 'Market Abuse Directive', or simply the 'Directive').

to trading on such a market has been made, irrespective of whether or not the transaction itself actually takes place on that market.

Articles 2, 3 and 4 shall also apply to any financial instrument not admitted to trading on a regulated market in a Member State, but whose value depends on a financial instrument as referred to in paragraph 1.

Articles 6(1) to (3) shall not apply to issuers who have not requested or approved admission of their financial instruments to trading on a regulated market in a Member State.

7.03   Article 1 of the Directive stated that:[3]

'Financial instrument' shall mean:
- transferable securities as defined in Council Directive 93/22/EEC of 10 May 1993 on investment services in the securities field,[4]
- units in collective investment undertakings,
- money-market instruments,
- financial-futures contracts, including equivalent cash-settled instruments,
- forward interest-rate agreements,
- interest-rate, currency and equity swaps,
- options to acquire or dispose of any instrument falling into these categories, including equivalent cash-settled instruments. This category includes particular options on currency and on interest rates,
- derivatives on commodities,
- any other instrument admitted to trading on a regulated market in a Member State or for which a request for admission to trading on such a market has been made.

7.04   It is to be noted in summary that Article 9 of the Directive was expressed to cover (1) any 'financial instrument admitted to trading on a regulated market in at least one Member State or for which a request for admission to trading on such a market has been made' and (2) any 'financial instrument' not so admitted but whose 'value depends' on financial instruments which have been so admitted. Despite the importance of the meaning of the phrase 'value depends', it was not defined in the Directive. Its limits are left to be determined by legislation, the regulators and the courts.

7.05   The coverage of the UK market abuse regime is set out in MAR 1.2.1–1.2.6. The COMC first refers to FSMA, s 118(1), which says:

For purposes of this Act, market abuse is behaviour (whether by one person alone or by two or more persons jointly or in concert) which —
(a) occurs in relation to:
    (i) qualifying investments admitted to trading on a prescribed market, or
    (ii) qualifying investments in respect of which a request for admission to trading on such a market has been made, or

---

[3] Directive, Art. 1, sub-para. 3. See also Proposal for a Directive, 30 May 2001, Annex, Section A, Financial Instruments, p. 24.

[4] Investment Services Directive, 93/22 (OJ L141, 11.6.1993), p. 27, as last amended by European Parliament and Council Directive 2000/64/EC (OJ L290, 17.11.2000, p. 27) ('ISD').

(iii) in the case of subsections (2) and (3) [market abuse by insider dealing and improper disclosure, respectively], investments which are related investments in relation to such qualifying investments, and

(b) falls within any one or more of the types of behaviour set out in subsections (2) to (8).[5]

In the above provisions, market abuse is thus behaviour in relation to financial instruments falling within Article 9 of the Directive. In the COMC these are referred to as '*qualifying investments*', being investments traded on, or subject to, the rules of a '*prescribed market*'. The COMC 'Glossary' defines both 'qualifying investments' and 'prescribed markets' as those: **7.06**

> prescribed by the Treasury in the Prescribed Markets and Qualifying Investments Order'[6] or 'the PMO'.

Pre-Directive, Article 4 of the PMO[7] originally defined 'prescribed markets' as 'all markets which are established under the rules of a UK recognised investment exchange'.[8] The definition was expanded by an amendment introduced by the Financial Services Markets Act 2000 (Market Abuse) Regulations 2005[9] to include the following: **7.07**

- UK 'recognised investment exchanges' ('RIEs');
- OFEX (now PLUS Markets plc),[10] and
- 'regulated markets' as defined by Article 1(13) of the Investment Services Directive.[11]

The markets concerned now include the London Stock Exchange plc, EDX London Ltd, LIFFE Administration and Management, ICE Futures Europe, the London Metal Exchange Ltd, and Plus Markets plc (formerly OFEX), a trading facility for unlisted and unquoted securities.[12] An up-to-date list of RIEs can be found at <www.fsa.gov.uk/register/exchanges.do>. **7.08**

---

[5] MAR 1.2.2.

[6] FSA *Handbook*, Glossary.

[7] See the Financial Services and Markets Act 2000 (Prescribed Markets and Qualifying Investments) Order 2001/996.

[8] *Ibid.*, Article 4.

[9] SI 2005/381.

[10] On 19 July 2007 the FSA conferred RIE status on Plus Markets.

[11] ISD; EU members communicate the names of markets which they have designated 'regulated markets' to an annual list published by the EU. See, e.g., the 'Annotated Presentation of Regulated Markets and National Provisions Implementing Relevant Requirements of ISD' (93/22) (2005/C 112/02).

[12] SWX Europe Ltd (formerly virt-x) was also an RIE but closed its London presence in 2009, relocating to Zurich.

7.09   Article 5 of the same Order defined 'qualifying investments' as follows:

> There are prescribed, as qualifying investments in relation to the markets described
> by Article 4, all financial instruments within the meaning given in Article 1(3) of
> Directive 2003/6/EC of the European Parliament and the Council of 28 January
> 2003 on insider dealing and market manipulation (market abuse).[13]

7.10   Now the regime applies to all regulated markets throughout the EEA, that is,
those listed by EEA jurisdiction regulators in accordance with Article 4(14) of the
Markets in Financial Instruments Directive 2004/39/EC of 21 April 2004.

7.11   The above definitions apply for the purposes of FSMA, s 118, subsections (2), (3),
(5), (6) and (7). In relation to the so-called 'legacy offences' in subsections (4) and
(8) the scope of coverage is extended.[14] For these offences, behaviour that occurs
in relation to anything that is the subject matter, or whose price or value is expressed
by reference to the price or value of the qualifying investments, or occurs in relation to investments (whether or not they are qualifying investments) whose subject matter is the qualifying investments, is to be regarded as 'occurring in relation
to qualifying investments'.[15]

7.12   Thus, in these 'legacy cases' behaviour occurring in 'relation' to qualifying investments, involving insider dealing or market distortion,[16] can include behaviour
which:

>   (a)   occurs in relation to anything which is the subject matter, or whose price
>   or value is expressed by reference to the price or value of qualifying invest-
>   ments; or
>   (b)   occurs in relation to investments (whether qualifying or not) whose subject
>   matter is qualifying investments.[17]

7.13   Putting the legacy cases to one side, more widely, the market abuse regime in any
event extends not only to 'qualifying investments' but also, in some cases, to
'related investments'. 'Related' is a catch-all term apt to bring in many investment
products, regardless of what market they are traded in, which are 'related' to qualifying investments.

7.14   This flows from the phrases in FSMA, s 118, 'occurs in relation to' and 'related
investments'. In other words, market abuse can occur not only when one is dealing in 'qualifying investments' on 'prescribed markets', but can also occur in transactions which 'relate' to those things.

---

[13] SI 2005/381, reg. 10.
[14] Note the discussion of the sunset provisions applying these subsections in Chapter 3, para. 3.11
et seq.
[15] FSMA 2000, s 118A(3).
[16] FSMA, s 118(4) and (8), SI 2005/381, Sch. 2, reg. 5, s 1. (All following references to the post-
Directive Implementation s 118 should be understood to refer to the amendments to that regulation
in SI 2005/381.)
[17] FSMA, s 118A(3).

In the FSA *Handbook* Glossary, the term 'investment' is defined as: **7.15**

(in accordance with sections 22(4) (The classes of activity and categories of investments) and 397(13) (Miscellaneous offences) of the Act) any investment, including any asset, right or interest.[18]

FSMA, s 130A(3) says: **7.16**

'related investment', in relation to a qualifying investment, means an investment whose price or value depends on the price or value of the qualifying investment.[19]

According to the FSA *Handbook* Glossary 'related investment': **7.17**

(as defined in section 130A(3) of the Act) in relation to a qualifying investment, means an investment whose price or value depends on the price or value of the qualifying investment.

Thus, Contracts for Difference relating to shares traded on the London Stock Exchange were treated as 'related investments' for s 118(1)(a)(iii) in *FSMT v Shevlin*.[20]

The FSA has adopted an increasingly broad approach to the concept of 'related **7.18** investments'. These were initially described as 'relevant products' in the pre-Directive Implementation Code—'relevant products' being defined as:

1. investments, which are not 'qualifying investments', but behaviour affecting them can damage confidence in 'prescribed markets' and 'qualifying investments'; and/or[21]
2. anything that is the subject matter of a 'qualifying investment', or whose price or value is referenced to the price or value of 'qualifying investments'.[22]

Thus, one FSA example of a 'relevant product' that the Authority previously **7.19** included in the Code was as follows. The price of an OTC contract which is referenced to the price of the Brent crude futures contract traded on the IPE (which is a 'qualifying investment' traded on a 'prescribed market') was said to be, by virtue of its *relation* to the qualifying investment, a relevant product.[23]

These sections have been eliminated from the post-1 July 2005 COMC, which **7.20** has had two effects. First, the reduced guidance makes it more difficult for market participants to understand the scope of the word 'relation' in connection with the market abuse regime. Second, the FSA has released itself from any limitation that the phrase 'referenced to the price or value of' may have placed on the definition of the word 'related' in the context of enforcing the market abuse regime.

---

[18] FSMA, Glossary.
[19] FSMA, s 130A(3).
[20] FSMT case 060, 12 June 2008.
[21] MAR 1.11.8 (revoked 30 June 2005).
[22] MAR 1.11.9–11 (revoked 30 June 2005).
[23] MAR 1.11.12 (revoked 30 June 2005).

Thus, the FSA has increased its flexibility in reaching non-qualifying investments and non-prescribed markets.

7.21 'Relation', on its own, can be interpreted very broadly. In theory, any financial product is in competition with any other financial product and, thus, the rise or fall in the price of one can affect market demand for the others. What, if any, are the limits placed on the potential reach of 'relation' by the UK market abuse regime? The FSA includes in the COMC a list of 'factors to be taken into account' with respect to 'prescribed markets and qualifying investments: "in relation to".' That list is as follows:

> In the opinion of the FSA, the following factors are to be taken into account in deter-mining whether or not behaviour prior to a request for admission to trading of the admission to or the commencement of trading satisfies section 118(1)(a) of the Act, and are indications that it does:
> (1) if it is in relation to qualifying investments in respect of which a request for admission to trading on a prescribed market is subsequently made; and
> (2) if it continues to have an effect once an application has been made for the qualify-ing investment to be admitted for trading on a prescribed market, respectively.[24]

7.22 MAR 1.2.6 E states:

> In the opinion of the FSA, the following factors are to be taken into account in deter-mining whether or not refraining from action amounts to behaviour which satisfies section 118(1)(a) of the Act and are indications that it does:
> (1) if the person concerned has failed to discharge a legal or regulatory obligation (for example to make a disclosure) by refraining from acting; or
> (2) if the person concerned has created a reasonable expectation of him acting in a particular manner, as a result of his representations (by word or conduct), in circumstances which give rise to a duty or obligation to inform those to whom he made the representations that they have ceased to be correct, and he has not done so.[25]

7.23 As can be seen, this does not really help very much in determining the reach of 'in relation'. In certain cases, market abuse can be committed in transactions that 'influence' qualifying investments on prescribed markets. For example an 'abusive squeeze' can be executed by trading 'related investments' and/or trading on a market or trading platform:

> with a view to influencing the price of the same or a related qualifying investment that is traded on another prescribed market.[26]

7.24 It appears that the outer reach of the market abuse regime, both in the UK and the EU, continues to depend on judicial determination of the meaning of the phrase

---

[24] MAR 1.2.5 E.
[25] MAR 1.2.6 E.
[26] MAR 1.6.4 E. See also MAR 1.6.10 E (behaviour securing an abnormal or artificial price), MAR 1.6.11 (abusive squeezes).

'value depends'. Will it extend as far as concluding that all investments are competitors, and, therefore, dependent for their values on the values of all others? If not, what will the limits be? Early jurisprudence has not yet given an answer to these questions.

C. Which 'Markets' Are Covered?

Post-MAD, the regime now applies to all regulated markets throughout the EEA, that is, those listed by EEA jurisdiction regulators in accordance with Article 4(14) of the Markets in Financial Instruments Directive 2004/39/EC of 21 April 2004. The Directive thus applies to a wide range of markets including: **7.25**

- regulated markets; [27]
- trading platforms;
- devices for dissemination of price information;
- off-market transactions;
- any other means or devices for effecting transactions, and
- primary, secondary and 'grey' markets.

D. Geographical Reach

The Directive is applicable to all actions within Member State territories. It is also applicable to actions where elements of prohibited behaviour are within such territories with other elements taking place in third countries. It is also applicable to financial instruments admitted or going to be admitted to trading in a Member State.[28] **7.26**

As discussed in this chapter, the FSA has taken a very broad view of the scope of the application of the market abuse regime. In its view it can apply to 'everyone' whose conduct *may* have an effect on the UK financial markets. In other words, there are very few people indeed whose conduct is not theoretically reached by the market abuse regime. FSMA, s 118A says, in pertinent part: **7.27**

> (1) Behaviour is to be taken into account for purposes of the Part only if it occurs —
>   (a) in the United Kingdom, or
>   (b) in relation to —

---

[27] Art. 1(13) of ISD. For application of the Market Abuse Directive to the other types of markets listed, see Proposal for a Directive of the European Parliament of the Council on Insider Dealing and Market Manipulation (Market Abuse), COM (2001) 281 final, 2001/118 (COD) 30 May 2001, Art. 9, pp. 9–10.

[28] Directive, Art. 10.

      (i) qualifying investments which are admitted to trading on a prescribed market situated in, or operating in, the United Kingdom,

      (ii) qualifying investments for which a request for admission to trade on such a prescribed market has been made, or

      (iii) in the case of section 118(2) and (3) [both inside information market abuse], investments which are related investments in relation to such qualifying investments.

(2) For the purposes of subsection (1), as it applies in relation to section 118(4) [relevant information market abuse] and (8) [misleading impressions or distortion], a prescribed market accessible electronically in the United Kingdom is to be treated as operating in the United Kingdom.

(3) For the purposes of section 118(4) and (8), the behaviour that is to be regarded as occurring in relation to qualifying investments includes behaviour which —

    (a) occurs in relation to anything that is the subject matter, or whose price or value is expressed by reference to the price or value of the qualifying investments, or

    (b) occurs in relation to investments (whether or not they are qualifying investments) whose subject matter is the qualifying investments.

7.28 The COMC reflects an expansive view of the application the market abuse regime. In response to the question 'APPLICATION: WHERE?', MAR 1.1.7 contains the following enigmatic statement:

> … The Code does not exhaustively describe all the factors to be taken into account in determining whether behaviour amounts to market abuse. If factors are described, they are not to be taken as conclusive indications, unless specified as such, and the absence of a factor mentioned does not, of itself, amount to a contrary indication.[29]

7.29 This is not to say that the FSA is likely to seek to enforce the market abuse regime against people from various walks of life all over the world. Rather, it is an indication that the FSA wants to give itself the flexibility to deal with any market disruption which may affect the UK. It does not want to be hampered by trying to prescribe in advance exactly how, and to whom, it will apply the market abuse regime.

7.30 Experiences over the last 15 years or so have made the UK regulators aware that the nature of market disruptions and their causes can be unpredictable. Consequently, they wish to have the flexibility to respond regardless of how and where market disruptions come about. It is worth noting that one of the principal reasons for introducing the market abuse regime was to avoid the kind of embarrassing situation that the FSA previously found itself in, during the Barings Bank collapse or the Sumitomo copper manipulation, where UK regulators found that they did not have the powers to respond with regulatory solutions as rapidly as they would have liked. Criminal prohibitions, such as FSA, s 47[30] and the insider

---

[29] MAR 1.1.7.
[30] Now FSMA, s 397.

trading prohibitions under the Criminal Justice Act 1993 proved too cumbersome to permit a rapid regulatory response. They required the bringing of a prosecution, and proof of the elements of the offence beyond reasonable doubt. These hurdles made regulatory response too slow to achieve what was wanted.

The market abuse regime in contrast gives the FSA the kind of regulatory flexibility **7.31** observable in regulatory agencies in the US to take administrative action to correct market problems, in addition to having the option to seek criminal sanctions.

E. Conclusions

The UK Government has taken a very broad view of the application of the market **7.32** abuse regime in terms of product, market and geographical coverage. In addition, sections 1.1.6 and 1.1.7 of the COMC make clear that the Code does not 'exhaustively' describe either the behaviour that may or may not amount to market abuse, or all the factors to be taken into account in determining whether behaviour constitutes market abuse.[31]

Consequently, the FSA has reserved for itself a very wide band of flexibility in **7.33** judging who, what, when and where contributed to market abuse within its jurisdiction.

Ultimately, the FSA's view of the reach of the market abuse regime may be tested **7.34** in the courts, but, for now, it must be regarded as very long.

---

[31] MAR 1.1.6 and 1.1.7.

8

JUDGING BEHAVIOUR

A. Introduction

As shown in the previous chapters, the basic standard of behaviour required of **8.01** market participants is that:

(a) they should conduct their affairs so as not to compromise the fair and efficient operation of the market, or act in a manner which unfairly damages the interests of investors;[1] and

(b) that if a market participant engages in insider dealing or market manipulation, he risks having sanctions imposed for having engaged in 'market abuse'.[2]

Once these basic concepts are known, market participants will still have questions **8.02** about how their behaviour in the market will be compared to the prevailing standards of market behaviour when deciding whether or not someone has committed market abuse. These questions will include:

(a) Who is the person being judged — the actor(s) who will be held responsible if market misconduct is found?

---

[1] See Chapter 2 above.
[2] See Chapter 3 above.

(b) What guides will they use to compare the conduct of the responsible actor against the behaviour expected of a market participant in the actor's position?

(c) Who will be judge(s) of whether market misconduct occurred?

8.03 Each of these is an important question for market participants concerned about how their behaviour will be viewed by regulators and other market parties. However, the answers to these issues are not entirely obvious from the FSMA sections on market abuse or the FSA Code of Market Conduct. Therefore, this chapter will attempt to explain them in more detail.

(1) Who is the 'actor' whose conduct is judged?

8.04 The prohibitions in the Directive apply to *any* person, whether natural or legal.[3] For the purposes of the market abuse regime, the person who is expected to adhere to the standard is the actor who has engaged in the behaviour in question, the 'behaviour'.

8.05 The standard of behaviour expected of him will vary with his level of experience, skill and knowledge. For example, the standard of behaviour expected of a retail investor is likely to differ from the standard expected of an industry professional. An industry professional will be held to a higher standard of conduct.[4]

8.06 Having established that there is no physical restriction on who is covered by the market abuse regime, is there any requirement of a particular mental state? Must the party in question have a particular mental state in order to be found to have committed market abuse? Must the party have intended to commit market abuse?

8.07 While under both the Directive and the UK market abuse regime, one can commit market abuse without intending to do so, 'intent' does nonetheless have some significance to both. It is useful therefore to examine the extent to which 'intent' has a role to play in both the Directive and the UK market abuse regime in a little more detail.

The role of intent

8.08 The Market Abuse Directive appears, like the UK market abuse regime, to be an 'effects'-based regulation. However, the presence of guilty intent does play a role in Directive prohibitions against market abuse. An example of this 'dual' approach can be seen in respect of market abuse by use of inside information. The Directive states that this type of market abuse can consist of transactions in

---

[3] Directive, Art. 1, para. 6.

[4] For examples, see MAR 1.2.8 E, 1.2.21 G, 1.9.4 E(1).

financial instruments by a person 'who knows, or *ought to have known*', that information is inside information.[5]

This seems to imply that this type of market abuse can consist of reckless, **8.09** negligent or inadvertent as well as intentional conduct. On the other hand, proper 'intent' can also provide a defence in some circumstances. With respect to 'market manipulation' the Directive says that the person whose conduct constitutes market manipulation:

> … may be able to establish that his reasons for entering into such transactions or issuing orders to trade were legitimate and that the transactions and orders to trade were in conformity with accepted market practice on the regulated market concerned.[6]

However, the Directive goes on to say that this is not a complete defence. If the **8.10** regulator establishes that there is another 'illegitimate' reason behind the transactions or orders, the regulator could still impose sanctions.[7] This seems to imply that some element of 'intent' must be established before a sanction of market manipulation can be imposed.

The market abuse regime in the UK does not require a finding of 'intention' to **8.11** commit market abuse. It applies an 'effects'-based standard rather than a standard based on a finding of intent. MAR 1.2.3 says:

> [The market abuse definition in FSMA section 118] does not require the person engaging in the behaviour in question to have intended to commit market abuse.[8]

It is important to note that this does actually mean that one can commit market **8.12** abuse by 'mistake' or 'inadvertence'. For example, a market trader entering an order into the market may add an extra zero to his order. That addition could affect market prices significantly. Even if the extra zero is a mistake, the FSA could still find that the trader was guilty of market abuse because he had failed to take reasonable care to prevent the mistake. In other words, one can negligently commit market abuse. When the original UK market abuse regime was first proposed, there was some support for a 'generalized' test of intent or 'principal purpose' in the Code, but that was rejected in favour of referring to specific 'principal purpose' tests relating to specific offences. It was decided that it would be better, in many cases, to consider all the circumstances surrounding a transaction including whether or not a firm had taken sufficient care to ensure that the market would not be disrupted at the time the transaction was executed. It was expressly

---

[5] Directive, Recital 18.
[6] Directive, Recital 20.
[7] Directive, Recital 20.
[8] MAR 1.2.3.

recognized that there would be occasions when 'negligent conduct' could result in breaches of the 'Code'.[9]

8.13 An example of how negligence can be an issue is found in MAR 1.2.8, which lists one of the factors for determining whether a person could reasonably be expected to know he possessed inside information as being:

> (2) if a normal and reasonable person in the position of the person who has inside information would know or should have known that it is inside information.[10]

8.14 As explained in paragraphs 8.07 and 8.08 above, however, this does not mean that 'intent' has no role in the UK market abuse regime. The FSA will take into consideration (as an evidentiary or mitigating factor) that one accused of abuse lacked an intention or purpose to commit market abuse.

8.15 In some cases, whether or not a person's behaviour constitutes market abuse will depend on the purpose for which he engaged in the behaviour in question. However, in such circumstances, the purpose is likely to be only one of the relevant considerations. And, it should be noted, improper purpose need not be the sole purpose in engaging in the behaviour, but there is more likely to be a finding of market abuse if it is an 'actuating' purpose.[11]

8.16 A number of provisions of the MAR introduce elements of intent into their definitions and interpretations. Such things as the 'purpose of the behaviour' or whether a person was 'influenced' to engage in improper conduct introduce requirements that, in some circumstances, a particular state of mind be present before a person can be found guilty of market abuse.[12]

8.17 Much concern has been expressed that the lack of a general requirement of intent in order to find market abuse is severe in that it gives rise to uncertainty and potentially to injustice. Commentators have expressed the view that the market abuse regime should not be based upon 'strict liability'.

8.18 The explanation for refusal to include a general requirement of intent is that the principal goal of the market abuse regime is to preserve the efficient operation of the market and not to establish the moral culpability of market participants. The argument is that market confidence is affected more by 'effects' rather than the off and on disclosed mental states of the market's participants. The FSA has stated that it is not its intention to punish people for 'accidental' offences. However, as pointed out above, one can be punished for negligent offences if it is shown that one did not take proper care to avoid the unwanted effects caused by one's behaviour.

---

[9] *FSA Feedback Statement on responses to Consultation Paper 10: Market Abuse* (March 1999), pp. 3–4, paras 14–17.

[10] MAR 1.2.8(2).

[11] For example, see MAR 1.6.5.

[12] See, e.g., MAR 1.2.22, 1.2.23, 1.4.2(2), 1.5.5(2), 1.5.10 and 1.6.4.

In such circumstances the FSA indicated that among the things it would take into consideration could be:

- whether the circumstances suggest that a person concerned took reasonable steps to avoid engaging in market abuse;
- the likelihood that the same type of misconduct (whether on the part of the person concerned or others) will recur if it is not deterred;
- steps that have been taken by the person concerned to address the misconduct. This might include action to compensate those who have suffered loss as a result of the misconduct or, in the case of a firm, action to put in place systems and controls to prevent a reoccurrence of the abuse;
- the extent to which the misconduct is capable of being adequately addressed by action by other market authorities. Where the conduct in question takes place on a market overseen by an RIE, the RIE may well be placed to deal with the misconduct. If the misconduct constitutes a breach of the rules of the RIE and the RIE has disciplinary and enforcement powers that are adequate to address the misconduct in question, the FSA would not normally propose to take action.[13]

8.19

The FSA indicated that where it appeared that a breach of the code was caused by negligence, it would pay particular attention to what the firm had done to prevent the abuse and what actions it had taken to prevent a reoccurrence.[14]

8.20

However, the Rules of MAR, which along with FSMA 2000 have implemented the Directive, do not simply describe general characteristics of relevant market participants (such as their intention or other state of mind). In some cases they narrow their focus to prescribe particular duties, and in some cases, new duties for particular classes of market participants. Three that are discussed below are issuers, transaction intermediaries and journalists.

8.21

FSA regulation of issuers

For example, with respect to issuers of shares, the FSA now requires compliance with the Disclosure and Transparency Rules (DTRs). These reflect certain obligations of the Directive:

8.22

1. requiring companies to disclose inside information;
2. requiring companies to keep lists of those with access to inside information; and
3. requiring directors and senior managers (and those 'connected' to them) to report their transactions in shares of companies for which they work.[15]

---

[13] FSA, *Feedback Statement on responses to Consultation Paper 10: Market Abuse*, p. 4, para. 16.
[14] *Ibid.*, para. 17.
[15] See the FSA *Handbook*, Disclosure and Transparency Rules, DTR 2 and DTR 3.

8.23   These provisions implement the requirements of Article 6 of the Directive, which regulates the flow of market information. The Article does this in a number of ways.[16] First, Articles 6.1 and 6.2 of the initial Directive requires the issuers to inform the public of inside information as soon as possible. To accord with Article 2(1) and (4) of the Directive, the FSA requires issuers to promptly disclose inside information to all investors in as synchronized a fashion as possible.[17] The FSA's stated intention is to prevent a minority of investors from gaining an advantage over the others by having early access to inside information. In addition, the FSA also proposes to require that issuers may not use the disclosure of inside information as part of their marketing activities in a manner that is likely to be misleading. Also, any significant changes to publicly disclose information will also be required to be promptly disclosed.

8.24   However, certain exemptions will be permitted to the requirements of prompt disclosure of inside information. The FSA states that such disclosure can be delayed to protect the legitimate interests of issuers. One example may be an instance where the issuer is engaged in a course of delicate negotiations. However, certain requirements must be met.[18] Confidentiality of the information must be ensured during the delay, and the delay must be conducted so that it would not be likely to mislead the public.[19]

8.25   Second, Article 6.3 of the Directive requires members of the management of issuers (and any persons 'closely associated' with them) to disclose their dealings in the shares (or other financial instruments linked to the shares) of the issuers. The FSA has introduced rules implementing this requirement.[20]

8.26   It should also be noted that many of the disclosure of information requirements will not apply to issuers who have not requested or approved an admission of their financial instruments to trading on a regulated market in an EU Member State.[21]

Intermediaries and suspicious transactions

8.27   Firms that arrange or execute investment transactions (in or through an appointed representative in the UK)[22] also receive special attention because the

---

[16] DTR 1.1.2R.
[17] DR 1.3., DTR 2.2.1R, DTR 2.2.9G, DTR 2.3, DTR 2.4.
[18] DTR 1.2R and 2.5R.
[19] DTR 2.5R.
[20] DTR 3R.
[21] DR 1.1.
[22] FSA *Handbook, Supervision Manual,* SUP 15.10.1.

new requirements impose on them a duty to report 'suspicious transactions' to the FSA. The relevant FSA requirement says:

> A firm which arranges or executes a transaction with or for a client in a qualifying investment admitted to trading on a prescribed market and which has reasonable grounds to suspect that the transaction might constitute market abuse must notify the FSA without delay.[23]

The firm has the burden of deciding on a case-by-case basis whether or not it has reasonable grounds to conclude that a transaction constitutes market abuse.[24] The firm has to be able to explain the basis of its suspicions when notifying the FSA.[25] More details of the obligations relating to suspicious transactions can be found in SUP 15.10 and SUP 15 Annex 5.   **8.28**

Journalists' conduct

Another group that comes in for particular scrutiny in the FSA's regulations is journalists. On a number of occasions, concerns have been raised about the position of journalists who deal in the shares of a company before publication of an article they have written containing recommendations to buy, sell or hold those shares. Generally, it is the FSA's position that it would 'promote public awareness' for market participants to appreciate the need to consider the journalists' motives before acting on their recommendations and, second, to work with the Press Complaints Commission (PCC) and the Editors' Code of Practice and Committee to tighten the self-regulation of journalists relating to share dealings.   **8.29**

After working with the above-named self-regulatory organizations, the FSA noted that the PCC Best Practice Guidelines did make changes to tighten up self-regulation in this area. Therefore, rather than taking direct action itself, the FSA decided that it would continue to try to work with the self-regulatory organizations to achieve the objectives it desires.[26]   **8.30**

FSMA, s 118A(4) incorporates this philosophy saying: **8.31**

> For the purposes of section 118(7),[27] the dissemination of information by a journalist acting in his professional capacity is to be assessed taking into account the codes

---

[23] SUP 15.10.2, referring to Directive Art. 6(9).
[24] SUP 15.10.3.
[25] SUP 15.10.4.
[26] FSA, Code of Market Conduct: Feedback on CP 59 and CP 76. April 2001, p. 19, paras 6.17–6.19.
[27] The form of market abuse comprising 'behaviour [which] consists of disseminating, or causing the dissemination of, information by any means which gives, or is likely to give, a false or misleading impression as to a qualifying investment or related investment by a person who knew or could reasonably be expected to have known that the information was false or misleading'. FSMA, s 118 (7), SI 2005/381.

governing his profession unless he derives, directly or indirectly, any advantage or profits from the dissemination of the information.

8.32 In other words, there is an important limitation on a journalist's ability to seek protection under the self-regulatory codes of his profession, when acting in his professional capacity—advantage or profit. If he derives either from the dissemination of false or misleading impressions, the FSA need not take the professional codes of journalists into account when assessing whether a journalist's conduct amounts to market abuse.[28]

8.33 The current Code of Practice promulgated by the Press Complaints Commission makes express reference to 'Financial journalism' at section 13. It states:

(i) Even where the law does not prohibit it, journalists must not use for their own profit financial information they receive in advance of its general publication, nor should they pass such information to others.

(ii) They must not write about shares or securities in whose performance they know that they or their close families have a significant financial interest without disclosing the interest to the editor or financial editor.

(iii) They must not buy or sell, either directly or through nominees or agents, shares or securities about which they have written recently or about which they intend to write in the near future.

8.34 However, there is a question as to how significant a deterrent a complaint to the PCC will be. The sanctions that the PCC says it will impose if it upholds a complaint appear limited. It says:

If we can not resolve the complaint to your satisfaction, the Commission will review all the circumstances—including any offers to resolve the complaint made by the editor—and take a decision as to whether it can adjudicate on a complaint. If the Commission upholds your complaint, the publication concerned will be obliged to publish our criticism of them in full and with due prominence. A copy of or adjudication will be contained in our regular Bulletin, and also published on our website.[29]

8.35 However, what the editor's code of practice seems to have done is to make journalists particularly open to punishment by the FSA for misconduct. Despite the relative lack of severe sanctions exercised by the PCC, section 13, relating to financial journalism, is even stricter than the market abuse regime against misuse of information. It states that '*even where the law does not prohibit it ...*', journalists must not profit from any financial information they receive in advance of its general publication, nor may they pass that information on to others. In other words, there is no 'market practice' within journalism that could be said to permit the use of such information for personal gain under any circumstances.

---

[28] FSMA, s 118A(4); SI 2005/381.
[29] Press Complaints Commission, 'Making a Complaint'. See <www.pcc.org.uk>.

This was the intention of the FSA even before the FSMA came into effect. An FSA **8.36**
Press Release as long ago as 25 July 2000 stated:

> Any journalist dealing as an 'insider' on information that is not generally available,
> or publishing misleading information with a view to influencing the price of shares,
> for example, will be covered by the regime and could be fined or publicly censured
> by the FSA.[30]

This has been made clear by the prosecution of the journalists responsible for the **8.37**
Daily Mirror's 'City Slickers' column, who were charged with a criminal offence
under the FS Act, s 47(2). The journalists responsible—Anil Bhoyrul and James
Hipwell—conspired to create a 'misleading impression as to the value of investments ...' by recommending shares in their column which they personally bought
before publishing their recommendations.

The prosecution, the result of a four-year investigation, ended in a successful con- **8.38**
viction of Hipwell in December 2005, Bhoyrul having pleaded guilty in August
2005. Hipwell's subsequent appeal against a six-month sentence of imprisonment
was unsuccessful.[31] Piers Morgan, who was then editor of the *Daily Mirror*, was
also questioned in connection with the investigation but was cleared of any
wrongdoing.

B. Who Judges Behaviour?

Who determines whether or not market abuse has been committed? Having **8.39**
reviewed what constitutes market abuse in the previous chapters, this section will
discuss who is responsible for determining whether the line into market abuse has
been crossed.

Under the Market Abuse Directive, the government of each EU Member State is **8.40**
responsible for implementing the provisions of the Directive as required by the
terms of the Directive. Article 10 says:

> Each Member State shall apply the prohibitions and requirements provided for in
> this Directive to:
> (a) actions carried out on its territory or abroad concerning financial instruments
> that are admitted to trading on a regulated market situated or operating within
> its territory or for which a request for admission to trading on such market has
> been made;

---

[30] FSA, *Keeping the UK Financial Markets Clean: FSA Proposals for Preventing Market Abuse*, 25
July 2000, p. 4.
[31] *R v Hipwell* [2006] 2 Cr App R (S) 636.

(b) actions carried out on its territory concerning financial instruments that are admitted to trading on a regulated market in a Member State or for which a request for admission to trading on such market has been made.[32]

8.41 The governments of the Member States do not, however, have a free hand in determining how the Directive is to be administered. Article 11 of the Directive requires that:

> Without prejudice to the competences of judicial authorities, each Member State shall designate a single administrative authority competent to ensure that the provisions adopted pursuant to this Directive are applied. Member States shall establish effective consultative arrangements and procedures with market participants concerning possible changes in national legislation. These arrangements may include consultative committees within each competent authority, the membership of which should reflect as far as possible the diversity of market participants, be they issuers, providers of financial services or consumers.[33]

8.42 There were thus three separate elements to the implementation of the provisions of the Directive under the authority of the government of a Member State. First, a single 'competent authority' was to have primary responsibility for the day-to-day implementation of the terms of the Directive. Second, the judiciary of each Member State retained the power to review and rule on the appropriateness of the implementation employed. Third, each Member State was *required* to ensure effective consultative arrangements for a diverse cross-section of market participants. What 'effective' means in this context is not stated. Presumably, any required determination of whether such arrangements are, in fact, effective will be left to the relevant judicial authorities.

(1) Competent authorities

8.43 The Directive leaves no doubt as to where a Member State should lodge the principal authority for enforcing its prohibitions against market abuse.

> A single competent authority should be designated in each Member State to assume at least final responsibility for supervising compliance with the provisions adopted pursuant to this Directive, as well as international collaboration. Such an authority should be of an administrative nature guaranteeing its independence of economic actors avoiding conflicts of interest.[34]

8.44 Note that the powers of the competent authority are not limited to 'final responsibility' for supervising compliance with the Directive. Member States were urged to grant their competent authorities 'at least' that responsibility.

---

[32] Directive, Art. 10.
[33] Directive, Art. 11.
[34] Directive, Recital 36.

Member States are directed to provide their competent authorities with sufficient **8.45**
powers to effectively enforce the provisions of the Market Abuse Directive.

> In accordance with national law, Member States should ensure appropriate financing
> of the competent authority. The authority should have adequate arrangements for
> consultation concerning possible changes in national legislation such as a consulta-
> tive committee composed of representatives of issuers, financial services providers
> and consumers, so as to be fully informed of their views and concerns.[35] A common
> set of effective tools and powers for the competent authority of each Member State
> will guarantee supervisory effectiveness.[36]

Article 12 of the Directive gave the following directions: **8.46**

1. The competent authority shall be given all supervisory and investigatory powers
   that are necessary for the exercise of its functions. It shall exercise such powers:
   (a) directly; or
   (b) in collaboration with other authorities or with the market undertakings; or
   (c) under its responsibility by delegation to such authorities or to the market
       undertakings; or
   (d) by application to the competent judicial authorities.
2. Without prejudice to Article 6(7) [the obligation of the competent authority to
   keep the public correctly informed about matters having to do with inside infor-
   mation], the powers referred to in paragraph 1 of this Article shall be exercised
   in conformity with national law and shall include at least the right to:
   (a) have access to any document in any form whatsoever; and to receive a copy
       of it;
   (b) demand information from any person, including those who are successively
       involved in the transmission of orders or conduct of the operations con-
       cerned, as well as their principals, and if necessary, to summon and hear any
       such person;
   (c) carry out on-site inspections;
   (d) require existing telephone and existing data traffic records;
   (e) require the cessation of any practice that is contrary to the provisions
       adopted in the implementation of this Directive;
   (f) suspend trading of the financial instruments concerned;
   (g) request the freezing and/or sequestration of assets;
   (h) request temporary prohibition of professional activity.[37]

As can be seen from the above, the grant of powers intended for competent **8.47**
authorities was expressed very broadly—indeed, commensurate with those
such as any body would have to investigate a criminal offence. Also, these powers
of investigation and punishment were not limited by the statements contained
in Article 12. Article 12 provided only that the competent authority should have

---

[35] Directive, Recital 36.
[36] Directive, Recital 37.
[37] Directive, Art. 12.

'at least the right' to exercise the powers listed in Article 12(2). More extensive powers were able to be granted, and, in the UK, they were.

8.48   The UK's 'competent authority' is the Financial Services Authority (FSA). The FSA was designated under the FSMA 2000 as the corporate body charged with carrying out the regulatory functions set out in that Act.[38] Consequently, many of the powers and procedures required by the Market Abuse Directive were already being exercised by the FSA.[39] In a number of cases, the powers of the FSA were more extensive than the minimum requirements of the Market Abuse Directive.[40]

8.49   In its implementation of the Market Abuse Directive, the UK Government discussed whether it would not be wise to narrow the scope of the FSA's regulatory remit in some areas so that it did not exceed the minimum requirements of the Directive.[41] There was some concern expressed that if the UK did not cut back its regulatory regime to the level of the minimum requirements of the Directive, it would be in danger of losing competitive advantage to countries that implemented the Directive by only complying with the minimum requirements. However, in the end this argument was rejected on the grounds that market integrity was an issue of primary importance to market participants.[42]

8.50   The actual result of the UK implementation was that the FSA's powers were extended beyond what they had been prior to the Directive. The FSA was given powers over certain issuers of investments which enable it to supervise the enforcement of the requirements of the Directive that:

- companies disclose inside information;
- they keep lists of those with access to inside information, and
- directors and senior managers (and those 'connected' to them) report their transactions in shares of companies for which they work.[43]

8.51   In the UK, the FSA is now in the position of judging whether or not behaviour constitutes market abuse along with the competent authorities of other EU Member States.[44] In implementing the requirements of the Directive, in preserving previous FSA powers that are outside the scope of the Directive, and in adding new powers thought necessary, the Government determined how the FSA would be expected to exercise its judgment in determining whether market abuse had occurred.

---

[38]   FSMA, Part I, s 1.
[39]   Joint Consultation Paper, Executive Summary, para. 3.
[40]   Joint Consultation Paper, Executive Summary, para. 3.
[41]   Joint Consultation Paper, Executive Summary, para. 3.
[42]   Joint Consultation Paper, Regulatory Impact Assessment, para. B29.
[43]   Joint Consultation Paper, Executive Summary, para. 5.
[44]   Directive, Art. 11.

Exactly what the FSA is entitled to take into consideration in exercising its judg- **8.52**
ment and what the limitations on that judgment are, are only sketchily outlined
in the Market Abuse Directive itself. The Directive was intended to introduce a
common framework in Member States for the prevention, detection, investigation and punishment of market abuse.[45] Although a 'framework' was provided,
there was very little detail of how those processes should be approached and
conducted.

Some guidance could be found in the discussion of the use of inside information **8.53**
where the Directive stated that:

> Use of inside information can consist in the acquisition or disposal of financial
> instruments by a person who knows, or ought to have known, that the information
> possessed is inside information. In this respect, *the competent authority should con-*
> *sider what a normal and reasonable person would know or should have known in the*
> *circumstances.*[46]

From this, one could see that the 'judge' of whether the information in question **8.54**
was 'inside information' was the hypothetical 'normal and reasonable person'.
Although this test is to apply in cases involving inside information, there was no
clear statement that this standard of judgment was intended to be the yardstick for
all issues covered in the Directive.

With respect to market manipulation, the Directive proposed that the competent **8.55**
authority should have the power to make the following judgment:

> A person who enters into transactions or issues orders to trade which are constitutive
> of market manipulation may be able to establish that his reasons for entering into
> such transactions or issuing orders to trade were legitimate and that the transactions
> and orders to trade were in conformity with accepted practice on the regulated mar-
> ket concerned. A sanction could still be imposed *if the competent authority established*
> *that there was another, illegitimate, reason behind these transactions or orders to*
> *trade.*[47]

With respect to this issue, a three-part test was therefore outlined. First, a judg- **8.56**
ment had to be made that the relevant transactions or orders constituted market
manipulation. Inferentially, this judgment was to be made by the competent
authority. In making that judgment the competent authority will refer to the definition of market manipulation found in Article 1.2(a) of the Directive:

> 2. 'Market manipulation' shall mean:
>   (a) transactions or orders to trade:
>   — which give, or are likely to give, false or misleading signals as to the
>   supply of, demand for or price of financial instruments, or

---

[45] Joint Consultation Paper, Introduction, s 1.5, p. 5.
[46] Directive, Recital 18.
[47] Directive, Recital 20.

> — which secure by a person or persons acting in collaboration, the price of one or several financial instruments at an abnormal or artificial level,

unless the person who entered into the transactions or issued the orders to trade establishes that his reasons for so doing are legitimate and that these transactions or orders to trade conform to accepted market practices on the regulated market concerned ...[48]

8.57 Under the terms of the Directive, it is a matter for the competent authority, in possession of the requisite devolved authority from its Member State government to interpret and implement the provisions of the Directive, which makes the initial judgment that behaviour constituting market abuse has occurred.[49] In making this judgment, the Directive itself did not provide any express guidance about how the behaviour was to be judged. For example, it did not say that:

(a) the competent authority must judge whether a normal and reasonable person would, or would have been likely to, have received the false and misleading signals; or

(b) whether such signals would have or would have been likely to have influenced anyone's actions; or

(c) what tests must be met to establish whether behaviour is '*likely*' to give false or misleading signals.

8.58 Such guidance was found in Implementing Directive 2003/124/EC, which stated:

> Reasonable investors base their investment decisions on information already available to them, that is to say, on *ex ante* available information. Therefore, the question whether, in making an investment decision, a reasonable investor would be likely to take into account a particular piece of information should be appraised on the basis of the *ex ante* available information. Such an assessment has to take into consideration the anticipated impact of the information in light of the totality of the related issuer's activity, the reliability of the source of the information and any other market variables likely to affect the related financial instrument or derivative financial instrument related thereto in the given circumstances.[50]

8.59 In other words, the judgment made by the competent authority was and is expected be based on:

(a) what would affect the investment decisions of a reasonable investor;

(b) what a reasonable investor would take into account in light of the total information he had available to him prior to a relevant investment decision;

(c) how a reasonable investor would judge the reliability of relevant information, and

(d) which market variables a reasonable investor would consider relevant.

---

[48] Directive, Art. 1.2(a).
[49] Directive, Recitals 28 and 36.
[50] Commission Directive 2003/124.

Second, the behaviour of the person in question is to be compared with 'the **8.60** accepted practice of the regulated market concerned'. In this instance the burden is on the person suspected of market abuse to establish a favourable comparison, and to propose that comparison either as a defence to or in mitigation of an allegation of market manipulation.

The Directive also provided that the competent authority 'may' issue some guid- **8.61** ance on the matters covered in the Directive stating that:

> The guidance should be in conformity with the provisions of the Directive and the implementing measures adopted in accordance with the comitology procedure.[51]

This has been undertaken by the FSA in the publication of the Code of Market Conduct—and in particular in its Guidance provisions.

(2) The Regulatory Decisions Committee

The allocation of decision making on regulatory issues, such as market abuse, is **8.62** set out in the Decision Procedure and Penalties Manual of the FSA *Handbook*.[52] Under FSMA, s 395:

(1) The Authority [FSA] must determine the procedure that it proposes to follow in relation to the giving of —
   (a) supervisory notices; and
   (b) warning notices and decision notices.
(2) That procedure must be designed to secure, among other things, that the decision which gives rise to the obligation to give any such notice is taken by a person not directly involved in establishing the evidence on which that decision is based.[53]

In response to this statutory requirement, which applies to notices to be given as **8.63** part of FSA market abuse investigations, the Board of the FSA has established the Regulatory Decisions Committee (RDC).

The RDC was established by the FSA because the FSMA requires investigation **8.64** and recommendation functions to be separate from the taking of decisions and issuing of statutory notices. The RDC takes supervisory, authorization and enforcement decisions that are materially significant for the firms and individuals in question. The RDC reports to the Board of the FSA – the Authority being

---

[51] Directive, Recital 21. 'Comitology procedure' refers to the process in the implementation of EU legislation where regulatory rules proposed by the European Commission are adopted after having been reviewed and approved by a committee of experts from Member States. In the case of the Market Abuse Directive, the committee of experts is the Committee of European Securities Regulation (CESR), established by Commission Decision 2001/527/EC (OJ L191.13.7.2001, p. 43).

[52] FSA *Handbook*, DEPP.

[53] FSMA, s 395.

responsible for the appointment of the chairman and members who are themselves chosen from market practitioners, and other appropriate individuals, to represent the public interest. The RDC issues Warning and Decision Notices relating to market abuse or other misconduct based on recommendations from FSA staff.[54]

(3) Other regulators

8.65 Although the FSA certainly has the lead role in judging whether or not behaviour has crossed the line into that constituting market abuse, it is not the only organization in the UK with responsibility for preventing and punishing market misconduct. There are a number of other bodies with regulatory responsibilities, including exchanges and specialized regulatory agencies also responsible for particular sectors of the financial market.

8.66 In many cases, it is necessary to take into account the rules of the market in question, the Takeover Code or the FSA Rules. The fact that a person suspected of market abuse is in compliance with such rules may not excuse market abuse. However, greater weight may be given to rules that require or permit specific sorts of behaviour. By the same token, the fact that the person concerned has not complied with a particular rule does not create a presumption of market abuse. However, an exemption from a market or Takeover Panel rule will be a factor to be taken into consideration. In this context, there are no rules in the Takeover Code which permit or require a person to behave in a way which amounts to market abuse.[55] Indeed, if disclosure, for example, is made in accordance with this Code, that will be taken into account by the FSA in determining whether it was made by a person in the proper course of the exercise of his employment;[56] further, behaviour which conforms to certain of the rules of the Takeover Code specified in the Table at MAR 1.10.5[57] will not then of itself be treated as amounting to market abuse[58] provided that, in addition, the behaviour is expressly required or expressly permitted by the rule in question and it conforms to any General Principle set out at Section B of the Takeover Code. Likewise, behaviour conforming to Rule 4.2 of the Takeover Code[59] will not, of itself, amount to market abuse provided these

---

[54] FSA, Regulatory Decisions Committee (RDC), <www.fsa.gov.uk>, 21 March 2005. For details of the regulations relating to the responsibilities of the RDC, see FSA *Handbook*, DEPP.
[55] MAR 1.10.3 G.
[56] MAR 1.4.5 E.
[57] These relate to the timing, dissemination or availability, content and standard of care applicable to a disclosure, announcement, communication or release of information
[58] MAR 1.10.4 C.
[59] This relates to restrictions on dealings by offerors and concert parties

same additional requirements are met.[60] Considerable weight will be accorded to the views of the Takeover Panel with respect to applying and interpreting the Takeover Code.

(4) Overseas markets

When the behaviour in question occurs on an overseas market, whether or not a   **8.67** person complied with the rules of the overseas market will not, of itself, determine whether or not there has been market abuse. However, whether or not the person in question is actually in the UK, the regular user test (to the extent it continues to be relevant)[61] will include consideration as to whether local rules, conventions and practices in the market in question have been complied with.[62]

Consequently, there are a number of agencies that have overlapping responsibili-   **8.68** ties for market abuse. To help avoid possible regulatory confusion, the FSA has entered into 'operating arrangements' with these other bodies. Operating arrangements which have been published include the following.

(5) Operating arrangements with Ofex[63]

Ofex plc—now Plus Markets plc—became a Recognised Investment Exchange   **8.69** (RIE) in July 2007. Issues relating to market abuse on that market now fall to be dealt with under the arrangements discussed below in paragraphs 8.74–8.80. The former regime will, however, be briefly described as of now historic interest. Ofex plc provided a market for the off-exchange trading of unlisted shares being then authorized and regulated by the FSA but at that time neither an RIE nor a Designated Investment Exchange (DIE) under the FSMA. It was a Prescribed Market for the purposes of the FSMA, s 118 and maintained its own rules for trading. Therefore it was in the position of policing misconduct in connection with transactions on its market.

In June of 2002, the FSA published its Operating Arrangements with Ofex.   **8.70** In that document the FSA and Ofex acknowledged the importance of protecting the integrity of the Ofex market. Therefore Ofex and the FSA agreed to maintain a close working relationship to deal with enforcement issues relating to possible market abuse.

---

[60] MAR 1.10.6 C
[61] See the discussion of the sunset provisions in Chapter 3, para. 3.11.
[62] MAR 1.5.7 E
[63] FSA, *Operating Arrangements Between the Financial Services Authority and Ofex plc*, June 2002.

8.71   Recognizing that the FSA and Ofex had overlapping regulatory responsibilities, they agreed that they would try to make certain that the party with the most appropriate regulatory duties and powers would be the one to conduct an investigation in any particular case. In order to achieve that, they agreed to consider cases of possible market abuse on a case-by-case basis.

8.72   The FSA pointed out that in cases where the market misconduct took place solely on Ofex, and all the perpetrators were members of Ofex, Ofex's own enforcement powers would be sufficient to deal with the misconduct. However, the FSA and Ofex would continue to communicate about any enforcement situation to determine whether FSA action was necessary.

(6) Operating arrangements with RIEs[64]

8.73   The RIEs also have regulatory responsibilities that require them to protect the integrity of their markets by discouraging and punishing market abuse. Recognizing the importance of this mandate, the FSA entered into operating arrangements with the RIEs to achieve effective operating arrangements to prevent and detect market misconduct.

8.74   The RIEs currently include EDX London Ltd, ICE Futures Europe, LIFFE Administration and Management, London Stock Exchange plc, Plus Markets plc and the London Metal Exchange Ltd. Their goal, in common with the FSA, is to keep their markets attractive to participants by hosting fair and transparent trading environments.

8.75   However, the RIEs and the FSA wish to avoid unnecessary duplication of investigation and enforcement arising out of the same incidents. They have agreed that they will keep each other informed about cases of joint interest and to hold regular meetings on common issues.

8.76   Suspected cases of market misconduct will be considered on a case-by-case basis. They will consider the seriousness of the misconduct, the jurisdiction of the FSA and the RIE, and the spectrum of regulatory powers available to each. The FSA and the relevant exchange will discuss which is best placed to take appropriate action.

8.77   Once again, in those cases where the effects of the misconduct are limited to a particular RIE, where all the perpetrators are members, and the RIE has sufficient powers to deal with the misconduct, the FSA will probably be content to let the RIE investigate and deal with the incident. However, the FSA and the RIE will

---

[64] FSA, *Operating Arrangements Between the Financial Services Authority and the Recognised Investment Exchanges on Market Misconduct.*

stay in contact during the investigation and the FSA will consider whether any subsequent enforcement action is necessary.

For the information of market participants and other interested parties, the FSA **8.78** provides appropriate enforcement guidance in its Code of Market Conduct ('MAR') and the RIEs provide their own guidance in their rules.

During the time that such cooperative arrangements have been in force between **8.79** the FSA and other regulatory bodies, there have been incidents where market misconduct has been alleged in the specialized markets covered by the rules of the specific markets discussed above. It is not within the scope of this book to discuss and analyse each of those incidents. This book only has room to discuss the FSA's resolution of market misconduct cases.[65] However, readers interested in the conduct and resolution of such an investigation can find an example in the International Petroleum Exchange's (now merged with ICE Futures Europe) investigation into and determination of certain market misconduct allegations discussed in *The Report of the Independent Complaints Commissioner into Mr. Cook's Allegations*, October 2002.[66]

(7) The Panel on Takeovers and Mergers[67]

Recognizing that both the FSA and the Panel on Takeovers and Mergers ('the **8.80** Panel') might be concerned with the possible impact of market misconduct on the UK financial markets, they agreed to work towards a common objective of putting in place effective mechanisms to deal with market abuse while avoiding unnecessary enforcement duplication.

In furtherance of the above objective, the FSA and the Panel agreed to liaise regu- **8.81** larly to discuss cases of mutual interest including, among other things, who should investigate and whether a joint investigation is appropriate. In relevant cases, they agreed to share information, and generally sought to prevent undue duplication of work. The FSA's Enforcement Guide continues this approach.[68]

With respect to issues of market misconduct that might arise during a takeover **8.82** bid, the FSA and the Panel acknowledged the importance of minimizing disruption of the bid. Consequently, during a bid, the FSA will exercise its powers relating to market abuse only in unusual circumstances. The circumstances under which the FSA might consider using its powers were originally described

---

[65] See Chapter 14, Market Abuse Cases.
[66] A pdf copy is obtainable from the ICE website.
[67] See the Enforcement Guide at paragraphs 2.15, 3.16 and 12.11; see further, DEPP 6.2.19 G to 6.2.28 G.
[68] See fn67 above

in the FSA's *Operating Guidelines Between the Financial Services Authority and the Panel on Takeovers and Mergers on Market Misconduct* and included the following:

1. where the Panel requests that the FSA use its powers to impose penalties, request a court to impose penalties, issue an injunction or order restitution;
2. where the Panel is unable to obtain the cooperation of a person important to an investigation;
3. where the suspected misconduct would constitute misuse of information under the FSMA, s 118(2)(a) or insider dealing under the Criminal Justice Act 1993, Part V;
4. where a person refuses to comply with a Panel ruling;
5. where the suspected misconduct relates to a class of securities outside the Panel's jurisdiction;
6. where the suspected misconduct threatens the stability of the financial system.

These are now summarised in DEPP 6.2.22 G which provides that:

> In relation to behaviour which may have happened or be happening in the context of a takeover bid, the FSA will refer to the Takeover Panel and give due weight to its views. Where the Takeover Code has procedures for complaint about any behaviour, the FSA expects parties to exhaust those procedures. The FSA will not, save in exceptional circumstances, take action under any of section 123 (FSA's power to impose penalties), section 129 (Power of court to impose penalties), section 381 (Injunctions), sections 383 or 384 (Restitution) in respect of behaviour to which the Takeover Code is relevant before the conclusion of the procedures available under the Takeover Code.

8.83   When considering a decision to intervene in a case, the FSA will have regard to the guidelines set out in its Decision Procedure and Penalties Manual and the views of the Panel.

8.84   If the FSA does decide to intervene, it will keep the Panel informed of its actions and give due weight to the Panel's views. As a case develops, the matter will be regularly reviewed to determine whether it is appropriate for the FSA or the Panel to take the lead in the investigation.

8.85   In general, in deciding which party should take the lead in an investigation, the FSA and the Panel will consider all relevant factors including:

1. whether the suspected misconduct may include criminal offences;
2. the scale of the misconduct and the severity of the consequences;
3. the need for consistency of enforcement and discipline;
4. the availability of appropriate resources;
5. whether the suspected misconduct is a breach of the Takeover Code or the SARs;
6. which regulator is able to act most quickly;

7. whether assistance of overseas regulators will be required;
8. whether the misconduct involves potential loss to consumers for whom restitution may be an appropriate remedy;
9. whether a financial penalty may be appropriate.

In cases where the FSA and the Panel are conducting concurrent investigations **8.86** arising from related conduct, the two regulators will seek to avoid prejudicing each other's actions. To that end they will notify each other of significant developments in their own investigations and any significant steps that they intend to take including:

1. interviewing key witnesses;
2. requiring production of significant volumes of documents;
3. executing search warrants;
4. instituting proceedings or disposing of a case.

If related investigations of the FSA or the Panel reach a point where it is considered **8.87** appropriate to bring disciplinary or enforcement proceedings, the decision to commence such proceedings will take into account whether the proceedings might prejudice the actions of the other regulator and whether separate proceedings are appropriate. The Panel and the FSA will communicate with each other before either makes a decision to commence such a proceeding.

Finally, each will inform the other of the outcome of any investigations or proceedings of joint interest and communicate any other helpful feedback. **8.88**

(8) *The regular user*

Ever since the FSMA market abuse prohibitions were first proposed, the role of **8.89** the 'regular user of the market' had been a topic of discussion. Given that this hypothetical person is now relevant only to certain so-called legacy offences as discussed in Chapter 3, a detailed discussion of this 'individual' is not apposite. We accordingly confine our consideration to a few issues of now largely historic interest.

First, with the implementation of the Directive in the UK, the role of the 'regular **8.90** user' changed. Originally, the FSMA, s 118(10) said that (for purposes of Part VIII) the term 'regular user':

> in relation to a particular market, means a reasonable person who regularly deals on market in investments of the kind in question.[69]

---

[69] The Implementation of the Directive has replaced FSMA, s 118 with a new s 118, and moved the above definition of 'regular user' to a new FSMA, s 130A(3) (SI 2005/381). See also MAR 1.2.20–1.2/21.

8.91   Behaviour would be market abuse only where it would be likely to be regarded by the regular user as a failure to observe the standard of behaviour reasonably expected of someone in their particular position in relation to that market.[70] The FSA pointed out that the 'regular user' was not a real person or a group of real people. He was not identified by taking a survey of market participants. The Authority expressed the view that the test was intended as an 'objective standard' to avoid the argument that the fact that 'everyone' does something in a market does not make it an acceptable market practice.

8.92   In its pre-Directive Code, the FSA said that the regular user, for purposes of the UK market abuse regime, was *not*:

- the FSA; or
- competitors or market co-participants of the person alleged to have committed market abuse in the market in question.[71]

8.93   The FSA said:

> Initially, we will have to form our own view about whether particular behaviour is acceptable. We are not the regular user but we do have to give guidance on the standards the regular user is likely to expect. Ultimately, the Tribunal will decide what standards the regular user expects.[72]

8.94   In its pre-Directive Code, the FSA stated that the statutory regular user is 'likely' to consider all the circumstances of the behaviour in question and that:

> it is expected that market users should conduct their affairs so as not to compromise fair and efficient market operation or so as to unfairly damage the interest of investors.[73]

8.95   The last point raised the very real question as to whether the UK provisions on market abuse were in fact ever governed by a regular user test. The regular user's view about the acceptability of market behaviour would still be judged against whether or not generally accepted behaviour promotes fair and efficient market operation and does not unfairly damage investors.

8.96   The FSA recognized that the standard of behaviour expected by the regular user was going to vary from market to market. For example. the disclosure standards of equities markets are different from the disclosure expected in commodities markets. As a result, there will be different expectations with respect to the use of non-public information in those different markets. Also the standard expected of a person will vary according to his knowledge, skill, experience and position.

---

[70] MAR 1.2.1 (revoked 30 June 2005).
[71] MAR 1 Annex 4G (1 May 2005).
[72] FSA, *Market Conduct Source Book, Feedback on CP 124*, June 2002, Annex B p. 1 Question 3.
[73] MAR 1.2.3 (revoked 30 June 2005).

As an example, the standards expected of public servants or public sector bodies will need to take into account their statutory or other official duties.[74]

The position of the FSA was that what the prevailing standards in a particular market were at a particular time was relevant, but may not coincide with the standards which the 'regular user' of the market expected to meet. This was because the FSA believed that standards expected by *actual users* of the market may not be deemed acceptable by the objective *regular user*. The FSA gave an example of a market in which the typical users tolerate misuse of information but a 'regular user' would not find this acceptable.[75] **8.97**

In its pre-Directive Code, the FSA said that behaviour that conformed to standards generally accepted by users of the market could still be market abuse.[76] The FSA gave an example of issues concerning the trading of property futures in 1991 on the London FOX market. This involved transactions intended to give the appearance of activity and liquidity in the property futures market. Such transactions were carried out at the request and with the encouragement of senior officials of the exchange but, in the FSA's view, fell below standards acceptable to the 'regular user'.[77] **8.98**

However, the FSA noted that the market codes and practices the regular user would take into account would include not only the rules, codes of conduct and good practice of UK RIEs and other UK markets, but also the relevant rules and standards of overseas markets.[78] The FSA stated that although reference to overseas market regulations may be an important factor, compliance with those standards will not automatically protect a market participant from a finding of market abuse. They will do so only when the overseas standards 'deliver broadly equivalent protection' to the FSA's own rules.[79] **8.99**

(9) The post-Directive regular user

The post-Directive definition of the 'regular user' is now moved from FSMA, s 118(10) to s 130A(3). One of the stated goals of the FSA during the Directive implementation process was to 'simplify the content of the Handbook …'.[80] As a result of those changes, the FSA says: **8.100**

> We reduced the amount of guidance provided on some aspects of the market abuse regime.[81]

---

[74] MAR 1.2.7 (revoked 30 June 2005).
[75] CP 59, p.15, para. 6.6.
[76] MAR 1.2.4 (revoked 30 June 2005).
[77] CP 59, pp. 16–17, paras. 6.8–6.10.
[78] CP 59, p. 25, para. 6.7.
[79] CP 59, p. 16, para. 6.8.
[80] FSA, *Implementation of the Market Abuse Directive*, 5 March 2005, p. 3.
[81] 'Implementation', 5 March 2005, p. 5.

8.101   In particular, with respect to the regular user, the Government noted:

> ... the UK does need to adjust its existing market abuse regime to implement the directive. We cannot retain the breadth of the current 'regular user test'. It may mean that behaviour prohibited by the directive would be exculpated currently in the UK. So for those offences which are included in the directive, we can only make available the defences that are included in the directive; this means that we will be reducing the current range of defences. To do otherwise would mean under-implementation of the directive.[82]

8.102   In the post-Directive Code the regular user was described as follows:

> The regular user is a hypothetical reasonable person who regularly deals on the market and in the investments of the kind in question. The presence of the regular user imports an objective element [...][83] while retaining some subjective features of the markets for the investments in question.[84]

8.103   In summary, the application of the regular user test was thus first reduced and now survives only in relation to the so-called legacy offences. As discussed in Chapter 3, the so-called legacy offences will disappear from 31 December 2009.

---

[82] Joint Consultation Paper, p. 17, para. 3.14.
[83] The omitted section says 'into the elements listed in MAR 1.2.15'. This does not appear to be correct because there are currently no elements 'listed' in 1.2.15.
[84] MAR 1.2.21.

9

ENFORCEMENT PROCEDURE

A. Enforcement in the UK

The Directive was not intended to replace national provisions regarding regula-   **9.01**
tory authorities. However, it was intended to support the creation of a single
competent authority for regulating market abuse within each Member State. That
authority was required to be given a minimum list of powers in order to correctly
implement and enforce the Directive provisions. Both before and after the
Directive, the 'Authority' charged with enforcing market abuse regulation in the
UK is the FSA.

The FSA enforcement underwent a substantial revision as a result of, among other   **9.02**
things, criticism by the Tribunal in the *Legal & General* case.[1] A number of changes
to the FSA *Handbook* were made thereafter.[2] At the end of August 2007, the FSA's
Enforcement and Decision Making sections of the Handbook ('DEC') were taken
out of force. A new Enforcement Guide ('EG') and a new Decision Procedure and
Penalties Manual ('DEPP') were introduced.

---

[1] FSA, *Enforcement Process Review: Report and Recommendations*, July 2005 ('*Enforcement Report*')
p. 5. For further discussion of *Legal & General*, see Chapter 14.
[2] FSA, *Enforcement Process Review: Handbook Changes*, July 2005 ('*Enforcement Changes*').

9.03   The purpose of this chapter is not to review the history of why those changes were made. It is to give the reader a basic understanding of how the FSA operates an enforcement proceeding related to market abuse, the statutory basis of enforcement and how that is reflected in the FSA *Handbook*.

9.04   With those things in mind, the reader should read the description of FSA enforcement in the next part of this chapter with an understanding that those parts of the FSA *Handbook* that deal with those procedures are continually being modified.

9.05   The FSA is not the only 'enforcer' of market abuse prohibitions in the UK.[3] The FSMA also gives a private right of action to parties who are damaged by a contravention of the rules. The final section of this book will give a brief description of the fundamental elements of such rights.

B. FSA Market Abuse Enforcement Powers

9.06   Essentially, the FSA has two powers under FSMA, s 128(3) which expressly relate to market abuse investigations. The first power is to impose penalties in conformity with s 123. The second power is to appoint a person to conduct an investigation as mandated under s 168 of the Act.

(1) Information gathering

9.07   The powers of the FSA to gather information and conduct an investigation are set out in Part XI of the Act, ss 165–177. Under s 165, the FSA can issue a written notice to an authorized person requiring him or it to provide information or documents of a specified description. The information or documents must be produced before the end of a specified reasonable period, and at a specified place.

9.08   The information or documents may be required to be produced 'without delay'.[4] The section applies only to information or documents reasonably required by the FSA to perform its functions under the Act. Information may be required in any reasonable form. And the FSA can require that the information or documents be verified or authenticated in any reasonable manner.[5] 'Documents' are widely defined to include 'information recorded in any form'.[6] It follows that the term

---

[3] There are also others with institutional enforcement duties such as recognized investment exchanges ('RIEs') and recognized clearing houses ('RCHs'). However, it is not within the scope of this book to discuss their functions and duties and how those may relate to market abuse regulation.

[4] FSMA, s 165(3).

[5] FSMA, s 165.

[6] FSMA, s 417(1).

will embrace tape recordings,[7] film and video recordings[8] and email communications. Further, the FSMA provides that references to production of documents include 'references to producing a copy of the information in legible form'.[9] This would require transcriptions of illegible hand-writing and decoding of encrypted material.

The persons who can be required to produce information or documents extend **9.09** beyond authorized persons. They can also include persons who are 'connected' with an authorized person; the operator, trustee or depository of a scheme recognized under ss 270 or 272 who is not an authorized person; a recognized investment exchange; or a recognized clearing house. The term 'authorized person' also includes a person who was at any time authorized but who may have ceased to be an authorized person. A 'connected' person can be a person who is a member of an authorized person's group, a controller of an authorized person, any member of a partnership of which an authorized person is a member; or persons mentioned in Part I or II of Schedule 15 of the Act.[10] Persons included in Part I of Schedule 15 are:

1. officers, managers, employees or agents of a corporate body which is an authorized person or its parent; an authorized person who is in a partnership with a person who has been a member, manager, employee or agent of the partnership;
2. if the unauthorized person is an unincorporated association, a person who has been an officer, manager, employee or agent of the unincorporated association;
3. if the unauthorized person is a friendly society, a person who has been an officer at, manager or employee of the friendly society in conformity with the Friendly Societies Act 1992, s 119(1);
4. if the authorized person is a building society, a person who has been an officer or employee of the building society in conformity with the meeting and meaning of the Building Societies Act 1986, s 119(1);
5. if the authorized person is an individual, a person who has been an employee or agent of the individual.

It is important to note that under some circumstances, a person under **9.10** investigation may not be an authorized person. If that is the case, the references in ss 171–172 of the Act, as to what an investigator may require of persons under

---

7 See *Grant v South Western and County Properties* [1985] Ch 185.
8 See *Senior v Holdsworth ex parte Independent Television News Ltd* [1976] QB 23.
9 FSMA, s 417(1).
10 FSMA, s 165 and FSMA, Sch. 15.

investigation, apply equally to the unauthorized persons under investigation.[11] Under Schedule 15, Part II such persons can also be:

1. the partner, manager, employee, agent, appointed representative, banker, auditor, actuary or solicitor of a person under investigation;
2. the parents of a person under investigation;
3. a subsidiary of a person under investigation;
4. a subsidiary undertaking of a parent undertaking of the person under investigation; or
5. a parent undertaking of a subsidiary undertaking of a person under investigation.

9.11   A refusal to supply information or documents pursuant to an investigator's request made formally under FSMA may be referred to the High Court and dealt with as a contempt. It is a defence to such proceedings that there was a 'reasonable excuse' for the lack of compliance. What amounts to a 'reasonable excuse' for this purpose is by no means clear. One example may arise where it is possible to show that the questioning sought to be pursued was 'unfair'.[12] This means of challenge must, however, be regarded as a high-risk strategy.

9.12   A person may not be required to produce, disclose or permit the inspection of so called 'protected items'.[13] The latter phrase is defined to embrace communications between a professional legal adviser, his client and/or any other person, which are made either in connection with the giving of legal advice to the client or in connection with or in contemplation of legal proceedings and tendered for the purposes of those proceedings.[14] This broadly protects documents and communications which would conventionally enjoy legal professional or litigation privilege. By creating a defined category of 'protected items', rather than adopting reference to the established concepts of legal and litigation privilege, it is clear that the decision to justify withholding any particular document or item of information must be justified by reference to the statutory criteria and not by reference to the common law ambit of privilege conventionally understood.

9.13   Information obtained by a bank and/or documents created in the course of the bank's instructions by a client are said to be confidential. The 'confidence' may be waived by the client or overridden by the court.[15] Limited respect to this principle is preserved by the FSMA. In short, no person may be required to disclose information or produce documents in respect of which he owes an obligation of

---

[11] FSMA, Sch. 15 Part I and FSMA, ss 171 and 172.
[12] See *In Re Mirror Group Newspapers plc* [2000] Ch 194.
[13] FSMA, s 413(1).
[14] FSMA, s 413(2), (3).
[15] See *Tournier v National Provisional and Union Bank of England* [1994] 1 KB 461.

confidence by virtue of carrying on the business of banking unless he is the person under investigation or the person to whom the obligation of confidence is owed is being investigated; otherwise disclosure may be given with the consent of the person to whom the obligation of confidence is owed or the investigating authority has specifically authorized disclosure.[16] The latter exception effectively extinguishes the scope of the right to object on this ground.

(2) Skilled persons reports

In addition to the general power to obtain documents and information from authorized persons, the FSA may also require to be provided with a report on any matter about which it has or could have required the provision of information or production of documents under s 165 discussed above.[17] The preconditions for such a requirement are that:

9.14

(a) the FSA must first give written notice to the person concerned of the requirement for such a report;[18]
(b) the 'skilled person' must be nominated or approved by the FSA and appear to have the skills necessary to make a report; and[19]
(c) the power must be exercised only in relation to an authorized person, any member of the authorized person's group or a partnership of which he is a member (or any person who has at any given time fallen within the above).

The FSA's Annual Report for 2008/09 revealed that it used this power in 56 cases in 2008/09 to examine a number of regulatory concerns including market abuse; this compares with 29 reports commissioned in 2007/08 to that end, 17 cases in 2005/06 and 19 in 2004/05 where the subjects of reports included controls to prevent market abuse.

9.15

Further, insofar as the report must relate to 'any matter about which the FSA has required or could require the provision of information or production of documents under Section 165', it follows that the report must be *reasonably* required in connection with the exercise by the FSA of its statutory functions. The FSMA also imposes a duty on any person who is providing or who has at any time provided services in relation to a matter on which a report is required to give the appointed skilled person 'all such assistance as [he] may reasonably require'.[20]

9.16

---

[16] FSMA, s 175(5).
[17] FSMA, s 166(1).
[18] FSMA, s 161(1).
[19] FSMA, s 166(4).
[20] FSMA, s 166(5).

The foregoing obligation is able to be enforced on the application of the FSA by an injunction.[21]

9.17 Where the FSA's objectives include obtaining expert analysis or recommendations for remedial action, the above power may well be regarded as appropriate either instead of or in conjunction with its remaining powers to obtain documents and information discussed here.[22]

9.18 Self-evidently, the skilled person must report competently and in good faith. He is protected against any breaches of the restrictions on disclosure of confidential information contained in the FSMA,[23] provided such disclosure to the FSA is made 'in good faith and the person disclosing the information reasonably believes that [it] is relevant to the discharge of public function by the Authority'.[24] It is a discrete and untested issue whether skilled persons might be protected by the traditional immunity from actions in negligence[25] which extends to experts preparing reports for use in litigation.[26]

(3) General investigations

9.19 The powers discussed above to compel production of information and documents where reasonably required by the FSA, in the exercise of its statutory functions (including the commissioning of reports by skilled persons), apply as between the FSA and the authorized concern (including connected parties). In addition the FSA has power to undertake a 'general investigation' into the nature, conduct or state of a business. These further powers are contained in FSMA, ss 167, 170 and 171 and apply more widely:

- first, they are available to both the FSA and the Secretary of State;
- second, they may be deployed in relation to both authorized persons and appointed representatives; and
- third, the definition of 'connected persons' in relation to whom these extended powers are also available is broader than that discussed above. It here includes not only officers, managers, partners, employees and agents but embraces appointed representatives, bankers, auditors, actuaries or solicitors of the

---

[21] FSMA, s 166(6).

[22] See SUP 5, which contains guidance on the FSA's use of the s 166 power including guidance on the terms of appointment, contractual duties and reporting processes.

[23] See FSMA, s 348.

[24] Financial Services and Markets Act 2000 (Disclosure of Information by Prescribed Persons) Regulations 2001 (SI 2001/1857), paragraph 3(2).

[25] *Stanton v Callaghan* [1999] 2 WLR 74: '… an expert witness who gives evidence at trial is immune from suit in respect of anything which he says in the Court and that immunity will extend to the contents of the report which he adopts as or incorporates in his evidence'.

[26] See, e.g., *Palmer v Durnford Ford* [1992] QB 483.

person under investigation, or a parent or subsidiary undertaking of the person under investigation.

The FSA's or Secretary of State's power to appoint 'one or more competent persons **9.20** to conduct an investigation on its behalf' arises in respect of:

- the nature, conduct, or state of the business of an authorized person or of an appointed representative;
- a particular aspect of that business; or
- the ownership or control of an authorized person.[27]

If the person so appointed thinks it necessary for the purposes of the investigation, **9.21** he may also investigate the business of a person who is or has at any relevant time been a member of the group of which the person under investigation is part or a partnership of which such person was a member. 'Business' is defined to include any part of a business even if it does not consist of carrying on regulated activities.[28]

The investigating authority (the FSA or the Secretary of State) must give written **9.22** notice of the appointment of an investigator to the person who is the subject of the investigation, specify the provisions under which and as a result of which the investigator was appointed and state the reason for the appointment.[29] Likewise, if the business of a connected concern is to be included in the investigation, written notice thereof must be provided.[30] The statutory threshold for instituting an investigation into the affairs of an authorized firm or appointed representative is that 'it appears to the Authority or the Secretary of State ... that there is good reason for doing so'.[31]

The investigating authority is empowered to control the scope of the investigation **9.23** which includes power to direct the appointed investigator(s) to 'extend the investigation to additional matters'.[32] The FSA is, however, here only obliged to notify the person under investigation of the change in the scope or conduct of the investigation if it forms the opinion that 'the person subject to investigation is likely to be significantly prejudiced by not being made aware of it'. It is difficult to reconcile the statutory requirement for initial notice as to the appointment of an investigator and the reason for it with the absence of any later requirement to notify a change in scope of the investigation save where in the opinion of the investigating authority the person under investigation would be 'significantly' prejudiced by

---

[27] FSMA, s 167(1)(a)(b) and (c).
[28] FSMA, s 167(5).
[29] FSMA, s 170(2), (4).
[30] FSMA, s 167(3).
[31] FSMA, s 167(1).
[32] FSMA, s 170(8)(b).

not being made aware of it. It is to be expected that written notice would be given where there may otherwise be unnecessary costs incurred by a firm dealing with an aspect of an investigation which the FSA no longer intended to pursue or where a person may inadvertently incriminate himself by not knowing of the change in scope.

9.24 The person appointed under the above regime is given the following statutory powers:

(a) a power to require the person under investigation or any person connected with him to attend upon the investigator and answer any questions;

(b) a power to require any of the above to provide information;

(c) a power to require 'any person' (that is, whether or not the subject of the investigation or a connected person) to provide documents; and

(d) subject to the proviso in each case that 'the investigator concerned *reasonably* considers the question, provision of information or provision of the document to be relevant to the purposes of the investigation'.[33]

(4) Search warrants

9.25 The final power available in the investigative armoury of the FSA is the right to obtain a search warrant from a Justice of the Peace. An application for a warrant may be made by the Secretary of State, the FSA or any investigator where information is able to be provided on oath that there are reasonable grounds for believing any one or more of three specific conditions may be satisfied.[34]

9.26 The first set of conditions arises where a person has been required to provide information and has failed wholly or partly to comply; if there are reasonable grounds to believe that there may be documents or information on the premises, specified in the warrant, a magistrate may authorize a constable to enter the premises to search for and seize relevant documents or information and to take copies or extracts therefrom.

9.27 A warrant may also be issued where the premises specified in it are those of an authorized person or an appointed representative and there are reasonable grounds to believe that if otherwise requested to produce documents or information, the recipient of the request would not comply with it or would remove, tamper with or destroy documents.

9.28 Finally, a warrant may also be issued where there are reasonable grounds for believing that an offence mentioned in FSMA, s 168 has been or is being committed

---

[33] FSMA, s 171(1), (2), and (3).
[34] FSMA, s 176.

and there are on the premises, specified in the warrant, documents or information which may be relevant to whether the offence has been or is being committed; in this instance, the court must also be satisfied that a simple requirement to produce the documents would either be ignored or result in documents or information being removed, tampered with or destroyed.

C. Basic FSA Enforcement Policy

The FSA is a 'risk-led' rather than 'enforcement-led' regulator. August 2006 saw **9.29** the publication of the FSA's Risk Assessment Framework. In paragraph 1.1 it stated:

> The Financial Services Authority (FSA) is a risk-based regulator and ARROW is the framework we use to make risk-based regulation operational. ARROW stands for the Advanced, Risk-Responsive Operating FrameWork and covers all of our risks, firm-specific, thematic and internal. As such, the ARROW framework has three main components:
> - ARROW Firms: used when assessing risks in individual firms (we sometimes call this 'vertical' supervision);
> - ARROW Themes: used when assessing cross-cutting risks, i.e. those involving several firms or relating to the market as a whole (we sometimes call this 'horizontal' work); and
> - Internal Risk Management: used when assessing the operational risks that might impact the FSA.

It aims to focus on those areas of regulation where it can make the greatest progress **9.30** towards fulfilling its statutory objectives.[35] Therefore, each year, it identifies 'enforcement priorities' in its Business Plan which relate to those market sectors where market misconduct is believed to be most likely.[36] The priority sectors are identified as 'high', 'medium high', 'medium low' and 'low'. The factors that the FSA brings to bear in choosing priorities include:[37]

(a) the relative importance attached to sending a message to a particular market sector, or to the financial services industry as a whole; and

(b) a concentration of resources on larger financial groups.

This is not to say that the FSA will ignore serious breaches in low-priority sectors **9.31** but it is more likely that market abuse violations will be identified in high-priority sectors, and in larger firms. The majority of enforcement cases has followed this pattern.[38]

---

[35] *Enforcement Report,* 1.7.
[36] *Enforcement Report,* 4.7–4.10.
[37] *Enforcement Report,* 4.9.
[38] *Enforcement Report,* 4.9–4.10.

9.32　From reviewing the market abuse cases discussed in Chapter 14, almost all have related to insider dealing in the share markets. Apparently, the FSA considers this is a high priority rule violation about which it wishes to send a strong message to the industry.[39]

D.　The Enforcement Referral Decision

9.33　The structure of the FSA is complex,[40] but it contains both Supervision and Enforcement divisions. The decision to undertake an enforcement action is the result of communications between the two. The Supervision divisions within the FSA that can make referrals to Enforcement are:[41]

1.　Major Retail Groups, Retail Firms, Small Firms and Wholesale Firms;
2.　Markets (particularly for market abuse and Listing Rule violations);
3.　Retail Themes[42] (relating to financial promotion or arising from FSA review visits);
4.　Contact Revenue and Information Management (relating to failures to pay fees or submit returns when due).

9.34　Questions of enforcement can be identified either by a firm's designated FSA supervisor or by some other FSA function in contact with a firm, but it is most likely to be raised by a supervisor. The supervisors will be aware of the enforcement priorities and that knowledge will serve as a guide regarding what issues they should be looking at. Each FSA supervisory division has an Enforcement Relationship Manager ('ERM') who is the contact point for referrals. The ERM advises the supervisor about enforcement procedures and helps draft the documentation that accompanies a referral.[43]

9.35　The criteria for making a referral are listed in the DEPP section of the FSA *Handbook*. The criteria for determining whether to take disciplinary action are set out in DEPP 6.2. When encountering conduct appearing to be a regulatory breach, the FSA is to consider the full circumstances of the matter. A non-exhaustive list of the factors it will consider includes:[44]

(1)　The nature, seriousness and impact of the suspected breach, including:
　　(a)　whether the breach was deliberate or reckless;

---

[39] See Chapter 14, Market Abuse Cases.
[40] *Enforcement Report*, Annex 5, FSA Organisation Chart.
[41] *Enforcement Report*, 4.17.
[42] Which involves reviewing a particular issue across a selection of firms: *Enforcement Report*, 4.13–4.16.
[43] *Enforcement Report*, 4.8.
[44] DEPP 6.2.1.

   (b) the duration and frequency of the breach;

   (c) the amount of any benefit gained or loss avoided as a result of the breach;

   (d) whether the breach reveals serious or systemic weaknesses of the management systems or internal controls relating to all or part of a person's business;

   (e) the impact or potential impact of the breach on the orderliness of markets including whether confidence in those markets has been damaged or put at risk;

   (f) the loss or risk of loss caused to consumers or other market users;

   (g) the nature and extent of any financial crime facilitated, occasioned or otherwise attributable to the breach; and

   (h) whether there are a number of smaller issues, which individually may not justify disciplinary action, but which do so when taken collectively.

(2) The conduct of the person after the breach, including the following:

   (a) how quickly, effectively and completely the person brought the breach to the attention of the FSA or another relevant regulatory authority;

   (b) the degree of co-operation the person showed during the investigation of the breach;

   (c) any remedial steps the person has taken in respect of the breach;

   (d) the likelihood that the same type of breach (whether on the part of the person under investigation or others) will recur if no action is taken;

   (e) whether the person concerned has complied with any requirements or rulings of another regulatory authority relating to his behaviour (for example, where relevant, those of the Takeover Panel or an RIE); and

   (f) the nature and extent of any false or inaccurate information given by the person and whether the information appears to have been given in an attempt to knowingly mislead the FSA.

(3) The previous disciplinary record and compliance history of the person including:

   (a) whether the FSA (or any previous regulator) has taken any previous disciplinary action resulting in adverse findings against the person;

   (b) whether the person has previously undertaken not to do a particular act or engage in particular behaviour;

   (c) whether the FSA (or any previous regulator) has previously taken protective action in respect of a firm, using its own initiative powers, by means of a variation of a Part IV permission or otherwise, or has previously requested the firm to take remedial action, and the extent to which such action has been taken; and

   (d) the general compliance history of the person, including whether the FSA (or any previous regulator) has previously issued the person with a private warning.

(4) ... The FSA will not take action against a person for behaviour that it considers to be in line with guidance, other materials published by the FSA in support of the Handbook or FSA-confirmed Industry Guidance which were current at the time of the behaviour in question. (The manner in which guidance and other published materials may otherwise be relevant to an enforcement case is described in EG 2.)

(5) Action taken by the FSA in previous similar circumstances.

(6) … Where other regulatory authorities propose to take action in respect of the breach which is under consideration by the FSA, or one similar to it, the FSA will consider whether the other authority's action would be adequate to address the FSA's concerns, or whether it would be appropriate for the FSA to take its own action.

9.36 The referral decision is supported by the Enforcement Referral Document (ERD). In the ERD, the referring entity is required to explain why the particular circumstances of the case make it appropriate for enforcement action. The ERD must be signed by the manager of the relevant manager of the referring division. If the referring division is different from the division supervising the firm in question, the ERD requires the supervisor to be informed. If the supervisor does not agree with the referral, his reasons must be stated.[45]

9.37 The FSA tries to make it clear that the nature of a firm's relationship with the FSA will be a factor in a decision to refer a matter to Enforcement. If a firm has a proven record of having senior management that takes its responsibilities seriously, being open and communicative with the FSA and taking prompt action to remedy regulatory problems, an Enforcement referral may be less likely. A firm's specific response to the particular situation that has attracted the FSA's concern will also be taken into consideration. On its website, the FSA gives specific examples of cases (without mentioning names) where it has decided not to take enforcement action, despite possible rule breaches, because of the ways the firms in question responded to the problems. The fact that a firm is conscientious about its regulatory duties will not change the FSA's priority sectors or the seriousness with which it regards breaches in those areas, but it may affect individual decisions about whether taking enforcement action in a particular case is the most efficient use of the FSA's resources.[46]

9.38 If Enforcement declines to act on a referral, the referring entity can take the matter to a higher authority in the FSA. Although usually settled at a lower level, such a disagreement can ultimately be resolved by the Case Referrals Committee (CRC). The CRC is chaired by an FSA Managing Director and is made up from Directors drawn from divisions across the FSA.[47]

9.39 Firms have complained that they are sometimes kept in the dark between the time that they are told an enforcement action is contemplated and the final decision to refer a matter to Enforcement. Poor communication between the FSA and a supervised firm at this stage was criticized in the *Enforcement Report*. It was suggested that, in future, the time gap between the first mention of possibility of

---

[45] *Enforcement Report*, 4.23.
[46] *Enforcement Report*, 4.24.
[47] *Enforcement Report*, 4.25.

referral and the final decision to refer to Enforcement should be kept to a minimum. Supervisors have also been admonished not to tell a firm that a matter will not be referred to Enforcement until that has been cleared with other interested parties at the FSA.[48]

E. Post-referral Investigation

Once a case is accepted by the Enforcement Division, a Project Sponsor, Project **9.40** Manager and case team are assigned. The case team will include a case lawyer. The size, composition and experience of the team will vary with the type and complexity of the investigation.[49]

At the start of a formal investigation, a Notice of Investigation is usually given to **9.41** the firm in question at an initial meeting. The other purpose of the meeting is to discuss with the firm, and any individuals involved, the nature of the investigation and how the FSA proposes to conduct it. The FSA will usually outline the names of individuals and the types of documents it believes it will need to examine. The FSA usually provides an 'information pack' to the firm explaining the main stages of enforcement and the possibilities for mediation and settlement.[50]

Before demanding production of information and documents from those under **9.42** investigation, the FSA investigators will try to get as much information as they can from the FSA's own records. This is to save duplication.[51]

Throughout the investigation, communication is between the case team and the **9.43** firm and individuals under investigation, with the appropriate FSA supervisor being informed of the progress of the investigation. The supervisor is usually not directly involved in the investigation.[52] As an investigation moves towards a conclusion, the case team will prepare a draft investigation report. Copies are sent to the firm and individuals under investigation to allow them to correct any factual errors.[53]

Usually, the legal issues that arise during an investigation are considered by **9.44** the case lawyers. Outside counsel are sometimes hired in more complex cases.[54] The FSA Chairman and senior management (such as the Chief Executive and the

---

[48] *Enforcement Report*, 4.26–4.27.
[49] *Enforcement Report*, 5.1.
[50] *Enforcement Report*, 5.2–5.4.
[51] *Enforcement Report*, 5.5.
[52] *Enforcement Report*, 5.13–5.16.
[53] *Enforcement Report*, 5.21.
[54] *Enforcement Report*, 5.24.

three Managing Directors) do sometimes become involved in investigations, depending on the importance, complexity and seriousness of the case.

9.45 During the course of an investigation, the FSA Enforcement Division will some-times employ experts, 'skilled persons', as defined in FSMA, s 166, to provide reports on specific subjects about which the FSA needs information to help them better understand particular aspects of the conduct under investigation.[55]

9.46 The FSA can direct an RIE or an RCH to terminate, suspend or limit its own enquiry while the FSA conducts an investigation of alleged market abuse.[56]

F. Informal Disciplinary Action

9.47 Many investigations are discontinued without any formal FSA disciplinary action. In some cases, the FSA will issue a 'private warning' to a firm or individual, as described in the Enforcement Guide to the FSA's approach to exercising its enforcement powers.[57] A private warning is not a determination that any misconduct or breach has been found. It is intended to indicate that there are issues about which the FSA is concerned which have not been resolved entirely to the FSA's satisfaction. They are given in cases where the FSA wishes to alert the persons under investigation that they have come close to disciplinary action, but, in the particular case, the FSA has decided not to take formal disciplinary action.[58]

9.48 Prior to issuing a private warning (unless the FSA has already done substantially the same thing by providing a draft investigation report with an invitation to com-ment), the FSA conducts a 'minded to' procedure in which it informs those under investigation that it is considering issuing a private warning, states its reasons, and invites comments.[59]

G. Formal Disciplinary Action

9.49 In other cases, the FSA will conclude a market abuse investigation by deciding to take formal disciplinary action. The first step in a formal FSA disciplinary action for market abuse is the issuance of a 'warning notice' to the persons concerned that

---

[55] *Enforcement Report*, 5.32–5.33. FSA Enforcement has done this about half a dozen times since December 2001.

[56] FSMA, s 128.

[57] Enforcement Guide 7.10–7.19.

[58] Enforcement Guide 7.10–7.19 and *Enforcement Report*, 5.44.

[59] *Enforcement Report*, 5.45.

the FSA proposes to take action against him. If the warning notice informs the target of an FSA proposal to impose a financial penalty, the amount of the proposed penalty must be stated. If the warning notice proposes to publish a statement, the terms of the statement must be given.[60]

The FSA is required to allow the persons concerned at least 28 days to respond to the warning notice by making representations.[61] The Warning Notice must inform the recipient that he has a right to inspect 'the material on which [the Authority] relied in taking the decision which gave rise to the [issue of] the Notice'.[62] The Warning Notice must also identify a similar inspection right in relation to what is described as 'secondary material which in the opinion of the Authority might undermine' its decision.[63] Secondary material is defined to mean 'material ... which (a) was considered by the Authority in reaching the decision or (b) obtained by the Authority in connection with the matter to which the Notice ... relates but which was not considered by it in reaching that decision'.[64] The material on which [the Authority otherwise] relied in taking the decision' to which the Notice relates is not separately defined. It is reasonable to assume that 'material' embraces (at least) documents and information made available to or collected by the FSA. Information may therefore include knowledge gained from discussions with third parties—whether or not recorded in writing. There are four categories of 'material' which the FSA may nonetheless withhold. These are:

(a) 'excluded material'—material which has been intercepted in obedience to a warrant issued under enactments relating to the interception of communications or which indicates that such a warrant was issued or that material was intercepted in obedience thereto;[65]

(b) 'comparison material'—material which relates to a case involving a person other than the recipient of the Notice and which was taken into account by the FSA in the instant case only for the purposes of comparison with other cases;

(c) 'protected items'—in essence materials attracting legal privilege as discussed above;

(d) 'public interest material'—material which in the opinion of the FSA it would not be in the public interest to disclose or it would be unfair to disclose having

9.50

---

[60] FSMA, s 126 and *Enforcement Report*, 6.2. Regarding the penalties which the FSMA may impose, see FSMA, s 123 and the discussion of penalties in Chapter 10, below.

[61] FSMA, s 387(2). See also DEC 4.4.

[62] FSMA, s 394(1).

[63] FSMA, s 391(1)(b).

[64] FSMA, s 394(6).

[65] FSMA, s 394(7).

regard to its significance to the recipient of the Notice and the potential prejudice to the commercial interests of the other person.[66]

9.51 In the latter two cases (protected items and public interest material) the FSA must nonetheless inform the recipient of the Notice of the existence of the material in question. It is difficult to understand why there is no similar requirement to disclose at least the existence of the first two categories of material. Further, it is to be regarded as a serious defect that the FSMA and the rules and regulations made under it by the FSA provide no effective mechanism for challenging decisions to withhold information.

9.52 After representations have been made, the FSA can either notify the persons concerned that it will take no further action[67] or issue a 'decision notice' informing the accused of the nature of the penalty the FSA has decided to impose.[68] The persons concerned[69] can refer the matter to the Financial Services and Markets Tribunal ('Tribunal') within 28 days of a decision notice.[70]

H. The Regulatory Decisions Committee

9.53 FSA regulatory decisions, such as the decisions to issue warning or decision notices, are made the Regulatory Decisions Committee ('RDC'). Under the FSMA, such decisions must be fair and must not be made by persons not directly involved in the investigation.[71]

9.54 FSMA, s 395 requires (among other things) that:

(1) The Authority [FSA] must determine the procedure that it proposes to follow in relation to the giving of —
   (a) supervisory notices; and
   (b) warning notices and decision notices.
(2) That procedure must be designed to secure, among other things, that the decision which gives rise to the obligation to give any such notice is taken by a person not directly involved in establishing the evidence on which the decision is based.[72]

---

[66] FSMA, s 394(3).
[67] DEC 2.2.6.
[68] FSMA, s 127.
[69] Please note that 'persons concerned' can also be third parties in some cases. *Enforcement Report,* 7.9–7.12.
[70] FSMA, s 133. For additional information about the Tribunal or market abuse cases before it, see Chapters 12 and 14.
[71] *Enforcement Report,* 6.3–6.5.
[72] FSMA, s 395.

In order to preserve the independence between the investigation and recommen-   **9.55**
dation functions which s 395 requires, the board of the FSA set up the RDC,
which takes those enforcement, authorization and supervisory decisions of
importance to the firms and individuals concerned. The RDC reports directly
to the board of the FSA, which appoints the chairman and members of the
RDC. They are charged with representing the public interest, and are chosen
from among industry practitioners and knowledgeable persons outside the
industry.[73]

The RDC had been criticized in the past for receiving information only from the   **9.56**
FSA investigative staff which the party being investigated did not see. It was argued
that this was inconsistent with the review process before the Tribunal which
involves a rehearing where each party hears the presentations of the other party.
The danger was that the RDC would make decisions not supported by adequate
evidence.

This was found to be the case in the two Tribunal decisions in the *Legal & General*   **9.57**
Assurance case, which involved allegations related to mis-selling of mortgages
rather than market abuse. However, the Tribunal's comments on the RDC process
were equally relevant to market abuse cases. The Tribunal said (among other
things relating to the RDC process): [74]

> We would not have taken the FSA's position. It is for FSA to establish its case and
> produce the evidence it relies on. The existence of delays and what FSA may see as
> unreasonableness on the part of the party challenged are no doubt frustrating if not
> infuriating. They are not however a justification for reaching a conclusion that FSA
> is '*obliged*' to rely on evidence as being 'strongly indicative' and arriving at its conclu-
> sions 'accordingly'. We see no such obligation. The issue should be—what is the
> evidence and what conclusions do we draw from it. If more evidence was needed FSA
> should have obtained it.[75]

However, noting that the FSA was conducting a wide-ranging review of its   **9.58**
enforcement procedure, including the RDC procedure, the Tribunal refused to
make further recommendations at the time.[76]

---

[73] FSA, Regulatory Decisions Committee ('RDC'), FSA website, 21 March 2005.
[74] Also discussed in Chapter 14, below.
[75] Legal & General First Decision, p 68, para. 212.
[76] As was noted above in the first section of this chapter, the FSA's review was completed in July
2005, and a number of *Handbook* changes followed; see *Enforcement Report*, 6.

I. Settlement

9.59   Settlement of an enforcement case is possible at any stage of the proceedings.[77] Most enforcement cases settle, and it is in the public interest to settle as early as possible. Discounts for early settlement are encouraged.[78] However, settlement with the FSA can be different from usual civil case settlements because the FSA will still need to make sure that its statutory objectives are met, and some publicity may result.

9.60   Sometimes, a settlement requires a decision notice because imposition of a financial penalty may be part of the settlement. In such cases, the RDC will be involved to make a decision. The case team will obtain 'settlement parameters' from the RDC and will try to settle within the parameters. Settlement may also follow mediation, which is sometimes used in difficult-to-settle enforcement cases.

J. Private Actions

9.61   As the focus on the control of market abuse is supposed to be equally on the protection of market integrity and the protection of investors, there should be a number of things that investors can do to obtain compensation in cases where they are victims of market abuse. Under the UK regulatory scheme there are several options that an aggrieved investor can use to pursue complaints about acts of market abuse that affect them.

9.62   Before proceeding, it may be advisable for an investor to consult a lawyer qualified to deal with financial services issues to get advice about which course to pursue and how to pursue it. In the first instance, an individual investor may complain to the supervisor or higher management of the company employing the person or persons that the investor feels has caused the market abuse. That may solve the problem.

9.63   If it does not, then the investor will have to decide whether to take his complaint outside the company that dealt with his investment to independent trade or regulatory bodies who are charged with looking into customer complaints. In the UK, there are a number of such options.

---

[77] *Enforcement Report*, 7.
[78] *Enforcement Report*, 7.13–7.22.

K. Complaints to the FSA

A person who thinks himself the victim of market abuse may complain to **9.64** the FSA. However, the FSA's function is to have overall responsibility to protect market integrity and investors generally. It is not really their function to adjudicate individual claims for the customers of financial firms. That is not to say that, if they do conclude that someone has committed market abuse, they will not order that compensation be made to affected investors, but that is a decision made more to protect the market as a whole than to repair damage to an individual investor.

The FSMA provides in this regard a wide range of injunctive and restitutionary **9.65** powers. Thus, at a general level, subject to the High Court being satisfied that there is a reasonable likelihood that any person will contravene or continue to contravene a requirement imposed by or under the FSMA or commit conduct constituting an offence for which the FSA or the Secretary of State has power to prosecute under the FSMA, it may on the application of the FSA or the Secretary of State make an order restraining the (relevant) contravention.[79] The remedy of an injunction is accordingly available in respect of 'any person' and not just authorized or approved persons.

In addition to the power to apply for a 'restraining order', the FSA or the Secretary **9.66** of State may also ask the court for an order directing any person who can be shown to have contravened a relevant requirement and further 'any other person who appears to have been knowingly concerned in the contravention' to take such steps as the court may direct to remedy it.[80] The court may also be asked to make an order restraining any person who has contravened a relevant requirement of the FSMA or been knowingly concerned in such a contravention from 'disposing of or otherwise dealing with any assets ... which it is satisfied [such person(s)] is reasonably likely to dispose of or otherwise deal with'.[81]

It is probably sufficient for a person to be said to have been 'knowingly concerned **9.67** in the contravention', to have had knowledge of the facts involved in the contravention without also having knowledge or any appreciation that the material facts amounted to a contravention of FSMA.[82]

---

[79] FSMA, s 380.
[80] FSMA, s 380(2).
[81] FSMA, s 380(3).
[82] See *per* Millett LJ in *Securities and Investments Board v Scandex Capital Management A/S* [1998] 1 WLR 712.

9.68 The FSA may also apply to the court for a restraining or remedial order to be made against any person where the court may be satisfied that there is a reasonable likelihood of conduct being committed, continued or repeated amounting to market abuse.[83] In this instance also, the Court may be asked to make an order restraining the disposal of assets.[84]

9.69 Further, where the High Court is satisfied (on the application of the FSA or the Secretary of State) that a person has contravened a requirement imposed on him under FSMA or any other person has been knowingly concerned in such a contravention, the court can make an order requiring such person to pay to the FSA such sum as appears to the court to be just. Before any such order may be made, the court must also be satisfied that either profits have accrued to him as a result of the contravention or one or more persons have suffered loss or been otherwise adversely affected as a result of the contravention.[85] Any amount paid to the FSA in pursuance of such an order must be paid to a 'qualifying person' or distributed among such 'qualifying persons' as the court may direct.[86] A 'qualifying person' here means 'a person appearing to the Court to be someone (a) to whom the profits mentioned [above] are attributable or (b) who has suffered the loss or adverse effect mentioned [above]'.[87] Similar powers may be exercised by the court, on the application of the FSA, in cases involving market abuse.[88] In exercising such powers in relation to a person 'who has been knowingly concerned in the contravention of a requirement', it is not necessary that the person concerned can be shown to have profited from the breach. Participation in the contravention without gain is sufficient to invoke the power to make a restitution order.[89]

9.70 The court may also be asked to make a declaration confirming the fact of contravention of the FSMA's requirements by the individual concerned and authorize the FSA to distribute effectively any money adjudged to be due to satisfy a restitutionary obligation.[90] The court is likely to grant a declaration of contravention by named individuals where it is satisfied an order should be made. Such a declaration will assist in determining whether the person concerned should be regarded as 'a fit and proper person to carry on investment business'; the declaration may be of assistance to overseas regulators and may aid individual investors considering bringing proceedings for compensation arising out of the breaches.[91]

---

[83] FSMA, s 381.
[84] FSMA, s 381(4).
[85] FSMA, s 382.
[86] FSMA, s 382(3).
[87] FSMA, s 382(8).
[88] FSMA, s 383.
[89] See *SIB v Pantell SA* No. 2 [1993] Ch 256.
[90] See *FSA v Lukka*, Ch D, 29 April 1999.
[91] See *per* Neuberger J in *FSA v Lukka*, above.

10

PENALTIES

A. Market Abuse Directive

In order to ensure that the Directive against market abuse was effective, the Directive itself required that any infringements needed to be promptly detected and sanctioned. Therefore, it provided that sanctions should be sufficiently dissuasive and proportionate to the gravity of the infringement and to the gains realized, and should be consistently applied by Member States.[1]   **10.01**

The Directive also called for cooperation between national authorities on such issues as exchanging information, rendering assistance to each other and cooperating in cross-border investigations.[2]   **10.02**

Under Article 14 of the Directive, Member States were directed to impose appropriate administrative measures and sanctions against people who failed to comply with the market abuse provisions. These measures were directed to be effective, proportionate and dissuasive. The Commission drew up a list of administrative   **10.03**

---

[1] Directive, Recital 38.
[2] Directive, Art. 16.

measures and sanctions to serve as guidance.[3] A number of explanatory instruments have been issued.[4]

10.04 The EU's Committee of European Securities Regulators ('CESR') has embraced the task of seeking to harmonize financial standards throughout Europe by setting a European Standard for Conduct of Business Rules. In July and October 2008 CESR published two consultation papers on the Market Abuse Directive. The first was entitled Market Abuse Directive Level 3 – Second Set of CESR Guidance. It covered insider lists and suspicious transaction reporting. The second consultation paper was entitled 'Information on the common operation of the Directive to the Market'. It dealt with stabilization and the notion of inside. Feedback statements covering both consultation papers were published and in May 2009 CESR published its third set of guidance and information on the common operation of MAD. The relevant measures are designed to 'promote market integrity' and to reduce Europe-wide financial services risk. This is achieved by establishing that if a person is found to be unfit to conduct financial services business in one jurisdiction, he should not be permitted to take advantage of the ISD passport to conduct business in other jurisdictions.

10.05 Under Article 15, persons subject to market abuse sanctions shall be entitled to an appeal before court against any decisions taken by the regulatory authority of a Member State.[5]

B. UK Penalties

(1) Introduction

10.06 As set out in the FSA *Enforcement Guide* ('EG'), Chapters 7–18, the range of penalties available to the FSA is extensive. They are applicable not only to

---

[3] Directive, Art. 14.

[4] Commission Regulation (EC) 2273/2003 of 22 December 2003, Implementing Directive 2003/6/EC of the European Parliament and of the Council as regards exemptions for buy-back programmes and stabilisation of financial Instruments, OJ L336/33, 23.12.2003; Commission Directive 2003/124; Commission Directive 2003/125/EC of 22 December 2003 Implementing Directive 2003/6/EC of the European Parliament and of the Council as regards the fair presentation of investment recommendations and disclosure of conflicts of interest, OJ L339/73, 24.12.2003; Commission Directive 2004/72/EC of 29 April 2004 Implementing Directive 2003/6/EC of the European Parliament and of the Council as regards accepted market practices, the definition of inside information in relation to derivatives on commodities, the drawing up of lists of insiders, the notification of managers' transactions and the notification of suspicious transactions, OJ L162/70, 30.4.2004; Committee of European Securities Regulators, Level 3 – First Set of CESR Guidance and Information on the Common Operation of the Directive, CESR/04-505b; Market Abuse Directive Level 3 – Third set of CESR guidance and information on the common operation of the Directive to the Market, 15 May 2009.

[5] Directive, Art. 15.

authorized persons but, in many cases, against anyone.[6] The possible penalties include:[7]

1. variation of a Part IV permission on the FSA's own initiative;
2. intervention against incoming firms;
3. cancellation of a Part IV permission on the FSA's own initiative;
4. injunctions;
5. withdrawal of approval;
6. prohibition of individuals;
7. restitution and redress;
8. insolvency proceedings and orders against debt avoidance;
9. public censures and public statements;
10. financial penalties;
11. prosecution of criminal offences;
12. disqualification of auditors and actuaries;
13. disqualification orders against members of the professions; and
14. directions against incoming electronic commerce providers.

10.07 Not all these penalties are specifically earmarked as 'market abuse penalties'. Indeed, it is s 6.3 of the FSA Decision Procedure and Penalties Manual ('DEPP') that is specifically labelled 'Penalties for market abuse'. However, it would be naïve for a market participant to think that the FSA will not look for justifications to impose any penalty it considered appropriate against a person it believed guilty of market misconduct, whether or not such penalty was specifically labelled a 'market abuse sanction'. Therefore it is instructive to examine each of the penalties within the power of the FSA.

(2) General factors

10.08 The general factors the FSA considers relevant in deciding whether to take action for suspected breaches of FSA rules are set out in s 6.2.1 of the DEPP. The list given in the DEPP is not exhaustive and different factors may be relevant in particular cases. Such factors include:

1. the nature and seriousness of the suspected behaviour including:
    (a) whether the behaviour was deliberate or reckless;
    (b) the duration and frequency of the behaviour;
    (c) the amount of any benefit gained or loss avoided as a result of the breach;
    (d) whether the breach reveals serious or systemic weaknesses of the management systems or internal control relating to a person's business;

---

[6] EG 7.2.
[7] EG 7–18.

(e) the impact or potential impact of the behaviour on the orderliness of markets, including whether confidence in those markets has been damaged or put at risk;

(f) the loss or risk of loss caused to consumers and market users generally;

(g) the nature and extent of any financial crime attributable to the breach; and

(h) whether there are smaller issues which taken cumulatively justify disciplinary action;

2. the conduct of the person following the breach, including:

    (a) how quickly, effectively and completely the person brought the behaviour to the attention of the FSA or another relevant regulatory authority;

    (b) the degree of co-operation the person showed during the FSA's investigation of the behaviour of concern or during those of any other regulatory authority (for example, the Takeover Panel or an RIE) which is allowed to share information obtained during an investigation with the FSA. In this context, persons are reminded that they may have a duty to co-operate with other regulatory authorities. For example, MAR 4.3.4 G requires firms to whom that rule applies to assist the Takeover Panel in certain circumstances. However, a person will not necessarily avoid action for market abuse or requiring or encouraging merely by fulfilling a duty to co-operate;

    (c) any remedial steps that the person has taken to address the behaviour, whether on his own initiative or in meeting the requirement of another regulatory authority, and how promptly that person has taken those steps. This might include identifying those who have suffered loss and compensating them, taking disciplinary action against staff (where appropriate), and taking action designed to ensure that similar problems do not arise in the future. It might also include (for example, in the context of a takeover bid) any steps taken to correct a misleading statement or misleading impression or distortion of the market. However, a person will not necessarily avoid a penalty merely by fulfilling a duty to take remedial action;

    (d) the likelihood that the same type of breach (by the person under investigation or by others) will recur if no action is taken;

    (e) whether the person concerned has complied with any requirements or rulings of another regulatory authority relating to his behaviour (for example, where relevant, those of the Takeover Panel or an RIE); and

    (f) the nature and extent of any false or inaccurate information given by the person and whether the information appears to have been given in an attempt knowingly to mislead the FSA;

3. the disciplinary record and general compliance history of the person, including:

    (a) whether the FSA or another regulator has taken any previous action against the person resulting in adverse findings;

    (b) whether the person has previously undertaken not to do a particular act or engage in particular behaviour;

(c) whether the FSA or any previous regulator previously took protective action in respect of a firm by means of a variation of a Part IV permission or otherwise, or has requested that the firm take remedial action, and the extent to which this action has been taken; and

(d) the general compliance history of the person, such as previous private warnings;

4. FSA guidance and other published materials;

5. action taken by the FSA in previous similar cases; and

6. action taken by other domestic or international regulatory authorities. Where other regulatory authorities propose to take action in respect of the breach under consideration by the FSA, the FSA will consider whether that action would be adequate to address the FSA's concerns, or whether it would be appropriate for the FSA to take its own action.8 For example, the FSA has the power to impose unlimited financial penalties, whereas an RIE's powers may be more limited in a particular case. Where the behaviour of the person concerned is also, in the opinion of the Takeover Panel, a breach of that person's responsibilities under the Takeover Code, the FSA would not expect to use its powers under the market abuse regime against that person, except in the circumstances described in DEPP 6.2.26. If the FSA considers that using its powers may be appropriate in those circumstances, it will not take action during the bid except in the circumstances described in DEPP 6.2.26G(1), DEPP 6.2.26G(3), DEPP 6.2.26G(4), and under certain circumstances, DEPP 6.2.26G(5).

(3) Market abuse factors

Under FSMA, s 124, the FSA is required to publish a statement of its policy with respect to the imposition of penalties under FSMA, s 123. This 'statement' is found in different parts of the FSA Handbook—in particular the Code of Market Conduct (MAR), the EG, and the DEPP.9   **10.09**

The FSA points out that in cases involving market abuse or requiring or encouraging someone else to engage in market abuse, it will take into consideration additional factors set out in 6.2.2 of the DEPP, which will have an impact on its decision whether to take enforcement action. Such factors include: **10.10**

1. the degree of sophistication of the users of the market in question, the size and liquidity of the market, and the susceptibility of the market to market abuse. For example, where the users of a market are generally not market

---

⁸ DEPP 6.2.1.

⁹ FSA Handbook, Code of Market Conduct ('MAR'), Decision Procedure and Penalties Manual ('DEPP'), and Enforcement Guide ('EG').

professionals, and they have suffered loss as a result of the behaviour and that loss has not been promptly or adequately compensated for by the person concerned, this may be a factor in favour of the imposition of a penalty (this does not, however, mean that the FSA will not take action to impose financial penalties on persons whose behaviour falls within the market abuse provisions where only market professionals have suffered);

2. the impact, having regard to the nature of the behaviour, that any financial penalty or public statement may have on the financial markets or on the interests of consumers:

   (a) a penalty may show that high standards of market conduct are being enforced in the financial markets, and may bolster market confidence;

   (b) a penalty may protect the interests of consumers by deterring future market abuse and improving standards of conduct in a market;

   (c) in the context of a takeover bid, the FSA may consider that the impact of the use of its powers is likely to have an adverse effect on the timing or outcome of that bid, and therefore it would not be in the interests of financial markets or consumers to take action for market abuse during the takeover bid. If the FSA considers that the proposed use of its powers may have that effect, it will consult the Takeover Panel and give due weight to its views.[10]

10.11 Separate and apart from the factors listed above, the FSA explicitly states that it will not impose a penalty on a person for possible market abuse if there are reasonable grounds to believe that:

1. the person believed, on reasonable grounds, that his behaviour did not amount to market abuse or requiring or encouraging; or

2. the person concerned took all reasonable precautions and exercised all due diligence to avoid engaging in market abuse or requiring or encouraging.[11]

10.12 In deciding whether one or both of the two above conditions have been met, the FSA may take into account several enumerated factors. These factors are set out in DEPP 6.3.2, but may vary depending on the case. The FSA says that the list given in DEPP 6.3.2 includes factors which it *may* consider when deciding whether to

---

[10] DEPP 6.2.2.

[11] By s 123(2) the FSA may not impose a penalty on a person if, having considered any representations made to it in response to a warning notice, there are reasonable grounds for it to be satisfied that—'(a) he believed, on reasonable grounds, that his behaviour did not fall within paragraph (a) or (b) of subsection (1), or (b) he took all reasonable precautions and exercised all due diligence to avoid behaving in a way which fell within paragraph (a) or (b) of that subsection'; See also, DEPP 6.3.1.

impose a financial penalty, but others may be considered as well.[12] The non-exclusive list given by the FSA includes:

1. whether and if so to what extent, the behaviour in question was analogous to the behaviour described in the Code of Market Conduct as amounting or not amounting to market abuse or requiring or encouraging;
2. whether the FSA has issued any guidance on the behaviour in question and if so, the extent to which the person sought to follow that guidance;
3. whether, and if so to what extent, the behaviour complied with the rules of any relevant prescribed market or any other relevant market or other regulatory requirements (including the Takeover Code or the SARs) or any relevant codes of conduct or best practice;
4. the level of knowledge, skill and experience to be expected of the person concerned;
5. whether, and if so to what extent, the person can demonstrate that the behaviour was engaged in for a legitimate purpose and in a proper way;
6. whether, and if so to what extent, the person followed internal consultation and escalation procedures in relation to the behaviour (for example, did the person discuss the behaviour with internal line management and/or internal legal or compliance departments);
7. whether, and if so the extent to which, the person sought any appropriate expert legal or other expert professional advice and followed that advice; and
8. whether, and if so to what extent, the person sought advice from the market authorities of any relevant prescribed market or, where relevant, consulted the Takeover Panel, and followed the advice received.[13]

C. Market Abuse Sanctions

10.13   Chapter 6 of the DEPP details certain penalties which are identified as 'market abuse sanctions'. Those penalties include 'financial penalty or public censure'.[14] The FSA's power to impose financial penalties on market abusers derives from the FSMA, s 123(1). Under that section, the FSA may impose a penalty if it is satisfied that a person ('A'):

1. (a)   is or has engaged in market abuse, or
2. (b)   by taking or refraining from taking any action has required or encouraged another person or persons to engage in behaviour which, if engaged in by A, would amount to market abuse.[15]

---

[12]   DEPP 6.3.2.
[13]   DEPP 6.3.2.
[14]   DEPP 6.4.
[15]   FSMA, s 123(1).

(1) Financial penalties for market abuse

10.14   If the FSA concludes that someone has committed market abuse:

it may impose on him a penalty in such amount as it considers appropriate.[16]

The extraordinary thing about this potential fine is that its amount is *unlimited*. There is no cap. The financial punishment can be as severe as the FSA deems it is sufficient to inflict.[17]

10.15   In deciding the size of the financial penalty, the FSA will be guided by a number of factors including:[18]

1. the principal purpose for which the FSA imposes sanctions, namely to promote high standards of regulatory and market conduct by deterring persons who have breached FSA rules from committing additional breaches, deterring others from committing similar breaches, and demonstrating the benefits of compliant business;

2. the nature, seriousness and impact of the breach in question, in regard to which the following considerations may be relevant:
   (a) the duration and frequency of the breach;
   (b) whether the breach revealed serious or systemic weaknesses in the person's procedures or of the management systems or internal controls relating to that person's business;
   (c) in market abuse cases, the FSA will take into consideration whether the breach had an adverse effect on markets and the seriousness of that effect;
   (d) the loss or risk of loss caused to consumers, investors and market users generally;
   (e) the nature and extent of any financial crime facilitated, occasioned or attributable to the breach; and
   (f) in the context of contraventions of Part VI of the Act, the extent to which the breach which constitutes the contravention departs from current market practice;

3. the extent to which the breach was deliberate or reckless. In determining whether a breach is deliberate or reckless (which would increase the penalty), the FSA may have regard to:
   (a) whether the breach was intentional, in that the person could foresee or intended the consequences of his actions;

---

[16]   FSMA, s 123(1).

[17]   Although the market abuse regime is intended to be a civil remedy for market misconduct, those accused of market abuse attract the protections afforded in criminal prosecutions in some cases. See the Court of Appeal's decision in the *Han & Yau* case (*Han & Yau, Martins & Martins Morris v Commissioners of Customs and Excise*, Court of Appeal's Decisions, Case No. A3/2001/0149A, 3 July 2001), and discussion of this issue in Chapter 13, below.

[18]   DEPP 6.5.

   (b) if the person has not followed a firm's internal procedures and/or FSA guidance, the reasons for this non-compliance;

   (c) where the person has taken decisions beyond its or his field of competence, the reasons for the decisions and for them being taken by that person;

   (d) whether the person gave no apparent consideration to the consequences of the behaviour that constitutes the breach;

   (e) in the context of a contravention of a rule or requirement imposed under Part VI of the Act, whether the person sought professional advice before the contravention occurred, and whether he followed that advice;

4. whether the person on whom the penalty is to be imposed is an individual, in that because individuals will not always have the resources of a body corporate, enforcement action may have a greater impact on an individual, and so it may be possible to achieve effective deterrence by imposing a smaller penalty on an individual, as opposed to a body corporate;

5. the size, financial resources and other circumstances of the person on whom the penalty is to be imposed:

   (a) the FSA may take into account whether there is verifiable evidence of serious financial hardship or difficulties if the person were to pay the penalty appropriate for the particular breach;

   (b) the FSA will consider whether a lower penalty would be appropriate, if a person might be rendered insolvent or be threatened with insolvency by an imposed penalty;

   (c) the degree of seriousness of a breach may be linked to the size of a firm. For example, a larger firm could cause damage with a breach to more people than smaller firm, so a larger penalty may be justified;

   (d) the size and resources of a person and what steps that person took after the breach;

   (e) the FSA may decide to impose a financial penalty on a mutual, even though this may have a direct impact on that mutual's customers;

6. the amount of benefit gained or loss avoided as a result of the breach, for example:

   (a) the FSA will propose a penalty consistent with the principle that a person should not benefit from a breach; and

   (b) the penalty should act as an incentive to the person and others to comply with regulatory standards and required standards of market conduct;

7. whether a person committed a breach in such a way as to avoid or reduce the risk that the breach would be discovered, or that the difficulty of detection may have affected the behaviour in question, in which case a higher penalty may be appropriate. The rationale behind this factor is that a person's incentive to commit a breach may be greater where the breach is hard to detect;

8. conduct following the breach, including:
    (a) the conduct of the person in bringing or failing to bring the breach to the attention of the FSA or other regulatory authorities;
    (b) the degree of cooperation the person showed during the investigation of the breach by the FSA or other regulatory authorities (cooperation tends to reduce the penalty);
    (c) any remedial steps taken once the breach was identified; and
    (d) whether the person concerned has complied with any requirements or rulings of another regulatory authority relating to the breach (e.g., the Takeover Panel);
9. disciplinary record and compliance history, including:
    (a) whether the FSA or a previous regulator has taken previous disciplinary action against the person;
    (b) whether the person has previously undertaken not to do a particular act or engage in a particular behaviour;
    (c) whether the FSA or any previous regulator has previously taken protective action in respect of a firm using its own initiative powers, by means of a variation of a firm's Part IV permission, or has previously requested the firm to take remedial action and the extent to which that action has been taken;
    (d) the general compliance history of that person, including previous private warnings;
10. other action taken by the FSA or a previous regulator, including previous actions in which the FSA and a person on whom a penalty is to be imposed have reached agreement as to the amount of the penalty. The FSA seeks to apply a consistent approach to determine the appropriate level of penalty;
11. action taken by other domestic or international authorities, including:
    (a) action taken or to be taken against a person by other regulatory authorities which may be relevant where that action relates to the breach in question; and
    (b) the degree to which any remedial or compensatory steps required by other regulatory authorities have been taken, and if so, how promptly;
12. FSA guidance and other published materials:
    (a) a person does not automatically commit a breach by not following FSA guidance, but if a breach has been established, the fact that guidance had raised relevant concerns may inform the seriousness with which the breach is to be regarded by the FSA when determining the level of penalty;
    (b) the FSA will consider the nature and accessibility of the guidance or other published materials when deciding if they are relevant to the level of penalty, and if so, what weight to give them in relation to other factors;

13. the timing of any agreement as to the amount of the penalty. The FSA and the person on whom the penalty will be imposed may seek to agree to the amount and terms of a financial penalty. The amount of the penalty will be reduced to reflect the stage at which the FSA and the person concerned reach an agreement.

A person who is required to pay a financial penalty can ask the FSA to let him pay **10.16** in instalments. If the person in question can produce verifiable evidence of serious financial hardship or financial difficulties, the FSA may grant such a request. The FSA has no wish render a person insolvent; however, generally any penalty must be paid in full within one year of the final notice of penalty.[19]

(2) Statement of censure for market abuse

As an alternative to imposing an unlimited fine, FSMA, s 123(3) permits the FSA **10.17** to publish a statement that a person has engaged in market abuse. This is sometimes called 'naming and shaming', and is described in DEPP 6.4. It is to be noted that whilst FSMA, s 123(3) is explicit in postulating alternative penalties of a fine or statement of public censure, the disciplinary measures against authorized firms in of FSMA, ss 205 and 206 contemplate the FSA having power to impose both sanctions. Notwithstanding the wording of the Act, however, in practice the FSA here too treats the penalties as alternatives.[20]

In making a choice between imposing a fine or issuing a public statement about a **10.18** person's behaviour, the FSA will take all the circumstances of a case into account. Among the factors it will consider (although this is not an exclusive list) are the following:[21]

1. whether deterrence would be effectively achieved by issuing a public censure;
2. whether or not the person in question made a profit or avoided a loss through his market misbehaviour. If so, the FSA will probably consider a fine appropriate so that the person will not financially benefit from the market abuse;
3. how serious was the market abuse? The more serious the conduct, the more likely it is that a fine will be imposed;
4. if the person brought the breach to the attention of the FSA, this factor may weigh in favour of a public censure, as opposed to a financial penalty;
5. if a person admits market abuse, provides full cooperation with the FSA and makes efforts to see that those who suffered loss as a result are fully

---

[19] EG 7.7.
[20] See DEPP 6.4.1 G.
[21] DEPP 6.4.

compensated, the FSA may be more inclined to issue a public statement rather than impose a fine, depending on the seriousness of the market abuse;

6. if the person has a poor disciplinary record or compliance history, the FSA may be more likely to impose a fine;

7 what the FSA has done in previous similar cases. The aim of the FSA is to maintain a consistent approach in market abuse cases;

8. the impact of a financial penalty on the person in question. In some cases, depending on the circumstances, the FSA may impose a smaller financial penalty of a person of genuinely modest means.

10.19 The above factors are relevant to all cases, including therefore market abuse cases.

D. The Wider Landscape

(1) High Level Principles

10.20 As pointed out above, sanctions which are specifically labelled 'market abuse penalties' are not the only ways that the FSA can punish market abuse. They have a wide range of sanctions at their disposal. These start with FSA's High Level Standards, including the Principles for Business ('the Principles').[22]

10.21 The FSA is very clear about the overlap between market abuse and violations of the Principles. Principle 5 requires a regulated entity to observe proper standards of market conduct. Therefore, any behaviour which constitutes market abuse or requiring or encouraging will also constitute a breach of Principle 5.

10.22 The FSA DEPP contains a specific subsection discussing policy on 'discipline' relating to breaches of the Principles.[23] There, the FSA reminds the firms it regulates that:

> The Principles are a general statement of the fundamental obligations of firms under the regulatory system. The Principles derive their authority from the FSA's rule-making powers set out in section 138 ... of the Act. A breach of a Principle will make a firm liable to disciplinary action.[24]

10.23 In determining whether a Principle has been breached, the FSA will compare the conduct under examination with the standard of conduct required by the Principle in question. In making that comparison, the FSA accepts that it has the burden of showing that a regulated party has been at fault. This burden will vary depending on the Principle. For example, with respect to Principle 5, the FSA will need to

---

[22] FSA *Handbook, High Level Standards, Principles for Businesses.*
[23] DEPP 6.2.14 and 6.2.15.
[24] DEPP 6.2.14.

show that the party in question failed to observe proper standards of market conduct.[25]

In many cases, of the kind described above, a regulated party is required to exercise 'reasonable care' to avoid unacceptable market behaviour, and the issue of whether reasonable care has been exercised may be a factor in mitigating the seriousness of the breach. In general terms, an authorized person must take reasonable care to put in place and maintain systems and controls adequate for the nature, scale and complexity of its business. To fail to do so would be a violation of Principle 3,[26] which requires a firm to take reasonable care to organize and control its affairs responsibly and effectively.[27] With respect to market abuse, there are also, as shown above, a number of cases in which it will be to the benefit of the party under investigation if it is found that his behaviour was not deliberate or reckless. **10.24**

(2) Private warnings

It is not everyone that need be particularly concerned about all the specifics of FSA discipline. In general they apply mostly to authorized persons and approved persons who are under the specific regulation of the FSA. The disciplinary provision that applies to every person is that dealing with 'private warnings'.[28] Private warnings may be issued by the FSA in cases where, despite having concerns about certain behaviour, the FSA decides that it is not appropriate to bring a formal disciplinary proceeding. However, the FSA still wants the party in question to know that they came close to triggering a formal disciplinary proceeding, so the FSA issues a 'private warning'.[29] **10.25**

Examples of circumstances where the FSA may be likely to give private warnings instead of taking formal disciplinary action (although the following circumstances will not necessarily determine the outcome on their own) include: **10.26**

1. where the matter in question is 'minor in nature or degree'; or
2. where the party in question has taken full or immediate action to correct the problem.[30]

Cases where a person, not authorized or approved by the FSA, could receive private warnings include: **10.27**

1. potential cases of market abuse;

---

[25] PRIN 2.1.1.
[26] PRIN 1.1.7.
[27] PRIN 2.1.1.
[28] EG 7.10–7.19.
[29] EG 7.10.
[30] EG 7.12.

2. cases where the FSA was considering making a prohibition order; or

3. cases where the FSA was considering making a disqualification order.[31]

10.28 The FSA requires that authorized or approved persons acknowledge receipt of the warning letter (and they may make comments in response if they wish). The letter will form part of a person's compliance history, and may be taken into account in deciding whether the FSA brings any disciplinary proceedings against the party in question in the future. The age of the warning is relevant but a long-standing warning may still matter.[32] However, if such a disciplinary action is commenced, a private warning will not be relied upon in determining whether a breach has taken place or in determining the level of sanction, if one is imposed.[33]

10.29 Private warnings to an approved person may also be sent to that person's employer.[34] Although not rising to the level of constituting formal 'private warnings', the FSA can also express concerns about the way a party conducts its business in ordinary correspondence. Despite not being a formal sanction in the sense that a 'private warning' is, this correspondence will also be a part of a party's compliance history.[35]

10.30 Of course, in certain cases, correspondence expressing concern and private warnings are not enough to counter the market misbehaviour in question and the FSA will feel compelled to take more positive disciplinary action. The *Enforcement Guide* section on discipline also explains the FSA's criteria for deciding to take such action.[36]

(3) Approved persons—sanctions

10.31 The statutory authority of the FSA to take action against approved persons is found in FSMA, s 66(1). In general, the FSA can take action against an approved person if they believe he is guilty of misconduct and they are satisfied that disciplinary action is appropriate.[37] Individual discipline will be imposed where it is shown that an approved person was personally responsible, and acted deliberately or unreasonably having regard to all the circumstances.[38] In the context of market abuse, approved persons may become exposed to disciplinary action in three ways: (1) by committing a primary act under FSMA, s 123(1)(a); (2) by engaging in

---

[31] EG 7.13.
[32] EG 7.16.
[33] EG 7.15.
[34] EG 7.14.
[35] EG 7.15.
[36] EG 7.19.
[37] DEPP 6.2.9. Further details about how the FSA can proceed against approved persons are found throughout the FSMA with particular reference to DEPP 6.2.
[38] DEPP 6.2.4.

conduct or behaviour that puts the firm in breach and constitutes a violation of APER (as mentioned in 10.34 below) or (3) by requiring or encouraging another person to engage in behaviour that would amount to market abuse under FSMA, s 123(1)(b). In the first and third cases the individual is dealt with as the 'person' concerned in the violation; in the second case, his conduct attracts disciplinary action because he is an approved person.

10.32 In order to assist approved persons with understanding what is expected of them, the FSA has, in accordance with FSMA, s 64, issued Statements of Principle describing what is expected of approved persons and a Code of Practice for Approved Persons.[39]

10.33 In considering whether in general disciplinary action against an approved person is more appropriate than disciplinary action against a firm, the FSA will take into account all the circumstances, but will particularly consider the following:

1. whether disciplinary action against an approved person would be more appropriate considering the responsibility of those individuals in the firm exercising 'significant influence functions';
2. whether in the case of market misconduct by a firm, the conduct of the individual approved person in question fell below the standard which would be reasonable given all the circumstances.[40]

10.34 In relation to market abuse the FSA also considers in most cases that firms, rather than individuals, will bear the primary responsibility for regulatory compliance. Therefore, when disciplinary action is considered appropriate in market abuse cases, the FSA's focus is more likely to fall on an authorized person ('firm') rather than an approved person ('individual') working for the firm.[41] However, some market misconduct by an approved person will trigger individual disciplinary response. For example:

1. where a firm shows that it took all reasonable steps to prevent market abuse; or
2. where a firm had taken reasonable steps to put in place appropriate systems and controls, but the market abuse occurred as the result of an approved person circumventing those firm compliance efforts.[42]

10.35 However, the FSA says it will not discipline approved persons (whether in relation to market abuse or more generally) on the basis of 'vicarious liability'. It will not

---

[39] FSA *Handbook, Statements of Principle and Code of Practice for Approved Persons*, APER 2, 3 and 4.
[40] DEPP 6.2.6 and 6.2.7.
[41] EG 2.32. See also DEPP 6.2.4.
[42] DEPP 6.2.5.

hold an individual approved person responsible for the acts of others, unless the person in question has improperly delegated his duties to others, or improperly influenced others to engage in market abuse. In general, in order to avoid personal liability, an approved person should exercise due and reasonable care when assessing information and acting upon it.[43]

10.36 Thus, the FSA considers that the primary responsibility for ensuring compliance with a firm's regulatory obligations rests with the firm itself. Accordingly, the FSA will only take disciplinary action against an approved person where there is evidence of personal culpability on the part of that approved person. Personal culpability arises where the behaviour was deliberate or where the approved person's standard of behaviour was below that which would be reasonable in all the circumstances. In setting the standard of reasonableness the FSA is likely to adopt a low threshold, that is, a *Bolam* standard of care[44] (being that of the averagely competent practitioner) rather than a *Wednesbury Corporation* test,[45] that is, conduct so unreasonable that no reasonable practitioner would have been guilty of it. This approach may be thought to be more consistent with serving the statutory objective of securing an appropriate degree of investor protection.

10.37 One very important limitation on the FSA's disciplinary power against approved persons lies in the limitation period introduced by the FSMA in respect of such proceedings. In short, the FSA may not take action against an approved person after the end of a period of two years beginning with the first day on which the FSA knew of the misconduct.[46] The 'knowledge requirement' may be satisfied by actual or constructive knowledge on the part of the FSA. The FSA is treated as knowing of misconduct if it has information from which misconduct can reasonably be inferred.[47]

10.38 In considering whether a limitation defence may be available in respect of any proceedings to discipline an individual for regulatory infringement, the following issues will therefore be critical:

- the extent of the FSA's first knowledge of misconduct alleged (whether actual or constructive knowledge);
- the date of commencement of proceedings to discipline.

10.39 As to the start date, no problem will arise where the FSA has discovered 'misconduct' of the kind mentioned in FSMA, s 66(2) that might attract action

---

[43] DEPP 6.2.8.
[44] See *Bolam v Friern Hospital Management Committee* [1957] 2 All ER 118.
[45] See *Wednesbury Corporation v Ministry of Housing and Local Government* (No 2) [1966] 2 QB 275.
[46] FSMA, s 66(4).
[47] FSMA, s 66(5)(a).

under s 66(1), for example, in the course of a routine monitoring visit and thus has actual knowledge; the more difficult issue will be to determine the date of constructive knowledge where the FSA can be shown to have had information from which misconduct could reasonably be inferred.

So far as the expiration of the two-year period is concerned, proceedings are treated **10.40** as begun 'when a warning notice is given'.[48] The date for the giving of such a notice is prescribed.[49] The Regulations provide for a deemed date of service depending on the method of service selected (for example, second business day after posting or the day after the day on which a document is transmitted by fax). It is to be assumed for this purpose that the notice will only be effective if it is itself a valid notice. The FSMA prescribes certain information the notice must contain.[50] In particular, the notice must:

- state the action the FSA proposes to take;
- give reasons for the proposed action;
- be in writing, and
- state whether the recipient is or is not entitled to access to certain materials in the possession of the FSA.[51]

Where proceedings are brought at about two years after the date of the original **10.41** infringement alleged, the timing and validity of the relevant notice could therefore be critical. Determining the date on which a notice is given ought to be a straightforward exercise; it is open to argument, however, whether in the context of disciplinary proceedings it would be right to allow the 'deemed date' to prevail over the actual date of service if the latter date was in truth later and took the proceedings past the two-year end date; further, whilst the notice may appear valid, it would also be open to argument that a notice served in bad faith ought not to be treated as a valid notice at all, for example where the FSA has insufficient evidence to justify proceedings but serves a notice to avoid a possible limitation defence arising. In the criminal law context, where prosecuting authority has tried to circumvent limitation periods applying to the date for the institution of proceedings or has by procedural devices sought to deprive a defendant of such a defence, these attempts have generally failed.[52]

---

[48] FSMA, s 66(5)(b); see further below.
[49] See Financial Services and Markets Act 2000 (Service of Notices) Regulations 2001 (SI 2001/1420).
[50] See FSMA, s 387.
[51] See s 387(1)(e).
[52] Cf. *R v Brentford Justices ex parte Wong* [1991] QB 445; *R v Newcastle upon Tyne Justices, ex parte Hindle* [1984] 1 All ER 770.

E. Other Measures

10.42   It is not the place of this book to discuss in detail each of the general (that is to say, not specifically labelled as 'market abuse') disciplinary penalties or other measures that the FSA may employ in response to regulatory breaches which, under appropriate circumstances, can include market abuse. However, because many of them will give the FSA alternative ways to sanction market abuse, it is worth saying a few words about some of the major ones and pointing the reader in the direction of more detailed information in the event that future reference is required.

(1) Variation of a Part IV permission

10.43   Under the FSMA, ss 45 and 47, the FSA has the power to vary, on its own initiative, a Part IV permission, to intervene against an incoming firm and to cancel a Part IV permission (with withdrawal of authorization).[53] The FSA's power to employ these sanctions can be used in cases 'where it has serious concerns about a firm, or about the way its business is being or has been conducted'.[54]

10.44   It is not hard to imagine that such concerns can relate to the commission of market abuse. Indeed the FSA goes on to say that it will consider varying a firm's Part IV permission when it has serious concerns about the way a firm's business is being conducted including when the firm:

> ... has breached requirements imposed on it by or under the Act [FSMA] (including the Principles and the rules) ... and the breaches are material in number or in individual seriousness.[55]

10.45   Under the FSMA, s 53, the FSA may exercise this variation power as a matter of urgency where:

1.   the information available to it indicates serious concerns about the firm or its business that need to be addressed immediately; and

2.   circumstances indicate that it is appropriate to use statutory powers immediately to require and/or prohibit certain actions by the firm in order to ensure the firm addresses these concerns.[56]

10.46   Examples of limitations which may be imposed include restricting the number or category of customers with which the firm can deal or limiting the number of specified investments in which a firm may deal. The FSA may, in addition to stating limitations on the scope of a permission, impose requirements on the firm to

---

[53] EG 8.
[54] EG 8.5.
[55] EG 8.5(1)(b)(iii).
[56] EG 8.7.

take or refrain from taking specified action.[57] Examples of requirements include a prohibition on holding client money or trading in certain categories of specified investment. Further, on granting a Part IV permission the FSA may impose 'assets requirements'.[58] This may include prohibiting dealings with specified assets held by the authorized firm. The FSA may then vary a Part IV permission by amending or introducing limitations, restrictions or requirements as described above; in addition, it may remove a regulated activity from the permission or vary the description of a permitted regulated activity.[59]

(2) Cancellation of Part IV permission

The FSA has similar powers and policies, also subject to FSMA, ss 45 and 47, to cancel a Part IV permission on its own initiative. It may exercise that power on the same grounds as those for a variation. The principal circumstance in which the FSA will consider cancelling a firm's Part IV permission, which may relate to market abuse, is: **10.47**

> where the FSA has very serious concerns about a firm, or the way its business is or has been conducted …[60]

If as a result of a variation of a Part IV permission there are no longer any regulated activities for which the authorized person concerned has permission, the FSA must cancel the permission 'once it is satisfied that it is no longer necessary to keep the permission in force'.[61] The reason for otherwise keeping a permission alive would be to institute disciplinary proceedings. Finally, once an authorized person's Part IV permission is cancelled and as a result there is no regulated activity for which the firm has permission, the FSA must give a direction withdrawing that firm's status as an authorized person.[62] Steps leading to the ultimate withdrawal of authorization will plainly be predicated upon the most serious concern as to a firm's ability to carry on business by way of regulated activities. Although as noted above, variations and proposals for cancellation are to be notified to the firm, the more serious course of cancellation and termination require the FSA to implement the more detailed Warning Notice and Decision Notice procedure (described in Chapter 9). Thus cancellation of a permission and withdrawal of authorization cannot be directed to take effect immediately. The FSA may, however, vary a permission by removing the regulated activities covered by it, in an appropriate case with immediate effect.   **10.48**

---

57 FSMA, s 43.
58 FSMA, s 48.
59 FSMA, ss 44(1), 45(2).
60 EG 8.13.
61 FSMA, s 44(4).
62 FSMA, s 33.

(3) Intervention against incoming firms

10.49   Pursuant to the FSMA, ss 194 and 195, the FSA has the power to take enforcement against firms coming in to operate in the UK that are authorized by an
overseas regulator in the EEA or which the UK recognizes by treaty.[63]

(4) Withdrawal of approval

10.50   The FSA has the power to withdraw approval from approved persons or to issue
prohibition orders in order to achieve its regulatory objectives in punishing and
deterring failures to comply with appropriate standards of conduct.[64] In general,
the FSA may withdraw approval only if it concludes that the person in question is
not a 'fit and proper person' to perform the function to which the approval
relates.[65] The factors which the FSA uses to assess fitness and propriety can certainly be affected by participation in the commission of market abuse. For example, the FSA says that the criteria it applies include 'honesty, integrity and
reputation'.[66] It is reasonable to conclude that withdrawal of approval is another
weapon in the FSA arsenal for the punishment of market abuse. It gives the FSA
additional flexibility where they conclude it is appropriate to punish approved
individuals as well as, or in addition to authorized firms.

(5) Prohibition of individuals

10.51   Another, and broader, power that the FSA has to punish individuals who are
involved in market abuse is its power to prohibit individuals from carrying out
functions related to regulated activities. This power can be used against anyone,
approved or unapproved. [67]

10.52   The FSA's power to make such prohibitions derives from FSMA, s 56(2). It may
order a prohibition when it concludes that an individual is not fit and proper to
carry out functions in relation to regulated activities.[68] In assessing whether
the imposition of a prohibition order is appropriate, the FSA will look at the
entire range of circumstances surrounding a particular case. One such issue will
be 'the severity of risk which he poses to consumers or the market generally'.[69]

---

[63] For more information, see FSMA, Sch. 3 (EEA passport rights) and FSMA Sch. 4 (Treaty
rights).
[64] EG 9.1.
[65] EG 9.2. For more details see EG 9 generally, and ss 60 and 61 of the FSMA regarding FSA
decisions about whether a person is 'fit and proper'.
[66] EG 9.9.
[67] EG 9.17.
[68] EG 9.1.
[69] EG 9.5.

There seems little doubt that such 'risks' can be posed by participation in market abuse.[70]

The power is not confined to approved persons but extends to individuals who are   **10.53**
not approved persons, and includes exempt persons and members of professional firms and unauthorized individuals. Any order made may relate to a particular description of activities, firms generally or any firm within a specified class of firm.[71] Breach by an individual of a prohibition order is made a criminal offence rendering such a person liable on summary conviction to a fine.[72] It is a defence for such an accused person, however, to show that he took all reasonable precautions and exercised all due diligence to avoid committing the offence.[73]

(6) The assistance of the court

Once the FSA has decided to take action for regulatory breaches—including mar-   **10.54**
ket abuse—it can call upon the assistance of the judiciary to make its sanctions effective. As pointed out in the Appendix to the EG, the FSA can apply to the court under FSMA, s 381 for an injunction restraining market abuse, or under FSMA, s 383 for an order of restitution requiring a guilty party to repay the losses of damage suffered by other parties because of the market misconduct in question.[74] Once it has issued a decision notice the FSA can, of its own authority, in compliance with FSMA, s 384, require a party to make restitution.[75]

(7) Injunctions

The FSA may apply to a court for injunctions to require any person to undertake   **10.55**
a particular act, or cease particular behaviour, whether or not that person is regulated by the FSA.[76] This tool can be used in many regulatory situations (see the FSMA, s 380) and, as has already been explained, to assist in enforcing sanctions against market abuse (FSMA, s 381).[77] In as much as the remedy of an injunction is accordingly available in respect of 'any person' and not just authorized or approved persons, the FSA or the Secretary of State may (in addition to the power to apply for a 'restraining order'), also ask the court for an order directing any person who can be shown to have contravened a relevant

---

[70] For more on prohibition of individuals, see EG 9, generally, and FSMA, s 56.
[71] FSMA, s 56(3).
[72] FSMA, s 56(4).
[73] FSMA, s 45(5).
[74] EG Appendix 1.4.
[75] FSMA, s 384.
[76] EG 11.8.
[77] EG 10.1.

requirement and 'any other person who appears to have been knowingly concerned in the contravention' to take such steps as the court may direct to remedy it.[78] The court may also be asked to make an order restraining any person who has contravened a relevant requirement of FSMA or been knowingly concerned in such a contravention from 'disposing of or otherwise dealing with any assets ... which it is satisfied [such person(s)] is reasonably likely to dispose of or otherwise deal with'.[79]

10.56 It is probably sufficient for a person to be said to have been 'knowingly concerned in the contravention', to have had knowledge of the facts involved in the contravention without also having knowledge or any appreciation that the material facts amounted to a contravention of the FSMA.[80]

10.57 The FSA may also apply to the court for a restraining or remedial order to be made against any person where the court may be satisfied that there is a reasonable likelihood of conduct being committed, continued or repeated amounting to market abuse.[81] In this instance also, the court may be asked to make an order restraining the disposal of assets.[82] It is recognized by the FSA that the grant of such injunctive relief will have serious consequences for those concerned. The broad test the FSA will apply when it decides whether to seek an injunction is whether the application would be the most effective way to deal with the FSA's concerns.

10.58 The FSA can in summary, therefore, apply for three types of injunction: (1) to restrain conduct; (2) to take remedial steps; (3) to secure assets.[83]

10.59 Under FSMA, s 380, the FSA can apply for an injunction restraining or prohibiting, or to take steps to remedy, a contravention of any requirement imposed by the FSMA, or imposed by any other Act which the FSA is empowered to enforce (such as insider dealing under Part V of the Criminal Justice Act 1993 or money laundering regulations).[84] The FSA may also apply for an injunction to freeze assets.[85]

10.60 Injunctions under FSMA, s 381 apply to market abuse cases. Again, the FSA may seek such injunctions against anyone, whether authorized or not.[86] In those

---

[78] FSMA, s 380(2).
[79] FSMA, s 380(3).
[80] See *per* Millett LJ in *Securities and Investments Board v Scandex Capital Management* A/S [1998] 1 WLR 712.
[81] FSMA, s 381.
[82] FSMA s 381(4).
[83] EG 10.2.
[84] EG 10.1, footnote 9.
[85] EG 10.4.
[86] EG 11.8.

cases, the court may grant an injunction restraining (or in Scotland, an interdict prohibiting) the market abuse where the FSA has evidence 'showing that there is a reasonable likelihood that a person will contravene a requirement of the Act and that the contravention will result in the dissipation of assets belonging to investors'.[87]

This provides the FSA with an opportunity to apply a powerful sanction in addi-   **10.61**
tion to the penalties that the FSA itself may impose on a party guilty of market misconduct. A person who disobeys an injunction may be held in contempt of court and liable to imprisonment, fine or seizure of assets.[88]

The FSA's policy in applying for injunctions takes into account that the granting   **10.62**
of an injunction entails serious consequences for those against whom the injunction applies. Therefore, the seriousness of the alleged offence is an impor-tant consideration in the FSA's determination of whether to apply for an injunc-tion. The principal factor in the FSA's decision to apply for an injunction is whether an injunction is the most effective way to deal with the FSA's concerns about particular market conduct. Among the other things that the FSA will take into consideration in making a determination to apply for any injunction relating to market abuse are the following:[89]

1. the nature and seriousness of the market misconduct or the expected misconduct;
2. the extent of the loss, risk of loss or risk to client assets threatened by the mis-conduct in question;
3. the number of consumers who may be affected and the size of the potential damage to them;
4. the potential impact of the misconduct in question on the financial system (including market distortion or disruption);
5. the losses or costs likely to be imposed on users of the financial system by the conduct;
6. whether the persons responsible for the misconduct are likely to take steps to stop it which will adequately protect consumers, and provide sufficient assur-ances that the conduct will not be repeated;
7. whether other relevant regulators can or will intervene to stop the misconduct, adequately protect innocent third parties and remedy any adverse conse-quences of the misconduct;
8. whether future steps will be adequate to prevent a repeat and remedy the con-sequences of the conduct in question;

---

[87] EG 10.5.
[88] EG 11.5(4).
[89] EG 10.3.

9. whether there is danger of assets being dissipated;
10. the balance between the costs of enforcing an injunction and the benefits to be gained by obtaining one;
11. the disciplinary and compliance record of the person in question;
12. whether the misconduct can be adequately dealt with by other disciplinary remedies;
13. whether the misconduct in question is connected with financial crime; and
14. whether action taken by the FSA will have consequences for other financial transactions, such as takeover bids.

10.63 Generally, the FSA will publish the details of successful injunction applications.[90] However, there may be times when the FSA will decide not to do so, such as when publication could harm confidence in the financial system.

(8) Restitution and redress

10.64 The FSA has two avenues to impose restitution and redress. It may apply to the court for an order of restitution or, in the case of regulated entities, it may use its administrative powers to require restitution.[91] The FSA's power to apply to the court for orders in cases of market abuse has been discussed above. However, the FSA has such powers that apply more broadly to other statutory and regulatory requirements which the FSA is charged with administering.

10.65 Under FSMA, s 382, a court may, on the application of the FSA, grant a restitution order. When deciding whether to apply for restitution, the FSA will consider 'whether this would be the best use of the FSA's limited resources taking into account, for example, the likely amount of the recovery and the costs of achieving and distributing any sums. It will also consider ... other ways that persons might obtain redress, and whether it would be more efficient or cost-effective for them to use these means instead; and any proposals by the person concerned to offer redress to any consumers or other persons who have suffered loss, and the adequacy of those proposals.'[92] Other factors the FSA may take into account include whether the profits are quantifiable and losses identifiable, the number of persons affected, the solvency of the firm, other powers available to the FSA, the behaviour of the persons suffering loss, and the context of the conduct in question.[93] The FSA notes that it expects to exercise its restitution powers only on rare occasions.[94]

---

[90] EG 6.16.
[91] EG 11.4.
[92] EG 11.1.
[93] EG 11.3.
[94] EG 11.1.

Any amount paid to the FSA in pursuance of such an order must be paid to a   **10.66**
'qualifying person' or distributed among such 'qualifying persons' as the court
may direct.[95] A 'qualifying person' here means 'a person appearing to the Court to
be someone (a) to whom the profits mentioned [above] are attributable or (b) who
has suffered the loss or adverse effect mentioned [above]'.[96] Similar powers may be
exercised by the court, on the application of the FSA, in cases involving market
abuse.[97] In exercising such powers in relation to a person 'who has been knowingly
concerned in the contravention of a requirement', it is not necessary that the person concerned can be shown to have profited from the breach. Participation in the
contravention without gain is sufficient to invoke the power to make a restitution
order.[98]

Under FSMA, s 384, the FSA is given administrative power to require restitution,   **10.67**
without a court order, if the FSA is satisfied that an authorized person has knowingly been involved in contravening a relevant requirement under the FSMA.
The factors taken into account by the FSA in deciding whether to exercise its
s 384 powers are the same as listed above for deciding whether to exercise its
s 382 powers. In addition, however, when deciding whether to apply to the court
for restitution under s 382 or require restitution from firms under s 384, the FSA
will take into consideration:

1. whether the FSA wishes to combine an application for an order for restitution
   with other court action against the firm;
2. whether the FSA wishes to bring related court proceedings against an unauthorized person where the factual basis of the proceeding is the same as the
   claim for restitution against the firm;
3. whether there is a danger that the assets of the firm may be dissipated (in which
   case the FSA may wish to combine an application to the court for an order for
   restitution with an application for an asset-freezing injunction); or
4. the FSA suspects that the firm may not comply with an administrative requirement to give restitution.[99]

The court may also be asked to make a declaration confirming the fact of contra-   **10.68**
vention of the FSMA's requirements by the individual concerned and authorizing
the FSA to distribute any money adjudged to be due to satisfy a restitutionary
obligation.[100] The court is likely to grant a declaration of contravention by named
individuals where it is satisfied an order should be made. Such a declaration will

---

[95] FSMA, s 382(3).
[96] FSMA, s 382(8).
[97] FSMA, s 383.
[98] See *SIB v Pantell SA* No 2 [1993] Ch 256.
[99] EG 11.5.
[100] See *FSA v Lukka* Ch D, 29 April 1999.

assist in determining whether the person concerned should be regarded as 'a fit and proper person to carry on investment business'; the declaration may be of assistance to overseas regulators and may aid individual investors considering bringing proceedings for compensation arising out of the breaches.[101]

(9) Prosecution of criminal offences

10.69 Under FSMA, ss 401 and 402, the FSA is given the power to prosecute criminal offences and to institute proceedings for certain other offences.[102] The relevant offences are as follows:

- unauthorized trading;[103]
- false claims to be authorized or exempt;[104]
- unlawful financial promotions;[105]
- performing or agreeing to perform functions in breach of a prohibition order;[106]
- a number of Listing Rule infringements;[107]
- provision of false information to FSA investigators;[108]
- failing to comply with provisions about control over authorized persons;[109]
- providing false or misleading information to an auditor or actuary;[110]
- false claims to exemption from the general prohibition;[111]
- disclosure of confidential information in contravention of statutory restrictions imposed by FSMA;[112]
- misleading statements and practices offences;[113]
- misleading the FSA;[114]
- offences of inside dealing under Part IV Criminal Justice Act 1993;[115] and
- money laundering infringements.[116]

10.70 The FSA does recognize that sanctions for market abuse are intended to complement existing criminal sanctions against insider dealing and misleading

---

[101] See *per* Neuberger J in *FSA v Lukka*, above.
[102] Such as the improper carrying on of a Consumer Credit Act business. EG 12.1.
[103] FSMA, s 23.
[104] FSMA, s 24.
[105] FSMA, s 25.
[106] FSMA, s 56(4).
[107] FSMA, ss 83(3), 85(2) and 98(2).
[108] FSMA, s 177.
[109] FSMA, s 191.
[110] FSMA, s 346.
[111] FSMA, s 333.
[112] FSMA, ss 348, 350 and 352.
[113] FSMA, s 397.
[114] FSMA, s 398.
[115] FSMA, s 402(1)(a).
[116] FSMA, s 402(1)(b).

statements and practices offences. It also recognizes that, in some cases, conduct can breach both the criminal law as well as FSMA market abuse offences. In such cases, the FSA can decide to commence criminal proceedings instead of bringing an administrative proceeding. In such cases, it will take into account the requirements of the Code for Crown Prosecutors.[117]

Among the factors which the FSA will take into account in deciding to bring a **10.71** criminal prosecution for market misconduct are the following:

1. the seriousness of the misconduct and whether prosecution would be likely to result in a significant criminal sentence;
2. whether there are victims who have suffered loss as a result of the misconduct;
3. the number of the victims and the sizes of the losses they suffered;
4. whether the misconduct affected the market so as to cause significant disruption to, or damage to confidence in, the market;
5. the size of any profits made or losses avoided by the misconduct;
6. whether the conduct is likely to be continued or repeated if a criminal penalty is not sought;
7. the previous disciplinary and compliance records of those involved in the market misconduct in question;
8. the extent to which those involved in the misconduct promptly and voluntarily provided restitution or redress to those who have suffered losses by the misconduct, and what steps they have taken to correct systemic failures related to the misconduct;
9. the effects of criminal prosecution on securing redress for those who have suffered losses, such as where a criminal prosecution might affect the solvency of a firm which owes compensation to consumers as a result of market misconduct;
10. how cooperative with the FSA parties connected with the market misconduct have been, above and beyond their bare statutory duties to co-operate;
11. the extent to which an individual's misconduct involved dishonesty, abuse or position or trust;
12. to what extent an individual played a leadership role in market misconduct by a group;
13. the personal circumstances of individuals involved in the market misconduct.[118]

---

[117] EG 12.2.
[118] EG 12.8.

10.72   Please note that the FSA emphasizes that the above is not an exhaustive list of the things they may consider.[119] A more detailed discussion of the role of the criminal law and examples of some of the more recent criminal prosecutions can be found in Chapter 13.

10.73   The FSA has decided to follow a policy of not simultaneously seeking criminal prosecution and civil sanctions against the same parties for the same conduct:

> It is the FSA's policy not to impose a sanction for market abuse where a person is being prosecuted for market misconduct or has finally been convicted or acquitted of market misconduct (following the exhaustion of all appeal processes) in a criminal prosecution arising from substantially the same allegations. Similarly, it is the FSA's policy not to commence a prosecution for market misconduct where the FSA has brought or is seeking to bring disciplinary proceedings for market abuse arising from substantially the same allegations.[120]

10.74   However, even if the FSA does not intend simultaneously to pursue criminal prosecution and market abuse sanctions, it may nevertheless pursue some of the other regulatory remedies discussed above, alongside market abuse sanctions or criminal prosecution, including:[121]

1. injunctions;
2. orders of restitution;
3. withdrawal of approval or authorization, or cancellation of permission; or
4. prohibitions of individuals.

10.75   In the prosecution of criminal offences, the FSA will cooperate with other authorities that have the prosecutorial powers including: the Secretary of State for Trade and Industry, the Director General of Fair Trading, the Crown Prosecution Service; the Serious Fraud Office, prosecutors in Northern Ireland. The FSA has no power to prosecute offences under the FSMA in Scotland. That remains the responsibility of the Crown Office.[122]

10.76   Finally, it is important to note that the imposition of a penalty in a market abuse case does not make a transaction void or unenforceable. The reason for this position is probably to prevent parties who have lost money in a transaction from raising a complaint of market abuse in the hopes of avoiding their obligations to perform a contract. Although a finding of market abuse may entitle a damaged party to compensation for its losses, that party may still be required to perform the original contract.[123]

---

[119] EG 12.9.
[120] EG 12.10.
[121] EG 12.4.
[122] EG Annex 2, 13.
[123] FSMA, s 131.

11

DEFENCES

A. Types of Defences—General Considerations

Defences to allegations of market abuse consist of five basic types: **11.01**

(a) objections to personal or subject matter jurisdiction. This will depend on the
    relationship between the subject matter and the UK financial markets. This
    issue is dealt with in discussions of the 'reach' of the UK market abuse regime
    in Chapter 8, above. It is mentioned in this chapter only to flag it as a possible
    issue;
(b) compliance with relevant regulatory rules;
(c) being within a 'safe harbour';
(d) evidential defences consisting of other factors indicating that behaviour did
    not constitute market abuse;
(e) the person in question is acting on behalf of a public authority with respect to:
    (i)   monetary policies;
    (ii) exchange rate or public debt management policies; or
    (iii) foreign exchange reserves policies.[1]

---

[1] FSMA, s 118A(5)(c), SI 2005/381.

B. Particular Defences—Detailed Considerations

(1) Compliance with regulatory rules

11.02   FSMA, s 118A(5)(a) states:

> Behaviour does not amount to market abuse for the purposes of this Act if —
> (a) it conforms with a rule which includes a provision to the effect that behaviour conforming with the rule does not amount to market abuse ...[2]

11.03   The FSA carefully points out in the Code that there are no regulatory rules that require a person to commit market abuse, although some rules may say that conduct which complies with the rule will not amount to market abuse. However, what these rules mean is that compliance with such a rule will not of itself constitute market abuse. This means that conduct complying with such a rule can still be market abuse if factors such as improper motivations or other market disrupting elements are present.[3]

11.04   Rules that come within this category, where compliance with them does not in itself amount to market abuse, include:

1. rules relating to Chinese walls (SYSC 10.2.2 R (see SYSC 10.2.2 R(4));[4] and
2. parts of the Part 6[5] rules relating to the timing, dissemination or availability, content and standard of care applicable to disclosure announcement, communication or release of information (see the Disclosure Rules).[6]

11.05   The FSA also emphasizes that there are no rules in the Takeover Code which require a person to commit market abuse. However, they point out that even someone acting in compliance may still be guilty of market abuse under certain circumstances.[7] Behaviour conforming with the rules of the Takeover Code (specified in MAR Table 1.10.5 C)[8] relating to the disclosure, announcement, communication or release of information will not, of itself, constitute market abuse if the behaviour is expressly required or expressly permitted by the rule in question (for these purposes, notes associated with the rules will be treated as part of the rules until notice otherwise); and it conforms to any General Principle set out in Section B of the Takeover Code relevant to the rule.[9]

---

[2] FSMA, s 118A(5)(a); SI 2005/381.
[3] MAR 1.10.2 G.
[4] FSMA *Handbook, Senior Management Arrangements, Systems and Controls* ('SYSC').
[5] As defined in FSMA, s 73A.
[6] MAR 1.10.2 G. See also FSA Implementation, Directive Instrument, Annex 2, Market Abuse Directive disclosure rules instrument 2005 ('Disclosure Rules'), in effect from 1 July 2005.
[7] MAR 1.10.3 G.
[8] MAR 1.10.5 C.
[9] MAR 1.10.4 C(1).

Behaviour conforming to Rule 4.2 of the Takeover Code relating to restrictions on **11.06** dealings by offerors or parties acting in concert with them will not of itself constitute market abuse to the extent that the behaviour is expressly permitted or required by that rule provided also that, in addition, the behaviour is expressly required or expressly permitted by the rule in question and it conforms to any General Principle set out at Section B of the Takeover Code.[10]

Thus, the exceptions in MAR 1.10.4 C and 1.10.6 C, discussed above, do not **11.07** apply to any behaviour conforming to a rule in the Takeover Code when such behaviour is in breach of any of the General Principles set out in Section B of the Takeover Code which is relevant to such rule.[11]

C. Safe Harbours

The term 'safe harbour' was not used in the Directive, which rather specified cer- **11.08** tain circumstances and events as situations to which the Directive was disapplied. Thus, Article 2(1) for example provided that '… Member States shall prohibit any person … who possesses inside information from using that information by acquiring or disposing of, or by trying to acquire or dispose of, for his own account or for the account of a third party, either directly or indirectly, financial instruments to which that information relates'; Article 2(3) then states: 'this Article shall not apply to transactions conducted in the discharge of an obligation that has become due to acquire or dispose of financial instruments where that obligation results from an agreement concluded before the person concerned possessed inside information.' The term 'safe harbour' is nonetheless useful as describing behaviour which could be interpreted as falling within the definitions of market abuse but which will not be treated by the regulators as market abuse as long as certain requirements are met.[12]

It is not a term with any diminished significance in post-Directive FSA regula- **11.09** tion.[13] Whilst the UK implementation of the Directive reduced the number of specific safe harbours from the nine identified in the pre-Implementation Code, FSMA, s 118A(5)(b) still specifies three specific safe harbours as follows:

Behaviour does not amount to market abuse for the purposes of this Act if –
(a) it conforms with a rule which includes a provision to the effect that behaviour conforming with the rule does not amount to market abuse,

---

[10] MAR 1.10.6 C.
[11] MAR 1.10.5 C and MAR 1.10.6 C.
[12] MAR. 1.10.1 G.
[13] FSA *Implementation*, 2.3.

(b) it conforms with the relevant provisions of Commission Regulation (EC) No 2273/2003 of 22 December 2003 implementing Directive 2003/6/EC of the European Parliament and of the Council as regards exemptions for buy-back programmes and stabilisation of financial instruments, or

(c) it is done by a person acting on behalf of a public authority in pursuit of monetary policies or policies with respect to exchange rates or the management of public debt or foreign exchange reserves.

11.10 The safe harbours preserved in relation to share buy-back and stabilization activities will be discussed in more detail, below, in this section of the chapter.

11.11 However, the pre-implementation safe harbours have not entirely vanished from the market abuse regime. The FSA has stated that:

> A number of the safe harbours in the original Code were deleted because they were no more than descriptions of behaviour that did not amount to market abuse.[14]

11.12 In other words, although they are eliminated as safe harbours, they may still provide a useful guide to certain behaviour that the FSA does not consider market abuse. They may still be useful as indications of the kinds of things that may be 'evidential defences'. Consequently, the old 'safe harbours' are discussed in the 'evidential defences' section of this chapter, below.

(1) Share buy-back programmes and new issue price stabilization

11.13 MAR 2.1.4 says:

> The purpose of this chapter is to describe the extent to which stabilisation activity has the benefit of a 'safe harbour' for market abuse under the Buy-back and Stabilisation Regulation ... and to specify by rules the extent to which stabilisation activity has the benefit of a 'safe harbour' for market abuse (misuse of information), market abuse (misleading behaviour) or market abuse (distortion) ... or [certain other] criminal offences ...[15]

(2) Share buy-back programmes

11.14 The first safe harbour relates to share buy-back programmes which meet, among other things, the following standards:[16]

- they accord with the Second Company Law Directive (77/91/EEC); [17]
- they are approved by a general meeting of shareholders;

---

[14] FSA *Implementation*, 2.3.
[15] MAR 2.1.4.
[16] Directive, Art. 8.
[17] OJ L026, 31.01.1977, pp. 1–13.

- prior to trading, full details of the buy-back programme are published;
- the programme is announced outside 'closed periods';
- the buy-back programme is able to fulfil required reporting obligations;
- the programme relates to no more than 10 per cent of a company's subscribed capital;
- the programme complies with price, volume and volatility restrictions;
- trades are closed within a specific time period, currently proposed as five minutes;
- restrictions on selling own shares, take-overs and other related issues are complied with; and
- all trading is in accordance with the announced programme.

The Directive's requirements regarding purchases of own shares required changes **11.15** to the Listing Rules—see now the Disclosure Rules and Transparency Rules ('DTR') and in particular DTR 5.5.1R and 5.11.2R.

In order to come within the safe harbour, buy-back programmes can have only **11.16** limited objectives. They must comply with the Directive Buyback and Stabilisation Regulation and must be undertaken to reduce the capital of an issuer (in value or in number of shares) or to meet obligations resulting from:

(a) debt financial instruments exchangeable into equity instruments;
(b) employee share option programmes or other allocations of shares to employ-ees of the issuer or of an associate company.[18]

Share buy-back programmes must comply with the conditions set out in **11.17** Article 19 (1) of the PLC Safeguards Directive, that is, the Second Council Directive of 13 December 1976 on the coordination of safeguards for the protec-tion of the interests of members and others in respect of the formation of public limited liability companies and the maintenance and alteration of their capital, with a view to making such safeguards equivalent (No. 77/91/EEC).[19]

Prior to the start of trading, full details of any buy-back programme must be **11.18** adequately disclosed to the public in EC Member States in which the issuer has requested a commission of shares to trading on a regulated market. Those details must include the objective of the programme, the maximum consideration, the maximum number of shares to be acquired and the length of the period for which authorization for the programme has been given. Any subsequent changes to the programme must be adequately disclosed in Member States. The issuer must

---

[18] MAR 1, Annex 1, 1.1.3.
[19] MAR 1, Annex 1, 1.1.5. Implemented in the UK by Companies Act 1985, s 166.

have in place mechanisms ensuring it fulfils the trade reporting obligations to the relevant authority of the regulated market on which the shares have been admitted to trading. Each transaction must be recorded and include certain specified information. The issuer must disclose the details of transactions no later than the end of the seventh daily market session following the date of the execution of such transactions.[20]

11.19　Other applicable regulations relating to conditions for trading and restrictions for the buy-back programme are set out in MAR 2. These are largely repetitions of the material of the provisions of the articles of the EU's Buy-back and Stabilisation Regulation ('the Regulation').[21]

(3) New issue price stabilization

11.20　This safe harbour applies to support for the price of new issues of certain securities. In order to qualify as a safe harbour the stabilization will have to meet, among others, the following requirements:[22]

- it can operate only during a defined period;
- it is applicable only to equity, debt and convertible securities;
- public disclosure of the stabilization must be made within one week of its completion;
- there must be an identified 'Stabilization Manager' who has a duty of reporting the activities under the stabilization programme to the appropriate national regulator.

11.21　MAR 2 of the FSA Handbook now sets out the regulations for stabilization.[23]

11.22　With respect to the 'criminal offences', MAR 2 also provides a safe harbour which can be a defence both to the criminal offences of insider dealing in the Criminal Justice Act 1993, Part V and market manipulation under FSMA, s 397.[24]

11.23　It is also worth pointing out that the FSA has said in the past that buy-back and stabilization activities which fall outside the safe harbour may not necessarily be abusive. Such behaviour might be entered into for legitimate reasons and it might be accepted practice of the market in question.[25]

---

[20] MAR 1, Annex 1, 1.1.5.
[21] Commission Regulation 2273/2003.
[22] Directive, Art. 8. See also MAR 2.3.4 and 2.3.5.
[23] MAR 2.
[24] MAR 2.1.2 (3) and (4). Regarding defences to other criminal offences, see MAR 2.3–2.5.
[25] Joint Consultation Paper, s 3.24, p. 19; Appendix C, 2.2.2D.

D. Evidential Defences

(1) General comments

'Evidential defences' are not as well defined or as certain as 'safe harbours'. They **11.24** rely entirely on the ability of the accused to produce proof which shows that:

(a) his actions were not motivated by an intention to commit market abuse; and/or

(b) his behaviour did not have the effect of constituting market abuse.

This statement alone demonstrates the complexity of the market abuse regime. **11.25** As discussed above in Chapter 9, the market abuse regime bears an uncertain relationship with the criminal law. In some cases, market abuse behaviour will be considered criminal, in others civil. It is not clear at the outset of any market abuse investigation which approach the FSA will take. Depending on which it is, the burden of proof will differ. Different evidence will be required.

To avoid conviction for a criminal charge, it may be sufficient for the accused to **11.26** show he did not intend to commit market abuse. However, to avoid a civil penalty he may have to show that his actions did not have the effect of constituting market abuse. It is not within the scope of this book to examine all the legal issues that relate to this criminal/civil distinction.

As to what factors a person suspected of market abuse should consider identifying **11.27** to show his innocence, the FSA does give some guidance in the Code. In a number of places, throughout the Code, the Authority lists some (but not all) of the factors they will take into account when deciding whether certain behaviour constitutes market abuse. The Code also provides examples of behaviour that the FSA does or does not consider apt to amount to market abuse. When seeking to put together an evidential defence, it is on these expressly identified factors and examples that an accused should first look to build.[26]

(2) 'Old safe harbours'—guidance from the past

There is no doubt that the FSA's examples of relevant factors and behaviour that **11.28** it considers to be or not to be market abuse are very helpful to market participants and their advisors in understanding the FSA's approach to market abuse enforcement. The importance of that knowledge cannot be overestimated. As stated above, the market abuse regime is a very flexible tool in the FSA. That is as it

---

[26] See, e.g., MAR 1.2.7–1.2.14, MAR 1.3.3–1.3.23 and many other sections throughout the Code.

should be in order to have effective regulation. However, its very flexibility means that market participants will be hard pressed to know exactly how the FSA is likely to react to any particular pattern of market behaviour. Consequently, at least some market activity is bound to be constricted by misplaced fear that the FSA could regard certain actions as market abuse. Given the fact that a finding of market abuse can attract disastrously severe civil and criminal penalties, that is not a concern to be regarded lightly.

11.29   The Joint Consultation Paper (UK Implementation of the EU Market Abuse Directive, June 2004) identified that certain previous safe harbours (in particular):

1. dealing or arranging required for other reasons;[27]
2. dealing or arranging not based on information;[28] and
3. relevant information held behind effective Chinese walls,[29]

did not 'fall within the definition of market abuse'. This was also true of various Listing Rules and City Code provisions treated as safe harbours.[30]

11.30   As the Implementation Directive 2005 pointed out:

> One of the key differences in the version of the Code we consulted on was the amendment and/or deletion of 'safe harbours'. A number of the safe harbours in the original Code were deleted because they were no more than descriptions of behaviour that did not amount to market abuse.[31]

11.31   Detailed guidance on the descriptions of behaviour, listed in paragraph 11.30 above, which could still be construed as not amounting to market abuse was formerly set out in MAR 1.4.20 C to MAR 1.4.31 C.[32] Although these are no longer strictly 'safe harbours', the cited provisions having now been revoked, it is useful to review them because of the strong possibility that the FSA may still consider such behaviour not to amount to market abuse.

(3) Dealing or arranging required for other reasons

11.32   This related to the market abuse category of insider dealing described as misuse of information. It comprised behaviour constituting dealing or arranging deals that was required for purposes of complying with legal (including contractual) or regulatory obligations that existed before the information in question was in

---

27 MAR 1.4.20 C (revoked 30 June 2005).
28 MAR 1.4.21 C (revoked 30 June 2005).
29 MAR 1.4.24 C (revoked 30 June 2005).
30 Joint Consultation Paper, Chapter 4, s 4.12.
31 FSA *Implementation*, Chapter 2, Feedback on the Code, s 2.3.
32 Joint Consultation Paper, Chapter 4, FSA Implementation, s 4.22.

the relevant person's possession.[33] In the Code, satisfaction of such a legal or regulatory obligation is now listed as a factor 'to be taken into account' in deciding whether behaviour is based on inside information.[34]

(4) Dealing or arranging not based on information

This did not constitute market abuse if relevant information not generally avail-   **11.33**
able, although in a person's possession, had not influenced that person's decision to engage in dealing or arranging.[35] Again, this is no longer a safe harbour, but a factor to be taken into account in judging whether the behaviour was on the basis of inside information.[36]

In cases where a limited number of individuals within an organization are in   **11.34**
possession of the relevant information, the FSA will consider the following factors in judging whether possession of the information influenced decisions to deal or arrange deals. These include whether any of the people who had the information:

(a) were involved in any way in relevant decisions to deal or arrange deals; or
(b) had any direct or indirect influence on the decisions to deal or arrange the deals; or
(c) had any contact with the people involved in making relevant decisions to deal or arrange deals whereby the relevant restricted information could have passed between them.[37]

(5) Trading information, takeover bids and other market operations

The industry raised a number of objections to the complete elimination of this   **11.35**
safe harbour. In response, the FSA reasserted that the 'safe harbour' would not continue. Under the Market Abuse Directive, transactions motivated by information about the planned trading activities of clients can certainly amount to market abuse, and can also be violations of other FSA regulations relating to 'front-running', dealing fairly and in due turn,[38] personal account dealing[39] or other breaches of duties relating to such things as takeover bids, new offers, issues placements or other primary market activity.

---

[33] Formerly designated a 'safe harbour' under MAR 1.4.20 C (revoked 30 June 2005).
[34] MAR 1.3.3 E (2).
[35] Formerly designated a 'safe harbour' under MAR 1.4.21 C (revoked 30 June 2005).
[36] MAR 1.3.3 E (1).
[37] MAR 1.3.3 E (3).
[38] MAR 1.3.2 E and COBS 11.
[39] COBS 11.7.

11.36 However, under some limited circumstances, the FSA has said that such transactions will not constitute market abuse solely because they were based on information relating to future transactions.[40] The Code clarifies that such activities would not be market abuse where they were clearly linked to legitimate trading by market makers and others acting in a similar capacity, and the dutiful execution of client orders.[41] They have placed in the Code lists of the factors they will take into account in deciding whether such activity was proper.[42]

11.37 One example of legitimate behaviour given by the FSA relates to takeover and merger activity.[43] The Code says:

> Behaviour, based on inside information relating to another company, in the context of a public takeover bid or merger for the purpose of gaining control of that company or proposing a merger with that company, does not of itself amount to market abuse (insider dealing) including:
> (1) seeking from holders of securities, issued by the target, irrevocable undertakings or expressions of support to accept an offer to acquire those securities (or not to accept such an offer);
> (2) making arrangements in connection with an issue of securities that are to be offered as consideration for the takeover or merger offer or to be issued in order to fund the takeover or merger offer, including making arrangements for the underwriting or placing of those securities and any associated hedging arrangements by underwriters or places which are proportionate to the risks assumed; and
> (3) making arrangements to offer cash as consideration for the takeover or merger offer as an alternative to securities consideration.[44]

11.38 Two categories of inside information relate to the above takeovers or mergers:
(1) information that an offeror or potential offeror is going to make, or is considering making, an offer for the target;
(2) information that an offeror or potential offeror may obtain through due diligence.[45]

11.39 Factors to be taken into account in judging whether or not a person's behaviour is for the purpose of him gaining control of the target company or him proposing a merger with that company (and which will be taken as indications that it is) are (1) whether the transactions concerned are in the target company's shares; or (2) whether the transactions concerned are for the sole purpose of gaining that control or effecting that merger.[46]

---

[40] MAR 1.4.26 C (revoked 30 June 2005).
[41] MAR 1.3.7C and 1.3.12C.
[42] See generally MAR 1.3.
[43] MAR 1.3.17 C.
[44] MAR 1.3.17 G.
[45] MAR 1.3.18 G.
[46] MAR 1.3.19 E.

However, there are some activities related to takeover bids which can constitute **11.40**
market abuse. These include dealing on the basis of inside information which is
not 'trading information'; front-running; dealing in other investments (such as
the shares of other companies in the target industry, or contracts for differences
which merely give an economic exposure to the effects of a takeover bid) on the
basis of information relevant to the takeover bid. Those acting as agents, or in
concert, with a bidder will also be guilty of market abuse if they deal in investments or participate in relevant transactions which have an economic exposure to
the bid for their own benefit when motivated by restricted information about
a bid.[47]

(6) Underwriting agreements

An agreement to underwrite an issue of securities or other legitimate market **11.41**
making activities will not, in itself, constitute market abuse by misuse of
information.[48]

(7) Chinese walls

Although information held behind 'Chinese walls', also referred to by the FSA as **11.42**
'information barriers',[49] formerly gave rise to 'safe harbour', this safe harbour status no longer obtains. This does not mean, however, that use of information held
behind Chinese walls will necessarily constitute market abuse. That category of
behaviour (and, indeed, other behaviour that was previously covered by a specific
safe harbour but no longer is) may be undertaken for legitimate market reasons
and may be an 'accepted market practice'. Also, behaviour not within a safe harbour may simply not be within the definition of market abuse.[50] This included the
behaviour formerly covered by a safe harbour for information held behind Chinese
walls.[51]

The 'descriptions of behaviour which is not abusive' was as follows: **11.43**

> Dealing or arranging deals will not amount to a misuse of information if the person's
> possession of relevant information that is not generally available did not influence
> the decision to engage in the dealing or arranging in question.[52]

---

[47] MAR 1.3.2 E.
[48] MAR 1.3.7 C.
[49] COBS 12.4.3.
[50] Joint Consultation Paper, s 3.24.
[51] Joint Consultation Paper, s 4.12.
[52] MAR 1.4.21 C (revoked 30 June 2005).

11.44 It was presumed for the purposes of MAR 1.4.21 C that the person's possession of the information in question did not influence his decision to deal or arrange deals if:

(1) the person had taken a firm decision to deal or arrange deals before the relevant information was in the person's possession; and

(2) the terms on which the person had proposed to enter into the transaction(s) did not alter after the receipt of the information.[53]

11.45 In the case of an organization and where one or more individuals within the organization was in possession of relevant information, it was presumed for the purposes of MAR 1.4.21 C that such possession had no influence on the person's decision to deal or arrange deals if none of the individuals in possession of the information:

(1) had any involvement in the decision to engage in the dealing or arranging; or

(2) behaved in such a way as to influence, directly or indirectly, the decision to engage in the dealing or arranging, or

(3) had any contact with those who were involved in the decision to engage in the dealing or arranging whereby the information could have been transmitted.[54]

11.46 The former safe harbour relating to Chinese walls in the context of market abuse behaviour labelled 'misuse of information' was as follows:[55]

Relevant information does not influence the decision to deal or arrange deals if:

(1) the information in question was held behind an effective Chinese wall and the individual or individuals who dealt or arranged deals was or were on the other side of the Chinese wall (see further COB 2.4); or

(2) arrangements equivalent to effective Chinese walls had been established and maintained in respect of the information, and the individuals who dealt or arranged deals did not, therefore, have access to the relevant information.

11.47 Issues relating to former safe harbours which were merely descriptions of behaviour that did not amount to market abuse, including use of information behind Chinese walls, is now covered in MAR section 1.9.5 E as follows:[56]

In the opinion of the FSA, the following factors are to be taken into account in determining whether or not behaviour that creates a false or misleading impression as to, or distorts the market for, a qualifying investment, has also failed to meet the standard expected by a regular user.

---

[53] MAR 1.4.22 E (revoked 30 June 2005).
[54] MAR 1.4.23 E (revoked 30 June 2005).
[55] MAR 1.4.24 C (revoked 30 June 2005), and see also MAR 1.4.25 G (revoked 30 June 2005) referring to another safe harbour relating to Chinese walls at MAR 1.7.3 E(2) (revoked 30 June 2005).
[56] MAR 1.9.5 E.

(1) ...

(6) if an organisation has created a false or misleading impression, whether the individuals responsible could only know they were likely to create a false or misleading impression if they had access to other information that was being held behind Chinese wall or similarly effective arrangements ...

Further reference to rules relating to Chinese walls, now described as 'the control of information rule', is found in new MAR 1.10.2 G:[57] **11.48**

> There are no rules which permit or require a person to behave in a way which amounts to market abuse. Some rules contain a provision to the effect that behaviour conforming to that rule does not amount to market abuse:
> (1) the control of information rule (SYSC 10.2.2 R(1) (see SYSC 10.2.2 R(4)));
> (2) those parts of the Part 6 rules which relate to the timing, dissemination or availability, content and standard of care applicable to a disclosure, announcement, communication or release of information (see in particular the Disclosure Rules and Transparency Rules).

More detailed rules governing the use of Chinese walls are found in s 10.2 of the Senior Management Arrangements, Systems and Controls in the FSA *Handbook*.[58] As stated there, Chinese walls have two principal purposes in the context of regulated investment business in the UK. The first is to fulfil the requirements of Principle 8 of the Principles of Business that: **11.49**

> [A] firm must manage conflicts of interest fairly, both between itself and its customers and between a customer and another client.[59]

One permitted method of managing potential conflicts is to set up and maintain 'Chinese walls' which are rules and procedures that restrict the movement of information within a firm. If a Chinese wall meets the necessary criteria, then the FSA may consider it proper for a firm to withhold or decline to use information that, without a proper Chinese wall, the firm would otherwise have to disclose to or use for the benefit of a particular client.[60] **11.50**

The second principal purpose is to comply with FSMA, s 147, which permits the FSA to make rules regarding the holding of information to the extent that that they meet the following criteria: **11.51**

> 147 ...
> (2) Control of information rules may —
> (a) require the withholding of information which A would otherwise have to disclose to a person ('B') for or with whom A does business in the course of carrying on any regulated or other activity;

---

[57] MAR 1.10.1 G.
[58] FSA *Handbook*, SYSC 10.2.
[59] PRIN 2.1.
[60] SYSC 10.2.3.

(b) specify circumstances in which A may withhold information which he would otherwise have to disclose to B;

(c) require A not to use for the benefit of B information A holds which A would otherwise have to use in that way;

(d) specify circumstances in which A may decide not to use for the benefit of B information A holds which A would otherwise have to use in that way.[61]

11.52 With respect to such control of information, the FSA requires the following. First it defines a 'Chinese wall' for purposes of regulation under the FSMA as being:

> an arrangement that requires information held by a person in the course of carrying on one part of the business to be withheld from, or not to be used for, persons with or for whom it acts in the course of carrying on another part of its business . . .[62]

11.53 If such an arrangement is properly made, than the creator of the Chinese wall may:

1. withhold, or not use, the information in question; and
2. for purposes of effectuating (1) above, permit persons employed in one part of its business to withhold such information from persons employed in another part of its business;

> to the extent that the above relates to business which, in at least one of its parts, involves doing designated investment business or relevant ancillary activities.[63]

11.54 The FSA goes on to say that such information may be withheld (or not used) when this is required by a Chinese wall established between different parts of a business in the same group. However, this would not excuse any failure to comply with any legal or regulatory requirement to transmit or use the information which arises outside the Conduct of Business rules.[64]

11.55 The FSA requires that adequate steps must be taken to ensure that Chinese walls remain effective and are properly monitored.[65] However, if the above requirements are met regarding the establishment and maintenance of a Chinese wall, then, for purposes of FSMA, s 118A(5)(a), behaviour required by the Chinese wall which results in the withholding or refusing to use information will not constitute market abuse.[66]

---

[61] FSMA, s 147.
[62] SYSC 10.2.2 R (1).
[63] SYSC 10.2.2 R (1).
[64] SYSC 10.2.2 R (2).
[65] SYSC 10.2.2 R (3).
[66] SYSC 10.2.2 R (4).

This means that: **11.56**

(1) conduct that complies with SYSC s 10.2.2 R(1) will constitute a defence against proceedings brought under FSMA, s 397(2) or (3);[67]
(2) behaviour in conformity with SYSC s 10.2.2 R does not amount to market abuse (see SYSC s 10.2.2(4)); and
(3) conduct that complies with SYSC s 10.2.2 R(1) will provide a defence for a firm against an FSA enforcement action or an action for damages under FSMA, s 150 based on breach of a relevant requirement to disclose or use information (this may be relevant to requirements of the SYSC, PRIN and MAR 3 regarding inter-professional conduct).[68]

When any SYSC rules or any CASS[69] rules apply to a firm which engages in acts **11.57** based on knowledge of restricted information, the information in question will not be attributed to the entire firm if the information used by the acting individuals is properly separated from the rest of the firm by a Chinese wall established under SYSC 10.2.2 R. In other words, when a firm manages a conflict of interest with a Chinese wall, properly set up and maintained in compliance with SYSC 10.2.2 R, individuals on 'the other side' of the Chinese wall will not be regarded as being in possession of information which the Chinese wall prevents them from having.[70]

---

[67] Behaviour constituting certain kinds of misleading statements or practices. SYSC 10.2.3 G (1).
[68] SYSC 10.2.3 G (3).
[69] FSA *Handbook, Business Standards, Client Assets*, CASS.
[70] SYSC 10.2.4 R and 10.2.5 G.

12

HEARINGS AND APPEALS

A. Financial Services and Markets Tribunal

(1) Outline

Any person who is subject to a 'notice of decision' may make a reference to the **12.01** Financial Services and Markets Tribunal ('the Tribunal'). The reference must be made before the end of 28 days of the date on which the notice of decision is given or other appropriate date if relevant.[1]

The Tribunal has broad powers with respect to FSA disciplinary decisions. A refer- **12.02** ence to the Tribunal is not really an 'appeal'. It is a new hearing on the issues before a new, and independent, forum. The Tribunal may consider any relevant evidence and may direct any decision which the FSA could originally have made. In effect, the review undertaken by the Tribunal is by way of a hearing *de novo*. Anything which the FSA could have considered (even if it did not) or which relates to

---

[1] FSMA, s 127(4) and 133(1).

the subject matter (even if it was unavailable to the FSA), the Tribunal may consider.[2]

12.03 A person appearing before the Tribunal in relation to market abuse cases has a right in certain circumstances to legal assistance.[3] The relevant circumstances are that he must be 'an individual who has referred the matter to the Tribunal under section 127(4)' of FSMA,[4] that is, he must be an individual against whom the FSA has decided to take action under s 123 of the Act.[5] However, this is different from the legal aid provided in most other situations. The legal assistance before the Tribunal is not paid for by taxpayers but from a fund which is collected from the fees of those regulated by the FSA.[6]

12.04 Subject to the constraints discussed below at paragraphs 12.69–12.73 any person who is unhappy with the decision of the Tribunal may, with permission of the Tribunal or the Court of Appeal,[7] appeal to the Court of Appeal. From the Court of Appeal, an appeal can be made to the House of Lords if leave to appeal is given by the Court of Appeal or the House of Lords.[8]

(2) The structure of the Tribunal

12.05 FSMA, Sch. 13 describes, in general terms, the composition of the Tribunal and its procedures. The Lord Chancellor is directed to appoint a panel of persons for purposes of serving as chairmen of the Tribunal.[9] Members of the panel must be persons with at least five years of particular legal qualifications.[10] From among this 'panel of chairmen', one member is to be appointed as 'President of the Financial Services and Markets Tribunal' and another as 'Deputy President'. The Deputy President has those functions which the President may assign to him. A person appointed as President or Deputy President must have seven years of particular legal qualifications.[11]

---

[2] FSMA, s 133.
[3] FSMA, s 134.
[4] FSMA, s 134(3)
[5] In contrast therefore the right to legal assistance would not apply to a person exercising a right to refer a matter to the Tribunal under other circumstances, such as a third party exercising referral rights under FSMA, s 393(9).
[6] FSMA, s 136.
[7] Or, in Scotland, the Court of Session.
[8] FSMA, s 137(4).
[9] FSMA, Sch. 13, s 2(1).
[10] FSMA, Sch. 13, s 2(2).
[11] FSMA, Sch. 13, s 2. The first (and to date only) President of the Tribunal is Stephen Oliver QC (who is also the judicial head of the VAT and Duties Tribunal, the Pension Regulator Tribunal and the Claims Management Services Tribunal).

In addition, the Lord Chancellor must also appoint a panel of persons who appear to him to be qualified by experience or otherwise to deal with matters of the kind that may be referred to the Tribunal.[12]   **12.06**

If the President is absent or unable to act, his functions can be discharged by the Deputy President or, if he is unable to act (or there is no Deputy President) by another person can be appointed for that purpose from the panel of chairmen by the Lord Chancellor.[13]   **12.07**

The Lord Chancellor has the power to set terms of office, pay remuneration and expenses and appoint staff for the Tribunal.[14]   **12.08**

When a reference is made to the Tribunal, persons are chosen to act as members of the Tribunal in accordance with arrangements made by the President.[15] These 'standing arrangements' must provide for at least one Tribunal member to be selected from the panel of chairmen.[16] If it appears to the Tribunal that the matter before it involves questions of fact of special difficulty, the Tribunal may appoint one or more experts to assist.[17]   **12.09**

(3) Procedure before the Tribunal

The Tribunal must sit at such times and in such places as the Lord Chancellor may direct.[18] In accordance with FSMA, s 132(3), the Lord Chancellor may by rules make such provision as appears to him to be necessary or expedient in respect of the conduct of proceedings before the Tribunal. These may include requirements: **12.10**

(a) as to the manner in which the references are to be instituted;
(b) for the holding of hearings in private in such circumstances as specified in the rules;
(c) as to the persons who may appear on behalf of the parties;
(d) for a member of the panel of chairman to hear and determined interlocutor arena matters arising on a reference;
(e) for the suspension of decisions of the FSA which have taken effect;
(f) as to the withdrawal of references;
(g) as to the registration, publication and proof of decisions and orders.[19]

---

[12] FSMA, Sch. 13, s 3(4).
[13] FSMA, Sch. 13, s 2(7).
[14] FSMA, Sch. 13, ss 4–6.
[15] FSMA, Sch. 13, s 7(1).
[16] FSMA, Sch. 13, s 7(2).
[17] FSMA, Sch. 13, s 7(4).
[18] FSMA, Sch. 13, s 8.
[19] FSMA, Sch. 13, s 9.

12.11   The President of the Tribunal may give directions as to the practice and procedure to be followed by the Tribunal with respect to references to it.[20] By summons, the Tribunal may require any person to attend to give oral evidence before it or to produce any document under his custody or control which the Tribunal considers it necessary to examine.[21] The Tribunal may take evidence either orally under oath, or require the person examined to make a signed declaration of the truth of the matters on which he is examined.[22] A person is guilty of an offence if he, without reasonable excuse, refuses to attend a proceeding following the issue of the summons by the Tribunal, fails to give evidence, or alters, suppresses, conceals, destroys, or refuses to produce documents which he is required to produce before the Tribunal.[23] A person guilty of such an offence may be subject to a fine or, if convicted on indictment in relation to a failure to give evidence or similar, a prison sentence up to two years, or both.[24]

12.12   A decision of the Tribunal is to be made by a majority. The decision must state whether it was unanimous or by at least a majority. It must be recorded in a document containing the reasons for the decision and be signed by the member of the panel of chairmen dealing with the reference in question.[25]

12.13   The Tribunal must inform each party of its decision and, as soon as reasonably practicable, send to each party and any authorized person concerned a copy of the decision. The Tribunal must also send the Treasury a copy of the decision.[26]

12.14   If the Tribunal considers that a party has acted vexatiously, frivolously or unreasonably in the proceedings, it may order that party to pay another party the whole, or part, of the costs and expenses incurred by the other party in connection with the proceedings.[27]

12.15   Although the courts are familiar with a jurisdiction to make wasted costs orders in civil proceedings against a party which has behaved 'unreasonably',[28] it is unclear whether the Tribunal's approach to the issue of 'reasonableness' will be informed by the same jurisprudence. Also, it is unclear what conduct will answer the description 'vexatious' which is not equally appropriately described as 'unreasonable'. Some guidance has emerged from the Tribunal's decision on costs in *Baldwin*[29] where, following a successful reference, the Tribunal found that the proceedings

---

[20] FSMA, Sch. 13, s 10.
[21] FSMA, Sch. 13, s 11(1).
[22] FSMA, Sch. 13, s 11(2).
[23] FSMA, Sch. 13, s 11(3).
[24] FSMA, Sch. 13, s 11(4)–(5).
[25] FSMA, Sch. 13, s 12(1)–(2).
[26] FSMA, Sch. 13, ss 12(3)–(4).
[27] FSMA, Sch. 13, s 13(1).
[28] Ridehalgh v Horsfield [1994] Ch 205.
[29] FSMT, Case 028, 5 April 2006.

initiated against the appellant for market abuse were not justified. An argument that costs should only be awarded against the Authority if it could be shown to have been *Wednesbury*[30] unreasonable in proceeding in the first place was rejected. The Tribunal considered it had simply to apply the words of the Act, that is, under Schedule 13, paragraph 13: had the FSA acted unreasonably? An application for wasted costs against the FSA was partially successful in *Davidson v FSA*,[31] where a hearing had to be adjourned on it coming to light that the chairman of the RDC had spoken with a member of the Tribunal about the case. The applicant recovered 50 per cent of the costs thrown away given the FSA's unreasonable conduct (via the RDC) in speaking with the Tribunal.

A further indication of the approach that the Tribunal will take on costs issues emerges from *Davidson & Tatham v FSA*.[32] At paragraph 59 of the Decision the Tribunal indicated that from the arguments of the parties 'we have identified three elements of the disputed decision which they claim were unreasonable, namely, the approach to the evidence and the facts; the approach to the law; and the level of the penalties'.[33] As to the FSA's approach to the facts it concluded that 'the decision-making process at the time of the disputed decision had the defects identified in the enforcement process review, namely that before the case was referred to the Committee there was no dedicated legal function independent of the Enforcement Division to assist the Committee in its decision-making'.[34]   **12.16**

On the approach to the law, it found 'we are of the view that the Committee should have further explored the concept of the regular user and should have asked for an analysis of the application of the relevant rules of the alternative investment market and the provisions of the Code of Market Conduct. The Code of Market Conduct states that it imposes no new disclosure obligations but neither the draft warning notice nor the Committee considered what disclosure rules were applicable and whether they had been breached. This was brand new legislation which had not previously been tested … In our view the lack of a thorough legal review of this important matter was unreasonable in all the circumstances'.[35]   **12.17**

Finally, as to its approach to penalties it determined: **12.18**

> Finally, we turn to the level of the penalties and first consider whether it was reasonable to decide not to take criminal proceedings on the ground that they would give rise to a lower penalty because of the three mitigating factors of no personal gain,

---

[30] [1948] 1 KB 223.
[31] FSMT, Case 10, 10 August 2004.
[32] FSMT, Case 040, 16 May 2006.
[33] *Ibid.*, para. 59.
[34] *Ibid.*, para 63.
[35] *Ibid.*, para. 64.

no financial loss to investors, and the loss suffered by Mr Tatham and Mr Davidson. In our view it was not reasonable to decide against criminal proceedings on the ground that a higher penalty could be imposed by a civil penalty. It was also unreasonable to proceed to ignore the same mitigating factors as would have applied in criminal proceedings to reduce the level of the penalty.[36]

12.19 The fact that a party referring the matter to the Tribunal will not, however, be automatically exposed to an order to pay the FSA's costs where the reference fails is an important factor in not deterring the use of the Tribunal machinery on 'economic' grounds only.

12.20 If the Tribunal considers that a decision of the FSA subject to reference was unreasonable, it may order the FSA to pay a whole or part of the costs and expenses incurred by the other party in connection with the proceedings.[37]

12.21 An outline of the Tribunal Rules follows. The complete Rules can be found on the Tribunal website.[38]

B. Tribunal Rules

(1) Preliminary matters

Reference notice

12.22 A reference to the Tribunal is begun by a written 'reference notice' filed by the applicant, and signed by him or on his behalf, before the end of 28 days beginning with the date on which a decision notice is given by the FSA.[39] The notice needs to contain a number of things including (but not limited to):[40]

1. the name and address of the applicant;
2. a statement that the notice is a reference notice;
3. the issues of concerning the FSA notice that the applicant wishes the Tribunal to consider.

12.23 A copy of the relevant FSA notice needs to be filed with the reference notice.[41] At the time of filing the reference notice, the applicant can also apply for certain 'directions' such as extension of time limits or suspension of the FSA's

---

[36] *Ibid.*, para. 65.
[37] FSMA, Sch. 13, s 13(2).
[38] <www.financeandtaxtribunals.gov.uk>.
[39] SI 2001/2476, Financial Services and Markets Tribunals, the Financial Services and Markets Tribunal Rules 2001, Rule 4(1)–(2).
[40] Tribunal Rule 4(3).
[41] Tribunal Rule 4(5).

proposed action.[42] At the time the reference notice is filed the applicant needs to send a copy of the notice (and any previously filed application for directions) to the FSA.[43]

Upon receiving the notice, the Secretary of the Tribunal is to inform the parties **12.24** that the reference has been received; the date it was received and the Tribunal's decision on any application for directions.[44]

FSA's statement of case

The FSA is then required to file a statement in support of its action ('statement of **12.25** case') no later than 28 days from the day on which the FSA received the written statement sent to it by the Secretary of the Tribunal. The FSA's statement of case needs to specify the statutory provisions upon which it bases its action, the reasons for the action, set out the matters and facts on which the FSA relies to support its action and specify the date on which the statement of case is filed.[45] The FSA needs to include a list of documents on which it relies for its action and any further material which, in the opinion of the FSA, may undermine the decision to take such action.[46] At the time the statement of case is filed, the FSA must send a copy of the statement of case and the accompanying list to the applicant.[47]

Applicant's reply

The applicant must file a notification to the FSA's statement of case so that it is **12.26** received by the Tribunal no later than 28 days after the date on which the applicant received a copy of the statement of case or the date on which the applicant received a copy of any amended statement of case.[48]

In his reply, the applicant must state the grounds on which he relies in his **12.27** reference; identify all matters and contained in the statement of case which the applicant disputes; state the applicant's reasons for disputing them; and specify the date on which the reply is filed.[49] The reply must be accompanied by a list of documents on which the applicant relies in support of his case.[50] At the same time that he files the reply, the applicant must send a copy to the FSA with the accompanying list of documents.[51]

---

[42] Tribunal Rule 4(6).
[43] Tribunal Rule 4(7).
[44] Tribunal Rule 4(9).
[45] Tribunal Rule 5(1)–(2).
[46] Tribunal Rule 5(3).
[47] Tribunal Rule 5(4).
[48] Tribunal Rule 6(1).
[49] Tribunal Rule 6(2).
[50] Tribunal Rule 6(3).
[51] Tribunal Rule 6(4).

12.28 Given the extent of mutual disclosure which is likely already to have taken place as between the FSA and the referring party, it is unlikely that any fresh material will be relied upon by either side. It is also reasonably clear that if a reference is to be made to the Tribunal, the grounds therefor will have already been identified by the applicant. It is accordingly a slightly curious procedure as described above which does not result in the applicant stating the grounds for challenge properly save via the reply.

Secondary disclosure by the FSA

12.29 The FSA is then required to file a list of any further material which might reasonably be expected to assist the applicant's case as described in the applicant's reply which has not previously been listed by the FSA.[52] This additional list (referred to in the Tribunal Rules as 'secondary disclosure') must be filed so that it is received no later than 14 days after the day on which the FSA received the applicant's reply.[53] At the same time, the FSA must send a copy to the applicant.[54]

Exceptions to disclosure

12.30 There are certain exceptions to disclosure.[55] The lists need not include:

- any document that relates to a case involving another person which was taken into account by the FSA only for the purposes of comparison with other cases;[56]
- any document that is material if the disclosure of such a document is prohibited by the Regulation of Investigatory Powers Act 2000, s 17 in connection with legal proceedings;[57]
- any document in respect of which an application is being made to ask the Tribunal to direct the exclusion of the said document;[58]
- documents which it would not 'be fair [to disclose] having regard to (i) the likely significance of the document to the applicant in relation to the matter referred to the tribunal and (ii) the potential prejudice to the commercial interests of the person other than the applicant which would be caused by disclosure ...';
- protected items.[59]

---

[52] Tribunal Rule 7(1).
[53] Tribunal Rule 7(2).
[54] Tribunal Rule 7(3).
[55] Tribunal Rule 8.
[56] Tribunal Rule 8(1).
[57] Tribunal Rule 8(2).
[58] Tribunal Rule 8(3).
[59] Rule 8(1)–(8).

A party may apply to the Tribunal (without notice) for a direction authorizing the **12.31** exclusion of a document if disclosure is not in the public interest or not fair having regard to the likely significance of the document to the applicant in relation to the matter referred and the potential prejudice to the commercial interests of persons other than the applicant because of disclosure of the document.[60] In deciding such an application, the Tribunal may require the document to be produced to the Tribunal together with a statement of the reasons why its inclusion on the list is not in the public interest or not fair, and invite the other party to make representations respecting said documents and reasons for its potential exclusion.[61] If the Tribunal refuses such an application, it shall direct the party to revise its list to include the document and to file a copy of that as revised and send a copy to the other party.[62]

A party who has filed a list shall, at the request of the other party, provide the other **12.32** party with a copy of any document specified on the list or make any such document available to that party for inspection and copying.[63]

Applications and directions

The Tribunal may give directions to enable the parties to prepare for the hearing **12.33** of the reference, to assist the Tribunal to determine the issues and generally ensure a just, expeditious and economical determination of the reference. The Tribunal may give such directions either upon application or upon its own initiative. Where it gives such directions on its own initiative, it need not give prior notice to the parties of its intention to do so.[64]

The party making an application must send a copy to the other party unless the **12.34** application is made at a pre-hearing review or during the hearing of a reference. In other cases the application needs to be filed. A copy needs to be sent to the other party unless the application is accompanied by the written consent of all parties or is an application without notice as permitted by the Tribunal Rules.[65] If a party objects to the application, the Tribunal shall give the parties an opportunity to make representations.[66]

Directions may be given orally or in writing. Unless the Tribunal directs other- **12.35** wise, notice of any written direction (or refusal to give a direction) shall be given

---

[60] Tribunal Rule 8(4).
[61] Tribunal Rule 8(5).
[62] Tribunal Rule 8(6).
[63] Tribunal Rule 8(7).
[64] Tribunal Rule 9(1)–(3).
[65] Tribunal Rule 9(4).
[66] Tribunal Rule 9(5).

to the parties.[67] Directions containing a requirement may specify a time limit for complying with the requirement and shall include a statement of the consequences of a party's failure to comply with the requirement.[68]

12.36 A person to whom a direction is given may apply to the Tribunal showing good cause why the direction should be set aside. However, before granting such an application, the Tribunal must notify the person who applied for the direction and give them an opportunity to make representations.[69]

12.37 The Chairman of the Tribunal may direct a pre-hearing review.[70] A 'pre-hearing review' is a review of the reference that may be held at any time before the hearing of the reference.[71] If a pre-hearing review is held, the Secretary must give the parties not less than 14 days notice of the time and place of the pre-hearing review.[72]

12.38 Pre-hearing reviews are held before the Chairman. At the pre-hearing review the Chairman shall give all directions necessary or desirable for the just, expeditious and economical conduct of the reference. He should also endeavour to persuade the parties to make all admissions and agreements as they reasonably ought to make in relation to the proceedings.[73]

Particular types of directions

12.39 The Tribunal may give a number of procedural directions, such as:[74]

(a) fixing the time and place of the reference hearing;

(b) providing for oral hearings relating to the reference;

(c) adjourning any oral hearing;

(d) extending time limits (including that for making a reference under the FSMA);

(e) suspending or preventing an FSA notice from taking effect until the reference, and/or an appeal from a Tribunal determination, is concluded;

(f) permitting or requiring any party to provide additional information, supplementary statements, or amended response documents or supplementary statements;

---

[67] Tribunal Rule 9(6).
[68] Tribunal Rule 9(7).
[69] Tribunal Rule 9(8).
[70] Tribunal Rule 9(9).
[71] Tribunal Rule 9(12).
[72] Tribunal Rule 9(10).
[73] Tribunal Rule 9(11).
[74] Tribunal Rule 10. This rule reviews a number of procedural details which it is not within the scope of this discussion to provide.

(g) requiring any to file any document with the Tribunal which it is within the authority of the Tribunal to demand;

(h) requiring statements of issues and facts identifying which are agreed or not agreed;

(i) requiring filing, or agreement between the parties as to filing, of documents for any hearing;

(j) requiring parties to file: lists of witnesses and witness statements of their evidence;

(k) make provisions as to expert witnesses and their evidence;

(l) provide for appointment of experts and distribution of copies of any reports they produce;

(m) provide for the manner of giving any evidence;

(n) provide for the use of any languages other than English;

(o) require that the register include no particulars about the reference;

(p) provide for consolidation of separate references where appropriate.

Filing of subsequent notices

The FSA must file, without delay, a copy of any notice it sends to an applicant in relation to the referred action after the filing of a reference notice.[75]   **12.40**

Summoning witnesses

Regarding witnesses, the Tribunal may summon any person to do the following:[76]   **12.41**

(a) attend and give evidence at a specified time and place;

(b) file any document in his custody or under his control within a specified time; or

(c) both attend and file as described above.

A witness summons shall be sent so as to be received by the person to whom it is addressed not less than seven days before the time of the appearance specified.[77] Every summons must contain a statement of the penalties for refusal or failure to attend or give evidence.[78] Any person summoned who needs to travel more than 16 kilometres from his place of residence shall be entitled to have the expenses of his attendance paid or tendered to him in advance. If a summons is issued at the request of a party, those expenses are to be paid by that party.[79]   **12.42**

---

[75] Tribunal Rule 11.
[76] Tribunal Rule 12(1).
[77] Tribunal Rule 12(3).
[78] Tribunal Rule 12(4).
[79] Tribunal Rule 12(5).

12.43 The Tribunal may exempt a person from filing a document if the Tribunal is satisfied that:[80]

(a) it is a protected item or would be exempted by Rule 8(1) or (2); or

(b) it should not be undisclosed on one of the grounds specified in Rule 8(4).

12.44 To make a determination with respect to the exclusion of any such document, the Tribunal may:[81]

(a) require the document to be produced by the Tribunal;

(b) conduct any hearing in the absence of any parties; and

(c) invite any party to make representations.

If a party to whom a summons is directed applies for such relief, the Tribunal may direct that the summons be set aside or varied.[82]

Preliminary hearing

12.45 The Tribunal may direct that any question of fact or other issue in relation to the reference be determined at a preliminary hearing.[83] If the Tribunal is of the opinion that a determination of any question at a preliminary hearing substantially disposes of the reference, the Tribunal may treat the preliminary hearing as the hearing of the reference and make an order disposing of the reference as the Tribunal sees fit.[84]

12.46 The Tribunal may determine questions without an oral hearing if the parties agree in writing. However, the Tribunal may not, at the same time, dispose of the reference unless the parties agree in writing.[85]

Withdrawal of/unopposed reference

12.47 The applicant may withdraw a reference at any time before the hearing of the reference, without permission, by filing a notice of withdrawal. At the hearing of the reference, the applicant may withdraw with the Tribunal's permission. The Tribunal may determine any reference so withdrawn.[86]

---

[80] Tribunal Rule 12(2).
[81] Tribunal Rule 12(2).
[82] Tribunal Rule 12(6).
[83] Tribunal Rule 13(1).
[84] Tribunal Rule 13(2).
[85] Tribunal Rule 13(3).
[86] Tribunal Rule 14(1).

The FSA may state that it does not oppose the reference or it may withdraw its opposition to a reference:

12.48

(a) at any time before the hearing of the reference, without permission, by filing a notice to that effect; or

(b) at the hearing of the reference, with the Tribunal's permission.[87]

In any case where the FSA makes a statement of non-opposition or withdrawal, or where the applicant does not file a reply within any time limits set under Tribunal Rule 6(1) or Tribunal Rule 10(1)(b), the Tribunal may determine the reference without an oral hearing in accordance with Tribunal Rule 16. However, the Tribunal may not dismiss a reference under such circumstances without notifying the applicant and giving him an opportunity to make representations.[88] In determining any such reference, as described above, the Tribunal may make a costs order pursuant to Tribunal Rule 21.[89]

12.49

References by third parties

Under FSMA ss 392–394, third parties have certain rights with respect to warning notices and decision notices issued by the FSA.[90] Under s 393, if a warning notice identifies a third party other than the person to whom the notice is given and, in the opinion of the FSA that notice is prejudicial to the third party, a copy of the notice must be given to the third party.

12.50

However, the third party need not be given a copy if he has been given a separate warning notice in relation to the same matter or the FSA gives him such a notice at the same time it gives the warning notice which identifies him. Any notice copied to a third party must give the third party a specified reasonable period within which he may make representations to the FSA. This reasonable period may not be less than 28 days.

12.51

A third party may apply for a reference under FSMA, s 393, with certain modifications. Among these is the fact that the FSA must set out information or list materials only if they are information, documents or material that relate to matters referred to the Tribunal either under s 393(9) or s 393(11).

12.52

Similar rules apply with respect to the decision notice.[91] The decision notice must be copied to a third party if it identifies the third party other than the person to

12.53

---

[87] Tribunal Rule 14(2).
[88] Tribunal Rule 14(3).
[89] Tribunal Rule 14(4).
[90] Tribunal Rule 15.
[91] FSMA, s 392.

whom the notice given and in the opinion of the FSA is prejudicial to the third party. If the decision notice was preceded by a warning notice, a copy of the decision notice must (unless it has previously been given) be given to each person to whom warning notice was copied.

12.54 A copy of the decision notice does not have to be given to a third party if he has received a separate decision notice in relation to the same matter or he has been given a copy of the decision notice at the same time as the decision notice which identifies him.[92] However, neither requires a copy of a notice to be given to the third party if the FSA 'considers it impracticable to do so'.

12.55 Under certain circumstances, a person has a right to refer a matter to the Tribunal if he has received a decision notice. If a third party has been mentioned in a decision notice and the decision notice relates to a matter which, in the opinion of the FSA, is prejudicial to third party, then the third party may refer the decision to the Tribunal insofar as it relates to him.[93] A form of legal assistance is available in connection with certain references as discussed in paragraph 12.3.

12.56 When a decision notice is sent to a third person, it must be accompanied by an indication that he has a right to make a reference under s 393(9) and the procedure for the reference.[94] If a person believes that a copy of a decision notice should have been given to him, but was not, or a warning notice, but was not, he may refer the alleged failure to give him the notice to the Tribunal. The Tribunal will review the alleged failure and the decision in question so far as it relates to him or any opinion expressed by the FSA in relation to him.[95]

12.57 Section 394 also relates to a third party in the same way that it applies to a person to whom the notice is given insofar as material which the FSA must disclose relates to a matter which identifies the third party. A copy of a notice given to a third party must be accompanied by a description of the effect of s 394 as it applies to him.[96]

12.58 Any person to whom a warning notice or decision notice is copied must be given a copy of any notice of discontinuance applicable to the warning notice or decision notice in question.[97]

12.59 Under s 394, if the FSA sends a person a relevant notice, it must allow him access to the material on which it replied in making the decision to give the notice; and it must also allow him access to any 'secondary material' which, in the opinion of

---

[92] FSMA, s 393(4)
[93] FSMA, s 393(8)–(11).
[94] FSMA, s 393(10).
[95] FSMA, s 393(11).
[96] FSMA, s 393(13).
[97] FSMA, s 393(14).

the FSA, might undermine the decision to give a notice.[98] The 'secondary material' means material which was considered by the FSA in reaching its decision to issue a notice, or was obtained by the FSA in connection with the matter to which the notice applies but which was not considered in reaching its decision.[99]

However, the FSA does not have to allow a person access to such material if the material is 'excluded material' or it relates to a case involving a person other than the one to whom the notice is given; and it was taken into account by the FSA only for purposes of comparison with other cases.[100] 'Excluded material' means material which:[101]   **12.60**

(a) has been intercepted in obedience to a warrant issued relating to the interception of communications;
(b) indicates that such a warrant has been issued for that material has been intercepted in obedience to such a warrant for; or
(c) is a protected item as defined by FSMA, s 413.

The FSA may refuse the person receiving the notice access to particular material to which it would otherwise have allowed him access[102] if, in its opinion, allowing him access to the material: **12.61**

(a) would not be in the public interest; or
(b) would not be fair, having regard to—
   (i) the likely significance of the material in relation to the matter to which the notice applies; and
   (ii) the prejudicial effect to the commercial interests of a person other than the person receiving the notice which would be caused by the disclosure of the material[103].

If the FSA does not allow the person receiving the notice access to material because it is excluded material consisting of a protected item, it must give that person written notice of the existence of the protected item and the decision not to allow him access to it.[104] If the authority refuses to allow a person receiving notice access to material on the grounds that it is not in the public interest or not fair having regard to the factors described above, it must give him written notice of the refusal and the reasons for it.[105]   **12.62**

---

[98] FSMA, s 394(1).
[99] FSMA, s 394(6).
[100] FSMA, s 394(2).
[101] FSMA, s 394(7).
[102] FSMA, s 394(3).
[103] FSMA, s394(3)
[104] FSMA, s 394(4).
[105] FSMA, s 394(5).

C. Hearings

12.63   The Tribunal can determine a reference without an oral hearing if the parties agree, or if the issue is an application for directions, or if one of the parties does not contest. In such cases, the Tribunal can decide not to publicize the decision.[106] Hearings will in the main take place in public. Although the Rules provide that 'the Tribunal may direct that all or part of a hearing shall be in private' either upon the applicant of all the parties or upon the application of any party if the Tribunal is satisfied that a tribunal in private is necessary having regard to the interests of public order, national security, protection of private lives or 'any unfairness to the applicant or prejudice to the interests of consumers that might result from a hearing in public'.[107]

12.64   In the first decision on this issue[108] by the Tribunal released in July 2002 the Tribunal addressed a request for a private hearing in respect of a decision to withdraw authorization to conduct new insurance business made in relation to Eurolife Assurance Company Limited. The general guidelines there laid down by the Tribunal indicated that to justify an order directing a hearing to be in private. The Tribunal must be satisfied (in particular) in respect of two matters:

(a)   that a hearing in private is *necessary* having regard to any unfairness to the applicant or prejudice to the interests of consumers that *might* result from a hearing in public; and

(b)   that a private hearing would not prejudice the interests of justice.

12.65   If these two conditions are satisfied then the Tribunal has a discretion to hear a reference in private. It was recognized that there is in any event a distinction between 'prejudice' and 'unfairness'. Prejudice is not necessarily to be regarded as 'unfair'. The Tribunal indicated that in the ordinary course of events the risk of damage to a firm's reputation will not in itself amount to unfairness (although in an extreme case it may do so). The Tribunal was nonetheless concerned with 'the risk' of unfairness rather than the reality of its occurrence. A decision as to whether to hear a reference in private will not have regard to the merits of the reference itself. The risk of unfairness arising from incomplete or inaccurate press reporting of proceedings may be overcome by permitting the firm to make a public statement in rebuttal of the FSA's case at an early stage of the proceedings on the morning of the first day of the hearing. This decision, providing as it does valuable

---

[106]   Tribunal Rule 16.
[107]   Rule 17(3).
[108]   *Eurolife Assurance Company Ltd v FSA*, 23 May 2002.

guidance, suggests that the Tribunal is likely to start from a position in which public hearings are the norm.

(1) Representation at hearings

A party can be represented by anyone at a hearing (whether legally qualified or not) unless the Tribunal concludes there are good and sufficient reasons to refuse to permit someone to represent them at a hearing.[109] **12.66**

(2) Procedure at hearings

In general, the Tribunal can conduct hearings in the way it deems most suitable to clarify the issues before it and for the just, expeditious and economical determination of the proceedings. The Tribunal can entertain evidence not admissible in court and whether or not it was available to the FSA. If a party, after sufficient notice, fails to attend a hearing without good reason, in the case of a reference, hear and determine in the party's absence, or in the case of any other hearing give any direction or adjourn.[110] **12.67**

(3) Decisions of the Tribunal

Tribunal decisions are public except in some cases where part or all of the hearings were held in private.[111] **12.68**

(4) Costs

Costs orders, as described at paragraphs 12.14 to 12.21 above, shall be made only after the paying party has had a chance to make representations.[112] **12.69**

(5) Review of the Tribunal's decision

If a Tribunal is satisfied that its previous decision was wrongly made, either on its own initiative or as a result of a party's application, it may set aside the decision.[113] **12.70**

---

[109] Tribunal Rule 18.
[110] Tribunal Rule 19.
[111] Tribunal Rule 20.
[112] Tribunal Rule 21.
[113] Tribunal Rule 22.

(6) Appeals from the Tribunal

12.71   A party to a reference to the Tribunal may, with permission, appeal to the Court of Appeal on a point of law arising from a decision disposing of the reference.[114] Permission may be given by the Tribunal or the Court of Appeal. An application for permission to the Tribunal should be made orally at the hearing after the decision is announced or by way of written application, filed not later than 14 days after the Decision Notice is sent to the party making the application.[115]

12.72   An application to the Tribunal for permission may be decided by the Chairman and will not generally involve an oral hearing specifically to consider the application. The Tribunal must give written reasons for any decision made on the application. Where it is refused, the putative appellant will be directed to renew an application for permission to appeal to the Court of Appeal within 14 days of the refusal. If the Court of Appeal considers the decision of the Tribunal was wrong in law, it may remit the matter to the Tribunal for re-hearing and determination by it or itself make a determination.[116] As indicated, the right to appeal only arises where it is arguable that the decision of the Tribunal was 'wrong in law'. This will involve demonstrating some misapplication of the law relevant to the determination of the reference or it may involve showing that the decision was perverse or unsupported by evidence. In practice, therefore, appeals turning on points of 'evidence' may be dressed up as issues of law. The Administrative Court is used to dealing with such kinds of jurisprudential sartorial subterfuge and in practice the Court of Appeal will be well able to distinguish between a genuine point of law and an issue based on facts/evidence alone.

12.73   This appellate jurisdiction has been recently invoked by the FSA in *Financial Services Authority v Fox Hayes*.[117] The case concerned an appeal by the Authority against a decision of the Tribunal exonerating Fox Hayes, a firm of solicitors, in relation to its approval of certain financial promotions between unauthorized overseas companies and potential buyers of shares in the United Kingdom (the UK). The Authority served a decision notice on the firm, which was an authorized entity, and imposed a penalty for breach of the Conduct of Business Rules. Fox Hayes referred the Authority's notice to the Tribunal, which concluded that it had taken reasonable steps to ensure that the financial promotions were clear, fair and not misleading and that it conducted its business with due skill, care and diligence. On appeal, the Authority contended that Fox Hayes had not acted

---

[114] FSMA, s 137.
[115] Rule 23(2).
[116] FSMA, s 137(3).
[117] [2009] EWCA Civ 76.

as described. The Court of Appeal was accordingly required to determine whether the Tribunal's findings were reasonable and justified.

The purpose of the promotions in this case was to enable overseas companies to **12.74** try to persuade UK investors to buy OTC Bulletin Board shares. The promotion was found to be disguised and was hidden behind the provision of a report on a UK-listed company in which the UK investors already held shares. The UK investors received protection of an escrow account ensuring that they obtained share certificates before paying for it well after the promotion. It was clear that there was an element of financial promotion to persuade UK investors to buy shares which were effectively disguised. The court considered that Fox Hayes had constructive knowledge that this was the case and did not proceed to comply with the COBRs to ensure that the promotion was clear, fair and not misleading. At the beginning of the promotions, there was reason to doubt whether the overseas companies would act reliably and honestly in respect to their UK clients but the firm had not taken the necessary steps to clarify that doubt. The court held that the firm had erred in being involved in the schemes without proper disclosure to the UK investors of the companies' true purpose. The Tribunal had therefore clearly erred in law with its findings in these respects.

Lawrence Collins LJ was particularly critical of the attempt to lend credibility to **12.75** the promotion by making use of a small firm of solicitors:

> It is impossible to resist the conclusion that the promoters were using a small firm without any relevant expertise, and with a senior partner who was (to put it at its lowest) less than scrupulous and who had a substantial personal stake in the success of their efforts, because a substantial firm with real expertise would not have touched this business. They were using the firm not only to purport to comply with FSA rules, but to add an air of respectability to their documents. Fox Hayes knew that the whole purpose of the offer of free research reports was to act as a prelude to the solicitation of purchases of the OTC Bulletin Board shares. Mr Jones should have been alert to the fact that the use of the firm's name facilitated the approaches to potential investors.[118]

(7) Miscellaneous rules

Tribunal Rules 26–31 deal with various issues such as powers of the Tribunal and **12.76** the Chairman, failures to comply, irregularities, proof of documents and sending of notices.

---

[118] *Ibid.*, para. 63.

13

CRIMINAL LAW

A. Background

13.01 The FSMA market abuse regime has two relationships to criminal law. First, the market abuse regime was not intended to replace existing criminal laws but conceived to work alongside them—while covering a wider range of activities. Indeed, the FSA is empowered to institute criminal proceedings for a range of offences under FSMA and in respect of certain other offences arising under related legislation. Principally these comprise:

- carrying on a regulated activity without authorization or exemption;[1]
- making false claims to authorization or exemption;[2]
- breaching the restrictions on financial promotions;[3]
- failing to cooperate with and/or the provision of false information to FSA investigators;[4]
- failing to comply with provisions about control over authorized persons;[5]
- making false claims to be exempt from the general prohibition as a result of Part XX of the Act;[6]

---

[1] FSMA, s 23.
[2] FSMA, s 24.
[3] FSMA, s 25.
[4] FSMA, s 117.
[5] FSMA, s 191.
[6] FSMA, s 333.

- providing false or misleading information to an auditor or actuary;[7]
- disclosing confidential information in breach of the statutory restriction;[8]
- making false and misleading statements and engaging in misleading practices;[9]
- misleading the FSA;[10]
- breaching prescribed regulations relating to money laundering, insider dealing under Part V of the Criminal Justice Act 1993;[11]
- contraventions in relation to the exercise of treaty rights.[12]

The market abuse regime sits within this broad regulatory landscape. The offences mentioned above are a necessary part of the UK Government's regulation of the financial market and assist in securing an orderly regime of regulation. We consider below two particular criminal sanctions that specifically relate to market abuse.

13.02   Second, although this was not originally intended, the market abuse prohibitions are *part* of criminal law. Although the market abuse regime was originally created to provide the FSA with a flexible administrative remedy for market misconduct, the range of available enforcement options makes it legally impossible not to treat at least some market abuse cases as criminal proceedings.

B. Relation to Existing Criminal Law

13.03   In the UK, the market abuse prohibitions relate principally to two existing criminal offences. First, the Criminal Justice Act makes 'insider dealing' an offence. Under s 52 of that Act, a person may be found guilty of insider dealing if he is an individual who has 'inside information', and deals in securities that are 'price-affected' by the information, encourages another person to deal in 'price-affected' securities or discloses inside information to another person otherwise than in the proper performance of the functions of his employment, office or profession. Second, under FSMA, s 397 (replacing the old FS Act, s 47), a person is guilty of an offence who induces or discourages investment decisions by:

- knowingly or recklessly misleading false or deceptive statements; or
- concealment of material facts; or

---

[7]   FSMA, s 346.
[8]   FSMA, s 352.
[9]   FSMA, s 397.
[10]   FSMA, s 398.
[11]   FSMA, s 402.
[12]   FSMA, Sch. 4, para. 6.

- creating a false or misleading impression of the market price or value of any investment.

Each of these offences carries potential penalties of fines or imprisonment of up to seven years. However, the authorities have not found it easy to apply these sanctions because of the difficulty of proving criminal offences. First, a formal prosecution must be commenced. Second, the defendant must be proved to have committed the offence with 'criminal intent'. Finally, the offence must be proved by evidence which establishes the defendant's guilt 'beyond a reasonable doubt'. In other words, proving criminal offences requires meeting a very high standard. As a result, there have been very few successful criminal prosecutions under these statutes. **13.04**

With the implementation of the Directive in the UK, these prohibitions against criminal insider dealing and market manipulation will continue to be in effect. Prior to the original implementation of the FSMA, it was thought that the difficulties with the above criminal provisions diminished their regulatory usefulness. It was therefore thought that a new civil framework should be included in the FSMA to complement the above criminal provisions. A significant amount of market damaging did not need the full sanction of criminal law. It was decided that the criminal sanctions would remain in place. However, to achieve full protection for the financial markets, a 'civil' regime was created to extend the FSMA's regulation to all markets. It was feared that if the Government did not create this flexible regime the damage market abuse did to financial markets could damage the UK economy as a whole.[13] **13.05**

One of the principal aims of the FSMA market abuse regime is to provide the FSA with a more flexible administrative remedy for market disruption which required a lower standard of proof to be applied. The combination of criminal and administrative remedies for market abuse gave the FSA two methods to investigate and punish these offences: **13.06**

1. bringing a criminal prosecution (requiring a criminal standard of proof, a jury trial and holding up the possibility of a prison sentence); and
2. the civil remedies under the FSMA.

This gives the FSA far more flexibility in dealing with market abuse offences than it has had in the past. In the first place, it was not possible to punish firms for the criminal offence of insider dealing. Only individuals could be held accountable for criminal insider dealing. Under the civil market abuse provisions, firms can be disciplined. In addition, the FSA is now in a position to bring **13.07**

---

[13] *FSA Feedback Statement on responses to Consultation Paper 10: Market Abuse*, March 1999, p. 2, paras. 6–9.

criminal prosecutions. In the past, only the Serious Fraud Office or the Crown Prosecution Service had such powers. Now violations of the criminal market abuse provisions can be investigated and prosecuted by the FSA. Civil market abuse investigations can be brought only by the FSA.

C. Proceedings by the FSA

(1) Market abuse

13.08 In general terms, FSA market abuse investigations will start with a Notice of Appointment of Investigators. The Notice states who is under investigation, the legislative provisions that authorize the appointment of the investigators and the conduct which is being investigated.[14] At this point, it is not clear whether, when the investigation is concluded, the FSA will be pursuing a criminal prosecution or a civil enforcement case. This is of course different from an SFO or police investigation. Those will always be criminal. In certain cases, investigations may be pursued by both simultaneously but there are guidelines designed to encourage cooperation and coordination of the investigations between the different authorities pursuing firms suspected of market abuse.

(2) Criminal proceedings

13.09 The FSA has described its policy for deciding whether to bring a criminal prosecution as follows:

> It is our policy to pursue through the criminal justice system all those cases where a criminal prosecution is appropriate. These will be cases where:
> - there is enough evidence to provide a realistic prospect of convicting the defendant; and
> - a criminal prosecution is in the public interest, considering the seriousness of the offence and the circumstances surrounding it.[15]

13.10 The FSA *Handbook* states that decisions to begin criminal prosecutions authorized by the FSMA are to be made by the Chairman of the FSA's Regulatory Decisions Committee.[16]

13.11 In February 2004, the FSA commenced its first criminal prosecution for market abuse against three former directors of AIT, a company based in

---

[14] For more details on market abuse enforcement procedure, see Chapter 9, above.
[15] FSA, Enforcing the Code of Market Conduct (23 March 2005).
[16] Unless the Chairman is unavailable: FSA *Handbook*, DEC 1.1.3 G and DEC 4.1.6 G. Further details related to the FSA policy and procedure in prosecuting criminal cases are found in Chapter 12, above, and in FSA *Handbook*, EG 12.

Henley-on-Thames. The charges against the directors Rigby, Bailey and Rowley related to allegedly misleading statements made in May 2002 that AIT's profits would meet forecasts of £6.7 m. The statements were said to be false in that the projected profits depended on the existence of certain lucrative contracts which did not in fact exist at the date the statements were made. The charges were framed as violations of FSMA, ss 397(1)(a) and (1)(c), that is, that the directors had made statements they knew to be false or alternatively had been reckless as to the accuracy of the forecasts made. Rigby and Bailey were convicted by a jury of recklessly making false statements; Rowley was acquitted of both allegations. On 7 October 2005 Rigby was sentenced to a term of imprisonment of three and a half years and disqualified from acting as a company director for six years; Bailey received a custodial sentence of two years and was disqualified from being a company director for four years. On 20 December 2005 these sentences of imprisonment were reduced by the Court of Appeal to 18 months and nine months respectively.

D. Compatibility with the Human Rights Act 1998

One awkward issue which has arisen in recent years for government bodies, including regulators like the FSA, was whether the 'civil penalties' that they were authorized to invoke are consistent with the European Convention for the Protection of Human Rights and Fundamental Freedoms 1950 (ECHR). In the UK, the ECHR was brought into effect by the Human Rights Act 1998 (HRA), which came into effect on 2 October 2000.   **13.12**

Under the HRA, UK courts are required to take into account judgments by the European Court of Human Rights and to interpret UK legislation consistently with the ECHR. It is also unlawful under the HRA for public bodies to act inconsistently with the ECHR unless required to do so by domestic law.[17]   **13.13**

Since the passage of the HRA the area which has been subject to the most scrutiny by the courts is the ECHR's guarantee of the right to a fair trial. Regulatory authorities such as the FSA are certainly public authorities under the HRA. Therefore they must not act in a manner inconsistent with the greater protections which the ECHR grants to those facing criminal allegations as opposed to those facing civil disciplinary proceedings. For example, those facing criminal penalties are protected against self-incrimination and legal aid is to be made available to them.   **13.14**

In two cases in 2001, the Court of Appeal considered what the standards should be in determining whether an apparently 'civil' disciplinary proceeding brought   **13.15**

---

[17] HRA, s 6.

by a public body was in fact 'criminal' and therefore subject to the higher level of protection afforded to those accused of criminal offences. In the case of *R (on the application of Fleurose) v Securities and Futures Authority Ltd*,[18] the Court of Appeal upheld an administrative court decision that SFA disciplinary proceedings were not infringements of the right of the appellant to a fair trial under Article 6 of the ECHR. In that case, the Court of Appeal examined three basic criteria to determine whether the allegation should be classified as 'criminal' or 'civil'. The first test is how domestic law classifies the allegation. The second is whether the allegation is of a civil or criminal 'nature' and the third is the potential severity of the penalty. Where the application of the offence is to a specific group (that is, members of the SFA) rather than to the general public, the matter should not usually be classified as criminal unless there is a threat of imprisonment.

13.16 In *Fleurose*, the court concluded that members of the SFA were a specific group and that the prospect of an unlimited fine was not enough, by itself, to make the allegation a criminal charge. The court also noted that no objection had been raised by the appellant either at the disciplinary or appeals tribunal hearings and that the information that the appellant had given to the London Stock Exchange was done without the compulsion of a legal obligation.

13.17 About six months later the Court of Appeal considered an appeal by the Customs & Excise Commissioners from the decision of the VAT Duties Tribunal, Stephen Oliver QC, Chairman ('the Tribunal'). In that case, *Han and Yau v Customs & Excise Commissioners*,[19] the Tribunal had found that penalties for the alleged dishonest evasion of tax gave rise to criminal charges within the meaning of Article 6(1) of the ECHR and that therefore the person alleged to be guilty of such evasion was entitled to certain rights as provided in Article 6(3) of the ECHR.

13.18 Applying the three basic criteria for judging whether a person is the subject of a 'criminal charge' the court concluded that although under UK domestic law the penalty was characterized as 'civil', that categorization was not decisive. Moving on to the second test, the court concluded that the nature of the penalty was designed to punish and deter members of the public generally with respect to fraud or dishonest conduct. Noting that with respect to this kind of conduct, the Commissioners had discretion as to whether to impose a civil penalty or to bring a criminal prosecution, the conduct being investigated seemed to be by its nature more 'criminal' than 'civil'. Regarding the third test, the conclusion was that the penalty was substantial in that its purpose was to punish or deter the 'criminal' type of conduct in question and therefore it was not necessary that the taxpayer be subject to imprisonment for the allegation to be characterized

---

[18] [2001] ALL ER (D) 361 (Dec).
[19] [2001] 1 WLR 2253.

as criminal. Therefore the Court of Appeal upheld the finding of the Tribunal that the penalties for alleged dishonest evasion of tax were in the nature of criminal charges.

A similar analysis was applied by the High Court of Justiciary in its decision in **13.19** *King v Walden*,[20] in which it was found that penalties for fraudulent or negligent delivery of incorrect tax returns is a 'criminal' charge under the ECHR. The judge justified his findings for the following reasons:

1. the penalty was intended to punish and deter defaulting taxpayers;
2. the fine can be very large;
3. the fine is not related to administrative or other costs incurred by dealing with the taxpayer;
4. the amount of the fine can be mitigated if the taxpayer is found less culpable. Mitigation was found to be an element of a criminal rather than a civil charge.

Comparing the above analysis to the market abuse penalties available to the FSA, **13.20** there are a number of factors which point towards a finding that such penalties are also of a 'criminal' rather than a 'civil' nature. First, although the market abuse penalties are characterized as 'civil', the Court of Appeal has recognized that this characterization is not determinative. Second, the penalties can include an 'unlimited' fine. That leaves little doubt that the penalties can be very substantial indeed.

Third, the nature of the penalty leaves little doubt that its purpose is to punish and **13.21** deter market abusers. Consequently, it is not determinative that the alleged market abusers are not facing imprisonment. Fourth, there are substantial parallels between 'criminal' market abuse charges under the FSMA, s 397 and under the Insider Dealing Provisions of the Criminal Justice Act 1993 and the market abuse regime of the FSMA. Comparing these similarities, it is not difficult to draw a conclusion that the FSA has significant discretion as to whether to bring civil or criminal proceedings based on precisely the same market behaviour. The fact that what originate as 'civil' administrative enquiries may turn into 'criminal' proceedings seems to indicate that those being investigated should be afforded the protections available to those subject to criminal allegations.

Fifth, those accused of market abuse are permitted to argue 'mitigation' to reduce **13.22** penalties imposed on them by bringing in such factors as evidence that they had no intention to permit abuse, or that they took reasonable care to avoid the commission of market abuse. This use of mitigation seems to argue that it is 'criminal'-type behaviour that is under consideration, and not 'civil'. Sixth, the size of the

---

[20] [2001] STC 822.

penalty is not related to any specific administrative costs or provable market losses. It is related purely to the FSA's judgment as to how severely the market abuse should be punished.

13.23 Finally, the FSMA market abuse regime is not directed solely against persons regulated by the FSMA:

> The Code affects everyone who participates in, or whose conduct affects, the UK's financial markets. It makes no difference whether or not the person is regulated by the FSA, or based in the UK or overseas, or whether they are professional or retail investors.[21]

13.24 Consequently, the market abuse penalties are not directed only against a specific group, as was true in the *Fleurose* case, above. The above factors made it almost certain that the Financial Services and Markets Tribunal ('the Tribunal') and the courts would conclude that market abuse allegations could constitute 'criminal' cases.[22]

13.25 This issue was considered by the Tribunal in its 29 March 2005 decision in the appeal of *Arif Mohammed* against an FSA decision finding Mr Mohammed guilty of market abuse by trading shares while in possession of confidential information by nature of his employment as an audit manager with PricewaterhouseCoopers. This was the first market abuse case to be appealed to the Tribunal.[23] Arif Mohammed asserted that market abuse is similar to a criminal charge and that the FSA should be required to prove its case beyond reasonable doubt. The FSA argued that, in line with previous Tribunal decisions (in non-market abuse cases) the burden should operate on a 'sliding scale' requiring that the more serious the case, the more evidence should be required to prove it.[24]

13.26 On this issue, the Tribunal agreed with the FSA that a 'sliding scale' should be applied. However, they noted that in this case the allegations and potential penalties were serious enough that, as a practical matter, the Tribunal's application of a sliding scale would probably make no difference.[25] A year later the Tribunal was invited again to consider the proper characterization of market abuse proceedings in *Paul Davidson and Ashley Tatham v FSA*.[26] It concluded that although not criminal under domestic law, the penalties for market abuse were criminal in character

---

[21] FSA, 'Why market abuse could cost you money—the Code of Market Conduct is here to help protect you', December 2001.

[22] And perhaps one might also note, in passing, that the President of the Financial Services Markets Tribunal is the very same Stephen Oliver QC who was president of the VAT Tribunal in the *Han & Yaw* case.

[23] See further discussion of this case in Chapter 14, below.

[24] Citing *Hoodless and Blackwell v FSA*, FS & M Tribunal, 3 October 2003, at [21]; *Legal & General Assurance Soc Ltd v FSA*, FS & M Tribunal, January 2005, at [19].

[25] *Arif Mohammed*, p. 3, lines 6–10.

[26] FSMT Case 031, 16 May 2006.

for the purposes of the ECHR. This conclusion did not, however, require that the standard of proof be the criminal one. There was nothing in Article 6 to stipulate that proof beyond reasonable doubt was a prerequisite to any proceedings for market abuse being ECHR-compliant. Three months later the FSA attempted to persuade the Tribunal in *James Parker v FSA*[27] to treat the regime as 'civil'. The attempt was unsuccessful. It must be regarded now as settled that defendants to proceedings for market abuse are accordingly entitled to the protective measures secured by Article 8 of the ECHR as they are expressed to apply to criminal proceedings.

The Government was aware of concerns about the impact of the ECHR on the FSMA since the Act was first published as a draft Bill in July 1998. In November 1998 an initial Committee of both Houses of Parliament was set up to review the Bill. The proposed market abuse provisions were always a prominent part of the scrutiny and debate around the Bill. The Joint Committee published its first report on 29 April and its Second Report on 2 June. Its discussion of market abuse in the first report focused heavily on the relationship between the proposed market abuse regime and existing criminal offences. The first point they made was that the regime did not focus on a specific or restricted class of persons. The regime was to apply to everyone whether authorized or not and whether they were in the UK or not. **13.27**

The Committee recognized that the classification of the market abuse regime as civil under domestic law was not determinative for the ECHR and, therefore, it was likely to be regarded as criminal. This was based on analysis of the nature and scope of the regime and the severity of the penalties. At this early stage it was recognized that the special safeguards provided by Article 6 of the ECHR for criminal charges would apply with respect to the market abuse regime. The Committee urged the Government to publish its reviews as to whether market abuse was civil or criminal and pointed out that the necessary safeguards did not appear in the original draft Bill. **13.28**

In their Second Report, the Joint Committee again focused on the issue of whether market abuse allegations were criminal allegations for ECHR purposes. Again they pointed out that the implications of this were that market abuse proceedings would require an extra set of safeguards including: **13.29**

1. the privilege against self-incrimination;
2. a right to legal aid where appropriate; and
3. a high degree of clarity as to which behaviour is forbidden.

---

[27] FSMT Case 037, 18 August 2006

13.30 The Committee found that the Bill was lacking in these respects. They argued that this could leave market abuse cases open to challenge in the courts and could result in the legislation being declared incompatible with the ECHR. They urged the Government to publish its views as soon as possible.

13.31 On 19 May 1999, the Government did so. The Government's position was that it believed that the courts would treat market abuse allegations as civil proceedings under the ECHR. However, the Government recognized that proceedings where a fine might be imposed might be classified as criminal. Therefore, the Government decided to include additional safeguards in market abuse investigations including:

1. a provision that compelled statements will not be able to be used against the person who made them;[28]
2. that subsidized legal assistance would be available to the accused where appropriate;[29] and
3. that the Government would provide greater certainty as to what behaviour would constitute market abuse.

13.32 On 19 May 1999, the Joint Committee took testimony from Patricia Hewitt MP, then Economic Secretary to the Treasury. Although Patricia Hewitt maintained that she believed that market abuse would be regarded as a civil offence, she recognized that there were two characteristics of the regime which made it uncertain whether the courts would rule that the criminal protections required by the ECHR should apply to market abuse. The first characteristic was the fact that the market abuse regime covered all market participants and not just that restricted group of members of the regulated community. The second was that there were significant similarities between behaviour covered by the regime and that covered by the criminal offences of insider dealing and market manipulation.[30]

13.33 Changes were made to the draft legislation and to the FSA enforcement powers to provide what it believed to be compliance with the criminal allegation protections provided for in the ECHR. A scheme to provide legal assistance before the Tribunal was set out in FSMA, ss 134–136. Under s 134, the Lord Chancellor was given the power to promulgate regulations establishing a scheme providing legal assistance before the Tribunal. Only individuals are eligible for legal assistance. To be eligible, an individual must have a matter referred to the Tribunal. Under s 135, certain criteria for eligibility were set out.

---

[28] FSMA, s 174(2).
[29] FSMA, s 134(1).
[30] Minutes of Evidence taken before the Joint Committee on Financial Services and Markets, Wednesday 19 May 1999, Question 1, p. 8.

Under s 136 the FSA is required to pay to the Lord Chancellor sums covering the **13.34** anticipated or actual cost of legal assistance provided under the scheme. In order to find the money to do that, the FSA is required to obtain payments from authorized persons. There are certain provisions for the Lord Chancellor to repay any excess to the FSA. The FSA is required to distribute this fund to authorized persons or others in certain circumstances. Section 134 gives the Lord Chancellor the power to promulgate regulations establishing the legal assistance scheme. It sets out who was eligible for the scheme. This is limited to individuals (as opposed to companies) who have had an FSA decision imposing a penalty for market abuse, that the decision has been referred to the Tribunal and that it meets other eligibility criteria to be established under s 135. Section 135 gives examples of the types of provisions the Lord Chancellor should make respecting legal assistance. Examples of these provisions are:

• the form that the legal assistance may take;
• the persons that may be hired to provide the assistance;
• what the eligibility criteria will be; and
• procedure as to how to make an application, to whom, and what is required once assistance is granted.

Section 136 sets out how the legal assistance scheme will be funded. It is not the **13.35** ordinary kind of legal aid; it is a wholly independent scheme which is to be paid for by charges to authorized persons. It is up to the Lord Chancellor to determine the potential or actual cost of the legal assistance scheme. The FSA will have responsibility for collecting the appropriate charges from authorized persons and paying them to the Ministry of Justice. The money collected is to be paid into the Consolidated Fund. The costs of administering the scheme will be paid out of the operating costs of the Tribunal. If, in any year, the amount paid to the Lord Chancellor exceeds the cost of the legal assistance scheme the Lord Chancellor must either repay the excess to the FSA or take the excess into account when he makes his next cost determination by reducing the amount which the FSA has to charge authorized persons during the next year. If any excess is repaid to the FSA, it has the discretion to either distribute the excess among the authorized persons from whom charges were originally collected to offset the excess against further charges or to partly distribute and partly offset. If the FSA considers it inappropriate to deal with the excess in this way, it can apply to the Lord Chancellor for permission to use the excess in some other appropriate way.

Second, in order to avoid the use of compelled testimony in enforcement proceed- **13.36** ings, the FSA decided to divide its Supervision and Enforcement functions so they are handled totally independently with respect to disciplinary action. Forums are to be notified when a case is passed from the Supervision to the Enforcement Department. In the first instance, an Enforcement Committee will determine whether there is a case to answer. It will not impose a final decision, unless the forum/individual accepts the action proposed by the FSA. As part of this decision making, the person subject to investigation may make both written and oral submissions and early settlement negotiations would be attempted. If settlement negotiations fail, independent mediation will be used. No member of the Enforcement Committee (apart from the Chairman) is to be employed by the FSA. The Committee will operate with complete independence from the FSA as a regulatory body and will not be involved in establishing evidence on which it bases its decisions.

E. Conclusions

13.37   In addition to its powers to bring regulatory proceedings for market abuse, the FSA further has the power to institute criminal prosecutions both for FSMA market abuse style violations (for example, in respect of misleading statements and practices under s 397) and for violations of certain other statutes (for example, insider dealing under the Criminal Justice Act 1993). This puts the FSA in the powerful position of being the regulator, the prosecutor, and (in the first instance) the judge of market misconduct.

13.38   In order to permit the FSA to fill all these roles, and retain the flexibility it needs to be an effective market regulator, a complex 'sliding scale' has been adopted to judge which protections an alleged 'market abuser' should be allowed to invoke.[31] What are the gradations on this scale, and when do they change the position of the accused from 'civil' to 'criminal' defendant? That question will probably only be answered over time through decisions of the Tribunal and the courts.

---

[31] See discussion of *Arif Mohammed* appeal, above, and in Chapter 14, below.

14

MARKET ABUSE CASES

A. Introduction

Market abuse, and the need to control it, did not suddenly come into existence **14.01** with the FSMA. The FSA, and its predecessor organizations, have been struggling to control disruptive market behaviour since financial markets first made their appearance in England.[1] Ever since the FSMA came into effect, there has considerable anticipation as to how the FSA will interpret and enforce the sections of the FSMA relating to market abuse. Now, the implementation of the Market Abuse Directive raises concerns as to how the FSA's interpretation and enforcement will change.

The UK implementation of the Directive has indeed changed the breadth of the **14.02** FSA's jurisdiction with respect to whom and which activities are reached by the mandate to enforce sanctions against market abuse. As discussed in Chapter 2, the FSA's interpretation of what constitutes market abuse because of the implementation of the Directive is likely to be quite flexible. Further, one should keep

---

[1] The original author gives a number of early examples of market misbehaviour in an earlier book: *Building the Global Market: a Four Thousand Year History of Derivatives* (Kluwer Law International, London, 2000).

in mind that the most potent penalties that the FSA can impose on a party they believe to have engaged in improper market behaviour will continue to exist, largely unchanged, regardless of any changes brought about by the Market Abuse Directive. These include the FSA's power to bar a party from any financial services business for violation of its 'High Level Standards' including Principles for Business which require:

1. integrity;
2. skill, care and diligence;
3. proper management and control;
4. financial prudence;
5. proper market conduct;
6. regard for customers' interests;
7. proper communications with clients;
8. fair management of conflicts of interest;
9. regard for customers' trust;
10. protection of client's assets; and
11. open and cooperative relationships with regulators.[2]

14.03 Since early 2006, the FSA has repeatedly emphasized that it is moving its enforcement policy away from 'rule-based' regulation towards 'principles-based' regulation. What this has meant, in practice, is that in situations where the FSA believes that market misconduct has occurred, they are relying less on specific regulations, such as the market abuse regime, and more on the above Principles to impose penalties for misconduct. It remains to be seen, however, whether the FSA's expressed commitment to principles-based enforcement survives the impetus of the global crash for a return to rules-based regulation.[3]

14.04 The Principles approach offers the FSA a number of advantages. First, the Principles must be complied with by every FSA-regulated firm. Second, the standard for proving non-compliance is very low when compared with the specific requirements of proving market abuse. Third, the scope of definition of what is covered by the Principles is largely within the FSA's subjective control. Fourth, the Principles are general enough to cover any kind of market misconduct: past, present or future.

14.05 An example of punishing market abuse by reference to breaches of the High Level Principles is the £900,000 penalty imposed by the FSA in April 2003 on *ABN AMRO Equities (UK) Limited*.[4] The proceedings concerned a failure to comply

---

[2] FSA *Handbook*, PRIN 2, 2.1.1 R.
[3] A move back to a hard-edged rules-based regime is suggested by the Turner Review—A regulatory response to the global banking crisis (FSA, March 2009).
[4] *FSA v ABN AMRO Equities (UK) Ltd* (Final Notice), 15 April 2003.

with Rule 7.23A(3) of the Rules of the Securities and Futures Authority (which obliged SFA members to comply with, *inter alia*, provisions made under the Financial Services Act 1986). The High Level Principles concerned were Principle 3, which stated that 'a firm should observe high standards of market conduct ...' and Principle 9, which required that 'a firm should organise and control its internal affairs in a responsible manner ... [and] ... should have adequate arrangements to ensure [staff] are suitable, adequately trained and properly supervised, and that it has well-defined compliance procedures'.

In this instance, on 30 April 1998 and between 28 and 30 September and 16 and **14.06**
23 October 1998, these High Level Principles were breached by ABN AMRO in relation to the equity trading of three of its traders: the joint head of the UK Equity Trading Desk, a senior trader on the Cross-Border Equity Trading Desk, and a director of UK Equities. In particular, the joint Head of Trading had accepted and executed trading instructions on behalf of a customer in circumstances where he had a strong reason to suspect that those instructions were given to pursue an improper strategy to move the price of Carlton Communications plc to close higher; on 30 September 1998 the senior Cross-Border trader likewise accepted and acted on improper instructions on behalf of a customer to move the price of Volkswagen AG and Metro AG to close higher; on two separate occasions in September and October 1998 one of the directors of UK Equities accepted and executed improper instructions on behalf of another customer to move the price of British Biotech plc to close higher.

The FSA relied on earlier Guidance issued by the Securities and Investments **14.07**
Board,[5] which identified that: 'There are two situations in which a trade effected for a customer may be an improper trade. The first is where the firm has its own improper purpose in effecting the trade. The second is where the firm is taken to share the improper purpose of its customer, either because it is aware of that improper purpose or because it would have been, if it had not closed its eyes to it'.

The improper trading conduct resulted in the distortion of share prices for Carlton **14.08**
and British Biotech over a number of days in September and October 1998. Distortion of share prices for Metro and Volkswagen was avoided because of the auction system for calculating closing prices on the German exchange. In nonetheless imposing a substantial financial penalty, the FSA stated:[6] 'The main purpose of imposing a financial penalty is to promote high standards of regulatory conduct (which includes expressing condemnation of the wrongdoing) by deterring firms who have breached regulatory requirements from committing further

---

[5] Guidance Release 1/93 on *Proper Trades in Relation to On-Exchange Derivatives.*
[6] *FSA v ABN AMRO Equities (UK) Ltd* (Final Notice), 15 April 2003.

breaches, helping to deter others from committing contraventions and demonstrating generally to firms the benefits of compliant behaviour'.

14.09   A limit on application of the Principles is the fact that they apply only to regulated firms.[7] The market abuse regime has no such limitation. In considering these issues it is useful to review and comment on the market abuse decisions which the FSA has issued since the introduction of the FSMA market abuse regime, and how some of those decisions have been viewed by the Tribunal.

B. FSA Decisions

(1) Robert Middlemiss

14.10   On 10 February 2004, the FSA announced that it had fined Robert Middlemiss £15,000 for market abuse.[8] The FSA alleged the following. Mr Middlemiss was the Company Secretary at Profile Media Group (PMG).[9] The FSA alleged that he became aware, in April 2002, that PMG's revenues were probably going to be significantly below expectations.[10] Before this information was made public, Mr. Middlemiss sold some of his own shares, avoiding the loss of over £6,800.[11]

14.11   The FSA found that Mr Middlemiss had abused his position of trust for his own personal financial gain. The FSA found this to be a violation of the FSMA, s 118(2)(a) (as it existed at the time in question).[12] The FSA considered that a reasonable person who regularly dealt on the Alternative Investment Market would regard Mr Middlemiss' behaviour as a failure to observe the standard of behaviour reasonably to be expected of any investor and certainly that of a chartered accountant employed as Company Secretary of an AIM-listed company. Being in such a position, the FSA concluded that Mr Middlemiss was well aware of the sensitivity of the information available to him and the impropriety of exploiting that information to his own advantage before it had been made available to investors in accordance with PMG's obligation under the AIM Rules. The Code indicated that where market users rely on the timely dissemination of relevant information, those who possess relevant information ahead of its general dissemination should refrain from acting on that information.[13] Confidence in such markets depends in part on market users' confidence that they can deal with

---

[7] FSA *Handbook*, PRIN 3, 3.1.1 R.
[8] FSA, Final Notice to Robert Middlemiss, 10 February 2004.
[9] *Middlemiss* Notice, para. 12.
[10] *Middlemiss* Notice, paras. 20–21.
[11] *Middlemiss* Notice, paras. 28 and 46.
[12] *Middlemiss* Notice, paras. 32–43.
[13] MAR 1.4.3E.

each other on the basis that they have equal, simultaneous access to information that is required to be disclosed. The FSA considered the imposition of a penalty of £20,000 appropriate but reduced it to £15,000 to take into account Mr Middlemiss' financial resources and personal circumstances.

(2) Arif Mohammed

By a Decision Notice dated 30 April 2004, the FSA Regulatory Decisions Committee imposed a penalty of £10,000 on Mr Mohammed for committing market abuse under FSMA, s 118 by engaging in behaviour that constituted misuse of information.[14] The FSA alleged the following. Mr Mohammed was an audit manager employed by PricewaterhouseCoopers. In the course of that employment he was involved in providing accounting services to a company called Delta plc. The FSA found that, based on information he had obtained during his employment about the proposed sale of the electrical division of Delta, he had purchased shares in Delta shortly before the sale was announced in late 2002. Immediately after the announcement, he had sold the shares gaining a profit of over £3,500.

14.12

The FSA concluded that Mr Mohammed purchased the shares while in possession of confidential information that a sale of a substantial portion of Delta's business was likely to be announced shortly, and that such conduct was market abuse. Mr Mohammed referred that decision to the Financial Services and Markets Tribunal ('the Tribunal') challenging the FSA's decision on a number of grounds. On 29 March 2005, the Tribunal issued a decision unanimously upholding the FSA's decision. The Tribunal's decision is discussed in the 'Tribunal' section of this chapter, below.

14.13

(3) Peter Bracken

In July 2004, the FSA fined Peter Bracken, former head of communications of the Whitehead Mann Group plc (WMG) £15,000 for market abuse.[15] The FSA alleged the following. In September 2002, Mr Bracken learned that WMG would probably release a negative trading statement.[16] Mr Bracken thereafter placed an order to sell the company's shares short.[17] When the negative statement was subsequently made, Mr Bracken closed out his short position making a profit

14.14

---

[14] FSA, Decision Notice to Arif Mohammed, 30 April 2004.
[15] FSA, Final Notice to Peter Bracken, 7 July 2004.
[16] *Bracken* Notice, paras. 10–17 and 24–27.
[17] *Bracken* Notice, paras. 18–21.

of over £2,400.[18] On a subsequent occasion in November 2002, Mr Bracken also profited from short positions he took prior to the release of information which he believed would result in the decline of the company's share price. He realized an additional profit on the second transaction.[19]

14.15   Again, the FSA found such behaviour to be misuse of information in a violation of FSMA, s 118(2)(a).[20] In Bracken's case, the FSA imposed a fine of £15,000. The FSA apparently felt that the seriousness of the case was exacerbated by the fact that Bracken, as head of communications for a publicly listed company, was trusted with highly sensitive information. The FSA concluded he had deliberately abused that trust.[21] In particular the FSA observed:

> The fact that Mr Bracken's trading was contrary to Whitehead Mann's Share Dealing Code … does not of itself amount to market abuse. However, the FSA considers that Mr Bracken's failure to seek permission for his trading prior to the First Announcement and the Second Announcement, his failure to use Whitehead Mann's designated brokers, and the fact that his trading in November 2002 occurred during a close period, all provide evidence that Mr Bracken's trading was based on his misuse of relevant information and therefore amounted to abusive behaviour.

(4) Michael Thomas Davies

14.16   On 28 July 2004 the FSA issued a fine for market abuse relating to shares traded on OFEX (a UK market for trading shares that are not traded on the London Stock Exchange).[22] Essentially, the FSA found that Mr Davies, at relevant times the Group Financial Controller of Berkeley Morgan Group plc (BMG), had misused non-public information that he gained during his employment with BMG.[23]

14.17   The FSA alleged as follows. Mr Davies had helped to prepare the interim results which BMG was due to announce for the six months ended 31 October 2003. Thinking that the announcement would be followed by a price rise, Mr Davies placed an order with his broker to purchase BMG shares prior to the announcement. Following the announcement, the share price rose by almost 30 per cent resulting in a net profit for Mr Davies.[24]

14.18   The FSA found that Mr Davies was dealing on the basis of non-public information which a regular user of the market would be likely to regard as relevant when deciding the terms of transactions and which would ordinarily be disclosed to the market.

---

[18] *Bracken* Notice, paras. 22–23.
[19] *Bracken* Notice, paras. 28–34.
[20] *Bracken* Notice, paras. 41–53.
[21] *Bracken* Notice, paras. 54–58.
[22] FSA, Final Notice to Michael Thomas Davies, 28 July 2004.
[23] *Davies* Notice, paras. 1 and 11.
[24] *Davies* Notice, paras. 12–19.

This was held to be a violation of FSMA, s 118(2)(a).[25] The FSA initially imposed a penalty of £4,000 but subsequently reduced this to £1,000 as a result of the accused's full and frank admissions of his wrongdoing, his cooperation with the investigation, his personal circumstances and limited financial means.[26]

(5) Shell

In September 2004, the FSA fined two companies within the Royal Dutch/Shell Group ('Shell') £17 million for market abuse and for breaching the UK Listing Rules.[27] The US Securities and Exchange Commission (SEC) fined Shell an additional £65 million (US$120 million) for the same acts. Neither regulator has ruled out additional actions against individuals who were involved.

14.19

Although the particular facts are complicated, the regulators generally found that Shell had made false or misleading statements relating to its energy reserves between 1998 and 2003. It was not until the beginning of January 2004 that Shell set the record straight by announcing that its reserves were approximately 25 per cent less than previously represented.[28]

14.20

The relevant section of the FSMA was s 118(2)(b) which, at the time in question, stated that market abuse may be found where a party engages in:

14.21

> behaviour … likely to give a regular user of the market a false or misleading impression as to supply of, or demand for, or as to the price or value of investments of the kind in question.

Because the energy reserves in question related to futures contracts traded on regulated markets they were found to be within the jurisdiction of the Act. The FSA also referred to sections 1.2 and 1.5 of the Code of Market Conduct ('the Code'),[29] which set out the rules relating to false or misleading statements.[30] Chapters 9 and 17 of the Listing Rules required that issuers:

14.22

> must take all reasonable care to ensure that any statement or forecast or other information it notifies to a Regulatory Information Service or makes available to the UK Listing Authority is not misleading, false or deceptive and does not omit anything likely to affect the import of such statement, forecast or other information.[31]

In this case, the FSA considered £17 million to be appropriate.

14.23

---

[25] *Davies* Notice, paras. 21–34. As the FSMA and the Code were written at the time in question.

[26] *Davies* Notice, paras. 35–38.

[27] FSA, Final Notice to the 'Shell' Transport and Trading Company plc, and Royal Dutch Petroleum Company NV, 24 August 2004.

[28] *Shell* Notice, pp. 1–2.

[29] As it was written at the time in question.

[30] *Shell* Notice, paras. 49–54 and 60–69.

[31] *Shell* Notice, para. 56.

(6) *Evolution Beeson Gregory and Christopher Potts*

14.24   On 12 November 2004, the FSA announced that it had fined Evolution Beeson Gregory (EBG), a stock brokerage firm, £500,000, and its head of marketing, Mr Christopher Potts, £75,000, for distortion amounting to market abuse.[32] This was the first case in which the FSA imposed a financial penalty for market distortion amounting to market abuse.[33]

14.25   The FSA said the penalty was a result of a situation where, the FSA alleged, an individual investor was sold some shares of an Alternative Investment Market (AIM)-listed company. However, the FSA said the broker was unable to deliver the shares because it had sold shares of that company short to such a significant degree that it had sold over half the total of issued shares. The FSA found that the broker had sold shares it didn't own without making any reasonable provision for delivery. The FSA found this to constitute 'distorting' the supply, demand or price of a regulated investment and consequently market abuse under the Act.[34] What the FSA considered to be the serious nature of the distortion led to the large fine of £500,000.[35]

14.26   Andrew Procter, then Director of Enforcement at the FSA, said:

> The serious distortion of the Alternative Investment Market led to numerous investors being disadvantaged and was a direct result of the trading strategy engaged in by EBG and Mr Potts. The FSA expects firms and individuals to ensure their business activities do not interfere with the smooth operation of the market or unfairly damage the interests of investors and the FSA will not hesitate to take action in any instance where this occurs … Market users should be clear: we will not tolerate conduct that undermines the UK's reputation for maintaining clean, fair and efficient markets.[36]

(7) *Robin Mark Hutchings*

14.27   On 13 December 2004, the FSA announced that it had decided to impose an £18,000 penalty on Mr Robin Mark Hutchings ('Hutchings') for market abuse.[37] The FSA said that the time of the incidents in questions, Mr Hutchings was an FSA-Approved Person working as an equity financial analyst for EBG.[38] The FSA alleged as follows. In April and May of 2003, I Feel Good (Holdings) plc (IFG),

---

[32] FSA, Final Notice to Evolution Beeson Gregory and Mr Christopher Potts, 12 November 2004, paras. 1–4.

[33] EBG *Potts* Notice, para. 47.

[34] EBG *Potts* Notice, paras. 31–43.

[35] EBG *Potts* Notice, paras. 44–48.

[36] Quoted at <www.fsa.gov.uk/pages/library/communication/pr/2004/097.shtml>.

[37] FSA, Final Notice to Robin Mark Hutchings, 13 December 2004.

[38] See the previous case involving EBG and Christopher Potts.

a publishing company the shares of which traded on the AIM, received an acquisition bid from Dennis Publishing Limited ('Dennis') which, after some discussion, it accepted.

The bid approach by Dennis was first announced to the market by IFG on 15 April 2003. Approval by IFG's Board of the recommended cash offer was announced on 2 May 2003. During April 2003, Mr Hutchings had frequent contacts with a person close to the takeover discussions. Between 11 April 2003 and 30 April 2003, Hutchings purchased a number of IFG shares. When he sold his shares on 6 May 2003, he made a profit of £4,924.

14.28

The FSA concluded that Hutchings was in possession of information relating to the Dennis bid for IFG, its price and likely success, and that:

14.29

> This information had a material influence on Mr Hutchings' decision to deal in IFG shares on 28, 29 and 30 April 2003 …[39]

It found:

14.30

> [T]hat a reasonable person who regularly deals on AIM would regard Mr Hutchings' behaviour in respect of the relevant trades as a failure to observe the standard of behaviour reasonably to be expected of any investor and certainly that of an Approved Person as an analyst with a firm regulated by the FSA.[40]

The FSA found Hutchings' behaviour to constitute market abuse under FSMA, s 118(1) in that it:[41]

14.31

(a) occurred in relation to IFG shares, which are qualifying investments traded on AIM which is a prescribed market for purposes of the Act,

(b) was based on information which was not generally available to those using the market but which, if available to a regular user of the market, would or would have been likely to be regarded by him as relevant when deciding the terms on which transactions in investments in the kind in question should be effected; and

(c) was likely to be regarded by a regular user of AIM as a failure on the part of Mr Hutchings to observe the standards of behaviour reasonably expected of a person in his position in relation to the market.

Their Final Notice to Mr Hutchings also referred to MAR 1.4.3E, which indicates that:

14.32

> Where market users rely on timely dissemination of relevant information (as in this case on AIM), those who possess relevant information ahead of its general dissemination should refrain from acting on that information. Confidence in such markets depends, in part, on market users' confidence that they can deal with each other on

---

[39] *Hutchings* Notice, para. 36.
[40] *Hutchings* Notice, para. 40.
[41] *Hutchings* Notice, para. 35.

the basis that they have equal, simultaneous access to information that is required to be disclosed.[42]

14.33 The FSA said that the seriousness of this case was aggravated by the facts that:

1. Mr Hutchings was an Approved Person and employed as an analyst;[43]
2. his behaviour was deliberate;[44] and
3. he initially provided inconsistent explanations to the FSA.[45]

14.34 However, Mr Hutchings had no previous disciplinary history, was no longer working as an Approved Person in the financial services industry and had recently cooperated with the FSA investigation so as to enable the FSA to work expeditiously.[46] Under the circumstances, the FSA considered that a penalty of £18,000 was appropriate.[47]

(8) Jason Smith

14.35 Also on 13 December 2004, the FSA announced that it had decided to impose a penalty of £15,000 on Jason Smith for market abuse.[48] Mr Smith was also punished in connection with the Dennis bid for IFG, discussed with respect to the finding of market abuse against Robin Mark Hutchings discussed above.[49] The FSA said that Mr Smith and Mr Hutchings were friends and former colleagues.[50] During the time in question, Mr Smith was a Chartered Accountant who was Finance Director and Company Secretary of IFG. During April 2003, Mr Smith provided Mr Hutchings with information about the Dennis acquisition approach and bid for IFG.[51]

14.36 On the basis of the above facts, it appeared to the FSA that:

Mr Smith engaged in market abuse by disclosing to someone outside the company information which was likely to be regarded by a regular market user as relevant in determining the terms on which transactions in qualifying investments should be effected ...[52]

---

[42] *Hutchings* Notice, para. 41.
[43] *Hutchings* Notice, para. 44(c).
[44] *Hutchings* Notice, para. 44(e).
[45] *Hutchings* Notice, para. 44(d).
[46] *Hutchings* Notice, para. 44(j).
[47] *Hutchings* Notice, para. 45.
[48] FSA, Final Notice to Jason Smith, 13 December 2004.
[49] *Smith* Notice, para. 1.
[50] *Smith* Notice, para. 32.
[51] *Smith* Notice, paras. 36–38.
[52] *Smith* Notice, para. 7(a).

This was held to be market abuse in violation of FSMA, s 118(1) in that it:[53]   **14.37**

    (a) occurred in relation to IFG shares;

    (b) was based on information about two announcements which were relevant and which were not generally available;

    (c) is likely to be regarded by a regular user as a failure on the part of Mr Smith to observe the standards of behaviour reasonably expected of a person in his position in relation to the market; [and, therefore,] …

a reasonable person who regularly deals on AIM would regard Mr Smith's behaviour in respect of his disclosures of 14 and 28 April 2003 as a failure to observe the standard of behaviour reasonably to be expected of a Finance Director and Company Secretary of an AIM traded company. Being in such a position, Mr Smith was acutely aware of the sensitivity of the information that he possessed by reason of his employment and the impropriety of selectively disclosing such information before it had been made available to investors in accordance with IFG's obligations under the City Code on Takeovers and Mergers rules.

Taking into account that Smith was in a position of trust at the time he made the   **14.38**
disclosures in question, that he provided inconsistent explanations of the relevant events to the FSA, that his behaviour was deliberate, and that a penalty of market abuse would affect his professional futures, the FSA considered that its penalty was an appropriately serious response to its findings regarding Smith's behaviour.[54]

In commenting on the penalties imposed on Mr Hutchings and Mr Smith of   **14.39**
£18,000 and £15,000 respectively, the then Director of Enforcement at the FSA, Andrew Procter, observed:

> The selective dissemination of confidential information and its misuse by market participants will not be tolerated by the FSA. We have previously taken action against those who misuse relevant information for personal gain; however, this action demonstrates that we view equally seriously the activities of those who pass on that information. This action should concentrate the minds of all those who handle relevant information on their responsibilities.

(9) *Indigo Capital LLC and Robert Johan Henri Bonnier*

On 21 December 2004, the FSA announced that it had issued a Decision Notice   **14.40**
to Indigo Capital LLC (ICL) and Robert Johan Henri Bonnier that the FSA would impose financial penalties of £65,000 on ICL and £290,000 on Mr Bonnier for market abuse comprising 12 inaccurate disclosures related to deals in shares of Regus plc ('Regus'). The FSA alleged the following.[55]

---

[53] *Smith* Notice, para. 41.
[54] *Smith* Notice, paras. 55–56.
[55] FSA, Final Notice, *Indigo Capital LLC and Robert Johan Henri Bonnier*, December 21, 2004.

14.41   ICL had affiliates incorporated in both New York and France. ICL's main business had been financial services and investment. Mr Bonnier was a shareholder and full-time managing partner between July 2002 and September 2003. Regus was a public company traded on the London Stock Exchange. Its principal business was providing managed office space. Mr Bonnier was principally responsible for the investment decisions of ICL, and he conducted the dealing between ICL and Regus.[56]

14.42   The FSA said that the market abuse committed by Mr Bonnier and ICL came about as follows. Between mid-November 2002 and January 2003, Mr Bonnier opened brokerage accounts and purchased numbers of shares of Regus, and contracts for differences (CFDs) related to the shares of Regus.[57] The shares and CFDs were variously held in the names of Mr Bonnier or ICL. During that period, the registrar of Regus sent Mr Bonnier a notice requesting clarification of those holdings in Regus. In response, Mr Bonnier made statements to the registrar inaccurately representing the size and nature of the ICL/Bonnier holdings. Mr Bonnier's representations were reflected in statements Regus made to the market.[58]

14.43   In essence, Mr Bonnier had given the impression that by 6 January 2003, ICL had built up a holding of just over 15 per cent of Regus's shares.[59] In early January 2003, Bonnier had a number of discussions with the Panel on Takeovers and Mergers (POTAM) related to the purported stake that ICL had acquired in Regus. At POTAM's request, ICL issued a statement that it was exploring many options with Regus, one of which may have been a recommended takeover.[60] In fact, ICL's stake in Regus never amounted to more than 2.3 per cent of Regus shares, and, by January 2003, it was only 0.07 per cent.[61]

14.44   In total, during the period in question, Mr Bonnier made 12 materially inaccurate notifications ('Notifications') to Regus. According to the FSA Mr Bonnier made

---

[56]   ICL *Bonnier* Notice, Section 2.

[57]   A CFD is a contract under which one party agrees to pay the difference between the opening value and the closing value of an underlying asset. The asset can be anything of economic value such as a share, gold, wheat, etc. A CFD gives its purchaser an economic interest in the price of the asset (in this case, shares in Regus) without buying the asset itself. Of course, a CFD related to shares does not actually give the holder any voting rights or other beneficial interest in the underlying shares.

[58]   ICL *Bonnier* Notice, paras. 2.7–2.18.

[59]   ICL *Bonnier* Notice, para. 2.19.

[60]   ICL *Bonnier* Notice, para. 2.20.

[61]   ICL *Bonnier* Notice, para. 2.18.

the Notifications and signed them.[62] The FSA found this conduct to be market abuse under FSMA, s 118(2)(b),[63] which prohibits behaviour:

> likely to give the regular user of the market a false or misleading impression as to the supply of, or demand for, or as to the price or value of, investments of the kind in question.[64]

The FSA concluded that: **14.45**

> Mr Bonnier was the author of the Notifications [relating to the purported ICL share-holdings]. A regular user of the market in listed securities would reasonably expect a person in Mr Bonnier's position to make Notifications which stated correctly the number of Regus shares held. The Notifications did not state correctly the number of Regus shares held, and the FSA considers that it was likely that a regular user would regard Mr Bonnier as having failed to observe the standard of behaviour reasonably expected of him.[65]

It found that the market abuse in this case was 'serious and merit[ed] a significant **14.46** financial penalty'.[66] Because the principal responsibility for the market abuse in question lay with Mr Bonnier, it was decided that he would bear the principal financial responsibility for the penalty. The FSA stated that it believed the size of the penalty would be significant for Mr Bonnier but that it had no reason to believe it would cause him serious financial hardship.[67]

In commenting on the case, the then Director of Enforcement at the FSA, Andrew **14.47** Procter, observed:

> The smooth operation of the financial markets relies on the provision of accurate information to enable participants to make reasoned investment decisions about a company's shares. The announcements made by Regus, which were based exclusively on the notifications made by Mr Bonnier, were a substantive source of information for the market in Regus shares. In providing inaccurate information, Mr Bonnier created a false and misleading impression as to the supply of, demand for or the price or value of Regus shares. Investors need to have confidence in the integrity of the processes by which shares are traded on the market and that information disclosed to the market is accurate.

(10) David Isaacs

The FSA described David Isaacs as an experienced company executive and private **14.48** investor.[68] He was found to have engaged in market abuse in September 2003 by

---

[62] ICL *Bonnier* Notice, para. 3.16.
[63] ICL *Bonnier* Notice, para. 3.6.
[64] ICL *Bonnier* Notice, para. 3.3. As the FSMA, s 118 was then written.
[65] ICL *Bonnier* Notice, para. 3.7.
[66] ICL *Bonnier* Notice, para. 4.9.
[67] ICL *Bonnier* Notice, paras. 4.8–4.13.
[68] FSA, Final Notice to David Isaacs, 28 February 2005, para. 13.

making disclosures on a bulletin board website of information relating to Trafficmaster plc ('Trafficmaster') which was not generally available. The FSA imposed a £15,000 financial penalty on Isaacs.

14.49 Mr Isaacs was found by the FSA to have committed market abuse in violation of FSMA, s 118(2)(a) in that his improper behaviour was:

> based on information which is not generally available to those using the market but which, if available to a regular user of the market, would or would likely to be regarded by him as relevant when deciding the terms on which transactions in investments of the kind in question should be effected.[69]

14.50 The FSA said that Trafficmaster is a company in the satellite navigation and digital traffic information. In August and September of 2003, Trafficmaster held internal management meetings to discuss future installations of its products in popular automobiles. While visiting an acquaintance who had access to such minutes, the FSA found that Mr Isaacs saw these minutes and subsequently published information about their contents on an internet bulletin board. He also made purchases of shares in Trafficmaster.[70]

14.51 The FSA concluded that Mr Isaacs' behaviour was deliberate, that he had obtained the information in a dishonest and surreptitious manner, and that he had intended to affect the price of Trafficmaster shares.[71]

14.52 However, deciding the level of financial penalty, the FSA took into account that Mr Isaacs had not previously been subject to enforcement action and that he cooperated fully with the FSA's investigation.[72]

(11) Jonathan Malins

14.53 By a Decision Notice dated 20 December 2005, the FSA imposed a penalty of £25,000 on Jonathan Malins for market abuse.[73] The penalty was imposed in connection with Mr Malins' behaviour relating to his purchase of shares in Cambrian Mining plc ('Cambrian') ahead of announcements concerning Cambrian's placing of shares and its interim results.

14.54 At the relevant time, Cambrian was a mining company the shares of which traded on AIM. Malins was a co-founder of Cambrian, the only executive director based in the UK and its Finance Director. Malins was also a director of a number of other AIM companies. The FSA found that on 23 March 2005, Malins bought

---

[69] *Isaacs* Notice, para. 8. FSMA, s 118(2)(a), as it was then written.
[70] *Isaacs* Notice, paras. 16–29.
[71] *Isaacs* Notice, paras. 43–46.
[72] *Isaacs* Notice, para. 52.
[73] FSA/PN/141/2005 (21 December 2005). Final Notice dated 20 December 2005.

50,000 shares in Cambrian, prior to a 'share placing'[74] announcement made by Cambrian at 4.10 p.m. on the same day ('Placing').

On the morning of 23 March 2005, Malins chaired a board meeting to finalize the **14.55** Placing announcement. The Placing was to be at a premium to the then share price. After he had purchased the 50,000 shares, Malins asked Cambrian's broker to release the announcement to the market as soon as possible.

When he purchased the 50,000 shares in question, Malins knew that the Placing **14.56** announcement had not been made, that Cambrian was in a 'close period',[75] and he also knew the likely contents of Cambrian's as yet unannounced interim results. He had not applied for permission to purchase the shares, and, if he had, such permission would not have been granted.

The day after the Placing announcement, Cambrian's share price opened higher, **14.57** and closed much higher than the prices Malins had paid for the 50,000 shares. If he had chosen to sell the shares that day (he held on to them), his profit would have been £6,000.

On 31 March 2005, more than an hour and a half before the announcement of **14.58** Cambrian's interim results, Malins purchased an additional 20,000 Cambrian shares. The day before, 30 March 2005, Malins chaired a board meeting to formalize acceptance of the accounts and agree the making of the interim results announcement to be made on the next day. The results showed an increase in profitability and an increase in the value of Cambrian's investments. Malins understood the price sensitivity of the proposed announcement.

Malins had been given permission to purchase an additional 20,000 Cambrian **14.59** shares, on the condition that purchase be made **after** the interim results announcement. However, Malins purchased his shares at 9.22 a.m., before the time at which interim results are usually announced (10.00 a.m.), and did not check that Cambrian's interim results had actually been announced (in this case, at 11.02 a.m.).

After the interim results announcement, Cambrian's share price rose to a level **14.60** at which Malins would have realized a profit of £400 if he had sold the shares on 31 March 2005 (again, he continued to hold them).

The FSA took the view that the share purchases, separately or together, amounted **14.61** to market abuse in violation of FSMA, ss 118(1) and 118(2)(a).

---

[74] Sale of shares to a number of investors, but not to the public.
[75] A period before the announcement a company's preliminary or interim financial results (normally two months) during which the directors are barred from trading the company's shares.

14.62 The FSA's conclusion was that the seriousness of the market abuse in this case warranted a financial penalty of £25,000. In imposing a penalty of £25,000 the FSA considered:

> ... that a reasonable person who regularly deals on AIM would regard Mr Malins' behaviour as a failure to observe the standard of behaviour reasonably to be expected of an investor and certainly that of a finance director of an AIM company ... [he] was well aware of the sensitivity of the information available to him and the impropriety of exploiting [it] to his own advantage ... further, [his] failure to comply with Cambrian's rules and requirements regarding share dealing by employees [was] additional evidence of his failure to observe the standards reasonably expected of an employee in his position.

(12) GLG Partners LP and Philippe Jabré

14.63 The territorial reach of the market abuse regime is illustrated by the proceedings against GLG Partners LP and Philippe Jabré.[76] On 11 February 2003 Mr Jabré was 'wall crossed' by Goldman Sachs International as part of the pre-marketing of a new issue of convertible preference shares in Sumitomo Mitsui Financial Group Inc (SMFG). Mr Jabré was given confidential information and agreed to be restricted from dealing SMFG Securities until the issue was announced. Mr Jabré breached this restriction by short selling around $16m of SMFG ordinary shares on 12–14 February 2003. When the new issue was announced on 17 February 2003, Mr Jabré made a substantial profit for the GLG Markets Neutral Fund. In entertaining the proceedings—ultimately referred to the Financial Services and Markets Tribunal—it was made clear that it is not possible for someone with inside information on a UK traded stock to circumvent the market abuse regime by trading in that stock on an overseas market. Thus the transactions undertaken on the Tokyo market in respect of shares which were also listed on the LSE were found to have occurred in relation to qualifying investments 'traded' on a prescribed market.

14.64 The decision is also important in rejecting Mr Jabré's assertion that the transactions were part of a pre-existing trading strategy. He had asserted that it was public knowledge that major Japanese banks were under pressure from the Bank of Japan to bring their Tier 1 Ratios back in line with internationally required standards. He said that he had started to borrow shares in Japanese banks and subsequently started to short sell shares in SMFG. The FSA did not consider such stock borrowing to be evidence of a 'trading pattern' or that a single short trade evidenced any such 'trading pattern'. No definite orders to execute sales or trades at predetermined market price levels had been given and Mr Jabré's subsequently claimed intention to sell or trade at a particular price level was insufficient to show a

---

[76] *FSA v GLG Partners and Jabré* (Final Notice), 1 August 2006.

'pre-existing trading pattern' which justified the short selling which occurred between his move across and the public announcement by SMFG, whose intentions had been disclosed to him in advance in confidence.

(13) *Sean Pignatelli*

The flexibility of the FSA's enforcement powers to discipline approved persons who fail to observe proper standards of market conduct is well illustrated by *FSA v Sean Pignatelli*.[77] Mr Pignatelli was a US equity salesman employed by Credit Suisse First Boston (Europe) Ltd. On 24 May 2005 he received an analyst's email in which there were warning signals that it might contain inside information about a US company named Boston Scientific Corporation ('BSX'). In fact the email did not contain inside information but Mr Pignatelli did not turn his mind to whether or not it did. On receiving the analyst's communication Mr Pignatelli immediately relayed its contents to several people by telephone, including four clients who then sold or short sold BSX shares that evening. A financial penalty of £20,000 was imposed on him. This figure was considered appropriate, even although no disciplinary action had previously been taken against him; he did not stand to make any profit from his behaviour and the FSA had formed the view that when talking to clients Mr Pignatelli did not have a positive belief that he was in possession of inside information and did not seek deliberately to convey any such impression to clients.

14.65

(14) *Woolworths Group Plc*

Guidance as to information which 'would, if generally available, be likely to have a significant effect' on price is given in *FSA v Woolworths Group plc*.[78] The proceedings concerned a delay in disclosing a significant variation to the terms of a major supply contract of one of Woolworths' subsidiaries, Entertainment UK Ltd (EUK). On 9 August 2004 Woolworths and EUK entered into an agreement with Tesco Stores Ltd for the wholesale provision of entertainment products. On 20 December 2005 a variation agreement was concluded which increased the amount of retrospective discount that would be paid by EUK to Tesco by an estimated £8 m for the 12-month period from 1 March 2006. The consequential reduction in profits represented over 10 per cent of Woolworths' anticipated profits for the following financial year, which were expected to be approximately £68 m. The FSA considered that due to the size of reduction in profit in comparison to Woolworths' anticipated group profits, the information about

14.66

---

[77] *FSA v Pignatelli* (Final Notice), 20 November 2006.
[78] *FSA v Woolworths Group Ltd* (Final Notice), 11 June 2008.

the variation constituted inside information and as a result a disclosure obligation arose under Disclosure Rule 2.2.1 when the agreement was signed on 20 December 2005. Disclosure was not in fact made until 18 January 2006, which led to the creation of a false market in Woolworths' shares in the interim (a breach of Listing Principle 4).

14.67 Woolworths sought to argue that information as to the variation would not have been likely to have a significant effect. When the announcement was eventually made, the share price fell from 36.75p to 32.25p—a fall of 12.24 per cent. Woolworths pointed to other cases where action had followed significant share price movements in the range of 36 per cent to 67 per cent and suggested the price fall in this instance was not 'significant'. Further, it argued that inasmuch as the announcement also referred to the possibility of the Tesco/EUK supply contract not being renewed, the latter could well explain or have materially contributed to the fall in value. Woolworths contended that before the offence could be made out, the FSA would need to be satisfied that a share price fall of 10 per cent or more was able to be attributed to a particular piece of information for there to have been a 'significant effect on price' from that piece of information. This submission was rejected.

14.68 The FSA concluded that 'the materials available to the FSA, including the views of an appropriate market professional, do not support Woolworths' suggestion. The FSA is satisfied that the variation resulted in a profit reduction of more than 10 per cent and that this is, on any view, information of a type the reasonable investor would be likely to use as part of his investment decisions.' Although this case turned largely on the Listing Principles and Rules the issues raised were akin to market abuse ones and the decision can be seen as more widely informative as to those as well.

(15) Stewart McKegg

14.69 A further example of proceedings for abusive dealing based on inside information is *FSA v Stewart McKegg*.[79] In that case, Mr McKegg was a private retail investor who had regularly dealt in shares in Amerisur Resources plc. Blue Oar Securities plc was the appointed NOMAD for Amerisur and acted as broker for the company in a share placing which took place in May 2007. On 23 May that year, Blue Oar contacted Mr McKegg and made him an insider in relation to the proposed placing, to be announced to the market the following day. Blue Oar advised Mr McKegg that the placing price was 6p and would be announced the next day. He was told not to speak to anyone about the placing, nor trade until it was

---

[79] *FSA v McKegg* (Final Notice), 16 October 2008.

announced to the market on 24 May 2007. Following receipt of this inside information, Mr McKegg sold 549,000 Amerisur shares, constituting his entire holding, at 8.625p per share. He then purchased 750,000 shares at 6p in the placing.
Following the announcement of the placing, the price of Amerisur's shares fell to
7.5p. By his actions, Mr McKegg realized a profit of £14,411.25. The penalty
imposed was £34,411.25, made up as to £14,411.25 representing disgorgement
of the profit made and a penalty of £20,000. The FSA took into account that
Mr McKegg's behaviour was deliberate but that he had never been an insider
before and was not a professional market investor. Nonetheless, the FSA identified the penalty as 'intended to have a deterrent effect on those who may consider
engaging in market abuse'.

(16) Boyen and Boyen

An interesting example of 'inside information' arose in *FSA v Filip Boyen*.[80] There,   **14.70**
Mr Boyen was an experienced businessman who had become close friends with
Richard Ralph when the latter was British Ambassador to Peru. In the latter capacity Mr Ralph established close links with British mining companies in Peru,
including Monterrico Metals plc. On retirement from the diplomatic service,
Mr Ralph was appointed Executive Chairman of the company. In early 2007
Mr Ralph asked Mr Boyen to buy shares in the company on his behalf. Mr Boyen
was aware from company announcements that it was involved in takeover discussions and that Mr Ralph was the Executive Chairman. As an experienced investor
and businessman, Mr Boyen knew there were restrictions on dealings by company
directors in their companies' shares, including periods when dealing was not permitted. He did not express any concerns about Mr Ralph's request. He also bought
shares on his own behalf. Following the purchases, further announcements were
made relating to the prospective takeover which contributed to the company
share price increasing. Mr Boyen then sold his shares, making a profit of £29,482.
These transactions constituted market abuse in that Mr Boyen knew of Mr Ralph's
intention to deal clandestinely in the company's shares at a time when it was publicly known that the company had engaged in takeover discussions. He also knew
he had been asked to buy a substantial number (in total £30,000 worth) of shares
on behalf of the company's Executive Chairman. This information was 'inside
information' in that it was 'precise' information which was not generally available;
the information related directly to the company and would, if generally available,
have been likely to have had a significant effect on the price of the company's
shares. The financial penalty imposed consisted of, in the result, two elements:
disgorgement of profits, that is, £29,482, and an additional penalty of £52,500.

---

[80] *FSA v Boyen* (Final Notice), 12 November 2008.

The latter component reflected a 30 per cent discount for early settlement against the level of penalty the FSA would otherwise have regarded as appropriate, that is, £75,000.

14.71   In further proceedings against Mr Boyen's brother, Erik Boyen, the latter was also found guilty of market abuse. Filip Boyen had passed inside information to his brother which had been the basis for further dealings in the company's shares. In this instance, Erik Boyen personally profited by £127,254. In *FSA v Erik Boyen*,[81] Mr Boyen was required to disgorge the profits made and pay an additional penalty of £49,000.

C. Observations

14.72   Despite the fact that the FSA's regulatory remit covers a wide variety of financial instruments, the vast majority of market abuse cases concluded so far have to do with insider dealing relating to the trading of shares.[82] It is hard to know whether this is because the FSA finds market abuse related to insider dealing easier to prove, or because those involved in share transactions are more prone to insider dealing than market manipulation, or because those dealing in other investment products such as commodity derivatives or interest rate futures are less prone to market abuse, or because the FSA considers insider dealing its top priority.

14.73   In the UK, it must be the case that manipulation of the price of commodity derivatives based on such things as energy and foodstuffs could pose serious dangers to the national economy. Unlike insider dealing, the immediate impact of which reaches only those involved in a particular company or its shares, market manipulation of commodity derivatives could impact on a wide spectrum of consumers.

The FSA often states that its aims are:

> to promote efficient, orderly and fair markets, help retail consumers achieve a fair deal and improve its business capability and effectiveness.[83]

14.74   Clearly, deterring and punishing market abuse in the form of market manipulation is at least as important to achieving those aims as preventing and punishing insider trading. It has been said that the FSA has approximately 30 market abuse investigations going on at any one time, relating to a wide variety of financial

---

[81]   *FSA v Boyen* (Final Notice), 12 January 2009.

[82]   Two exceptions are the *EBG Potts* case (distortion) and the *Shell* case (misleading statements) discussed above.

[83]   See, e.g., FSA Statement regarding *Legal & General* Tribunal further decision, *Notes to editors*, note 6 (27 May 2005).

products including commodity futures and derivatives. Whilst it remains to be seen whether, in the future, there is a more even distribution of market abuse penalties between insider dealing and market manipulation, the FSA is clearly indicating that it takes all aspects of market abuse seriously. In February 2004 it launched its first prosecution under FSMA, s 397(1)(a) and (1)(c) against the directors of a company called AIT for making misleading statements. The case concerning these directors, Messrs Rigby, Bailey and Rowley, is considered in Chapter 13.

Indeed it is to be anticipated that the FSA will increasingly have regard to its powers to bring criminal prosecutions for market abuse-related offences. The comments made by Jamie Symington, head of Wholesale Department at the FSA, in a recent speech[84] is illustrative:

14.75

> There are a number of initiatives which the FSA has adopted over the last year or so to enhance enforcement against market abuse ... particularly ... the use of criminal prosecution powers ... one of the most significant changes in our approach to have occurred in the last year ... in the last year we have commenced three criminal prosecutions and expect to continue to bring more in the future ... there are three points in particular that I would like to emphasize. The first is that our aim here is to get people to take the threat of the consequences of their actions more seriously, and for the conduct to be viewed for what it really is: criminal ... The stigma that goes with a criminal conviction and the loss of liberty is not something that professionals want to have ... So the objective is to up the stakes for people who might risk committing market abuse so that they are deterred by the fact that they face a real prospect of a spell in prison and the publicity and stigma of a criminal conviction. The second point, which is very important, is that the move towards bringing more criminal prosecutions does not mean that we will not still bring civil market abuse proceedings ... That is why you will have seen that our success this year in launching three criminal prosecutions has been complemented by successes in concluding action under the civil market abuse regime against two other individuals, Mr Shevlin and Mr Harrison, in separate cases. So the strategy of bringing more criminal prosecutions is not to be regarded in isolation. We can and will continue to bring civil proceedings as well.

---

[84] 6 November 2008; see <www.fsa.gov.uk/pages/Library/Communication/Speeches/2008/1106_js.shtml>.

15

US JURISDICTION

A. Why It Matters

15.01 US courts and investment regulators take an extremely expansive view of the application of US law to non-US transactions. This is nowhere more true than with US antitrust, fraud and anti-manipulation rules. Indeed, the exemptions which have been created to exempt foreign issuers from US registration requirements do not create exemptions from US antitrust, fraud and anti-manipulation rules and individuals or corporations who breach these rules can be held liable under both US criminal and civil statutes.

15.02 Firms and individuals outside the US are often surprised by the reach of US jurisdiction over such activities. Accordingly, it is worth remembering that a US Federal Court held that:

> any market that is not exclusively a foreign market is part of US commerce.[1]

---

[1] Judge William C. Conner, US District Judge, Southern District of New York in the *Transnor* case.

15.03 It is also worth remembering that one is not immunized from US law suits or regulatory action simply by the fact that the same area is covered by UK or other non-US financial services regulations. The US Supreme Court has held that where a party is subject to both:

(1) if compliance with US (in that case, antitrust) law is not made impossible by British law;

(2) there is no excuse for not complying with US law.[2]

15.04 The news gets worse. Financial services in the US are regulated by a confusing patchwork of Federal (SEC, CFTC, Federal Reserve, Comptroller of the Currency, etc.) and State (for example, New York with State Attorney General Andrew Cuomo) agencies. All administer a complicated matrix of statutes and regulations which can apply to non-US transactions. In addition, many US statutes, for example, the Foreign Corrupt Practices Act of 1977,[3] target foreign financial activities directly. It is not within the scope of this book to even attempt to describe them all.

15.05 However, to give the reader an introduction to how US laws may apply to UK financial services activities, this chapter will briefly discuss aspects of four specific areas: antitrust, securities, commodity futures law and the relatively recent Sarbanes–Oxley Act of 2002.

B. Principles of US Jurisdiction: An Overview

15.06 Extraterritorial jurisdiction over non-US transactions generally focuses on several principles that will run throughout this chapter. First, there is a general presumption in US law against extraterritorial application of laws enacted by Congress that do not have an express provision relating to foreign jurisdiction. Thus, as in the case of certain Sarbanes–Oxley provisions, US courts will refuse to apply US laws to activities abroad unless some other basis for jurisdiction exits.

15.07 This presumption is linked to the idea of international comity, or the showing of respect and goodwill by one nation towards the laws and interests of other nations and other states' nationals. However, where domestic interests are significantly at stake, the principle of comity and the presumption against extraterritorial application are set aside. In such cases, US courts generally exercise jurisdiction:

(1) where the wrongful conduct occurs in the United States,

---

[2] US Supreme Court in *Hartford Fire Insurance v California* 509 U.S. 764 (1993).

[3] 15 U.S.C. §§ 78dd-1. (making it a federal crime to (1) make a payment to any foreign official in order to gain business or influence the decisions of that official and (2) requiring that foreign companies listed on US securities exchanges comply with certain accounting and record-keeping practices with respect to transactions).

or

(2) where the wrongful conduct has had substantial effect in the United States or upon United States citizens or shareholders.[4]

These two aspects of the extraterritorial jurisdiction test do not necessarily have to be applied separately from each other, and US courts have recognized that these concepts are interlinked. Further elaboration of these tests is provided below in relation to particular subject areas.

C. Combinations and Conspiracies in Restraint of Trade

Surprisingly, one of the most potent weapons that the US Government, or a non-US private litigant in a US Federal court, can use against a financial services market party is US antitrust (anti-competition) law.   **15.08**

The law and the rules governing its application are complicated. It is not within the scope of this book to do anything more than alert the reader to its existence. However, it has a long reach into international commerce, and it allows plaintiffs to seek triple damages.   **15.09**

There is little question that some, perhaps a significant portion, of the cases of insider dealing or market manipulation that constitute market abuse in the UK involve cooperation between two or more persons. As such they can also be 'combinations or conspiracies in restraint of trade'. That is to say, they are joint actions that harm competition through unfair, and illegal, conduct. The Sherman Antitrust Act, s 1 says: **15.10**

> Every contract, combination in the form of trust or otherwise, or conspiracy, in restraint of trade among the several States, or with foreign nations, is declared to be illegal.[5]

As can be seen, this law covers an extremely wide range of activities. It gives a complainant, or the US Government, the opportunity to file an action in a US Federal court regarding many financial services transactions involving combinations or conspiracies between two or more parties, whose actions together damage a private plaintiff and/or the market generally, if they occur in the international markets (many of them off-exchange) that make up much of the financial services business. The only transactions that are clearly excluded are transactions in wholly foreign markets with a wholly non-US impact. In the modern financial world, such markets are rare.

---

[4] See *SEC v Berger*, 322 F.3d 187, 192-93 (2d Cir. 2003).
[5] 15 U.S.C. 1.

15.11   Foreigners have standing to sue under US antitrust laws if a combination or conspiracy in restraint of trade has the requisite impact, or 'effect' on US commerce. The so-called 'effects test', touched upon briefly above, has a long history in US antitrust litigation, and says that if the effects of a conspiracy in restraint of trade are felt within the US, the US has jurisdiction, whether or not the activities that contributed to the effects occurred within US borders.[6]

15.12   One example of such a case is *Transnor (Bermuda) Ltd v BP North America Petroleum*, in which a Bermuda plaintiff, trading in the Brent 15-day market[7] from an office in London, brought suit in a US federal court alleging violations of s 1 of the Sherman Act. On the issue of the Bermuda-based plaintiff's standing to bring the suit, the court held:

> The fact that Transnor purchased the contracts at issue through the London branch of the Brent Market, rather than in New York or Houston, does not lessen Transnor's ability to vindicate Congress's clearly expressed desire that foreigners have standing to sue under US antitrust laws if the alleged course of anti-competitive conduct has the requisite impact on US commerce.[8]

More recently, in 2004, the Supreme Court reaffirmed the effects principle, while simultaneously holding that claims by foreign litigants regarding the effects felt in foreign jurisdictions of antitrust activities was not a sufficient independent basis for jurisdiction in a US forum. Therefore, where price-fixing conduct significantly and adversely affected customers both outside and within the United States, claimants could only sue based on the effects felt in the US—the extraterritorial claims were not covered by the Sherman Act.[9]

15.13   The Sherman Act is not the only US antitrust regulation that can be applied to international financial services transactions. Conduct that constitutes market abuse in the EU could be actionable in US courts under a number of statutes and regulations, provided that such activities meet the jurisdictional requirements laid out by US courts. Financial market participants, especially those coordinating projects with other market participants that are located in or may have effects in international markets with US links should certainly be aware of this potential for extraterritorial liability.

---

[6] See, e.g., *United States v Aluminum Co. of America*, 377 U.S. 271 (1964).
[7] At the time in question, an international market for the trading of contracts for North Sea Oil for future delivery.
[8] *Transnor (Bermuda) Ltd v BP North America Petroleum et al.*, 666 F. Supp. 584 (USDC SDNY 1987).
[9] See *F. Hoffmann-La Roche Ltd v Empagran S.A.* 542 U.S. 155 (2004) (Antitrust class action was brought on behalf of foreign and domestic purchasers of vitamins, alleging international price-fixing conspiracy by manufacturers and distributors).

D. Application of US Securities Laws to Non-US Transactions

The United States Securities Exchange Act,[10] s 10(b), is the most widely applied **15.14** federal securities law regulation against market fraud or manipulation (although it is not the only one). Section 10(b) makes it illegal for any person to use the post or other means of 'interstate commerce':

> To use or employ, in connection with the purchase or sale of any security … any manipulative or deceptive device or contrivance in contravention of such rules and regulations as the Commission may prescribe … in the public interest or for the protection of investors.

Prohibitions against market misconduct relating to securities (such as shares and bonds) and many derivatives related to them, in violation of Federal law, is enforced by the US Securities Exchange Commission[11] (SEC). The SEC, like the FSA in the UK, is empowered to bring either civil or criminal actions against alleged wrongdoers.

Because this s 10(b) only makes illegal those things which the SEC has made a rule **15.15** prohibiting, the SEC introduced Rule 10b-5, which states:

> It shall be unlawful for any person, directly or indirectly, by the use of any means or instrumentality of interstate commerce, or of the mails, or of any facility of any national securities exchange,
>
> (1) to employ any device, scheme or artifice to defraud,
> (2) to make any untrue statement of a material fact or to omit to state a material fact necessary in order to make the statements made, in the light of circumstances under which they were made, not misleading, or
> (3) to engage in any act, practice, or course of business which operates or would operate as a fraud or deceit upon any person, in connection with the purchase or sale or any security.

In the 60 years since it has been adopted, this rule has been applied by the SEC to a startling breadth of securities transactions, including those relating to insider trading and price manipulation.

However, this rule is used not only by the SEC, but also by private litigants seeking **15.16** redress. The US Supreme Court has held that 'a private right of action is implied' by s 10(b),[12] particularly in cases that involve misrepresentation or omission of corporate information, insider trading, or intentional manipulation.

---

[10] 15 U.S.C. 78a, I.
[11] Note that the individual states have their own enforcement agencies for violations of state law.
[12] *Herman v MacLean, Huddleston*, 459 U.S. 375 (1983).

15.17   The fact that transactions are in foreign securities outside the United States does not exempt them from the reach of federal securities anti-fraud provisions. There is no exclusion for foreign securities issuers from liability for conduct that violates, and meets the jurisdictional requirements of, the anti-fraud provisions of the federal securities laws.[13] The SEC has made it clear that, unless a specific exemption is granted, US securities regulations can even apply to foreign sovereign debt issuers.

15.18   With respect to foreign securities transactions, US courts have likewise found two bases for jurisdiction:

(1) where some of the actions alleged to comprise the violations took place within the US;[14]
(2) where US shareholders have been harmed by the alleged fraud.[15]

15.19   A court has also held that the securities anti-fraud prohibitions would apply in the following cases:

(1) where there were sales to Americans residing in the US;
(2) where there were sales to Americans residing overseas if things done in the US significantly added to their losses; and
(3) if the losses of foreigners outside the US were contributed to by acts in the US.[16]

15.20   One should also take note of the fact that any contract holding that disputes are to be resolved in non-US courts under non-US law will be upheld only if that agreement is not found to be 'unreasonable' and that foreign law does not underline the US requirement of 'full and fair disclosure and preventing fraud on US investors'.[17]

E. Commodity Exchange Act

15.21   Under US law, fraud and market manipulation with respect to commodities futures and many other kinds of derivatives is principally regulated under the Commodity Exchange Act (CEA).

---

[13] Securities Exchange Commission, *Final Rule: Selective Disclosure and Insider Trading*, Release No. 33-7881, II. B. 5.
[14] *US Leasco v Maxwell*, 468 F. 2d 1326 (2d Cir. 1972); *Travis v Anthes Imperial*, 473 F.2d 515 (8th Cir. 1973).
[15] *Schoenbaum v Firstbrook*, 405 F. 2d 200 (2d Cir. 1968).
[16] *Bersch v Drexel Firestone*, 519 f. 2d 974 (2d Cir. 1975).
[17] *Bonny v Lloyd's*, 3 F.3d 156 (7th Cir. 1993); *Roby v Lloyd's*, 996 F. 2d 1353 (2d Cir. 1993).

Under the CEA, the principal regulator of commodity futures (and other derivatives) trading, the Commodity Futures Trading Commission (CFTC), has the option of pursuing either civil or criminal remedies. **15.22**

Foreign plaintiffs can, under some circumstances, bring actions in US courts seeking compensation for damages resulting from violations of the CEA. A threshold requirement is that the claims be related to transactions on a market which is not 'wholly foreign'.[18] Very few international financial markets do not involve US commerce. **15.23**

The CEA provisions above prohibit actual or attempted manipulation of 'any commodity in interstate commerce or for future delivery on or subject to the rules of any contract market …' For example, for purposes of US regulation, it is undisputed that Brent System Blend Crude Oil ('Brent Oil')[19] is both a commodity in interstate commerce and a commodity for future delivery on a contract market within the meaning of the CEA. **15.24**

There is no precise statutory definition of 'market manipulation' in the CEA. Working definitions have evolved from the decisions of courts and other tribunals when considering a variety of intentional conduct which results in an 'artificial price'. The courts have recognized that the means and ways of market manipulation are as wide as imagination can make them. According to the United States Supreme Court in *Santa Fe Industries, Inc. v Green*: **15.25**

> Manipulation is virtually a term of art which is used in connection with securities markets. The term refers generally to such practices as wash sales, matched orders, or rigged prices that intended to mislead investors by artificially affecting market activity …[20]

A finding of manipulation and violation of the CEA requires a finding that the party engaged in conduct with the intention of affecting the market price of a commodity, which is determined by the forces of supply and demand, and as a result of such conduct an artificial price was created. **15.26**

The conduct complained of can consist of such things as deceit, trickery through the spreading of false rumours, concealment of position, and the violation of express anti-manipulation controls, to create an 'artificial price' not in accordance with the forces of supply and demand. **15.27**

---

[18] *Transnor*, above, and *de Atucha v Commodity Exchange, Inc.*, 608 F. Supp. 510 (USDC SDNY, 1985).

[19] A kind of oil produced in the North Sea in UK and Norwegian fields. It was the subject of the *Transnor* case, above.

[20] 430 U.S. 462, 476–477(1977).

15.28 The courts have found that the prohibited felony of market manipulation will have occurred if there is:

(1) 'conduct';
(2) 'intentionally engaged in';
(3) 'which resulted in a price ... which does not reflect the basic forces of supply and demand'.[21]

15.29 Manipulation can result in 'corners' or 'squeezes'. A 'corner' (for purposes of the CEA) may generally be defined as a programme of manipulation of the prices of a particular commodity whereby a trader or group of traders gains control of the supply or the future demand for a commodity and requires the 'shorts' to settle their obligations either by purchase of deliverable qualities of the commodity or a supply of offsetting 'long' contracts at an abnormal price imposed by the 'cornerer'. A 'squeeze' is maintaining, during a particular delivery month, a large long position of a commodity's known deliverable supplies together with ownership or control over a substantial part of the deliverable supplies for the purposes of pressuring prices upward in order to 'squeeze' the shorts by requiring them to pay artificial prices in order to settle their contractual obligations.

15.30 Under CEA, s 4c, it is made unlawful for any person to offer to enter into, to enter into, or to confirm the execution of a transaction that 'is of the character of, or is commonly known to the trade as, a "wash sale" or "accommodation trade"; or is a fictitious sale; or is used to cause any price to be reported, registered, or recorded that is not a true a *bona fide* price'.

15.31 The CFTC defined 'market risk' as follows:

> To be 'fictitious' within the meaning of Section 4c(a)(A), ... [i]t is sufficient if the transaction is structured to negate price competition or market risk. [Citation omitted]. For these purposes, price competition or market risk is negated when it is reduced to a level that has no practical impact on the transaction at issue. [For example], [a] (wash sale under Section 4c(a)(A)) [was found when a] broker was instructed to fill buy and sell orders for the same commodity futures contract for the same account with no more than a three point loss.[22]

CEA, s 13(a) makes any person who commits, or who wilfully aids, abets, counsels, commands, induces or procures the commission of a violation of *any* of the provisions of the CEA responsible for such violations 'as a principal'.

15.32 However, an important difference to note between the CEA treatment of market manipulation and the UK treatment under the FSMA is that a finding

---

[21] *Cargill Inc. v Harden*, 452 F.2d 1154, 1162-63 (8th Cir. 1971).
[22] US Commodity Futures Trading Commission, *In re Gimbel* [1987–1990 Transfer Binder] Comm. Fut. L. Rep. (CCH) 24,213 at 35,003, n. 7 (CFTC 14 April 1988).

of market manipulation under the CEA requires a finding of intent or wilfulness. It is not sufficient that the conduct has a distorting 'effect' on the market in question.

F. The Sarbanes–Oxley Act[23]

The Sarbanes–Oxley Act ('SOX' or 'the Act') is a United States Federal law enacted in 2002 in response to a number of corporate governance and accounting scandals including those affecting Tyco, Enron and Worldcom. These scandals caused upheaval within the US financial services industry and prompted public outcry against the reporting procedures of US corporations. Thus the purpose of the Act is 'to protect investors by improving the accuracy and reliability of corporate disclosures made pursuant to the securities laws'.[24]   **15.33**

Primarily, SOX enhances reporting standards for the boards and management bodies of all US public companies and public accounting firms. It is one of the most far-reaching corporate governance provisions to be passed since the 1930s and it is also the most extensive foreign corporate governance reform since the Foreign Corrupt Practices Act (FCPA) of 1977.[25] As a result, immediately after SOX was enacted, the international community, and particularly representatives from countries within the European Union, became concerned about the extra-territorial applicability of the Act. To date, only one case has directly addressed the applicability of SOX abroad.[26] Therefore, seven years after the enactment of the Act, the extent of its international reach is still unresolved.   **15.34**

(1) The extraterritorial applicability of SOX: overview

The SEC has declared that SOX is applicable to all foreign firms that are listed or registered on a US securities exchange, despite the historical presumption against extraterritorial application of US regulatory frameworks.[27] In 2002, at the time that the Act was passed, approximately 1,300 foreign corporations were listed on   **15.35**

---

[23] Pub. L. No. 107–204, 116 Stat. 745 (2002) (codified as amended in various sections of 15, 28 U.S.C.).

[24] *Ibid.*

[25] See Clyde Stoltenberg *et al.*, *A Comparative Analysis of Post-Sarbanes–Oxley Corporate Governance Developments in the US and European Union: The Impact of Tensions Created by Extraterritorial Application of Section 404*, 53 Am. J. Comp. L. 457 (2005).

[26] See *Carnero v Boston Scientific Corporation*, 433 F.3d 1 (1st Cir. 2006) (holding that the whistleblower protection provision of the Sarbanes–Oxley Act does not have extraterritorial application to protect foreign employees working abroad for foreign subsidiaries).

[27] Corinne A. Falencki, *Sarbanes–Oxley: Ignoring the Presumption Against Extraterritoriality*, 36 Geo. Wash. Int'l L. Rev. 1211, 1216 (2004).

the American stock exchanges, and most of the largest EU companies are dual-listed in the United States.[28]

15.36   Prior to the enactment of SOX, non-US companies listed in the United States were simply required to disclose their corporate governance arrangements.[29] These disclosure rules were, therefore, naturally compatible with foreign legal systems. The same is not true, however, in relation to SOX.

15.37   Controversy over the extraterritorial reach of SOX tends to focus on the extent to which the United States should have regulatory power over companies that are organized under the laws of other states. Justification for US jurisdiction emanates from the principle that conduct which occurs extraterritorially, but nonetheless has effects within the United States, is a valid basis for jurisdiction.[30] This general principle applies both to civil and criminal codes. From the United States perspective US courts would therefore have a basis for jurisdiction over the conduct of the boards of directors of companies listed on US stock exchanges and who have US-based investors.

15.38   However, from the perspective of foreign companies, US jurisdiction over the conduct of directors of non-US companies is more controversial. Congress, unlike the office of the President, the SEC or the New York Stock Exchange, does not have any international constituency and has almost no contact with or accountability among the international community.[31] Thus, particularly with regard to the Act's non-criminal provisions and to conduct in foreign jurisdictions that might actually be condemned under SOX but encouraged under foreign rules, the reach of SOX is more questionable.

(2) Application of SOX with respect to specific titles

15.39   The Sarbanes–Oxley Act is divided into 11 different titles.[32] All the provisions are applicable to non-US companies; however, certain provisions have had more of an

---

[28]   See Mindora D. Vancea, *Exporting US Corporate Governance Standards Through the Sarbanes–Oxley Act: Unilateralism or Cooperation?*, 53 *Duke L. J.* 833, 839 (2003).

[29]   See Maria Camilla Cardilli, *Regulation Without Borders: The Impact of Sarbanes–Oxley on European Companies*, 27 *Fordham Int'l L. J.* 785, 792 (2004).

[30]   See generally Vancea, above n. 28, at note 3.

[31]   See Vancea, above n. 28, at note 8.

[32]   (1) Public Company Accounting Oversight Board (PCAOB) (establishing the PCAOB to provide independent oversight of public auditors); (2) Auditor Independence (laying out standards for auditor independence and restricting auditors from providing non-audit services to the same companies to which it provides auditing services); (3) Corporate Responsibility (mandating that senior executives take individual responsibility for the accuracy and completeness of corporate financial reports); (4) Enhanced Financial Disclosures (describing enhanced reporting requirements for financial transactions); (5) Analyst Conflicts of Interest (defining the codes of conduct for securities analysts and requiring disclosure of knowable conflicts of interest); (6) Commission Resources

impact on foreign companies than others. In particular, whistleblower protections for employees, the strengthening of criminal and civil penalties for violations of securities laws, and the additional reporting requirements imposed by SOX have been particularly relevant for foreign entities and members of foreign corporate boards.

(3) Whistleblower protections and international jurisdiction

Perhaps the most significant development in assessing the extraterritorial jurisdiction of SOX came in the context of s 1107 of the Act, which established criminal penalties for retaliation against whistleblowing employees. This provision reads: **15.40**

> Whoever knowingly, with the intent to retaliate, takes any action harmful to any person, including interference with the lawful employment or livelihood of any person, for providing to a law enforcement officer any truthful information relating to the commission or possible commission of any federal offense, shall be fined under this title, imprisoned not more than 10 years, or both.[33]

However, in *Carnero v Boston Scientific Corporation*, a 2006 case, the United States First Circuit declared that this section of the Act does not have extraterritorial application to protect foreign employees working abroad for foreign subsidiaries.[34] The First Circuit pointed out that Congress was silent on how to apply the whistleblower provision of SOX abroad, and, citing several Supreme Court cases, reasoned that, 'where a statute is silent as to its territorial reach, and no contrary congressional intent clearly appears, there is generally a presumption against its extraterritorial application'.[35] This reasoning, and its presumption against application of criminal sanctions, could easily be extended to other sections of SOX which are silent on extraterritoriality, thereby significantly limiting the application of SOX to foreign companies.

---

and Authority (defining SEC authority to censure or bar securities professionals from practice); (7) Studies and Reports (requiring the Comptroller General and the SEC to perform various studies and report their findings); (8) Corporate and Criminal Fraud Accountability (describes specific criminal penalties for fraud by manipulation, destruction or alteration of financial records or other interference with investigations, and provides protections for whistle-blowers); (9) White Collar Crime Penalty Enhancement (increasing criminal penalties associated with white-collar crimes and conspiracies); (10) Corporate Tax Returns (stating that the CEO should sign the company tax return) and (11) Corporate Fraud Accountability (identifying corporate fraud and records tampering as criminal offences).

[33] 18 U.S.C. § 1513(e).
[34] See *Carnero v Boston Scientific Corporation*, 433 F.3d 1 (1st Cir. 2006).
[35] See *ibid.*, at 7.

(4) Stronger criminal penalties for violations of securities laws

15.41 Titles 8 and 9 of SOX set forth various increases in the penalties associated with criminal activity in the securities industry, particularly in relation to wire and mail fraud contemplated by s 10(b) of the Securities Exchange Act of 1934 (the 'Exchange Act'). SOX, s 802(a), for example, provides that:

> Whoever knowingly alters, destroys, mutilates, conceals, covers up, falsifies, or makes a false entry in any record, document, or tangible object with the intent to impede, obstruct, or influence the investigation or proper administration of any matter within the jurisdiction of any department or agency of the United States or any case filed under title 11, or in relation to or contemplation of any such matter or case, shall be fined under this title, imprisoned not more than 20 years, or both.[36]

This provision, as well as other similar criminal provisions, increased fines and also increased the prison sentences under these statutes from five to 20 years. However, as implied above, following the First Circuit *Carnero* decision, the extent to which US courts would apply these provisions extraterritorially is not clear.

15.42 SOX also amended the Exchange Act to enable the SEC to remove any officer or director who has been found in violation of any provision of s 10(b).[37] Again, this provision seems to be directed primarily at domestic (US) companies, but it is possible that this would have implications for any company listed on US exchanges.

(5) Implementation of internal controls, certification of reports and the Independent Auditing Committee

15.43 Another controversial aspect of SOX relates to the expensive and sometimes incompatible reporting requirements it imposes on foreign companies. Under SOX, CEOs and CFOs of a company must (i) personally certify that the company's annual and quarterly reports are accurate, and that they do not contain any material misstatements or misleading information (s 302) and (ii) along with the external auditor, report on the adequacy of the company's internal control over financial reporting (s 404). Failure to comply with these rules can result in both civil liability and criminal sanctions under s 906.

15.44 These provisions have been problematic for foreign companies. The implementation of such internal controls under s 404 of the Act can be prohibitively costly

---

[36] 18 U.S.C. § 1519.

[37] See 15 U.S.C. § 78 (u-3). The Securities Exchange Act of 1934 amended by the Sarbanes–Oxley Act of 2002 ('the Commission may issue an order to prohibit, conditionally or unconditionally, and permanently or for such period of time as it shall determine, any person who has violated section 10(b) … from acting as an officer or director').

and, some argue, have had the effect of foreign companies, especially the smaller ones that may be less likely to afford a reporting overhaul, delisting from US exchanges. In addition, English corporate governance rules require that all directors, rather than just the CFO and CEO, collegially certify company records.

A further provision imposing the requirement of an independent audit committee under s 301 of the Act has also come into direct conflict with civil law systems. Under s 301, the independent audit committee is 'directly responsible for the appointment, compensation, and oversight' of the work of any accounting firm employed by the company. The provision also requires the members of the audit committee to receive no compensation from the company. Because many civil-law companies, under codetermination laws, have employees who sit on boards, it is difficult for civil law issuers to comply with this aspect of the Act's stringent independence requirements.[38]   **15.45**

G. Conclusion

US legislation and regulations give the US Government, and private litigants, a   **15.46**
broad range of remedies for financial market misconduct which may have occurred wholly outside the borders of the US. To give financial market participants some idea of the breadth and long reach of US financial market regulation, some of the laws and enforcement issues are described above. It is, of course, not possible to discuss all the possible applicable state and federal regulations here, or all the pitfalls.

A US judgment of market misconduct can result in the imposition of a variety of   **15.47**
civil and criminal fines, injunctions, restitutions, imprisonment, and/or heavy civil damages (sometimes treble). It is also worth remembering that, unlike the UK, the prevailing party does not usually get significant costs (such as attorneys' fees), most civil trials can be tried before a local jury, and 'no win, no fee' arrangements are common. Thus, it would be mistake for any international financial market participant to lose sight of the possible application of US law with respect to any non-US transaction which could have a foreseeable US impact.

---

[38] See John C. Coffee, Jr., *Racing Towards the Top?: The Impact of Cross-Listings and Stock Market Competition on International Corporate Governance*, 102 *Colum. L. Rev.* 1757, 1825 (2002).

16

CONCLUSIONS

A. UK Market Abuse Regulation

Reviewing the work that has been done, and the regulatory material that has been **16.01** issued since the Bill that became the FSMA was originally introduced, it is undeniable that the FSA has made a determined effort to install a flexible and effective regime to deter and punish market abuse.

The very fact that the market abuse regime causes so much comment in the finan- **16.02** cial services industry is one measure of its success. Every market professional seems aware of its potential scope and serious intent.

It is not a simple regime. To many, it is worryingly complex. But so is market **16.03** abuse. To keep pace with the chameleon-like changeability of schemes to win unfair profits in the financial markets, the FSA needs a significant degree of indeterminate flexibility. If the methods of market abuse were certain, the FSA's potential responses could be made entirely predictable. The international financial markets are essential, but not ideal. To keep them strong and fair, the FSA must have the flexibility to respond rapidly to, as yet unknown, market threats.

At the moment, it looks as though the UK has managed to put a pretty good sys- **16.04** tem in place. It remains relatively new, so changes will probably be necessary as the Government and the courts review its workings over time. However, the response of the FSA to the Tribunal decisions in the *Legal & General* case, discussed above, and to more recent financial market problems, show that the FSA is committed to moving rapidly to improve its regulatory approach when changes are found to be necessary. Such a response is praise-worthy and can only contribute to enhancing confidence in the market abuse regime.

B. And Beyond

16.05   In the past, much financial services business has been subject to 'self' or 'light-handed' regulation. This is no longer true for market abuse or for financial market regulation generally. The introduction of the new UK regime, as modified by the even more recent EU Market Abuse Directive, and subject to additional changes as a result of the 2008/09 financial market problems, means that all financial services activity is now subject to increased scrutiny of market abuse regulation in major market centres around the world.

16.06   In essence, the current market abuse regulations mean that financial market participants have an overriding duty to ensure that the markets are run 'efficiently and fairly'. This duty is superior to the duty that financial market participants owe to their owners. They have a duty to run the markets not only for their own benefit, but for the benefit of market participants, investors and the public generally. With the wide reach of the UK market abuse regime, that of the EU Directive, and regulations such as those in the US (all due to become increasingly tougher), this duty now applies to all financial markets whether they are traded on-exchange, OTC or in 'grey' or 'black' form.

16.07   This creates a complicated situation for traders operating in an international market. Market participants will need to think carefully about how these regimes apply to them and how they will affect their businesses.

16.08   In summary, the regulation of market abuse imposes a serious new duty on market participants to make sure the markets are fairly run, and the coverage of that duty now appears inescapably wide.

APPENDIX I

Financial Services and Markets Act 2000 (selected sections)

An Act to make provision about the regulation of financial services and markets; to provide for the transfer of certain statutory functions relating to building societies, friendly societies, industrial and provident societies and certain other mutual societies; and for connected purposes.

[14th June 2000]

PART I
THE REGULATOR

The Financial Services Authority.

1.—(1) The body corporate known as the Financial Services Authority ("the Authority") is to have the functions conferred on it by or under this Act.

(2) The Authority must comply with the requirements as to its constitution set out in Schedule 1.

(3) Schedule 1 also makes provision about the status of the Authority and the exercise of certain of its functions.

The Authority's general duties

The Authority's general duties.

2.—(1) In discharging its general functions the Authority must, so far as is reasonably possible, act in a way—

(a) which is compatible with the regulatory objectives; and

(b) which the Authority considers most appropriate for the purpose of meeting those objectives.

(2) The regulatory objectives are—

(a) market confidence;

(b) public awareness;

(c) the protection of consumers; and

(d) the reduction of financial crime.

(3) In discharging its general functions the Authority must have regard to—

(a) the need to use its resources in the most efficient and economic way;

(b) the responsibilities of those who manage the affairs of authorised persons;

(c) the principle that a burden or restriction which is imposed on a person, or on the carrying on of an activity, should be proportionate to the benefits, considered in general terms, which are expected to result from the imposition of that burden or restriction;

(d) the desirability of facilitating innovation in connection with regulated activities;

(e) the international character of financial services and markets and the desirability of maintaining the competitive position of the United Kingdom;

(f) the need to minimise the adverse effects on competition that may arise from anything done in the discharge of those functions;

(g) the desirability of facilitating competition between those who are subject to any form of regulation by the Authority.

(4) The Authority's general functions are—

(a) its function of making rules under this Act (considered as a whole);

(b) its function of preparing and issuing codes under this Act (considered as a whole);

(c) its functions in relation to the giving of general guidance (considered as a whole); and

(d) its function of determining the general policy and principles by reference to which it performs particular functions.

(5) "General guidance" has the meaning given in section 158(5).

The regulatory objectives

Market confidence. **3.**—(1) The market confidence objective is: maintaining confidence in the financial system.

(2) "The financial system" means the financial system operating in the United Kingdom and includes—

(a) financial markets and exchanges;

(b) regulated activities; and

(c) other activities connected with financial markets and exchanges.

Public awareness. **4.**—(1) The public awareness objective is: promoting public understanding of the financial system.

(2) It includes, in particular—

(a) promoting awareness of the benefits and risks associated with different kinds of investment or other financial dealing; and

(b) the provision of appropriate information and advice.

(3) "The financial system" has the same meaning as in section 3.

The protection of consumers. **5.**—(1) The protection of consumers objective is: securing the appropriate degree of protection for consumers.

(2) In considering what degree of protection may be appropriate, the Authority must have regard to—

(a) the differing degrees of risk involved in different kinds of investment or other transaction;

(b) the differing degrees of experience and expertise that different consumers may have in relation to different kinds of regulated activity;

(c) the needs that consumers may have for advice and accurate information; and

(d) the general principle that consumers should take responsibility for their decisions.

(3) "Consumers" means persons—

(a) who are consumers for the purposes of section 138; or

(b) who, in relation to regulated activities carried on otherwise than by authorised persons, would be consumers for those purposes if the activities were carried on by authorised persons.

The reduction of financial crime. **6.**—(1) The reduction of financial crime objective is: reducing the extent to which it is possible for a business carried on—

(a) by a regulated person, or

254

(b) in contravention of the general prohibition, to be used for a purpose connected with financial crime.

(2) In considering that objective the Authority must, in particular, have regard to the desirability of—

(a) regulated persons being aware of the risk of their businesses being used in connection with the commission of financial crime;

(b) regulated persons taking appropriate measures (in relation to their administration and employment practices, the conduct of transactions by them and otherwise) to prevent financial crime, facilitate its detection and monitor its incidence;

(c) regulated persons devoting adequate resources to the matters mentioned in paragraph (b).

(3) "Financial crime" includes any offence involving—

(a) fraud or dishonesty;

(b) misconduct in, or misuse of information relating to, a financial market; or

(c) handling the proceeds of crime.

(4) "Offence" includes an act or omission which would be an offence if it had taken place in the United Kingdom.

(5) "Regulated person" means an authorised person, a recognised investment exchange or a recognised clearing house.

Corporate governance

Duty of Authority to follow principles of good governance.
7.—In managing its affairs, the Authority must have regard to such generally accepted principles of good corporate governance as it is reasonable to regard as applicable to it.

Arrangements for consulting practitioners and consumers

The Authority's general duty to consult.
8.—The Authority must make and maintain effective arrangements for consulting practitioners and consumers on the extent to which its general policies and practices are consistent with its general duties under section 2.

The Practitioner Panel.
9.—(1) Arrangements under section 8 must include the establishment and maintenance of a panel of persons (to be known as "the Practitioner Panel") to represent the interests of practitioners.

(2) The Authority must appoint one of the members of the Practitioner Panel to be its chairman.

(3) The Treasury's approval is required for the appointment or dismissal of the chairman.

(4) The Authority must have regard to any representations made to it by the Practitioner Panel.

(5) The Authority must appoint to the Practitioner Panel such—

(a) individuals who are authorised persons,

(b) persons representing authorised persons,

(c) persons representing recognised investment exchanges, and

(d) persons representing recognised clearing houses, as it considers appropriate.

Reviews

Reviews.
12.—(1) The Treasury may appoint an independent person to conduct a review of the economy, efficiency and effectiveness with which the Authority has used its resources in discharging its functions.

(2) A review may be limited by the Treasury to such functions of the Authority (however described) as the Treasury may specify in appointing the person to conduct it.

(3) A review is not to be concerned with the merits of the Authority's general policy or principles in pursuing regulatory objectives or in exercising functions under Part VI.

(4) On completion of a review, the person conducting it must make a written report to the Treasury—

(a) setting out the result of the review; and

(b) making such recommendations (if any) as he considers appropriate.

(5) A copy of the report must be—

(a) laid before each House of Parliament; and

(b) published in such manner as the Treasury consider appropriate.

(6) Any expenses reasonably incurred in the conduct of a review are to be met by the Treasury out of money provided by Parliament.

(7) "Independent" means appearing to the Treasury to be independent of the Authority.

Right to obtain documents and information.

13.—(1) A person conducting a review under section 12—

(a) has a right of access at any reasonable time to all such documents as he may reasonably require for purposes of the review; and

(b) may require any person holding or accountable for any such document to provide such information and explanation as are reasonably necessary for that purpose.

(2) Subsection (1) applies only to documents in the custody or under the control of the Authority.

(3) An obligation imposed on a person as a result of the exercise of powers conferred by subsection (1) is enforceable by injunction or, in Scotland, by an order for specific performance under section 45 of the Court of Session Act 1988.

Part II
Regulated and Prohibited Activities

The general prohibition

The general prohibition.

19.—(1) No person may carry on a regulated activity in the United Kingdom, or purport to do so, unless he is—

(a) an authorised person; or

(b) an exempt person.

(2) The prohibition is referred to in this Act as the general prohibition.

Requirement for permission

Authorised persons acting without permission.

20.—(1) If an authorised person carries on a regulated activity in the United Kingdom, or purports to do so, otherwise than in accordance with permission—

(a) given to him by the Authority under Part IV, or

(b) resulting from any other provision of this Act,

he is to be taken to have contravened a requirement imposed on him by the Authority under this Act.

(2) The contravention does not—

(a) make a person guilty of an offence;

(b) make any transaction void or unenforceable; or

(c) (subject to subsection (3)) give rise to any right of action for breach of statutory duty.

(3) In prescribed cases the contravention is actionable at the suit of a person who suffers loss as a result of the contravention, subject to the defences and other incidents applying to actions for breach of statutory duty.

Financial promotion

Restrictions on financial promotion.

21.—(1) A person ("A") must not, in the course of business, communicate an invitation or inducement to engage in investment activity.

(2) But subsection (1) does not apply if—

    (a) A is an authorised person; or

    (b) the content of the communication is approved for the purposes of this section by an authorised person.

(3) In the case of a communication originating outside the United Kingdom, subsection (1) applies only if the communication is capable of having an effect in the United Kingdom.

(4) The Treasury may by order specify circumstances in which a person is to be regarded for the purposes of subsection (1) as—

    (a) acting in the course of business;

    (b) not acting in the course of business.

(5) The Treasury may by order specify circumstances (which may include compliance with financial promotion rules) in which subsection (1) does not apply.

(6) An order under subsection (5) may, in particular, provide that subsection (1) does not apply in relation to communications—

    (a) of a specified description;

    (b) originating in a specified country or territory outside the United Kingdom;

    (c) originating in a country or territory which falls within a specified description of country or territory outside the United Kingdom; or

    (d) originating outside the United Kingdom.

(7) The Treasury may by order repeal subsection (3).

(8) "Engaging in investment activity" means—

    (a) entering or offering to enter into an agreement the making or performance of which by either party constitutes a controlled activity; or

    (b) exercising any rights conferred by a controlled investment to acquire, dispose of, underwrite or convert a controlled investment.

(9) An activity is a controlled activity if—

    (a) it is an activity of a specified kind or one which falls within a specified class of activity; and

    (b) it relates to an investment of a specified kind, or to one which falls within a specified class of investment.

(10) An investment is a controlled investment if it is an investment of a specified kind or one which falls within a specified class of investment.

(11) Schedule 2 (except paragraph 26) applies for the purposes of subsections (9) and (10) with references to section 22 being read as references to each of those subsections.

(12) Nothing in Schedule 2, as applied by subsection (11), limits the powers conferred by subsection (9) or (10).

(13) "Communicate" includes causing a communication to be made.

(14) "Investment" includes any asset, right or interest.

(15) "Specified" means specified in an order made by the Treasury.

Regulated activities

The classes of
activity and
categories of
investment.

22.—(1) An activity is a regulated activity for the purposes of this Act if it is an activity of a specified kind which is carried on by way of business and—

(a) relates to an investment of a specified kind; or

(b) in the case of an activity of a kind which is also specified for the purposes of this paragraph, is carried on in relation to property of any kind.

(2) Schedule 2 makes provision supplementing this section.

(3) Nothing in Schedule 2 limits the powers conferred by subsection (1).

(4) "Investment" includes any asset, right or interest.

(5) "Specified" means specified in an order made by the Treasury.

Offences

Contravention
of the general
prohibition.

23.—(1) A person who contravenes the general prohibition is guilty of an offence and liable—

(a) on summary conviction, to imprisonment for a term not exceeding six months or a fine not exceeding the statutory maximum, or both;

(b) on conviction on indictment, to imprisonment for a term not exceeding two years or a fine, or both.

(2) In this Act "an authorisation offence" means an offence under this section.

(3) In proceedings for an authorisation offence it is a defence for the accused to show that he took all reasonable precautions and exercised all due diligence to avoid committing the offence.

False claims to be
authorised or
exempt.

24.—(1) A person who is neither an authorised person nor, in relation to the regulated activity in question, an exempt person is guilty of an offence if he—

(a) describes himself (in whatever terms) as an authorised person;

(b) describes himself (in whatever terms) as an exempt person in relation to the regulated activity; or

(c) behaves, or otherwise holds himself out, in a manner which indicates (or which is reasonably likely to be understood as indicating) that he is—

(i) an authorised person; or

(ii) an exempt person in relation to the regulated activity.

(2) In proceedings for an offence under this section it is a defence for the accused to show that he took all reasonable precautions and exercised all due diligence to avoid committing the offence.

(3) A person guilty of an offence under this section is liable on summary conviction to imprisonment for a term not exceeding six months or a fine not exceeding level 5 on the standard scale, or both.

(4) But where the conduct constituting the offence involved or included the public display of any material, the maximum fine for the offence is level 5 on the standard scale multiplied by the number of days for which the display continued.

25.—(1) A person who contravenes section 21(1) is guilty of an offence and liable —

(a) on summary conviction, to imprisonment for a term not exceeding six months or a fine not exceeding the statutory maximum, or both;

(b) on conviction on indictment, to imprisonment for a term not exceeding two years or a fine, or both.

(2) In proceedings for an offence under this section it is a defence for the accused to show—

(a) that he believed on reasonable grounds that the content of the communication was prepared, or approved for the purposes of section 21, by an authorised person; or

Contravention of section 21.	(b) that he took all reasonable precautions and exercised all due diligence to avoid committing the offence.

Enforceability of agreements

Agreements made by unauthorised persons.	**26.**—(1) An agreement made by a person in the course of carrying on a regulated activity in contravention of the general prohibition is unenforceable against the other party.

(2) The other party is entitled to recover—

(a) any money or other property paid or transferred by him under the agreement; and

(b) compensation for any loss sustained by him as a result of having parted with it.

(3) "Agreement" means an agreement—

(a) made after this section comes into force; and

(b) the making or performance of which constitutes, or is part of, the regulated activity in question.

(4) This section does not apply if the regulated activity is accepting deposits.

Agreements made through unauthorised persons.	**27.**—(1) An agreement made by an authorised person ("the provider")—

(a) in the course of carrying on a regulated activity (not in contravention of the general prohibition), but

(b) in consequence of something said or done by another person ("the third party") in the course of a regulated activity carried on by the third party in contravention of the general prohibition, is unenforceable against the other party.

(2) The other party is entitled to recover—

(a) any money or other property paid or transferred by him under the agreement; and

(b) compensation for any loss sustained by him as a result of having parted with it.

(3) "Agreement" means an agreement—

(a) made after this section comes into force; and

(b) the making or performance of which constitutes, or is part of, the regulated activity in question carried on by the provider.

(4) This section does not apply if the regulated activity is accepting deposits.

Agreements made unenforceable by section 26 or 27.	**28.**—(1) This section applies to an agreement which is unenforceable because of section 26 or 27.

(2) The amount of compensation recoverable as a result of that section is—

(a) the amount agreed by the parties; or

(b) on the application of either party, the amount determined by the court.

(3) If the court is satisfied that it is just and equitable in the circumstances of the case, it may allow—

(a) the agreement to be enforced; or

(b) money and property paid or transferred under the agreement to be retained.

(4) In considering whether to allow the agreement to be enforced or (as the case may be) the money or property paid or transferred under the agreement to be retained the court must—

(a) if the case arises as a result of section 26, have regard to the issue mentioned in subsection (5); or

(b) if the case arises as a result of section 27, have regard to the issue mentioned in subsection (6).

(5) The issue is whether the person carrying on the regulated activity concerned reasonably believed that he was not contravening the general prohibition by making the agreement.

(6) The issue is whether the provider knew that the third party was (in carrying on the regulated activity) contravening the general prohibition.

(7) If the person against whom the agreement is unenforceable—

    (a) elects not to perform the agreement, or

    (b) as a result of this section, recovers money paid or other property transferred by him under the agreement, he must repay any money and return any other property received by him under the agreement.

(8) If property transferred under the agreement has passed to a third party, a reference in section 26 or 27 or this section to that property is to be read as a reference to its value at the time of its transfer under the agreement.

(9) The commission of an authorisation offence does not make the agreement concerned illegal or invalid to any greater extent than is provided by section 26 or 27.

Accepting deposits in breach of general prohibition.

29.—(1) This section applies to an agreement between a person ("the depositor") and another person ("the deposit-taker") made in the course of the carrying on by the deposit-taker of accepting deposits in contravention of the general prohibition.

(2) If the depositor is not entitled under the agreement to recover without delay any money deposited by him, he may apply to the court for an order directing the deposit-taker to return the money to him.

(3) The court need not make such an order if it is satisfied that it would not be just and equitable for the money deposited to be returned, having regard to the issue mentioned in subsection (4).

(4) The issue is whether the deposit-taker reasonably believed that he was not contravening the general prohibition by making the agreement.

(5) "Agreement" means an agreement—

    (a) made after this section comes into force; and

    (b) the making or performance of which constitutes, or is part of, accepting deposits.

Enforceability of agreements resulting from unlawful communications.

30.—(1) In this section-"controlled agreement" means an agreement the making or performance of which by either party constitutes a controlled activity for the purposes of that section; and "controlled investment" has the same meaning as in section 21.

(2) If in consequence of an unlawful communication a person enters as a customer into a controlled agreement, it is unenforceable against him and he is entitled to recover—

    (a) any money or other property paid or transferred by him under the agreement; and

    (b) compensation for any loss sustained by him as a result of having parted with it.

(3) If in consequence of an unlawful communication a person exercises any rights conferred by a controlled investment, no obligation to which he is subject as a result of exercising them is enforceable against him and he is entitled to recover—

    (a) any money or other property paid or transferred by him under the obligation; and

    (b) compensation for any loss sustained by him as a result of having parted with it.

(4) But the court may allow—
  (a) the agreement or obligation to be enforced, or
  (b) money or property paid or transferred under the agreement or obliga-
      tion to be retained, if it is satisfied that it is just and equitable in the
      circumstances of the case.

(5) In considering whether to allow the agreement or obligation to be enforced
    or (as the case may be) the money or property paid or transferred under the
    agreement to be retained the court must have regard to the issues mentioned
    in subsections (6) and (7).

(6) If the applicant made the unlawful communication, the issue is whether he
    reasonably believed that he was not making such a communication.

(7) If the applicant did not make the unlawful communication, the issue is
    whether he knew that the agreement was entered into in consequence of such
    a communication.

(8) Applicant" means the person seeking to enforce the agreement or obligation
    or retain the money or property paid or transferred.

(9) Any reference to making a communication includes causing a communica-
    tion to be made.

(10) The amount of compensation recoverable as a result of subsection (2) or
     (3) is—
  (a) the amount agreed between the parties; or
  (b) on the application of either party, the amount determined by the court.

(11) If a person elects not to perform an agreement or an obligation which (by virtue
     of subsection (2) or (3)) is unenforceable against him, he must repay any money
     and return any other property received by him under the agreement.

(12) If (by virtue of subsection (2) or (3)) a person recovers money paid or prop-
     erty transferred by him under an agreement or obligation, he must repay any
     money and return any other property received by him as a result of exercising
     the rights in question.

(13) If any property required to be returned under this section has passed to a
     third party, references to that property are to be read as references to its value
     at the time of its receipt by the person required to return it.

Part III
Authorisation and Exemption
Authorisation

Authorised persons.

31.—(1) The following persons are authorised for the purposes of this
Act —
  (a) a person who has a Part IV permission to carry on one or more
      regulated activities;
  (b) an EEA firm qualifying for authorisation under Schedule 3;
  (c) a Treaty firm qualifying for authorisation under Schedule 4;
  (d) a person who is otherwise authorised by a provision of, or made
      under, this Act.

Partnerships and unincor-
porated associations.

(2) In this Act "authorised person" means a person who is authorised for
the purposes of this Act.

32.—(1) If a firm is authorised—
  (a) it is authorised to carry on the regulated activities concerned in the
      name of the firm; and
  (b) its authorisation is not affected by any change in its
      membership.

(2) If an authorised firm is dissolved, its authorisation continues to have effect in relation to any firm which succeeds to the business of the dissolved firm.

(3) For the purposes of this section, a firm is to be regarded as succeeding to the business of another firm only if—

(a) the members of the resulting firm are substantially the same as those of the former firm; and

(b) succession is to the whole or substantially the whole of the business of the former firm.

(4) "Firm" means—

(a) a partnership; or

(b) an unincorporated association of persons.

(5) "Partnership" does not include a partnership which is constituted under the law of any place outside the United Kingdom and is a body corporate.

Ending of authorisation

Withdrawal of authorisation by the Authority.

33.—(1) This section applies if—

(a) an authorised person's Part IV permission is cancelled; and

(b) as a result, there is no regulated activity for which he has permission.

(2) The Authority must give a direction withdrawing that person's status as an authorised person.

EEA firms.

34.—(1) An EEA firm ceases to qualify for authorisation under Part II of Schedule 3 if it ceases to be an EEA firm as a result of—

(a) having its EEA authorisation withdrawn; or

(b) ceasing to have an EEA right in circumstances in which EEA authorisation is not required.

(2) At the request of an EEA firm, the Authority may give a direction cancelling its authorisation under Part II of Schedule 3.

(3) If an EEA firm has a Part IV permission, it does not cease to be an authorised person merely because it ceases to qualify for authorisation under Part II of Schedule 3.

Treaty firms.

35.—(1) A Treaty firm ceases to qualify for authorisation under Schedule 4 if its home State authorisation is withdrawn.

(2) At the request of a Treaty firm, the Authority may give a direction cancelling its Schedule 4 authorisation.

(3) If a Treaty firm has a Part IV permission, it does not cease to be an authorised person merely because it ceases to qualify for authorisation under Schedule 4.

Persons authorised as a result of paragraph 1(1) of Schedule 5.

36.—(1) At the request of a person authorised as a result of paragraph 1(1) of Schedule 5, the Authority may give a direction cancelling his authorisation as such a person.

(2) If a person authorised as a result of paragraph 1(1) of Schedule 5 has a Part IV permission, he does not cease to be an authorised person merely because he ceases to be a person so authorised.

Exercise of EEA rights by UK firms

Exercise of EEA rights by UK firms.

37.—Part III of Schedule 3 makes provision in relation to the exercise outside the United Kingdom of EEA rights by UK firms.

PART IV
PERMISSION TO CARRY ON REGULATED
ACTIVITIES

Application for permission

Application for permission.

40.—(1) An application for permission to carry on one or more regulated activities may be made to the Authority by—

(a) an individual;

(b) a body corporate;

(c) a partnership; or

(d) an unincorporated association.

(2) An authorised person may not apply for permission under this section if he has a permission—

(a) given to him by the Authority under this Part, or

(b) having effect as if so given,

which is in force.

(3) An EEA firm may not apply for permission under this section to carry on a regulated activity which it is, or would be, entitled to carry on in exercise of an EEA right, whether through a United Kingdom branch or by providing services in the United Kingdom.

(4) A permission given by the Authority under this Part or having effect as if so given is referred to in this Act as "a Part IV permission".

The threshold conditions.

41.—(1) "The threshold conditions", in relation to a regulated activity, means the conditions set out in Schedule 6.

(2) In giving or varying permission, or imposing or varying any requirement, under this Part the Authority must ensure that the person concerned will satisfy, and continue to satisfy, the threshold conditions in relation to all of the regulated activities for which he has or will have permission.

(3) But the duty imposed by subsection (2) does not prevent the Authority, having due regard to that duty, from taking such steps as it considers are necessary, in relation to a particular authorised person, in order to secure its regulatory objective of the protection of consumers.

Permission

Giving permission.

42.—(1) "The applicant" means an applicant for permission under section 40.

(2) The Authority may give permission for the applicant to carry on the regulated activity or activities to which his application relates or such of them as may be specified in the permission.

(3) If the applicant—

    (a) in relation to a particular regulated activity, is exempt from the general prohibition as a result of section 39(1) or an order made under section 38(1), but

    (b) has applied for permission in relation to another regulated activity,

the application is to be treated as relating to all the regulated activities which, if permission is given, he will carry on.

(4) If the applicant—

    (a) in relation to a particular regulated activity, is exempt from the general prohibition as a result of section 285(2) or (3), but

    (b) has applied for permission in relation to another regulated activity, the application is to be treated as relating only to that other regulated activity.

(5) If the applicant—

    (a) is a person to whom, in relation to a particular regulated activity, the general prohibition does not apply as a result of Part XIX, but

    (b) has applied for permission in relation to another regulated activity, the application is to be treated as relating only to that other regulated activity.

(6) If it gives permission, the Authority must specify the permitted regulated activity or activities, described in such manner as the Authority considers appropriate.

(7) The Authority may—

    (a) incorporate in the description of a regulated activity such limitations (for example as to circumstances in which the activity may, or may not, be carried on) as it considers appropriate;

    (b) specify a narrower or wider description of regulated activity than that to which the application relates;

    (c) give permission for the carrying on of a regulated activity which is not included among those to which the application relates.

Imposition of requirements.

43.—(1) A Part IV permission may include such requirements as the Authority considers appropriate.

(2) A requirement may, in particular, be imposed—

    (a) so as to require the person concerned to take specified action; or

    (b) so as to require him to refrain from taking specified action.

(3) A requirement may extend to activities which are not regulated activities.

(4) A requirement may be imposed by reference to the person's relationship with—

    (a) his group; or

    (b) other members of his group.

(5) A requirement expires at the end of such period as the Authority may specify in the permission.

(6) But subsection (5) does not affect the Authority's powers under section 44 or 45.

Variation and cancellation of Part IV permission

44.—(1) The Authority may, on the application of an authorised person with a Part IV permission, vary the permission by—

   (a) adding a regulated activity to those for which it gives permission;

   (b) removing a regulated activity from those for which it gives permission;

   (c) varying the description of a regulated activity for which it gives permission;

   (d) cancelling a requirement imposed under section 43; or

   (e) varying such a requirement.

(2) The Authority may, on the application of an authorised person with a Part IV permission, cancel the permission.

(2A) Without prejudice to the generality of subsections (1) and (2), the Authority may, in relation to an authorized Person who is an investment firm, exercise its power under this section to cancel the Part IV permission of the firm if it appears to it that—

   (a) the firm has failed, during a period of at least six months, to carry on a regulated activity which is an investment service or activity for which it has a Part IV permission;

   (b) the firm obtained at the Part IV permission by making a false statement or by other irregular means;

   (c) the firm no longer satisfies the requirements for authorization pursuant to Chapter I of Title II of the markets in financial instruments directive, or pursuant to or contained in any Community legislation made under that Chapter, in relation to a regulated activity which is an investment service or activity for which it has a Part IV permission; or

   (d) The firm has seriously and systematically infringe to the operating conditions pursuant to Chapter II of Title II of the markets in financial instruments directive, or pursuant to or contained in any Community legislation made under that Chapter, in relation to a regulated activity which is an investment service or activity for which it has a Part IV permission.

(2B) for purposes of subsection (2A) A. regulated activity is an investment service or activity if it falls within the definition of "investment services and activities" in section 417 (1).

(3) The Authority may refuse an application under this section if it appears to it—

    (a) that the interests of consumers, or potential consumers, would be adversely affected if the application were to be granted; and

    (b) that it is desirable in the interests of consumers, or potential consumers, for the application to be refused.

(4) If, as a result of a variation of a Part IV permission under this section, there are no longer any regulated activities for which the authorised person concerned has permission, the Authority must, once it is satisfied that it is no longer necessary to keep the permission in force, cancel it.

(5) The Authority's power to vary a Part IV permission under this section extends to including any provision in the permission as varied that could be included if a fresh permission were being given in response to an application under section 40.

Variation etc. on the Authority's own initiative.

45.—(1) The Authority may exercise its power under this section in relation to an authorised person if it appears to it that—

    (a) he is failing, or is likely to fail, to satisfy the threshold conditions;

    (b) he has failed, during a period of at least 12 months, to carry on a regulated activity for which he has a Part IV permission; or

    (c) it is desirable to exercise that power in order to protect the interests of consumers or potential consumers.

(2) The Authority's power under this section is the power to vary a Part IV permission in any of the ways mentioned in section 44(1) or to cancel it.

(3) If, as a result of a variation of a Part IV permission under this section, there are no longer any regulated activities for which the authorised person concerned has permission, the Authority must, once it is satisfied that it is no longer necessary to keep the permission in force, cancel it.

(4) The Authority's power to vary a Part IV permission under this section extends to including any provision in the permission as varied that could be included if a fresh permission were being given in response to an application under section 40.

(5) The Authority's power under this section is referred to in this Part as its own-initiative power.

Variation of permission on acquisition of control.

46.—(1) This section applies if it appears to the Authority that—

    (a) a person has acquired control over a UK authorised person who has a Part IV permission; but

    (b) there are no grounds for exercising its own-initiative power.

(2) If it appears to the Authority that the likely effect of the acquisition of control on the authorised person, or on any of its activities, is uncertain the Authority may vary the authorised person's permission by—

    (a) imposing a requirement of a kind that could be imposed under section 43 on giving permission; or

    (b) varying a requirement included in the authorised person's permission under that section.

(3) Any reference to a person having acquired control is to be read in accordance with Part XII.

Exercise of power in support of overseas regulator.

47.—(1) The Authority's own-initiative power may be exercised in respect of an authorised person at the request of, or for the purpose of assisting, a regulator who is—

    (a) outside the United Kingdom; and

    (b) of a prescribed kind.

(2) Subsection (1) applies whether or not the Authority has powers which are exercisable in relation to the authorised person by virtue of any provision of Part XIII.

(3) If a request to the Authority for the exercise of its own-initiative power has been made by a regulator who is—

    (a) outside the United Kingdom,

    (b) of a prescribed kind, and

    (c) acting in pursuance of provisions of a prescribed kind, the Authority must, in deciding whether or not to exercise that power in response to the request, consider whether it is necessary to do so in order to comply with a Community obligation.

(4) In deciding in any case in which the Authority does not consider that the exercise of its own-initiative power is necessary in order to comply with a Community obligation, it may take into account in particular—

    (a) whether in the country or territory of the regulator concerned, corresponding assistance would be given to a United Kingdom regulatory authority;

    (b) whether the case concerns the breach of a law, or other requirement, which has no close parallel in the United Kingdom or involves the assertion of a jurisdiction not recognised by the United Kingdom;

(c) the seriousness of the case and its importance to persons in the United Kingdom;

(d) whether it is otherwise appropriate in the public interest to give the assistance sought.

(5) The Authority may decide not to exercise its own-initiative power, in response to a request, unless the regulator concerned undertakes to make such contribution towards the cost of its exercise as the Authority considers appropriate.

(6) Subsection (5) does not apply if the Authority decides that it is necessary for it to exercise its own-initiative power in order to comply with a Community obligation.

(7) In subsections (4) and (5) "request" means a request of a kind mentioned in subsection (1).

Prohibitions and restrictions.

48.—(1) This section applies if the Authority—

(a) on giving a person a Part IV permission, imposes an assets requirement on him; or

(b) varies an authorised person's Part IV permission so as to alter an assets requirement imposed on him or impose such a requirement on him.

(2) A person on whom an assets requirement is imposed is referred to in this section as "A".

(3) "Assets requirement" means a requirement under section 43—

(a) prohibiting the disposal of, or other dealing with, any of A's assets (whether in the United Kingdom or elsewhere) or restricting such disposals or dealings; or

(b) that all or any of A's assets, or all or any assets belonging to consumers but held by A or to his order, must be transferred to and held by a trustee approved by the Authority.

(4) If the Authority—

(a) imposes a requirement of the kind mentioned in subsection (3)(a), and

(b) gives notice of the requirement to any institution with whom A keeps an account,

the notice has the effects mentioned in subsection (5).

(5) Those effects are that—

(a) the institution does not act in breach of any contract with A if, having been instructed by A (or on his behalf) to transfer any sum or otherwise make any payment out of A's account, it refuses to do so in the reasonably held belief that complying with the instruction would be incompatible with the requirement; and

(b) if the institution complies with such an instruction, it is liable to pay to the Authority an amount equal to the amount transferred from, or otherwise paid out of, A's account in contravention of the requirement.

(6) If the Authority imposes a requirement of the kind mentioned in subsection (3)(b), no assets held by a person as trustee in accordance with the requirement may, while the requirement is in force, be released or dealt with except with the consent of the Authority.

(7) If, while a requirement of the kind mentioned in subsection (3)(b) is in force, A creates a charge over any assets of his held in accordance with the requirement, the charge is (to the extent that it confers security over the assets) void against the liquidator and any of A's creditors.

(8) Assets held by a person as trustee ("T") are to be taken to be held by T in accordance with a requirement mentioned in subsection (3)(b) only if—

   (a) A has given T written notice that those assets are to be held by T in accordance with the requirement; or

   (b) they are assets into which assets to which paragraph (a) applies have been transposed by T on the instructions of A.

(9) A person who contravenes subsection (6) is guilty of an offence and liable on summary conviction to a fine not exceeding level 5 on the standard scale.

(10) "Charge" includes a mortgage (or in Scotland a security over property).

(11) Subsections (6) and (8) do not affect any equitable interest or remedy in favour of a person who is a beneficiary of a trust as a result of a requirement of the kind mentioned in subsection (3)(b).

Connected persons

Persons connected with an applicant.

49.—(1) In considering—

   (a) an application for a Part IV permission, or

   (b) whether to vary or cancel a Part IV permission,

the Authority may have regard to any person appearing to it to be, or likely to be, in a relationship with the applicant or person given permission which is relevant.

(2) Before—

   (a) giving permission in response to an application made by a person who is connected with an EEA firm, or

   (b) Varying any permission given by the Authority to such a person, where the effect of the variation is to grant permission for purposes of a single market directive other than the one for purposes of which the existing permission was granted, the Authority must consult the firm's home state regulator.

(2A) But subsection (2) does not apply to the extent that the permission relates to—

(a) and insurance mediation activity (within the meaning given by paragraph 2 (5) of Schedule 6); or

(b) a regulated activity involving a regulated mortgage contract, a regulated home reversion plan or a regulated home purchase plan.

(3) A person ("A") is connected with an EEA firm if—

(a) A is a subsidiary undertaking of the firm; or

(b) A is a subsidiary undertaking of a parent undertaking of the firm.

Additional permissions

Authority's duty to consider other permissions etc.

50.—(1) "Additional Part IV permission" means a Part IV permission which is in force in relation to an EEA firm, a Treaty firm or a person authorised as a result of paragraph 1(1) of Schedule 5.

(2) If the Authority is considering whether, and if so how, to exercise its own-initiative power under this Part in relation to an additional Part IV permission, it must take into account—

(a) the home State authorisation of the authorised person concerned;

(b) any relevant directive; and

(c) relevant provisions of the Treaty.

Procedure

Applications under this Part.

51.—(1) An application for a Part IV permission must—

(a) contain a statement of the regulated activity or regulated activities which the applicant proposes to carry on and for which he wishes to have permission; and

(b) give the address of a place in the United Kingdom for service on the applicant of any notice or other document which is required or authorised to be served on him under this Act.

(2) An application for the variation of a Part IV permission must contain a statement—

(a) of the desired variation; and

(b) of the regulated activity or regulated activities which the applicant proposes to carry on if his permission is varied.

(3) Any application under this Part must—

(a) be made in such manner as the Authority may direct; and

(b) contain, or be accompanied by, such other information as the Authority may reasonably require.

(4) At any time after receiving an application and before determining it, the Authority may require the applicant to provide it with such further information as it reasonably considers necessary to enable it to determine the application.

(5) Different directions may be given, and different requirements imposed, in relation to different applications or categories of application.

(6) The Authority may require an applicant to provide information which he is required to provide under this section in such form, or to verify it in such a way, as the Authority may direct.

Determination of applications.

52.—(1) An application under this Part must be determined by the Authority before the end of the period of six months beginning with the date on which it received the completed application.

(2) The Authority may determine an incomplete application if it considers it appropriate to do so; and it must in any event determine such an application within twelve months beginning with the date on which it received the application.

(3) The applicant may withdraw his application, by giving the Authority written notice, at any time before the Authority determines it.

(4) If the Authority grants an application for, or for variation of, a Part IV permission, it must give the applicant written notice.

(5) The notice must state the date from which the permission, or the variation, has effect.

(6) If the Authority proposes—

   (a) to give a Part IV permission but to exercise its power under section 42(7)(a) or (b) or 43(1), or

   (b) to vary a Part IV permission on the application of an authorised person but to exercise its power under any of those provisions (as a result of section 44(5)),

   it must give the applicant a warning notice.

(7) If the Authority proposes to refuse an application made under this Part, it must (unless subsection (8) applies) give the applicant a warning notice.

(8) This subsection applies if it appears to the Authority that—

   (a) the applicant is an EEA firm; and

   (b) the application is made with a view to carrying on a regulated activity in a manner in which the applicant is, or would be, entitled to carry on that activity in the exercise of an EEA right whether through a United Kingdom branch or by providing services in the United Kingdom.

(9) If the Authority decides—

   (a) to give a Part IV permission but to exercise its power under section 42(7)(a) or (b) or 43(1),

   (b) to vary a Part IV permission on the application of an authorised person but to exercise its power under any of those provisions (as a result of section 44(5)), or

   (c) to refuse an application under this Part,

it must give the applicant a decision notice.

Exercise of own-ini tiative
power: procedure.

53.—(1) This section applies to an exercise of the Authority's own-initiative power to vary an authorised person's Part IV permission.

(2) A variation takes effect—

(a) immediately, if the notice given under subsection (4) states that that is the case;

(b) on such date as may be specified in the notice; or

(c) if no date is specified in the notice, when the matter to which the notice relates is no longer open to review.

(3) A variation may be expressed to take effect immediately (or on a specified date) only if the Authority, having regard to the ground on which it is exercising its own-initiative power, reasonably considers that it is necessary for the variation to take effect immediately (or on that date).

(4) If the Authority proposes to vary the Part IV permission, or varies it with immediate effect, it must give the authorised person written notice.

(5) The notice must—

(a) give details of the variation;

(b) state the Authority's reasons for the variation and for its determination as to when the variation takes effect;

(c) inform the authorised person that he may make representations to the Authority within such period as may be specified in the notice (whether or not he has referred the matter to the Tribunal);

(d) inform him of when the variation takes effect; and

(e) inform him of his right to refer the matter to the Tribunal.

(6) The Authority may extend the period allowed under the notice for making representations.

(7) If, having considered any representations made by the authorised person, the Authority decides—

(a) to vary the permission in the way proposed, or

(b) if the permission has been varied, not to rescind the variation, it must give him written notice.

(8) If, having considered any representations made by the authorised person, the Authority decides—

(a) not to vary the permission in the way proposed,

(b) to vary the permission in a different way, or

(c) to rescind a variation which has effect, it must give him written notice.

(9) A notice given under subsection (7) must inform the authorised person of his right to refer the matter to the Tribunal.

(10) A notice under subsection (8)(b) must comply with subsection (5).

(11) If a notice informs a person of his right to refer a matter to the Tribunal, it must give an indication of the procedure on such a reference.

(12) For the purposes of subsection (2)(c) , whether a matter is open to review is to be determined in accordance with section 391(8).

Cancellation of Part IV permission: procedure.

54.—(1) If the Authority proposes to cancel an authorised person's Part IV permission otherwise than at his request, it must give him a warning notice.

(2) If the Authority decides to cancel an authorised person's Part IV permission otherwise than at his request, it must give him a decision notice.

References to the Tribunal

Right to refer matters to the Tribunal.

55.—(1) An applicant who is aggrieved by the determination of an application made under this Part may refer the matter to the Tribunal.

(2) An authorised person who is aggrieved by the exercise of the Authority's own-initiative power may refer the matter to the Tribunal.

PART V
PERFORMANCE OF REGULATED ACTIVITIES
Prohibition orders

Prohibition orders.

56.—(1) Subsection (2) applies if it appears to the Authority that an individual is not a fit and proper person to perform functions in relation to a regulated activity carried on by an authorised person.

(2) The Authority may make an order ("a prohibition order") prohibiting the individual from performing a specified function, any function falling within a specified description or any function.

(3) A prohibition order may relate to—

(a) a specified regulated activity, any regulated activity falling within a specified description or all regulated activities;

(b) authorised persons generally or any person within a specified class of authorised person.

(4) An individual who performs or agrees to perform a function in breach of a prohibition order is guilty of an offence and liable on summary conviction to a fine not exceeding level 5 on the standard scale.

(5) In proceedings for an offence under subsection (4) it is a defence for the accused to show that he took all reasonable precautions and exercised all due diligence to avoid committing the offence.

(6) An authorised person must take reasonable care to ensure that no function of his, in relation to the carrying on of a regulated activity, is performed by a

person who is prohibited from performing that function by a prohibition order.

(7) The Authority may, on the application of the individual named in a prohibition order, vary or revoke it.

(8) This section applies to the performance of functions in relation to a regulated activity carried on by—

(a) a person who is an exempt person in relation to that activity, and

(b) a person to whom, as a result of Part XX, the general prohibition does not apply in relation to that activity, as it applies to the performance of functions in relation to a regulated activity carried on by an authorised person.

(9) "Specified" means specified in the prohibition order.

Prohibition orders: procedure and right to refer to Tribunal.

57.—(1) If the Authority proposes to make a prohibition order it must give the individual concerned a warning notice.

(2) The warning notice must set out the terms of the prohibition.

(3) If the Authority decides to make a prohibition order it must give the individual concerned a decision notice.

(4) The decision notice must—

(a) name the individual to whom the prohibition order applies;

(b) set out the terms of the order; and

(c) be given to the individual named in the order.

(5) A person against whom a decision to make a prohibition order is made may refer the matter to the Tribunal.

Applications relating to prohibitions: procedure and right to refer to Tribunal.

58.—(1) This section applies to an application for the variation or revocation of a prohibition order.

(2) If the Authority decides to grant the application, it must give the applicant written notice of its decision.

(3) If the Authority proposes to refuse the application, it must give the applicant a warning notice.

(4) If the Authority decides to refuse the application, it must give the applicant a decision notice.

(5) If the Authority gives the applicant a decision notice, he may refer the matter to the Tribunal.

Approval

Approval for particular arrangements.

59.—(1) An authorised person ("A") must take reasonable care to ensure that no person performs a controlled function under an arrangement entered into by A in relation to the carrying on by A of a regulated activity, unless the Authority approves the performance by that person of the controlled function to which the arrangement relates.

(2) An authorised person ("A") must take reasonable care to ensure that no person performs a controlled function under an arrangement entered into by a contractor of A in relation to the carrying on by A of a regulated activity, unless the Authority approves the performance by that person of the controlled function to which the arrangement relates.

(3) "Controlled function" means a function of a description specified in rules.

(4) The Authority may specify a description of function under subsection (3) only if, in relation to the carrying on of a regulated activity by an authorised person, it is satisfied that the first, second or third condition is met.

(5) The first condition is that the function is likely to enable the person responsible for its performance to exercise a significant influence on the conduct of the authorised person's affairs, so far as relating to the regulated activity.

(6) The second condition is that the function will involve the person performing it in dealing with customers of the authorised person in a manner substantially connected with the carrying on of the regulated activity.

(7) The third condition is that the function will involve the person performing it in dealing with property of customers of the authorised person in a manner substantially connected with the carrying on of the regulated activity.

(8) Neither subsection (1) nor subsection (2) applies to an arrangement which allows a person to perform a function if the question of whether he is a fit and proper person to perform the function is reserved under any of the single market directives to an authority in a country or territory outside the United Kingdom.

(9) In determining whether the first condition is met, the Authority may take into account the likely consequences of a failure to discharge that function properly.

(10) "Arrangement"—

    (a) means any kind of arrangement for the performance of a function of A which is entered into by A or any contractor of his with another person; and

    (b) includes, in particular, that other person's appointment to an office, his becoming a partner or his employment (whether under a contract of service or otherwise).

(11) "Customer", in relation to an authorised person, means a person who is using, or who is or may be contemplating using, any of the services provided by the authorised person.

Applications for approval.

60.—(1) An application for the Authority's approval under section 59 may be made by the authorised person concerned.

(2) The application must—

    (a) be made in such manner as the Authority may direct; and

    (b) contain, or be accompanied by, such information as the Authority may reasonably require.

(3) At any time after receiving the application and before determining it, the Authority may require the applicant to provide it with such further information as it reasonably considers necessary to enable it to determine the application.

(4) The Authority may require an applicant to present information which he is required to give under this section in such form, or to verify it in such a way, as the Authority may direct.

(5) Different directions may be given, and different requirements imposed, in relation to different applications or categories of application.

(6) "The authorised person concerned" includes a person who has applied for permission under Part IV and will be the authorised person concerned if permission is given.

Determination of applications.

61.—(1) The Authority may grant an application made under section 60 only if it is satisfied that the person in respect of whom the application is made ("the candidate") is a fit and proper person to perform the function to which the application relates.

(2) In deciding that question, the Authority may have regard (among other things) to whether the candidate, or any person who may perform a function on his behalf—

    (a) has obtained a qualification,

    (b) has undergone, or is undergoing, training, or

    (c) possesses a level of competence, required by general rules in relation to persons performing functions of the kind to which the application relates.

(3) The Authority must, before the end of the period of three months beginning with the date on which it receives an application made under section 60 ("the period for consideration"), determine whether—

    (a) to grant the application; or

    (b) to give a warning notice under section 62(2).

(4) If the Authority imposes a requirement under section 60(3), the period for consideration stops running on the day on which the requirement is imposed but starts running again—

    (a) on the day on which the required information is received by the Authority; or

    (b) if the information is not provided on a single day, on the last of the days on which it is received by the Authority.

(5) A person who makes an application under section 60 may withdraw his application by giving written notice to the Authority at any time before the Authority determines it, but only with the consent of—

    (a) the candidate; and

    (b) the person by whom the candidate is to be retained to perform the function concerned, if not the applicant.

Applications for approval: procedure and right to refer to Tribunal.

62.—(1) If the Authority decides to grant an application made under section 60 ("an application"), it must give written notice of its decision to each of the interested parties.

(2) If the Authority proposes to refuse an application, it must give a warning notice to each of the interested parties.

(3) If the Authority decides to refuse an application, it must give a decision notice to each of the interested parties.

(4) If the Authority decides to refuse an application, each of the interested parties may refer the matter to the Tribunal.

(5) "The interested parties", in relation to an application, are—

    (a) the applicant;

    (b) the person in respect of whom the application is made ("A"); and

    (c) the person by whom A's services are to be retained, if not the applicant.

Withdrawal of approval.

63.—(1) The Authority may withdraw an approval given under section 59 if it considers that the person in respect of whom it was given is not a fit and proper person to perform the function to which the approval relates.

(2) When considering whether to withdraw its approval, the Authority may take into account any matter which it could take into account if it were considering an application made under section 60 in respect of the performance of the function to which the approval relates.

(3) If the Authority proposes to withdraw its approval, it must give each of the interested parties a warning notice.

(4) If the Authority decides to withdraw its approval, it must give each of the interested parties a decision notice.

(5) If the Authority decides to withdraw its approval, each of the interested parties may refer the matter to the Tribunal.

(6) "The interested parties", in relation to an approval, are—

    (a) the person on whose application it was given ("A");

    (b) the person in respect of whom it was given ("B"); and

    (c) the person by whom B's services are retained, if not A.

Conduct

Conduct: statements and codes.

64.—(1) The Authority may issue statements of principle with respect to the conduct expected of approved persons.

(2) If the Authority issues a statement of principle under subsection (1), it must also issue a code of practice for the purpose of helping to determine whether or not a person's conduct complies with the statement of principle.

(3) A code issued under subsection (2) may specify—

    (a) descriptions of conduct which, in the opinion of the Authority, comply with a statement of principle;

    (b) descriptions of conduct which, in the opinion of the Authority, do not comply with a statement of principle;

    (c) factors which, in the opinion of the Authority, are to be taken into account in determining whether or not a person's conduct complies with a statement of principle.

(4) The Authority may at any time alter or replace a statement or code issued under this section.

(5) If a statement or code is altered or replaced, the altered or replacement statement or code must be issued by the Authority.

(6) A statement or code issued under this section must be published by the Authority in the way appearing to the Authority to be best calculated to bring it to the attention of the public.

(7) A code published under this section and in force at the time when any particular conduct takes place may be relied on so far as it tends to establish whether or not that conduct complies with a statement of principle.

(8) Failure to comply with a statement of principle under this section does not of itself give rise to any right of action by persons affected or affect the validity of any transaction.

(9) A person is not to be taken to have failed to comply with a statement of principle if he shows that, at the time of the alleged failure, it or its associated code of practice had not been published.

(10) The Authority must, without delay, give the Treasury a copy of any statement or code which it publishes under this section.

(11) The power under this section to issue statements of principle and codes of practice—

    (a) includes power to make different provision in relation to persons, cases or circumstances of different descriptions; and

    (b) is to be treated for the purposes of section 2(4)(a) as part of the Authority's rule-making functions.

(12) The Authority may charge a reasonable fee for providing a person with a copy of a statement or code published under this section.

(13) "Approved person" means a person in relation to whom the Authority has given its approval under section 59.

Statements and codes: procedure.

65.—(1) Before issuing a statement or code under section 64, the Authority must publish a draft of it in the way appearing to the Authority to be best calculated to bring it to the attention of the public.

(2) The draft must be accompanied by—

    (a) a cost benefit analysis; and

    (b) notice that representations about the proposal may be made to the Authority within a specified time.

(3) Before issuing the proposed statement or code, the Authority must have regard to any representations made to it in accordance with subsection (2)(b).

(4) If the Authority issues the proposed statement or code it must publish an account, in general terms, of—

    (a) the representations made to it in accordance with subsection (2)(b); and

    (b) its response to them.

(5) If the statement or code differs from the draft published under subsection (1) in a way which is, in the opinion of the Authority, significant-

    (a) the Authority must (in addition to complying with subsection (4)) publish details of the difference; and

    (b) those details must be accompanied by a cost benefit analysis.

(6) Neither subsection (2)(a) nor subsection (5)(b) applies if the Authority considers—

    (a) that, making the appropriate comparison, there will be no increase in costs; or

(b) that, making that comparison, there will be an increase in costs but the increase will be of minimal significance.

(7) Subsections (1) to (6) do not apply if the Authority considers that the delay involved in complying with them would prejudice the interests of consumers.

(8) A statement or code must state that it is issued under section 64.

(9) The Authority may charge a reasonable fee for providing a copy of a draft published under sub section (1).

(10) This section also applies to a proposal to alter or replace a statement or code.

(11) Cost benefit analysis" means an estimate of the costs together with an analysis of the benefits that will arise —

(a) if the proposed statement or code is issued; or

(b) if subsection (5)(b) applies, from the statement or code that has been issued.

(12) "The appropriate comparison" means—

(a) in relation to subsection (2)(a), a comparison between the overall position if the statement or code is issued and the overall position if it is not issued;

(b) in relation to subsection (5)(b), a comparison between the overall position after the issuing of the statement or code and the overall position before it was issued.

Disciplinary powers.   66.—(1) The Authority may take action against a person under this section if—

(a) it appears to the Authority that he is guilty of misconduct; and

(b) the Authority is satisfied that it is appropriate in all the circumstances to take action against him.

(2) A person is guilty of misconduct if, while an approved person—

(a) he has failed to comply with a statement of principle issued under section 64; or

(b) he has been knowingly concerned in a contravention by the relevant authorised person of a requirement imposed on that authorised person by or under this Act.

(3) If the Authority is entitled to take action under this section against a person, it may—

(a) impose a penalty on him of such amount as it considers appropriate; or

(b) publish a statement of his misconduct.

(4) The Authority may not take action under this section after the end of the period of two years beginning with the first day on which the Authority knew of the misconduct, unless proceedings in

respect of it against the person concerned were begun before the end of that period.

(5) For the purposes of subsection (4)—

   (a) the Authority is to be treated as knowing of misconduct if it has information from which the misconduct can reasonably be inferred; and

   (b) proceedings against a person in respect of misconduct are to be treated as begun when a warning notice is given to him under section 67(1).

(6) "Approved person" has the same meaning as in section 64.

(7) "Relevant authorised person", in relation to an approved person, means the person on whose application approval under section 59 was given.

67.—(1) If the Authority proposes to take action against a person under section 66, it must give him a warning notice.

(2) A warning notice about a proposal to impose a penalty must state the amount of the penalty.

(3) A warning notice about a proposal to publish a statement must set out the terms of the statement.

(4) If the Authority decides to take action against a person under section 66, it must give him a decision notice.

(5) A decision notice about the imposition of a penalty must state the amount of the penalty.

(6) A decision notice about the publication of a statement must set out the terms of the statement.

(7) If the Authority decides to take action against a person under section 66, he may refer the matter to the Tribunal.

68. After a statement under section 66 is published, the Authority must send a copy of it to the person concerned and to any person to whom a copy of the decision notice was given.

69.—(1) The Authority must prepare and issue a statement of its policy with respect to—

   (a) the imposition of penalties under section 66; and

   (b) the amount of penalties under that section.

(2) The Authority's policy in determining what the amount of a penalty should be must include having regard to—

   (a) the seriousness of the misconduct in question in relation to the nature of the principle or requirement concerned;

   (b) the extent to which that misconduct was deliberate or reckless; and

   (c) whether the person on whom the penalty is to be imposed is an individual.

(3) The Authority may at any time alter or replace a statement issued under this section.

(4) If a statement issued under this section is altered or replaced, the Authority must issue the altered or replacement statement.

(5) The Authority must, without delay, give the Treasury a copy of any statement which it publishes under this section.

(6) A statement issued under this section must be published by the Authority in the way appearing to the Authority to be best calculated to bring it to the attention of the public.

(7) The Authority may charge a reasonable fee for providing a person with a copy of the statement.

(8) In exercising, or deciding whether to exercise, its power under section 66 in the case of any particular misconduct, the Authority must have regard to any statement of policy published under this section and in force at the time when the misconduct in question occurred.

Statements of policy: procedure.

70.—(1) Before issuing a statement under section 69, the Authority must publish a draft of the proposed statement in the way appearing to the Authority to be best calculated to bring it to the attention of the public.

(2) The draft must be accompanied by notice that representations about the proposal may be made to the Authority within a specified time.

(3) Before issuing the proposed statement, the Authority must have regard to any representations made to it in accordance with subsection (2).

(4) If the Authority issues the proposed statement it must publish an account, in general terms, of—

　(a) the representations made to it in accordance with subsection (2); and

　(b) its response to them.

(5) If the statement differs from the draft published under subsection (1) in a way which is, in the opinion of the Authority, significant, the Authority must (in addition to complying with subsection (4)) publish details of the difference.

(6) The Authority may charge a reasonable fee for providing a person with a copy of a draft published under subsection (1).

(7) This section also applies to a proposal to alter or replace a statement.

Breach of statutory duty

Actions for damages.

71.—(1) A contravention of section 56(6) or 59(1) or (2) is actionable at the suit of a private person who suffers loss as a result of the contravention, subject to the defences and other incidents applying to actions for breach of statutory duty.

(2) In prescribed cases, a contravention of that kind which would be actionable at the suit of a private person is actionable at the suit of a person who is not a private person, subject to the defences and other incidents applying to actions for breach of statutory duty.

(3) "Private person" has such meaning as may be prescribed.

PART VIII
PENALTIES FOR MARKET ABUSE
Market abuse

Market abuse.

[**118.**—(1) For the purposes of this Act, market abuse is behaviour (whether by one person alone or by two or more persons jointly or in concert) which—

(a) occurs in relation to—

(i) qualifying investments admitted to trading on a prescribed market,

(ii) qualifying investments in respect of which a request for admission to trading on such a market has been made, or

(iii) in the case of subsection (2) or (3) behaviour, investments which are related investments in relation to such qualifying investments, and

(b) falls within any one or more of the types of behaviour set out in subsections (2) to (8).

(2) The first type of behaviour is where an insider deals, or attempts to deal, in a qualifying investment or related investment on the basis of inside information relating to the investment in question.

(3) The second is where an insider discloses inside information to another person otherwise than in the proper course of the exercise of his employment, profession or duties.

(4) The third is where the behaviour (not falling within subsection (2) or (3))—

(a) is based on information which is not generally available to those using the market but which, if available to a regular user of the market, would be, or would be likely to be, regarded by him as relevant when deciding the terms on which transactions in qualifying investments should be effected, and

(b) is likely to be regarded by a regular user of the market as a failure on the part of the person concerned to observe the standard of behaviour reasonably expected of a person in his position in relation to the market.

(5) The fourth is where the behaviour consists of effecting transactions or orders to trade (otherwise than for legitimate reasons and in conformity with accepted market practices on the relevant market) which —

    (a) give, or are likely to give, a false or misleading impression as to the supply of, or demand for, or as to the price of, one or more qualifying investments, or

    (b) secure the price of one or more such investments at an abnormal or artificial level.

(6) The fifth is where the behaviour consists of effecting transactions or orders to trade which employ fictitious devices or any other form of deception or contrivance.

(7) The sixth is where the behaviour consists of the dissemination of information by any means which gives, or is likely to give, a false or misleading impression as to a qualifying investment by a person who knew or could reasonably be expected to have known that the information was false or misleading.

(8) The seventh is where the behaviour (not falling within subsection (5), (6) or (7))—

    (a) is likely to give a regular user of the market a false or misleading impression as to the supply of, demand for or price or value of, qualifying investments, or

    (b) would be, or would be likely to be, regarded by a regular user of the market as behaviour that would distort, or would be likely to distort, the market in such an investment, and the behaviour is likely to be regarded by a regular user of the market as a failure on the part of the person concerned to observe the standard of behaviour reasonably expected of a person in his position in relation to the market.

(9) Subsections (4) and (8) and the definition of "regular user" in section 130A(3) cease to have effect on [31 December 2009] and subsection (1)(b) is then to be read as no longer referring to those subsections.]

(10) In this section—

"behaviour" includes action or inaction;

"investment" is to be read with section 22 and Schedule 2;

"regular user", in relation to a particular market, means a reasonable person who regularly deals on that market in investments of the kind in question.

[Supplementary provision about certain behaviour]

[118A.—(1) Behaviour is to be taken into account for the purposes of this Part only if it occurs—

(a) in the United Kingdom, or

(b) in relation to—

    (i) qualifying investments which are admitted to trading on a prescribed market situated in, or operating in, the United Kingdom,

    (ii) qualifying investments for which a request for admission to trading on such a pre-scribed market has been made, or

    (iii) in the case of section 118(2) and (3), invest-ments which are related investments in rela-tion to such qualifying investments.

(2) For the purposes of subsection (1), as it applies in relation to section 118(4) and (8), a prescribed market accessible electronically in the United Kingdom is to be treated as operating in the United Kingdom.

(3) For the purposes of section 118(4) and (8), the behaviour that is to be regarded as occurring in rela-tion to qualifying investments includes behaviour which —

(a) occurs in relation to anything that is the subject matter, or whose price or value is expressed by reference to the price or value of the qualifying investments, or

(b) occurs in relation to investments (whether or not they are qualifying investments) whose sub-ject matter is the qualifying investments.

(4) For the purposes of section 118(7), the dissemina-tion of information by a person acting in the capac-ity of a journalist is to be assessed taking into account the codes governing his profession unless he derives, directly or indirectly, any advantage or profits from the dissemination of the information.

(5) Behaviour does not amount to market abuse for the purposes of this Act if—

(a) it conforms with a rule which includes a provi-sion to the effect that behaviour conforming with the rule does not amount to market abuse,

(b) it conforms with the relevant provisions of Commission Regulation (EC) No 2273/2003 of 22 December 2003 implementing Directive 2003/6/EC of the European Parliament and of the Council as regards exemptions for buy-back programmes and stabilisation of financial instruments, or

(c) it is done by a person acting on behalf of a pub-lic authority in pursuit of monetary policies or policies with respect to exchange rates or the management of public debt or foreign exchange reserves.

(6) Subsections (2) and (3) cease to have effect on [31 December 2009].]

[Insiders]

[**118B.**—For the purposes of this Part an insider is any person who has inside information—

(a) as a result of his membership of an administrative, management or supervisory body of an issuer of qualifying investments,

(b) as a result of his holding in the capital of an issuer of qualifying investments,

(c) as a result of having access to the information through the exercise of his employment, profession or duties,

(d) as a result of his criminal activities, or

(e) which he has obtained by other means and which he knows, or could reasonably be expected to know, is inside information.]

[Inside information]

[**118C.**—(1) This section defines "inside information" for the purposes of this Part.

(2) In relation to qualifying investments, or related investments, which are not commodity derivatives, inside information is information of a precise nature which—

(a) is not generally available,

(b) relates, directly or indirectly, to one or more issuers of the qualifying investments or to one or more of the qualifying investments, and

(c) would, if generally available, be likely to have a significant effect on the price of the qualifying investments or on the price of related investments.

(3) In relation to qualifying investments or related investments which are commodity derivatives, inside information is information of a precise nature which—

(a) is not generally available,

(b) relates, directly or indirectly, to one or more such derivatives, and

(c) users of markets on which the derivatives are traded would expect to receive in accordance with any accepted market practices on those markets.

(4) In relation to a person charged with the execution of orders concerning any qualifying investments or related investments, inside information includes information conveyed by a client and related to the client's pending orders which—

(a) is of a precise nature,

(b) is not generally available,

(c) relates, directly or indirectly, to one or more issuers of qualifying investments or to one or more qualifying investments, and

(d) would, if generally available, be likely to have a significant effect on the price of those qualifying investments or the price of related investments.

(5) Information is precise if it—

(a) indicates circumstances that exist or may reasonably be expected to come into existence or an event that has occurred or may reasonably be expected to occur, and

(b) is specific enough to enable a conclusion to be drawn as to the possible effect of those circumstances or that event on the price of qualifying investments or related investments.

(6) Information would be likely to have a significant effect on price if and only if it is information of a kind which a reasonable investor would be likely to use as part of the basis of his investment decisions.

(7) For the purposes of subsection (3)(c), users of markets on which investments in commodity derivatives are traded are to be treated as expecting to receive information relating directly or indirectly to one or more such derivatives in accordance with any accepted market practices, which is—

(a) routinely made available to the users of those markets, or

(b) required to be disclosed in accordance with any statutory provision, market rules, or contracts or customs on the relevant underlying commodity market or commodity derivatives market.

(8) Information which can be obtained by research or analysis conducted by, or on behalf of, users of a market is to be regarded, for the purposes of this Part, as being generally available to them.]

The code

The code.

119.—(1) The Authority must prepare and issue a code containing such provisions as the Authority considers will give appropriate guidance to those determining whether or not behaviour amounts to market abuse.

(2) The code may among other things specify—

(a) descriptions of behaviour that, in the opinion of the Authority, amount to market abuse;

(b) descriptions of behaviour that, in the opinion of the Authority, do not amount to market abuse;

(c) factors that, in the opinion of the Authority, are to be taken into account in determining whether or not behaviour amounts to market abuse;

(d) descriptions of behaviour that are accepted market practices in relation to one or more specified markets;

(e) descriptions of behaviour that are not accepted market practices in relation to one or more specified markets].

[(2A) In determining, for the purposes of subsections (2)(d) and (2)(e) or otherwise, what are and what are not accepted market practices, the Authority must have regard to the factors and procedures laid down in Articles 2 and 3 respectively of Commission Directive 2004/72/EC of 29 April 2004 implementing Directive 2003/6/EC of the European Parliament and of the Council.]

(3) The code may make different provision in relation to persons, cases or circumstances of different descriptions.

(4) The Authority may at any time alter or replace the code.

(5) If the code is altered or replaced, the altered or replacement code must be issued by the Authority.

(6) A code issued under this section must be published by the Authority in the way appearing to the Authority to be best calculated to bring it to the attention of the public.

(7) The Authority must, without delay, give the Treasury a copy of any code published under this section.

(8) The Authority may charge a reasonable fee for providing a person with a copy of the code.

Provisions included in the Authority's code by reference to the City Code.

120.—(1) The Authority may include in a code issued by it under section 119 ("the Authority's code") provision to the effect that in its opinion behaviour conforming with the City Code—

(a) does not amount to market abuse;

(b) does not amount to market abuse in specified circumstances; or

(c) does not amount to market abuse if engaged in by a specified description of person.

(2) But the Treasury's approval is required before any such provision may be included in the Authority's code.

(3) If the Authority's code includes provision of a kind authorised by subsection (1), the Authority must keep itself informed of the way in which the Panel on Takeovers and Mergers interprets and administers the relevant provisions of the City Code.

(4) "City Code" means the City Code on Takeovers and Mergers issued by the Panel as it has effect at the time when the behaviour occurs.

(5) "Specified" means specified in the Authority's code.

Codes: procedure.

121.—(1) Before issuing a code under section 119, the Authority must publish a draft of the proposed code in the way appearing to the Authority to be best calculated to bring it to the attention of the public.

(2) The draft must be accompanied by—

  (a) a cost benefit analysis; and

  (b) notice that representations about the proposal may be made to the Authority within a specified time.

(3) Before issuing the proposed code, the Authority must have regard to any representations made to it in accordance with subsection (2)(b) .

(4) If the Authority issues the proposed code it must publish an account, in general terms, of—

  (a) the representations made to it in accordance with subsection (2)(b); and

  (b) its response to them.

(5) If the code differs from the draft published under subsection (1) in a way which is, in the opinion of the Authority, significant—

  (a) the Authority must (in addition to complying with subsection (4)) publish details of the difference; and

  (b) those details must be accompanied by a cost benefit analysis.

(6) Subsections (1) to (5) do not apply if the Authority considers that there is an urgent need to publish the code.

(7) Neither subsection (2)(a) nor subsection (5)(b) applies if the Authority considers—

  (a) that, making the appropriate comparison, there will be no increase in costs; or

  (b) that, making that comparison, there will be an increase in costs but the increase will be of minimal significance.

(8) The Authority may charge a reasonable fee for providing a person with a copy of a draft published under subsection (1).

(9) This section also applies to a proposal to alter or replace a code.

(10) "Cost benefit analysis" means an estimate of the costs together with an analysis of the benefits that will arise—

  (a) if the proposed code is issued; or

  (b) if subsection (5)(b) applies, from the code that has been issued.

(11) "The appropriate comparison" means—

  (a) in relation to subsection (2)(a), a comparison between the overall position if the code is issued and the overall position if it is not issued;

(b) in relation to subsection (5)(b), a comparison between the overall position after the issuing of the code and the overall position before it was issued.

Effect of the code.

122.—(1) If a person behaves in a way which is described (in the code in force under section 119 at the time of the behaviour) as behaviour that, in the Authority's opinion, does not amount to market abuse that behaviour of his is to be taken, for the purposes of this Act, as not amounting to market abuse.

(2) Otherwise, the code in force under section 119 at the time when particular behaviour occurs may be relied on so far as it indicates whether or not that behaviour should be taken to amount to market abuse.

Power to impose penalties

Power to impose penalties in cases of market abuse.

123.—(1) If the Authority is satisfied that a person ("A") —

(a) is or has engaged in market abuse, or

(b) by taking or refraining from taking any action has required or encouraged another person or persons to engage in behaviour which, if engaged in by A, would amount to market abuse, it may impose on him a penalty of such amount as it considers appropriate.

(2) But the Authority may not impose a penalty on a person if, having considered any representations made to it in response to a warning notice, there are reasonable grounds for it to be satisfied that—

(a) he believed, on reasonable grounds, that his behaviour did not fall within paragraph (a) or (b) of subsection (1), or

(b) he took all reasonable precautions and exercised all due diligence to avoid behaving in a way which fell within paragraph (a) or (b) of that subsection.

(3) If the Authority is entitled to impose a penalty on a person under this section it may, instead of imposing a penalty on him, publish a statement to the effect that he has engaged in market abuse.

Statement of policy

Statement of policy.

124.—(1) The Authority must prepare and issue a statement of its policy with respect to—

(a) the imposition of penalties under section 123; and

(b) the amount of penalties under that section.

(2) The Authority's policy in determining what the amount of a penalty should be must include having regard to—

(a) whether the behaviour in respect of which the penalty is to be imposed had an adverse effect on the market in question and, if it did, how serious that effect was;

(b) the extent to which that behaviour was deliberate or reckless; and

(c) whether the person on whom the penalty is to be imposed is an individual.

(3) A statement issued under this section must include an indication of the circumstances in which the Authority is to be expected to regard a person as—

(a) having a reasonable belief that his behaviour did not amount to market abuse; or

(b) having taken reasonable precautions and exercised due diligence to avoid engaging in market abuse.

(4) The Authority may at any time alter or replace a statement issued under this section.

(5) If a statement issued under this section is altered or replaced, the Authority must issue the altered or replacement statement.

(6) In exercising, or deciding whether to exercise, its power under section 123 in the case of any particular behaviour, the Authority must have regard to any statement published under this section and in force at the time when the behaviour concerned occurred.

(7) A statement issued under this section must be published by the Authority in the way appearing to the Authority to be best calculated to bring it to the attention of the public.

(8) The Authority may charge a reasonable fee for providing a person with a copy of a statement published under this section.

(9) The Authority must, without delay, give the Treasury a copy of any statement which it publishes under this section.

Statement of policy: procedure.

125.—(1) Before issuing a statement of policy under section 124, the Authority must publish a draft of the proposed statement in the way appearing to the Authority to be best calculated to bring it to the attention of the public.

(2) The draft must be accompanied by notice that representations about the proposal may be made to the Authority within a specified time.

(3) Before issuing the proposed statement, the Authority must have regard to any representations made to it in accordance with subsection (2).

(4) If the Authority issues the proposed statement it must publish an account, in general terms, of—

(a) the representations made to it in accordance with subsection (2); and

(b) its response to them.

(5) If the statement differs from the draft published under subsection (1) in a way which is, in the opinion of the Authority, significant, the Authority must (in addition to complying with subsection (4)) publish details of the difference.

(6) The Authority may charge a reasonable fee for providing a person with a copy of a draft published under subsection (1).

(7) This section also applies to a proposal to alter or replace a statement.

Procedure

Warning notices.

126.—(1) If the Authority proposes to take action against a person under section 123, it must give him a warning notice.

(2) A warning notice about a proposal to impose a penalty must state the amount of the proposed penalty.

(3) A warning notice about a proposal to publish a statement must set out the terms of the proposed statement.

Decision notices and
right to refer to Tribunal.

127.—(1) If the Authority decides to take action against a person under section 123, it must give him a decision notice.

(2) A decision notice about the imposition of a penalty must state the amount of the penalty.

(3) A decision notice about the publication of a statement must set out the terms of the statement.

(4) If the Authority decides to take action against a person under section 123, that person may refer the matter to the Tribunal.

Miscellaneous

Suspension of investigations.

128.—(1) If the Authority considers it desirable or expedient because of the exercise or possible exercise of a power relating to market abuse, it may direct a recognised investment exchange or recognised clearing house—

(a) to terminate, suspend or limit the scope of any inquiry which the exchange or clearing house is conducting under its rules; or

(b) not to conduct an inquiry which the exchange or clearing house proposes to conduct under its rules.

(2) A direction under this section—

(a) must be given to the exchange or clearing house concerned by notice in writing; and

(b) is enforceable, on the application of the Authority, by injunction or, in Scotland, by an order under section 45 of the Court of Session Act 1988.

(3) The Authority's powers relating to market abuse are its powers—

(a) to impose penalties under section 123; or

(b) to appoint a person to conduct an investigation under section 168 in a case falling within subsection (2)(d) of that section.

Power of court to impose penalty in cases of market abuse.

129.—(1) The Authority may on an application to the court under section 381 or 383 request the court to consider whether the circumstances are such that a penalty should be imposed on the person to whom the application relates.

(2) The court may, if it considers it appropriate, make an order requiring the person concerned to pay to the Authority a penalty of such amount as it considers appropriate.

Guidance.

130.—(1) The Treasury may from time to time issue written guidance for the purpose of helping relevant authorities to determine the action to be taken in cases where behaviour occurs which is behaviour—

(a) with respect to which the power in section 123 appears to be exercisable; and

(b) which appears to involve the commission of an offence under section 397 of this Act or Part V of the Criminal Justice Act 1993 (insider dealing).

(2) The Treasury must obtain the consent of the Attorney General and the Secretary of State before issuing any guidance under this section.

(3) In this section "relevant authorities"—

(a) in relation to England and Wales, means the Secretary of State, the Authority, the Director of the Serious Fraud Office and the Director of Public Prosecutions;

(b) in relation to Northern Ireland, means the Secretary of State, the Authority, the Director of the Serious Fraud Office and the Director of Public Prosecutions for Northern Ireland.

(4) Subsections (1) to (3) do not apply to Scotland.

(5) In relation to Scotland, the Lord Advocate may from time to time, after consultation with the Treasury, issue written guidance for the purpose of helping the Authority to determine the action to be taken in cases where behaviour mentioned in subsection (1) occurs.

[Interpretation and supplementary provision]

[**130A.**—(1) The Treasury may by order specify (whether by name or description)—

(a) the markets which are prescribed markets for the purposes of specified provisions of this Part, and

(b) the investments that are qualifying investments in relation to the prescribed markets.

(2) An order may prescribe different investments or descriptions of investment in relation to different markets or descriptions of market.

(3) In this Part—

"accepted market practices" means practices that are reasonably expected in the financial market or markets in question and are accepted by the Authority or, in the case of a market situated in another EEA State, the competent authority of that EEA State within the meaning of Directive 2003/6/EC of the European Parliament and of the Council of 28 January 2003 on insider dealing and market manipulation (market abuse),

"behaviour" includes action or inaction,

"dealing", in relation to an investment, means acquiring or disposing of the investment whether as principal or agent or directly or indirectly, and includes agreeing to acquire or dispose of the investment, and entering into and bringing to an end a contract creating it,

"investment" is to be read with section 22 and Schedule 2,

"regular user", in relation to a particular market, means a reasonable person who regularly deals on that market in investments of the kind in question,

"related investment", in relation to a qualifying investment, means an investment whose price or value depends on the price or value of the qualifying investment.

(4) Any reference in this Act to a person engaged in market abuse is to a person engaged in market abuse either alone or with one or more other persons.]

Effect on transactions.

131. The imposition of a penalty under this Part does not make any transaction void or unenforceable.

[Protected Disclosures]

[**131A.**—(1) A disclosure which satisfies the following three conditions is not to be taken to breach any restriction on the disclosure of information (however imposed).

(2) The first condition is that the information or other matter —

(a) causes the person making the disclosure (the discloser) to know or suspect, or

(b) gives him reasonable grounds for knowing or suspecting, that another person has engaged in market abuse.

(3) The second condition is that the information or other matter disclosed came to the discloser in the course of his trade, profession, business or employment.

(4) The third condition is that the disclosure is made to the Authority or to a nominated officer as soon as is practicable after the information or other matter comes to the discloser.

(5) A disclosure to a nominated officer is a disclosure which is made to a person nominated by the discloser's employer to receive disclosures under this section, and is made in the course of the discloser's employment and in accordance with the procedure established by the employer for the purpose.

(6) For the purposes of this section, references to a person's employer include any body, association or organisation (including a voluntary organisation) in connection with whose activities the person exercises a function (whether or not for gain or reward) and references to employment must be construed accordingly.]

PART IX
HEARINGS AND APPEALS

The Financial Services and Markets Tribunal.

132.—(1) For the purposes of this Act, there is to be a tribunal known as the Financial Services and Markets Tribunal (but referred to in this Act as "the Tribunal").

(2) The Tribunal is to have the functions conferred on it by or under this Act.

(3) The Lord Chancellor may by rules make such provision as appears to him to be necessary or expedient in respect of the conduct of proceedings before the Tribunal.

(4) Schedule 13 is to have effect as respects the Tribunal and its proceedings (but does not limit the Lord Chancellor's powers under this section).

Proceedings: general provision.

133.—(1) A reference to the Tribunal under this Act must be made before the end of—
    (a) the period of 28 days beginning with the date on which the decision notice or supervisory notice in question is given; or
    (b) such other period as may be specified in rules made under section 132.

(2) Subject to rules made under section 132, the Tribunal may allow a reference to be made after the end of that period.

(3) On a reference the Tribunal may consider any evidence relating to the subject-matter of the reference, whether or not it was available to the Authority at the material time.

(4) On a reference the Tribunal must determine what (if any) is the appropriate action for the Authority to take in relation to the matter referred to it.

(5) On determining a reference, the Tribunal must remit the matter to the Authority with such directions (if any) as the Tribunal considers appropriate for giving effect to its determination.

(6) In determining a reference made as a result of a decision notice, the Tribunal may not direct the Authority to take action which the Authority would not, as a result of section 388(2), have had power to take when giving the decision notice.

(7) In determining a reference made as a result of a supervisory notice, the Tribunal may not direct the Authority to take action which would have otherwise required the giving of a decision notice.

(8) The Tribunal may, on determining a reference, make recommendations as to the Authority's regulating provisions or its procedures.

(9) The Authority must not take the action specified in a decision notice—

    (a) during the period within which the matter to which the decision notice relates may be referred to the Tribunal; and

    (b) if the matter is so referred, until the reference, and any appeal against the Tribunal's determination, has been finally disposed of.

(10) The Authority must act in accordance with the determination of, and any direction given by, the Tribunal.

(11) An order of the Tribunal may be enforced—

    (a) as if it were an order of a county court; or

    (b) in Scotland, as if it were an order of the Court of Session.

(12) "Supervisory notice" has the same meaning as in section 395.

Legal assistance before the Tribunal

Legal assistance scheme.

134.—(1) The Lord Chancellor may by regulations establish a scheme governing the provision of legal assistance in connection with proceedings before the Tribunal.

(2) If the Lord Chancellor establishes a scheme under subsection (1), it must provide that a person is eligible for assistance only if—

    (a) he falls within subsection (3); and

    (b) he fulfils such other criteria (if any) as may be prescribed as a result of section 135(1)(d).

(3) A person falls within this subsection if he is an individual who has referred a matter to the Tribunal under section 127(4).

(4) In this Part of this Act "the legal assistance scheme" means any scheme in force under subsection (1).

Provisions of the legal
assistance scheme.

135.—(1) The legal assistance scheme may, in particular, make provision as to—

(a) the kinds of legal assistance that may be provided;

(b) the persons by whom legal assistance may be provided;

(c) the manner in which applications for legal assistance are to be made;

(d) the criteria on which eligibility for legal assistance is to be determined;

(e) the persons or bodies by whom applications are to be determined;

(f) appeals against refusals of applications;

(g) the revocation or variation of decisions;

(h) its administration and the enforcement of its provisions.

(2) Legal assistance under the legal assistance scheme may be provided subject to conditions or restrictions, including conditions as to the making of contributions by the person to whom it is provided.

Funding of the legal
assistance scheme.

136.—(1) The Authority must pay to the Lord Chancellor such sums at such times as he may, from time to time, determine in respect of the anticipated or actual cost of legal assistance provided in connection with proceedings before the Tribunal under the legal assistance scheme.

(2) In order to enable it to pay any sum which it is obliged to pay under subsection (1), the Authority must make rules requiring the payment to it by authorised persons or any class of authorised person of specified amounts or amounts calculated in a specified way.

(3) Sums received by the Lord Chancellor under subsection (1) must be paid into the Consolidated Fund.

(4) The Lord Chancellor must, out of money provided by Parliament fund the cost of legal assistance provided in connection with proceedings before the Tribunal under the legal assistance scheme.

(5) Subsection (6) applies if, as respects a period determined by the Lord Chancellor, the amount paid to him under subsection (1) as respects that period exceeds the amount he has expended in that period under subsection (4).

(6) The Lord Chancellor must—

(a) repay, out of money provided by Parliament, the excess to the Authority; or

(b) take the excess into account on the next occasion on which he makes a determination under subsection (1).

(7) The Authority must make provision for any sum repaid to it under subsection (6)(a)—

  (a) to be distributed among—

    (i) the authorised persons on whom a levy was imposed in the period in question as a result of rules made under subsection (2); or

    (ii) such of those persons as it may determine;

  (b) to be applied in order to reduce any amounts which those persons, or such of them as it may determine, are or will be liable to pay to the Authority, whether under rules made under subsection (2) or otherwise; or

  (c) to be partly so distributed and partly so applied.

(8) If the Authority considers that it is not practicable to deal with any part of a sum repaid to it under subsection (6)(a) in accordance with provision made by it as a result of subsection (7), it may, with the consent the Lord Chancellor, apply or dispose of that part of that sum in such manner as it considers appropriate.

(9) "Specified" means specified in the rules.

Appeals

Appeal on a point of law.

137.—(1) A party to a reference to the Tribunal may with permission appeal—

  (a) to the Court of Appeal, or

  (b) in Scotland, to the Court of Session,

on a point of law arising from a decision of the Tribunal disposing of the reference.

(2) "Permission" means permission given by the Tribunal or by the Court of Appeal or (in Scotland) the Court of Session.

(3) If, on an appeal under subsection (1), the court considers that the decision of the Tribunal was wrong in law, it may—

  (a) remit the matter to the Tribunal for rehearing and determination by it; or

  (b) itself make a determination.

(4) An appeal may not be brought from a decision of the Court of Appeal under subsection (3) except with the leave of—

  (a) the Court of Appeal; or

  (b) the Supreme Court].

(5) An appeal lies, with the leave of the Court of Session or the House of Lords [Supreme Court], from any decision of the Court of Session under this section, and such leave may be given on such terms as to costs, expenses or otherwise as the Court of Session or the House of Lords [Supreme Court] may determine.

(6) Rules made under section 132 may make provision for regulating or prescribing any matters incidental to or consequential on an appeal under this section.

Part X
Rules and Guidance
Chapter I
Rule-Making Powers

General rule-making power.

138.—(1) The Authority may make such rules applying to authorised persons—

(a) with respect to the carrying on by them of regulated activities, or

(b) with respect to the carrying on by them of activities which are not regulated activities, as appear to it to be necessary or expedient for the purpose of protecting the interests of consumers.

[(1A) The Authority may also make such rules applying to authorised persons who are investment firms or credit institutions, with respect to the provision by them of a relevant ancillary service, as appear to the Authority to be necessary or expedient for the purpose of protecting the interests of consumers.

(1B) "Credit institution" means—

(a) a credit institution authorised under the banking consolidation directive, or

(b) an institution which would satisfy the requirements for authorisation as a credit institution under that directive if it had its registered office (or if it does not have a registered office, its head office) in an EEA State.

(1C) "Relevant ancillary service" means any service of a kind mentioned in Section B of Annex I to the markets in financial instruments directive the provision of which does not involve the carrying on of a regulated activity.]

(2) Rules made under this section are referred to in this Act as the Authority's general rules.

(3) The Authority's power to make general rules is not limited by any other power which it has to make regulating provisions.

(4) The Authority's general rules may make provision applying to authorised persons even though there is no relationship between the authorised persons to whom the rules will apply and the persons whose interests will be protected by the rules.

(5) General rules may contain requirements which take into account, in the case of an authorised person who is a member of a group, any activity of another member of the group.

(6) General rules may not—

    (a) make provision prohibiting an EEA firm from carrying on, or holding itself out as carrying on, any activity which it has permission conferred by Part II of Schedule 3 to carry on in the United Kingdom;

    (b) make provision, as respects an EEA firm, about any matter responsibility for which is, under any of the single market directives, reserved to the firm's home state regulator.

(7) "Consumers" means persons—

    (a) who use, have used, or are or may be contemplating using, any of the services provided by—

        (i) authorised persons in carrying on regulated activities; or [(ia) authorised persons who are investment firms or credit institutions in providing a relevant ancillary service; or]

        (ii) persons acting as appointed representatives;

    (b) who have rights or interests which are derived from, or are otherwise attributable to, the use of any such services by other persons; or

    (c) who have rights or interests which may be adversely affected by the use of any such services by persons acting on their behalf or in a fiduciary capacity in relation to them.

(8) If an authorised person is carrying on a regulated activity in his capacity as a trustee, the persons who are, have been or may be beneficiaries of the trust are to be treated as persons who use, have used or are or may be contemplating using services provided by the authorised person in his carrying on of that activity.

(9) For the purposes of subsection (7) a person who deals with an authorised person in the course of the authorised person's carrying on of a regulated activity is to be treated as using services provided by the authorised person in carrying on those activities.

Miscellaneous ancillary matters.

139.—(1) Rules relating to the handling of money held by an authorised person in specified circumstances ("clients' money") may—

    (a) make provision which results in that clients' money being held on trust in accordance with the rules;

    (b) treat two or more accounts as a single account for specified purposes (which may include the distribution of money held in the accounts);

    (c) authorise the retention by the authorised person of interest accruing on the clients' money; and

(d) make provision as to the distribution of such interest which is not to be retained by him.

(2) An institution with which an account is kept in pursuance of rules relating to the handling of clients' money does not incur any liability as constructive trustee if money is wrongfully paid from the account, unless the institution permits the payment—

(a) with knowledge that it is wrongful; or

(b) having deliberately failed to make enquiries in circumstances in which a reasonable and honest person would have done so.

(3) In the application of subsection (1) to Scotland, the reference to money being held on trust is to be read as a reference to its being held as agent for the person who is entitled to call for it to be paid over to him or to be paid on his direction or to have it otherwise credited to him.

(4) Rules may—

(a) confer rights on persons to rescind agreements with, or withdraw offers to, authorised persons within a specified period; and

(b) make provision, in respect of authorised persons and persons exercising those rights, for the restitution of property and the making or recovery of payments where those rights are exercised.

(5) "Rules" means general rules.

(6) "Specified" means specified in the rules.

Restriction on managers of [certain collective investment schemes]

140.—[(1) The Authority may make rules prohibiting an authorised person who has permission to act as—

(a) the manager of an authorised unit trust scheme, or

(b) the management company of an authorised UCITS open-ended investment company, from carrying on a specified activity.]

(2) Such rules may specify an activity which is not a regulated activity.

[(3) In this section—

(a) "authorised UCITS open-ended investment company" means an authorised open-ended investment company to which the UCITS directive applies; and

(b) "management company" has the meaning given by Article 1a.2 of the UCITS directive.]

Insurance business rules.

141.—(1) The Authority may make rules prohibiting an authorised person who has permission to effect or carry out contracts of insurance from carrying on a specified activity.

(2) Such rules may specify an activity which is not a regulated activity.

(3) The Authority may make rules in relation to contracts entered into by an authorised person in the course of carrying on business which consists of the effecting or carrying out of contracts of long-term insurance.

(4) Such rules may, in particular—

(a) restrict the descriptions of property or indices of the value of property by reference to which the benefits under such contracts may be determined;

(b) make provision, in the interests of the protection of policyholders, for the substitution of one description of property, or index of value, by reference to which the benefits under a contract are to be determined for another such description of property or index.

(5) Rules made under this section are referred to in this Act as insurance business rules.

Insurance business: regulations supplementing Authority's rules.

142.—(1) The Treasury may make regulations for the purpose of preventing a person who is not an authorised person but who—

(a) is a parent undertaking of an authorised person who has permission to effect or carry out contracts of insurance, and

(b) falls within a prescribed class,

from doing anything to lessen the effectiveness of asset identification rules.

(2) "Asset identification rules" means rules made by the Authority which require an authorised person who has permission to effect or carry out contracts of insurance to identify assets which belong to him and which are maintained in respect of a particular aspect of his business.

(3) The regulations may, in particular, include provision —

(a) prohibiting the payment of dividends;

(b) prohibiting the creation of charges;

(c) making charges created in contravention of the regulations void.

(4) The Treasury may by regulations provide that, in prescribed circumstances, charges created in contravention of asset identification rules are void.

(5) A person who contravenes regulations under subsection (1) is guilty of an offence and liable on summary conviction to a fine not exceeding level 5 on the standard scale.

(6) "Charges" includes mortgages (or in Scotland securities over property).

143. [repealed]

Specific rules

Price stabilising rules.

144.—(1) The Authority may make rules ("price stabilising rules") as to—

(a) the circumstances and manner in which,

(b) the conditions subject to which, and

(c) the time when or the period during which,

action may be taken for the purpose of stabilising the price of investments of specified kinds.

(2) Price stabilising rules—

(a) are to be made so as to apply only to authorised persons;

(b) may make different provision in relation to different kinds of investment.

(3) The Authority may make rules which, for the purposes of section 397(5)(b), treat a person who acts or engages in conduct—

(a) for the purpose of stabilising the price of investments, and

(b) in conformity with such provisions corresponding to price stabilising rules and made by a body or authority outside the United Kingdom as may be specified in the rules under this subsection,

as acting, or engaging in that conduct, for that purpose and in conformity with price stabilising rules.

(4) The Treasury may by order impose limitations on the power to make rules under this section.

(5) Such an order may, in particular—

(a) specify the kinds of investment in relation to which price stabilising rules may make provision;

(b) specify the kinds of investment in relation to which rules made under subsection (3) may make provision;

(c) provide for price stabilising rules to make provision for action to be taken for the purpose of stabilising the price of investments only in such circumstances as the order may specify;

(d) provide for price stabilising rules to make provision for action to be taken for that purpose only at such times or during such periods as the order may specify.

(6) If provisions specified in rules made under subsection (3) are altered, the rules continue to apply to those provisions as altered, but only if before the alteration the Authority has notified the body or authority concerned (and has not withdrawn its notification) that it is satisfied with its consultation procedures.

[(7) "Consultation procedures" means procedures designed to provide an opportunity for persons likely to be affected by alterations to those provisions to make representations about proposed alterations to any of those provisions.]

Financial promotion rules.

145.—(1) The Authority may make rules applying to authorised persons about the communication by them, or their approval of the communication by others, of invitations or inducements—

(a) to engage in investment activity; or

(b) to participate in a collective investment scheme.

(2) Rules under this section may, in particular, make provision about the form and content of communications.

(3) Subsection (1) applies only to communications which —

(a) if made by a person other than an authorised person, without the approval of an authorised person, would contravene section 21(1);

(b) may be made by an authorised person without contravening section 238(1).

[(3A) But subsection (3) does not prevent the Authority from making rules under subsection (1) in relation to a communication that would not contravene section 21(1) if made by a person other than an authorised person, without the approval of an authorised person, if the conditions set out in subsection (3B) are satisfied.

(3B) Those conditions are—

(a) that the communication would not contravene subsection (1) of section 21 because it is a communication to which that subsection does not apply as a result of an order under subsection (5) of that section;

(b) that the Authority considers that any of the requirements of—

(i) paragraphs 1 to 8 of Article 19 of the markets in financial instruments directive; or

(ii) any implementing measure made under paragraph 10 of that Article, apply to the communication; and

(c) that the Authority considers that the rules are necessary to secure that the communication satisfies such of the requirements mentioned in paragraph (b) as the Authority considers apply to the communication.]

(4) "Engage in investment activity" has the same meaning as in section 21.

(5) The Treasury may by order impose limitations on the power to make rules under this section.

Money laundering rules.

146. The Authority may make rules in relation to the prevention and detection of money laundering in connection with the carrying on of regulated activities by authorised persons.

Control of information rules.

147.—(1) The Authority may make rules ("control of information rules") about the disclosure and use of information held by an authorised person ("A").

(2) Control of information rules may—

    (a) require the withholding of information which A would otherwise have to disclose to a person ("B") for or with whom A does business in the course of carrying on any regulated or other activity;

    (b) specify circumstances in which A may withhold information which he would otherwise have to disclose to B;

    (c) require A not to use for the benefit of B information A holds which A would otherwise have to use in that way;

    (d) specify circumstances in which A may decide not to use for the benefit of B information A holds which A would otherwise have to use in that way.

Modification or waiver

Modification or waiver of rules.

148.—(1)...

[(2) The Authority may, on the application or with the consent of a person who is subject to rules made by the Authority, direct that all or any of those rules (other than rules made under section 247 (trust scheme rules) or section 248 (scheme particulars rules)) —

    (a) are not to apply to that person; or

    (b) are to apply to him with such modifications as may be specified in the direction.]

(3) An application must be made in such manner as the Authority may direct.

(4) The Authority may not give a direction unless it is satisfied that—

    (a) compliance by the ... person with the rules, or with the rules as unmodified, would be unduly burdensome or would not achieve the purpose for which the rules were made; and

    (b) the direction would not result in undue risk to persons whose interests the rules are intended to protect.

(5) A direction may be given subject to conditions.

(6) Unless it is satisfied that it is inappropriate or unnecessary to do so, a direction must be published by the Authority in such a way as it thinks most suitable for bringing the direction to the attention of—

    (a) those likely to be affected by it; and

    (b) others who may be likely to make an application for a similar direction.

(7) In deciding whether it is satisfied as mentioned in subsection (6), the Authority must—

(a) take into account whether the direction relates to a rule contravention of which is actionable in accordance with section 150;

(b) consider whether its publication would prejudice, to an unreasonable degree, the commercial interests of the … person concerned or any other member of his immediate group; and

(c) consider whether its publication would be contrary to an international obligation of the United Kingdom.

(8) For the purposes of paragraphs (b) and (c) of subsection (7), the Authority must consider whether it would be possible to publish the direction without either of the consequences mentioned in those paragraphs by publishing it without disclosing the identity of the … person concerned.

(9) The Authority may—

(a) revoke a direction; or

(b) vary it on the application, or with the consent, of the … person to whom it relates.

(10) "Direction" means a direction under subsection (2).

(11) "Immediate group", in relation to [a person] ("A"), means—

(a) A;

(b) a parent undertaking of A;

(c) a subsidiary undertaking of A;

(d) a subsidiary undertaking of a parent undertaking of A;

(e) a parent undertaking of a subsidiary undertaking of A.

Contravention of rules

Evidential provisions.

149.—(1) If a particular rule so provides, contravention of the rule does not give rise to any of the consequences provided for by other provisions of this Act.

(2) A rule which so provides must also provide—

(a) that contravention may be relied on as tending to establish contravention of such other rule as may be specified; or

(b) that compliance may be relied on as tending to establish compliance with such other rule as may be specified.

(3) A rule may include the provision mentioned in subsection (1) only if the Authority considers that it is appropriate for it also to include the provision required by subsection (2).

Actions for damages.

150.—(1) A contravention by an authorised person of a rule is actionable at the suit of a private person who suffers loss as a result of the contravention, subject to the defences and other incidents applying to actions for breach of statutory duty.

(2) If rules so provide, subsection (1) does not apply to contravention of a specified provision of those rules.

(3) In prescribed cases, a contravention of a rule which would be actionable at the suit of a private person is actionable at the suit of a person who is not a private person, subject to the defences and other incidents applying to actions for breach of statutory duty.

(4) In subsections (1) and (3) "rule" does not include—

    (a) [Part 6 rules]; or

    (b) a rule requiring an authorised person to have or maintain financial resources.

(5) "Private person" has such meaning as may be prescribed.

Limits on effect of contravening rules.

151.—(1) A person is not guilty of an offence by reason of a contravention of a rule made by the Authority.

(2) No such contravention makes any transaction void or unenforceable.

Procedural provisions

Notification of rules to the Treasury.

152.—(1) If the Authority makes any rules, it must give a copy to the Treasury without delay.

(2) If the Authority alters or revokes any rules, it must give written notice to the Treasury without delay.

(3) Notice of an alteration must include details of the alteration.

Rule-making instruments.

153.—(1) Any power conferred on the Authority to make rules is exercisable in writing.

(2) An instrument by which rules are made by the Authority ("a rule-making instrument") must specify the provision under which the rules are made.

(3) To the extent to which a rule-making instrument does not comply with subsection (2), it is void.

(4) A rule-making instrument must be published by the Authority in the way appearing to the Authority to be best calculated to bring it to the attention of the public.

(5) The Authority may charge a reasonable fee for providing a person with a copy of a rule-making instrument.

(6) A person is not to be taken to have contravened any rule made by the Authority if he shows that at the time of the alleged contravention the rule-making instrument concerned had not been made available in accordance with this section.

Verification of rules.

154.—(1) The production of a printed copy of a rule-making instrument purporting to be made by the Authority —

    (a) on which is endorsed a certificate signed by a member of the Authority's staff authorised by it for that purpose, and

(b) which contains the required statements, is evidence (or in Scotland sufficient evidence) of the facts stated in the certificate.

(2) The required statements are—

  (a) that the instrument was made by the Authority;

  (b) that the copy is a true copy of the instrument; and

  (c) that on a specified date the instrument was made available to the public in accordance with section 153(4).

(3) A certificate purporting to be signed as mentioned in subsection (1) is to be taken to have been properly signed unless the contrary is shown.

(4) A person who wishes in any legal proceedings to rely on a rule-making instrument may require the Authority to endorse a copy of the instrument with a certificate of the kind mentioned in subsection (1).

Consultation.

155.—(1) If the Authority proposes to make any rules, it must publish a draft of the proposed rules in the way appearing to it to be best calculated to bring them to the attention of the public.

(2) The draft must be accompanied by—

  (a) a cost benefit analysis;

  (b) an explanation of the purpose of the proposed rules;

  (c) an explanation of the Authority's reasons for believing that making the proposed rules is compatible with its general duties under section 2; and

  (d) notice that representations about the proposals may be made to the Authority within a specified time.

(3) In the case of a proposal to make rules under a provision mentioned in subsection (9), the draft must also be accompanied by details of the expected expenditure by reference to which the proposal is made.

(4) Before making the proposed rules, the Authority must have regard to any representations made to it in accordance with subsection (2)(d).

(5) If the Authority makes the proposed rules, it must publish an account, in general terms, of—

  (a) the representations made to it in accordance with subsection (2)(d); and

  (b) its response to them.

(6) If the rules differ from the draft published under subsection (1) in a way which is, in the opinion of the Authority, significant—

(a) the Authority must (in addition to complying with subsection (5)) publish details of the difference; and

(b) those details must be accompanied by a cost benefit analysis.

(7) Subsections (1) to (6) do not apply if the Authority considers that the delay involved in complying with them would be prejudicial to the interests of consumers.

(8) Neither subsection (2)(a) nor subsection (6)(b) applies if the Authority considers—

(a) that, making the appropriate comparison, there will be no increase in costs; or

(b) that, making that comparison, there will be an increase in costs but the increase will be of minimal significance.

(9) Neither subsection (2)(a) nor subsection (6)(b) requires a cost benefit analysis to be carried out in relation to rules made under—

(a) section 136(2);

(b) subsection (1) of section 213 as a result of subsection (4) of that section;

(c) section 234;

(d) paragraph 17 of Schedule 1.

(10) "Cost benefit analysis" means an estimate of the costs together with an analysis of the benefits that will arise—

(a) if the proposed rules are made; or

(b) if subsection (6) applies, from the rules that have been made.

(11) "The appropriate comparison" means—

(a) in relation to subsection (2)(a), a comparison between the overall position if the rules are made and the overall position if they are not made;

(b) in relation to subsection (6)(b), a comparison between the overall position after the making of the rules and the overall position before they were made.

(12) The Authority may charge a reasonable fee for providing a person with a copy of a draft published under subsection (1).

General supplementary powers.

156.—(1) Rules made by the Authority may make different provision for different cases and may, in particular, make different provision in respect of different descriptions of authorised person, activity or investment.

(2) Rules made by the Authority may contain such incidental, supplemental, consequential and transitional provision as the Authority considers appropriate.

Part XI
Information Gathering and Investigations

Powers to gather information

165.—(1) The Authority may, by notice in writing given to an authorised person, require him—

(a) to provide specified information or information of a specified description; or

(b) to produce specified documents or documents of a specified description.

(2) The information or documents must be provided or produced—

(a) before the end of such reasonable period as may be specified; and

(b) at such place as may be specified.

(3) An officer who has written authorisation from the Authority to do so may require an authorised person without delay—

(a) to provide the officer with specified information or information of a specified description; or

(b) to produce to him specified documents or documents of a specified description.

(4) This section applies only to information and documents reasonably required in connection with the exercise by the Authority of functions conferred on it by or under this Act.

(5) The Authority may require any information provided under this section to be provided in such form as it may reasonably require.

(6) The Authority may require—

(a) any information provided, whether in a document or otherwise, to be verified in such manner, or

(b) any document produced to be authenticated in such manner, as it may reasonably require.

(7) The powers conferred by subsections (1) and (3) may also be exercised to impose requirements on—

(a) a person who is connected with an authorised person;

(b) an operator, trustee or depositary of a scheme recognised under section 270 or 272 who is not an authorised person;

(c) a recognised investment exchange or recognised clearing house.

(8) "Authorised person" includes a person who was at any time an authorised person but who has ceased to be an authorised person.

(9) "Officer" means an officer of the Authority and includes a member of the Authority's staff or an agent of the Authority.

(10) "Specified" means—
    (a) in subsections (1) and (2), specified in the notice; and
    (b) in subsection (3), specified in the authorisation.

(11) For the purposes of this section, a person is connected with an authorised person ("A") if he is or has at any relevant time been—
    (a) a member of A's group;
    (b) a controller of A;
    (c) any other member of a partnership of which A is a member; or
    (d) in relation to A, a person mentioned in Part I of Schedule 15.

Reports by skilled persons.

166.—(1) The Authority may, by notice in writing given to a person to whom subsection (2) applies, require him to provide the Authority with a report on any matter about which the Authority has required or could require the provision of information or production of documents under section 165.

(2) This subsection applies to—
    (a) an authorised person ("A"),
    (b) any other member of A's group,
    (c) a partnership of which A is a member, or
    (d) a person who has at any relevant time been a person falling within paragraph (a), (b) or (c), who is, or was at the relevant time, carrying on a business.

(3) The Authority may require the report to be in such form as may be specified in the notice.

(4) The person appointed to make a report required by subsection (1) must be a person—
    (a) nominated or approved by the Authority; and
    (b) appearing to the Authority to have the skills necessary to make a report on the matter concerned.

(5) It is the duty of any person who is providing (or who at any time has provided) services to a person to whom subsection (2) applies in relation to a matter on which a report is required under subsection (1) to give a person appointed to provide such a report all such assistance as the appointed person may reasonably require.

(6) The obligation imposed by subsection (5) is enforceable, on the application of the Authority, by an injunction or, in Scotland, by an order for specific performance under section 45 of the Court of Session Act 1988.

Appointment of investigators

Appointment of persons
to carry out general investigations.

167.—(1) If it appears to the Authority or the Secretary of State ("the investigating authority") that there is good reason for doing so, the investigating authority may appoint one or more competent persons to conduct an investigation on its behalf into—

(a) the nature, conduct or state of the business of an authorised person or of an appointed epresentative;

(b) a particular aspect of that business; or

(c) the ownership or control of an authorised person.

(2) If a person appointed under subsection (1) thinks it necessary for the purposes of his investigation, he may also investigate the business of a person who is or has at any relevant time been—

(a) a member of the group of which the person under investigation ("A") is part; or

(b) a partnership of which A is a member.

(3) If a person appointed under subsection (1) decides to investigate the business of any person under subsection (2) he must give that person written notice of his decision.

(4) The power conferred by this section may be exercised in relation to a former authorised person (or appointed representative) but only in relation to—

(a) business carried on at any time when he was an authorised person (or appointed representative); or

(b) the ownership or control of a former authorised person at any time when he was an authorised person.

(5) "Business" includes any part of a business even if it does not consist of carrying on regulated activities.

(6) References in subsection (1) to a recognised investment exchange do not include references to an overseas investment exchange (as defined by section 313(1)).]

Appointment of persons to carry out
investigations in particular cases.

168.—(1) Subsection (3) applies if it appears to an investigating authority that there are circumstances suggesting that—

(a) a person may have contravened any regulation made under section 142; or

(b) a person may be guilty of an offence under section 177, 191, 346 or 398(1) or under Schedule 4.

(2) Subsection (3) also applies if it appears to an investigating authority that there are circumstances suggesting that—

(a) an offence under section 24(1) or 397 or under Part V of the Criminal Justice Act 1993 may have been committed;

(b) there may have been a breach of the general prohibition;

(c) there may have been a contravention of section 21 or 238; or

(d) market abuse may have taken place.

(3) The investigating authority may appoint one or more competent persons to conduct an investigation on its behalf.

(4) Subsection (5) applies if it appears to the Authority that there are circumstances suggesting that—

(a) a person may have contravened section 20;

(b) a person may be guilty of an offence under prescribed regulations relating to money laundering;

[(ba) a person may be guilty of an offence under Schedule 7 to the Counter-Terrorism Act 2008 (terrorist financing or money laundering);]

(c) an authorised person may have contravened a rule made by the Authority;

(d) an individual may not be a fit and proper person to perform functions in relation to a regulated activity carried on by an authorised or exempt person;

(e) an individual may have performed or agreed to perform a function in breach of a prohibition order;

(f) an authorised or exempt person may have failed to comply with section 56(6);

(g) an authorised person may have failed to comply with section 59(1) or (2);

(h) a person in relation to whom the Authority has given its approval under section 59 may not be a fit and proper person to perform the function to which that approval relates;

(i) a person may be guilty of misconduct for the purposes of section 66[; or

(j) a person may have contravened any provision made by or under this Act for the purpose of implementing the markets in financial instruments directive or by any directly applicable Community regulation made under that directive].

(5) The Authority may appoint one or more competent persons to conduct an investigation on its behalf.

(6) "Investigating authority" means the Authority or the Secretary of State.

Assistance to overseas regulators

Investigations etc. in support of overseas regulator.

169.—(1) At the request of an overseas regulator, the Authority may—

(a) exercise the power conferred by section 165; or

(b) appoint one or more competent persons to investigate any matter.

(2) An investigator has the same powers as an investigator appointed under section 168(3) (as a result of subsection (1) of that section).

(3) If the request has been made by a competent authority in pursuance of any Community obligation the Authority must, in deciding whether or not to exercise its investigative power, consider whether its exercise is necessary to comply with any such obligation.

(4) In deciding whether or not to exercise its investigative power, the Authority may take into account in particular—

(a) whether in the country or territory of the overseas regulator concerned, corresponding assistance would be given to a United Kingdom regulatory authority;

(b) whether the case concerns the breach of a law, or other requirement, which has no close parallel in the United Kingdom or involves the assertion of a jurisdiction not recognised by the United Kingdom;

(c) the seriousness of the case and its importance to persons in the United Kingdom;

(d) whether it is otherwise appropriate in the public interest to give the assistance sought.

(5) The Authority may decide that it will not exercise its investigative power unless the overseas regulator undertakes to make such contribution towards the cost of its exercise as the Authority considers appropriate.

(6) Subsections (4) and (5) do not apply if the Authority considers that the exercise of its investigative power is necessary to comply with a Community obligation.

(7) If the Authority has appointed an investigator in response to a request from an overseas regulator, it may direct the investigator to permit a representative of that regulator to attend, and take part in, any interview conducted for the purposes of the investigation.

(8) A direction under subsection (7) is not to be given unless the Authority is satisfied that any information obtained by an overseas regulator as a result of the interview will be subject to safeguards equivalent to those contained in Part XXIII.

(9) The Authority must prepare a statement of its policy with respect to the conduct of interviews in relation to which a direction under subsection (7) has been given.

(10) The statement requires the approval of the Treasury.

(11) If the Treasury approve the statement, the Authority must publish it.

(12) No direction may be given under subsection (7) before the statement has been published.

(13) "Overseas regulator" has the same meaning as in section 195.

(14) "Investigative power" means one of the powers mentioned in subsection (1).

(15) "Investigator" means a person appointed under subsection (1)(b).

Conduct of investigations

Investigations: general.

170.—(1) This section applies if an investigating authority appoints one or more competent persons ("investigators") under section 167 or 168(3) or (5) to conduct an investigation on its behalf.

(2) The investigating authority must give written notice of the appointment of an investigator to the person who is the subject of the investigation ("the person under investigation").

(3) Subsections (2) and (9) do not apply if—
 (a) the investigator is appointed as a result of section 168(1) or (4) and the investigating authority believes that the notice required by subsection (2) or (9) would be likely to result in the investigation being frustrated; or
 (b) the investigator is appointed as a result of subsection (2) of section 168.

(4) A notice under subsection (2) must—
 (a) specify the provisions under which, and as a result of which, the investigator was appointed; and
 (b) state the reason for his appointment.

(5) Nothing prevents the investigating authority from appointing a person who is a member of its staff as an investigator.

(6) An investigator must make a report of his investigation to the investigating authority.

(7) The investigating authority may, by a direction to an investigator, control—
 (a) the scope of the investigation;
 (b) the period during which the investigation is to be conducted;
 (c) the conduct of the investigation; and
 (d) the reporting of the investigation.

(8) A direction may, in particular—
 (a) confine the investigation to particular matters;
 (b) extend the investigation to additional matters;

(c) require the investigator to discontinue the investigation or to take only such steps as are specified in the direction;

(d) require the investigator to make such interim reports as are so specified.

(9) If there is a change in the scope or conduct of the investigation and, in the opinion of the investigating authority, the person subject to investigation is likely to be significantly prejudiced by not being made aware of it, that person must be given written notice of the change.

(10) "Investigating authority", in relation to an investigator, means—

(a) the Authority, if the Authority appointed him;

(b) the Secretary of State, if the Secretary of State appointed him.

Powers of persons appointed under section 167.

171.—(1) An investigator may require the person who is the subject of the investigation ("the person under investigation") or any person connected with the person under investigation—

(a) to attend before the investigator at a specified time and place and answer questions; or

(b) otherwise to provide such information as the investigator may require.

(2) An investigator may also require any person to produce at a specified time and place any specified documents or documents of a specified description.

(3) A requirement under subsection (1) or (2) may be imposed only so far as the investigator concerned reasonably considers the question, provision of information or production of the document to be relevant to the purposes of the investigation.

[(3A) Where the investigation relates to a recognised investment exchange, an investigator has the additional powers conferred by sections 172 and 173 (and for this purpose references in those sections to an investigator are to be read accordingly).]

(4) For the purposes of this section and section 172, a person is connected with the person under investigation ("A") if he is or has at any relevant time been—

(a) a member of A's group;

(b) a controller of A;

(c) a partnership of which A is a member; or

(d) in relation to A, a person mentioned in Part I or II of Schedule 15.

(5) "Investigator" means a person conducting an investigation under section 167.

(6) "Specified" means specified in a notice in writing.

Additional power of persons
appointed as a result of
section 168(1) or (4).

172.—(1) An investigator has the powers conferred by section 171.

(2) An investigator may also require a person who is neither the subject of the investigation ("the person under investigation") nor a person connected with the person under investigation—

(a) to attend before the investigator at a specified time and place and answer questions; or

(b) otherwise to provide such information as the investigator may require for the purposes of the investigation.

(3) A requirement may only be imposed under subsection (2) if the investigator is satisfied that the requirement is necessary or expedient for the purposes of the investigation.

(4) "Investigator" means a person appointed as a result of subsection (1) or (4) of section 168.

(5) "Specified" means specified in a notice in writing.

Powers of persons appointed
as a result of section 168(2)

173.—(1) Subsections (2) to (4) apply if an investigator considers that any person ("A") is or may be able to give information which is or may be relevant to the investigation.

(2) The investigator may require A—

(a) to attend before him at a specified time and place and answer questions; or

(b) otherwise to provide such information as he may require for the purposes of the investigation.

(3) The investigator may also require A to produce at a specified time and place any specified documents or documents of a specified description which appear to the investigator to relate to any matter relevant to the investigation.

(4) The investigator may also otherwise require A to give him all assistance in connection with the investigation which A is reasonably able to give.

(5) "Investigator" means a person appointed under subsection (3) of section 168 (as a result of subsection (2) of that section).

Admissibility of statements
made to investigators.

174.—(1) A statement made to an investigator by a person in compliance with an information requirement is admissible in evidence in any proceedings, so long as it also complies with any requirements governing the admissibility of evidence in the circumstances in question.

(2) But in criminal proceedings in which that person is charged with an offence to which this subsection applies or in proceedings in relation to action to be taken against that person under section 123—

(a) no evidence relating to the statement may be adduced, and

(b) no question relating to it may be asked, by or on behalf of the prosecution or (as the case may be) the Authority, unless evidence relating to it is adduced, or a question relating to it is asked, in the proceedings by or on behalf of that person.

(3) Subsection (2) applies to any offence other than one —

(a) under section 177(4) or 398;

(b) under section 5 of the Perjury Act 1911 (false statements made otherwise than on oath);

(c) under section 44(2) of the Criminal Law (Consolidation)(Scotland) Act 1995 (false statements made otherwise than on oath); or

(d) under Article 10 of the Perjury (Northern Ireland) Order 1979.

(4) "Investigator" means a person appointed under section 167 or 168(3) or (5).

(5) "Information requirement" means a requirement imposed by an investigator under section 171, 172, 173 or 175.

Information and documents: supplemental provisions.

175.—(1) If the Authority or an investigator has power under this Part to require a person to produce a document but it appears that the document is in the possession of a third person, that power may be exercised in relation to the third person.

(2) If a document is produced in response to a requirement imposed under this Part, the person to whom it is produced may—

(a) take copies or extracts from the document; or

(b) require the person producing the document, or any relevant person, to provide an explanation of the document.

(3) If a person who is required under this Part to produce a document fails to do so, the Authority or an investigator may require him to state, to the best of his knowledge and belief, where the document is.

(4) A lawyer may be required under this Part to furnish the name and address of his client.

(5) No person may be required under this Part to disclose information or produce a document in respect of which he owes an obligation of confidence by virtue of carrying on the business of banking unless—

(a) he is the person under investigation or a member of that person's group;

(b) the person to whom the obligation of confidence is owed is the person under investigation or a member of that person's group;

(c) the person to whom the obligation of confidence is owed consents to the disclosure or production; or

(d) the imposing on him of a requirement with respect to such information or document has been specifically authorised by the investigating authority.

(6) If a person claims a lien on a document, its production under this Part does not affect the lien.

(7) "Relevant person", in relation to a person who is required to produce a document, means a person who—

(a) has been or is or is proposed to be a director or controller of that person;

(b) has been or is an auditor of that person;

(c) has been or is an actuary, accountant or lawyer appointed or instructed by that person; or

(d) has been or is an employee of that person.

(8) "Investigator" means a person appointed under section 167 or 168(3) or (5).

Entry of premises under warrant.

176.—(1) A justice of the peace may issue a warrant under this section if satisfied on information on oath given by or on behalf of the Secretary of State, the Authority or an investigator that there are reasonable grounds for believing that the first, second or third set of conditions is satisfied.

(2) The first set of conditions is—

(a) that a person on whom an information requirement has been imposed has failed (wholly or in part) to comply with it; and

(b) that on the premises specified in the warrant—

(i) there are documents which have been required; or

(ii) there is information which has been required.

(3) The second set of conditions is—

(a) that the premises specified in the warrant are premises of an authorised person or an appointed representative;

(b) that there are on the premises documents or information in relation to which an information requirement could be imposed; and

(c) that if such a requirement were to be imposed—

(i) it would not be complied with; or

(ii) the documents or information to which it related would be removed, tampered with or destroyed.

(4) The third set of conditions is—

(a) that an offence mentioned in section 168 for which the maximum sentence on conviction on indictment is two years or more has been (or is being) committed by any person;

(b) that there are on the premises specified in the warrant documents or information relevant to whether that offence has been (or is being) committed;

(c) that an information requirement could be imposed in relation to those documents or information; and

(d) that if such a requirement were to be imposed—
  (i) it would not be complied with; or
  (ii) the documents or information to which it related would be removed, tampered with or destroyed.

(5) A warrant under this section shall authorise a constable—

(a) to enter the premises specified in the warrant;

(b) to search the premises and take possession of any documents or information appearing to be documents or information of a kind in respect of which a warrant under this section was issued ("the relevant kind") or to take, in relation to any such documents or information, any other steps which may appear to be necessary for preserving them or preventing interference with them;

(c) to take copies of, or extracts from, any documents or information appearing to be of the relevant kind;

(d) to require any person on the premises to provide an explanation of any document or information appearing to be of the relevant kind or to state where it may be found; and

(e) to use such force as may be reasonably necessary.

(6) In England and Wales, sections 15(5) to (8) and section 16 of the Police and Criminal Evidence Act 1984 (execution of search warrants and safeguards) apply to warrants issued under this section.

(7) In Northern Ireland, Articles 17(5) to (8) and 18 of the Police and Criminal Evidence (Northern Ireland) Order 1989 apply to warrants issued under this section.

(8) Any document of which possession is taken under this section may be retained—

(a) for a period of three months; or

(b) if within that period proceedings to which the document is relevant are commenced against any person for any criminal offence, until the conclusion of those proceedings.

(9) In the application of this section to Scotland—

(a) for the references to a justice of the peace substitute references to a justice of the peace or a sheriff; and

(b) for the references to information on oath substitute references to evidence on oath.

(10) "Investigator" means a person appointed under section 167 or 168(3) or (5).

(11) "Information requirement" means a requirement imposed —

    (a) by the Authority under section [87C, 87J,] 165 or 175; or

    (b) by an investigator under section 171, 172, 173 or 175.

Offences

Offences.

177.—(1) If a person other than the investigator ("the defaulter") fails to comply with a requirement imposed on him under this Part the person imposing the requirement may certify that fact in writing to the court.

(2) If the court is satisfied that the defaulter failed without reasonable excuse to comply with the requirement, it may deal with the defaulter (and in the case of a body corporate, any director or officer) as if he were in contempt [; and "officer", in relation to a limited liability partnership, means a member of the limited liability partnership].

(3) A person who knows or suspects that an investigation is being or is likely to be conducted under this Part is guilty of an offence if—

    (a) he falsifies, conceals, destroys or otherwise disposes of a document which he knows or suspects is or would be relevant to such an investigation, or

    (b) he causes or permits the falsification, concealment, destruction or disposal of such a document, unless he shows that he had no intention of concealing facts disclosed by the documents from the investigator.

(4) A person who, in purported compliance with a requirement imposed on him under this Part—

    (a) provides information which he knows to be false or misleading in a material particular, or

    (b) recklessly provides information which is false or misleading in a material particular, is guilty of an offence.

(5) A person guilty of an offence under subsection (3) or (4) is liable—

    (a) on summary conviction, to imprisonment for a term not exceeding six months or a fine not exceeding the statutory maximum, or both;

    (b) on conviction on indictment, to imprisonment for a term not exceeding two years or a fine, or both.

(6) Any person who intentionally obstructs the exercise of any rights conferred by a warrant under section 176 is guilty of an offence and liable on summary conviction to imprisonment for a term not exceeding [51 weeks] or a fine not exceeding level 5 on the standard scale, or both.

(7) "Court" means—

(a) the High Court;

(b) in Scotland, the Court of Session.

Part XIII

Incoming Firms: Intervention by Authority

Interpretation

Interpretation of this Part.

193.—(1) In this Part—

"additional procedure" means the procedure described in section 199;

"incoming firm" means—

(a) an EEA firm which is exercising, or has exercised, its right to carry on a regulated activity in the United Kingdom in accordance with Schedule 3; or

(b) a Treaty firm which is exercising, or has exercised, its right to carry on a regulated activity in the United Kingdom in accordance with Schedule 4; and

"power of intervention" means the power conferred on the Authority by section 196.

(2) In relation to an incoming firm which is an EEA firm, expressions used in this Part and in Schedule 3 have the same meaning in this Part as they have in that Schedule.

General grounds on which power of intervention is exercisable.

194.—(1) The Authority may exercise its power of intervention in respect of an incoming firm if it appears to it that—

(a) the firm has contravened, or is likely to contravene, a requirement which is imposed on it by or under this Act (in a case where the Authority is responsible for enforcing compliance in the United Kingdom);

(b) the firm has, in purported compliance with any requirement imposed by or under this Act, knowingly or recklessly given the Authority information which is false or misleading in a material particular; or

(c) it is desirable to exercise the power in order to protect the interests of actual or potential customers.

(2) Subsection (3) applies to an incoming EEA firm falling within sub-paragraph (a) or (b) of paragraph 5 of Schedule 3 which is exercising an EEA right to carry on any Consumer Credit Act business in the United Kingdom.

(3) The Authority may exercise its power of intervention in respect of the firm if [the Office of Fair Trading] has informed the Authority that—

(a) the firm,

(b) any of the firm's employees, agents or associates (whether past or present), or

(c) if the firm is a body corporate, a controller of the firm or an associate of such a controller,

has done any of the things specified in paragraphs [(a) to (e) of section 25(2A)] of the Consumer Credit Act 1974.

(4) "Associate", "Consumer Credit Act business" and "controller" have the same meaning as in section 203.

[Contravention by relevant EEA firm with UK branch of requirement under markets in financial instruments directive: Authority primarily responsible for securing compliance]

[**194A.**—(1) This section applies if—

(a) a relevant EEA firm has a branch in the United Kingdom; and

(b) the Authority ascertains that the firm has contravened, or is contravening, a requirement falling within subsection (3) (in a case to which Article 62.2 of the markets in financial instruments directive applies).

(2) "Relevant EEA firm" means an EEA firm falling within paragraph 5(a) or (b) of Schedule 3 which is exercising in the United Kingdom an EEA right deriving from the markets in financial instruments directive.

(3) A requirement falls within this subsection if it is imposed on the firm—

(a) by any provision of or made under this Act which implements the markets in financial instruments directive; or

(b) by any directly applicable Community regulation made under that directive.

(4) The Authority must give the firm written notice which —

(a) requires the firm to put an end to the contravention;

(b) states that the Authority's power of intervention will become exercisable in relation to the firm if the firm continues the contravention; and

(c) indicates any requirements that the Authority proposes to impose on the firm in exercise of its power of intervention in the event of the power becoming exercisable.

(5) The Authority may exercise its power of intervention in respect of the firm if—

    (a) a reasonable time has expired since the giving of the notice under subsection (4);

    (b) the firm has failed to put an end to the contravention within that time; and

    (c) the Authority has informed the firm's home state regulator of its intention to exercise its power of intervention in respect of the firm.

(6) Subsection (5) applies whether or not the Authority's power of intervention is also exercisable as a result of section 194.

(7) If the Authority exercises its power of intervention in respect of a relevant EEA firm by virtue of subsection (5), it must at the earliest opportunity inform the firm's home state regulator and the Commission of—

    (a) the fact that the Authority has exercised that power in respect of the firm; and

    (b) any requirements it has imposed on the firm in exercise of the power.]

Exercise of power in support of overseas regulator.

195.—(1) The Authority may exercise its power of intervention in respect of an incoming firm at the request of, or for the purpose of assisting, an overseas regulator.

(2) Subsection (1) applies whether or not the Authority's power of intervention is also exercisable as a result of section 194.

(3) "An overseas regulator" means an authority in a country or territory outside the United Kingdom—

    (a) which is a home state regulator; or

    (b) which exercises any function of a kind mentioned in subsection (4).

(4) The functions are—

    (a) a function corresponding to any function of the Authority under this Act;

    (b) a function corresponding to any function exercised by the competent authority under Part VI…;

    (c) a function corresponding to any function exercised by the Secretary of State under [the Companies Acts (as defined in section 2 of the Companies Act 2006)];

    (d) a function in connection with—

        (i) the investigation of conduct of the kind prohibited by Part V of the Criminal Justice Act 1993 (insider dealing); or

        (ii) the enforcement of rules (whether or not having the force of law) relating to such conduct;

    (e) a function prescribed by regulations made for the purposes of this subsection which, in the opinion of the Treasury, relates to companies or financial services.

(5) If—

    (a) a request to the Authority for the exercise of its power of intervention has been made by a home state regulator in pursuance of a Community obligation, or

    (b) a home state regulator has notified the Authority that an EEA firm's EEA authorisation has been withdrawn, the Authority must, in deciding whether or not to exercise its power of intervention, consider whether exercising it is necessary in order to comply with a Community obligation.

(6) In deciding in any case in which the Authority does not consider that the exercise of its power of intervention is necessary in order to comply with a Community obligation, it may take into account in particular—

    (a) whether in the country or territory of the overseas regulator concerned, corresponding assistance would be given to a United Kingdom regulatory authority;

    (b) whether the case concerns the breach of a law, or other requirement, which has no close parallel in the United Kingdom or involves the assertion of a jurisdiction not recognised by the United Kingdom;

    (c) the seriousness of the case and its importance to persons in the United Kingdom;

    (d) whether it is otherwise appropriate in the public interest to give the assistance sought.

(7) The Authority may decide not to exercise its power of intervention, in response to a request, unless the regulator concerned undertakes to make such contribution to the cost of its exercise as the Authority considers appropriate.

(8) Subsection (7) does not apply if the Authority decides that it is necessary for it to exercise its power of intervention in order to comply with a Community obligation.

[Contravention by relevant EEA firm of requirement under markets in financial instruments directive: home state regulator primarily responsible for securing compliance]

[195A.—(1) This section applies if the Authority has clear and demonstrable grounds for believing that a relevant EEA firm has contravened, or is contravening, a requirement falling within subsection (2) (in a case to which Article 62.1 or 62.3 of the markets in financial instruments directive applies).

(2) A requirement falls within this subsection if it is imposed on the firm—

    (a) by or under any provision adopted in the firm's home state for the purpose of implementing the markets in financial instruments directive; or

    (b) by any directly applicable Community regulation made under that directive.

(3) The Authority must notify the firm's home state regulator of the situation mentioned in subsection (1).

(4) The notice under subsection (3) must—

    (a) request that the home state regulator take all appropriate measures for the purpose of ensuring that the firm puts an end to the contravention;

    (b) state that the Authority's power of intervention is likely to become exercisable in relation to the firm if the firm continues the contravention; and

    (c) indicate any requirements that the Authority proposes to impose on the firm in exercise of its power of intervention in the event of the power becoming exercisable.

(5) The Authority may exercise its power of intervention in respect of the firm if—

    (a) a reasonable time has expired since the giving of the notice under subsection (3); and

    (b) conditions A to C are satisfied.

(6) Condition A is that—

    (a) the firm's home state regulator has failed or refused to take measures for the purpose mentioned in subsection (4)(a); or

    (b) any measures taken by the home state regulator have proved inadequate for that purpose.

(7) Condition B is that the firm is acting in a manner which is clearly prejudicial to the interests of investors in the United Kingdom or the orderly functioning of the markets.

(8) Condition C is that the Authority has informed the firm's home state regulator of its intention to exercise its power of intervention in respect of the firm.

(9) Subsection (5) applies whether or not the Authority's power of intervention is also exercisable as a result of section 194 or 195.

(10) If the Authority exercises its power of intervention in respect of a relevant EEA firm by virtue of subsection (5), it must at the earliest opportunity inform the Commission of—

    (a) the fact that the Authority has exercised that power in respect of the firm; and

    (b) any requirements it has imposed on the firm in exercise of the power.

(11) In this section—

"home state", in relation to a relevant EEA firm, means—

    (a) in the case of a firm which is a body corporate, the EEA State in which the firm has its registered office or, if it has no registered office, its head office; and

    (b) in any other case, the EEA State in which the firm has its head office;

"relevant EEA firm" has the same meaning as in section 194A.]

The power of intervention.

196. If the Authority is entitled to exercise its power of intervention in respect of an incoming firm under this Part, it may impose any requirement in relation to the firm which it could impose if—

    (a) the firm's permission was a Part IV permission; and

    (b) the Authority was entitled to exercise its power under that Part to vary that permission.

Exercise of power of intervention

Procedure on exercise of power of intervention.

197.—(1) A requirement takes effect—

    (a) immediately, if the notice given under subsection (3) states that that is the case;

    (b) on such date as may be specified in the notice; or

    (c) if no date is specified in the notice, when the matter to which it relates is no longer open to review.

(2) A requirement may be expressed to take effect immediately (or on a specified date) only if the Authority, having regard to the ground on which it is exercising its power of intervention, considers that it is necessary for the requirement to take effect immediately (or on that date).

(3) If the Authority proposes to impose a requirement under section 196 on an incoming firm, or imposes such a requirement with immediate effect, it must give the firm written notice.

(4) The notice must—

    (a) give details of the requirement;

    (b) inform the firm of when the requirement takes effect;

    (c) state the Authority's reasons for imposing the requirement and for its determination as to when the requirement takes effect;

    (d) inform the firm that it may make representations to the Authority within such period as may be specified in the notice (whether or not it has referred the matter to the Tribunal); and

    (e) inform it of its right to refer the matter to the Tribunal.

(5) The Authority may extend the period allowed under the notice for making representations.

(6) If, having considered any representations made by the firm, the Authority decides—

    (a) to impose the requirement proposed, or

    (b) if it has been imposed, not to rescind the requirement, it must give it written notice.

(7) If, having considered any representations made by the firm, the Authority decides—

    (a) not to impose the requirement proposed,

    (b) to impose a different requirement from that proposed, or

(c) to rescind a requirement which has effect, it must give it written notice.

(8) A notice given under subsection (6) must inform the firm of its right to refer the matter to the Tribunal.

(9) A notice under subsection (7)(b) must comply with subsection (4).

(10) If a notice informs a person of his right to refer a matter to the Tribunal, it must give an indication of the procedure on such a reference.

Power to apply to court for injunction in respect of certain overseas insurance companies.

198.—(1) This section applies if the Authority has received a request made in respect of an incoming EEA firm in accordance with—

(a) Article 20.5 of the first non-life insurance directive; or

[(b) Article 37.5 of the life assurance consolidation directive][; or

(c) Article 42.4 of the reinsurance directive].

(2) The court may, on an application made to it by the Authority with respect to the firm, grant an injunction restraining (or in Scotland an interdict prohibiting) the firm disposing of or otherwise dealing with any of its assets.

(3) If the court grants an injunction, it may by subsequent orders make provision for such incidental, consequential and supplementary matters as it considers necessary to enable the Authority to perform any of its functions under this Act.

(4) "The court" means—

(a) the High Court; or

(b) in Scotland, the Court of Session.

Additional procedure for EEA firms in certain cases.

199.—(1) This section applies if it appears to the Authority that its power of intervention is exercisable in relation to an EEA firm exercising EEA rights in the United Kingdom ("an incoming EEA firm") in respect of the contravention of a relevant requirement.

(2) A requirement is relevant if—

(a) it is imposed by the Authority under this Act; and

[(b) as respects its contravention, the single market directive in question provides that a procedure of the kind set out in the following provisions of this section (so far as they are relevant in the firm's case) is to apply].

(3) The Authority must, in writing, require the firm to remedy the situation.

[(3A) If the firm falls within paragraph 5(da) of Schedule 3, the Authority must at the same time as it gives notice to the firm under subsection (3) refer its findings to the firm's home state regulator.

(3B) Subsections (4) to (8) apply to an incoming EEA firm other than a firm falling within paragraph 5(da) of Schedule 3.]

(4) If the firm fails to comply with the requirement under subsection (3) within a reasonable time, the Authority must give a notice to that effect to the firm's home state regulator requesting it—

(a) to take all appropriate measures for the purpose of ensuring that the firm remedies the situation which has given rise to the notice; and

(b) to inform the Authority of the measures it proposes to take or has taken or the reasons for not taking such measures.

(5) Except as mentioned in subsection (6), the Authority may not exercise its power of intervention [before informing the firm's home state regulator and] unless satisfied—

(a) that the firm's home state regulator has failed or refused to take measures for the purpose mentioned in subsection (4)(a); or

(b) that the measures taken by the home state regulator have proved inadequate for that purpose.

(6) If the Authority decides that it should exercise its power of intervention in respect of the incoming EEA firm as a matter of urgency in order to protect the interests of consumers, it may exercise that power—

(a) before complying with subsections (3) and (4); or

(b) where it has complied with those subsections, before it is satisfied as mentioned in subsection (5).

(7) In such a case the Authority must at the earliest opportunity inform the firm's home state regulator and the Commission.

(8) If—

(a) the Authority has (by virtue of subsection (6)) exercised its power of intervention before complying with subsections (3) and (4) or before it is satisfied as mentioned in subsection (5), and

(b) the Commission decides under any of the single market directives [(other than the markets in financial instruments directive)] that the Authority must rescind or vary any requirement imposed in the exercise of its power of intervention, the Authority must in accordance with the decision rescind or vary the requirement.

[(9) In the case of a firm falling within paragraph 5(da) of Schedule 3, the Authority may not exercise its power of intervention before informing the firm's home state regulator and unless satisfied—

(a) that the firm's home state regulator has failed or refused to take all appropriate measures for the purpose of ensuring that the firm remedies the situation which gave rise to the notice under subsection (3); or

(b) that the measures taken by the home state regulator have proved inadequate for that purpose.]

Supplemental

Rescission and variation of requirements.

200.—(1) The Authority may rescind or vary a requirement imposed in exercise of its power of intervention on its own initiative or on the application of the person subject to the requirement.

(2) The power of the Authority on its own initiative to rescind a requirement is exercisable by written notice given by the Authority to the person concerned, which takes effect on the date specified in the notice.

(3) Section 197 applies to the exercise of the power of the Authority on its own initiative to vary a requirement as it applies to the imposition of a requirement.

(4) If the Authority proposes to refuse an application for the variation or rescission of a requirement, it must give the applicant a warning notice.

(5) If the Authority decides to refuse an application for the variation or rescission of a requirement—

(a) the Authority must give the applicant a decision notice; and

(b) that person may refer the matter to the Tribunal.

Effect of certain requirements on other persons.

201. If the Authority, in exercising its power of intervention, imposes on an incoming firm a requirement of a kind mentioned in subsection (3) of section 48, the requirement has the same effect in relation to the firm as it would have in relation to an authorised person if it had been imposed on the authorised person by the Authority acting under section 45.

Contravention of requirement imposed under this Part.

202.—(1) Contravention of a requirement imposed by the Authority under this Part does not—

(a) make a person guilty of an offence;

(b) make any transaction void or unenforceable; or

(c) (subject to subsection (2)) give rise to any right of action for breach of statutory duty.

(2) In prescribed cases the contravention is actionable at the suit of a person who suffers loss as a result of the contravention, subject to the defences and other incidents applying to actions for breach of statutory duty.

Powers of Director General of Fair Trading

Power to prohibit the carrying on of Consumer Credit Act business.

203.—(1) If it appears to [the Office of Fair Trading ("the OFT")] that subsection (4) has been, or is likely to be, contravened as respects a consumer credit EEA firm, [it] may by written notice given to the firm impose on the firm a consumer credit prohibition.

(2) If it appears to the [OFT] that a restriction imposed under section 204 on an EEA consumer credit firm has not been complied with, [it] may by written notice given to the firm impose a consumer credit prohibition.

(3) "Consumer credit prohibition" means a prohibition on carrying on, or purporting to carry on, in the United Kingdom any Consumer Credit Act business which consists of or includes carrying on one or more listed activities.

(4) This subsection is contravened as respects a firm if—

    (a) the firm or any of its employees, agents or associates (whether past or present), or

    (b) if the firm is a body corporate, any controller of the firm or an associate of any such controller,

does any of the things specified in paragraphs [(a) to (e) of section 25(2A)] of the Consumer Credit Act 1974.

(5) A consumer credit prohibition may be absolute or may be imposed—

    (a) for such period,

    (b) until the occurrence of such event, or

    (c) until such conditions are complied with,

as may be specified in the notice given under subsection (1) or (2).

(6) Any period, event or condition so specified may be varied by the [OFT] on the application of the firm concerned.

(7) A consumer credit prohibition may be withdrawn by written notice served by the [OFT] on the firm concerned, and any such notice takes effect on such date as is specified in the notice.

(8) Schedule 16 has effect as respects consumer credit prohibitions and restrictions under section 204.

(9) A firm contravening a prohibition under this section is guilty of an offence and liable—

    (a) on summary conviction, to a fine not exceeding the statutory maximum;

    (b) on conviction on indictment, to a fine.

(10) In this section and section 204—

"a consumer credit EEA firm" means an EEA firm falling within any of paragraphs (a) to (c) of paragraph 5 of Schedule 3 whose EEA authorisation covers any Consumer Credit Act business;

"Consumer Credit Act business" means consumer credit business, consumer hire business or ancillary credit business;

"consumer credit business", "consumer hire business" and "ancillary credit business" have the same meaning as in the Consumer Credit Act 1974;

"listed activity" means an activity listed in [Annex 1 to the banking consolidation directive] or the Annex to the investment services directive;

"associate" has the same meaning as in section [25(2A)] of the Consumer Credit Act 1974;

"controller" has the meaning given by section 189(1) of that Act.

Power to restrict the carrying on of Consumer Credit Act business.

204.—(1) In this section "restriction" means a direction that a consumer credit EEA firm may not carry on in the United Kingdom, otherwise than in accordance with such condition or conditions as may be specified in the direction, any Consumer Credit Act business which—

(a) consists of or includes carrying on any listed activity; and

(b) is specified in the direction.

(2) If it appears to the [OFT] that the situation as respects a consumer credit EEA firm is such that the powers conferred by section 203(1) are exercisable, the [OFT] may, instead of imposing a prohibition, impose such restriction as appears to [it] desirable.

(3) A restriction—

(a) may be withdrawn, or

(b) may be varied with the agreement of the firm concerned, by written notice served by the [OFT] on the firm, and any such notice takes effect on such date as is specified in the notice.

(4) A firm contravening a restriction is guilty of an offence and liable—

(a) on summary conviction, to a fine not exceeding the statutory maximum;

(b) on conviction on indictment, to a fine.

Part XIV
Disciplinary Measures

Public censure.

205. If the Authority considers that an authorised person has contravened a requirement imposed on him by or under this Act, [or by any directly applicable Community regulation made under the markets in financial instruments directive,] the Authority may publish a statement to that effect.

Financial penalties.

206.—(1) If the Authority considers that an authorised person has contravened a requirement imposed on him by or under this Act, [or by any directly applicable Community regulation made under the markets in financial instruments directive,] it may impose on him a penalty, in respect of the contravention, of such amount as it considers appropriate.

(2) The Authority may not in respect of any contravention both require a person to pay a penalty under this section and withdraw his authorisation under section 33.

(3) A penalty under this section is payable to the Authority.

Proposal to take disciplinary measures.	**207.**—(1) If the Authority proposes—

(a) to publish a statement in respect of an authorised person (under section 205), or

(b) to impose a penalty on an authorised person (under section 206),

it must give the authorised person a warning notice.

(2) A warning notice about a proposal to publish a statement must set out the terms of the statement.

(3) A warning notice about a proposal to impose a penalty, must state the amount of the penalty.

208.—(1) If the Authority decides—

Decision notice.

(a) to publish a statement under section 205 (whether or not in the terms proposed), or

(b) to impose a penalty under section 206 (whether or not of the amount proposed),

it must without delay give the authorised person concerned a decision notice.

(2) In the case of a statement, the decision notice must set out the terms of the statement.

(3) In the case of a penalty, the decision notice must state the amount of the penalty.

(4) If the Authority decides to—

(a) publish a statement in respect of an authorised person under section 205, or

(b) impose a penalty on an authorised person under section 206,

the authorised person may refer the matter to the Tribunal.

Publication.

209. After a statement under section 205 is published, the Authority must send a copy of it to the authorised person and to any person on whom a copy of the decision notice was given under section 393(4).

Statements of policy.

210.—(1) The Authority must prepare and issue a statement of its policy with respect to—

(a) the imposition of penalties under this Part; and

(b) the amount of penalties under this Part.

(2) The Authority's policy in determining what the amount of a penalty should be must include having regard to—

(a) the seriousness of the contravention in question in relation to the nature of the requirement contravened;

(b) the extent to which that contravention was deliberate or reckless; and

(c) whether the person on whom the penalty is to be imposed is an individual.

(3) The Authority may at any time alter or replace a statement issued under this section.

(4) If a statement issued under this section is altered or replaced, the Authority must issue the altered or replacement statement.

(5) The Authority must, without delay, give the Treasury a copy of any statement which it publishes under this section.

(6) A statement issued under this section must be published by the Authority in the way appearing to the Authority to be best calculated to bring it to the attention of the public.

(7) In exercising, or deciding whether to exercise, its power under section 206 in the case of any particular contravention, the Authority must have regard to any statement published under this section and in force at the time when the contravention in question occurred.

(8) The Authority may charge a reasonable fee for providing a person with a copy of the statement.

Statements of policy: procedure.

211.—(1) Before issuing a statement under section 210, the Authority must publish a draft of the proposed statement in the way appearing to the Authority to be best calculated to bring it to the attention of the public.

(2) The draft must be accompanied by notice that representations about the proposal may be made to the Authority within a specified time.

(3) Before issuing the proposed statement, the Authority must have regard to any representations made to it in accordance with subsection (2).

(4) If the Authority issues the proposed statement it must publish an account, in general terms, of—

(a) the representations made to it in accordance with subsection (2); and

(b) its response to them.

(5) If the statement differs from the draft published under subsection (1) in a way which is, in the opinion of the Authority, significant, the Authority must (in addition to complying with subsection (4)) publish details of the difference.

(6) The Authority may charge a reasonable fee for providing a person with a copy of a draft published under subsection (1).

(7) This section also applies to a proposal to alter or replace a statement.

Part XV
The Financial Services Compensation Scheme
The scheme manager

The scheme manager.

212.—(1) The Authority must establish a body corporate ("the scheme manager") to exercise the functions conferred on the scheme manager by or under this Part.

(2) The Authority must take such steps as are necessary to ensure that the scheme manager is, at all times, capable of exercising those functions.

(3) The constitution of the scheme manager must provide for it to have—

(a) a chairman; and

(b) a board (which must include the chairman) whose members are the scheme manager's directors.

(4) The chairman and other members of the board must be persons appointed, and liable to removal from office, by the Authority (acting, in the case of the chairman, with the approval of the Treasury).

(5) But the terms of their appointment (and in particular those governing removal from office) must be such as to secure their independence from the Authority in the operation of the compensation scheme.

(6) The scheme manager is not to be regarded as exercising functions on behalf of the Crown.

(7) The scheme manager's board members, officers and staff are not to be regarded as Crown servants.

The scheme

The compensation scheme.

213.—(1) The Authority must by rules establish a scheme for compensating persons in cases where relevant persons are unable, or are likely to be unable, to satisfy claims against them.

(2) The rules are to be known as the Financial Services Compensation Scheme (but are referred to in this Act as "the compensation scheme").

(3) The compensation scheme must, in particular, provide for the scheme manager—

(a) to assess and pay compensation, in accordance with the scheme, to claimants in respect of claims made in connection with regulated activities carried on (whether or not with permission) by relevant persons; and

(b) to have power to impose levies on authorised persons, or any class of authorised person, for the purpose of meeting its expenses (including in particular expenses incurred, or expected to be incurred, in paying compensation, borrowing or insuring risks).

(4) The compensation scheme may provide for the scheme manager to have power to impose levies on authorised persons, or any class of authorised person, for the purpose of recovering the cost (whenever incurred) of establishing the scheme.

(5) In making any provision of the scheme by virtue of subsection (3)(b), the Authority must take account of the desirability of ensuring that the amount of the levies imposed on a particular class of authorised person reflects, so far as practicable, the amount of the claims made, or likely to be made, in respect of that class of person.

(6) An amount payable to the scheme manager as a result of any provision of the scheme made by virtue of subsection (3)(b) or (4) may be recovered as a debt due to the scheme manager.

(7) Sections 214 to 217 make further provision about the scheme but are not to be taken as limiting the power conferred on the Authority by subsection (1) [(except where limitations are expressly stated)].

(8) In those sections "specified" means specified in the scheme.

(9) In this Part (except in sections 219, 220 or 224) "relevant person" means a person who was—

(a) an authorised person at the time the act or omission giving rise to the claim against him took place; or

(b) an appointed representative at that time.

(10) But a person who, at that time—

(a) qualified for authorisation under Schedule 3, and

(b) fell within a prescribed category,

is not to be regarded as a relevant person in relation to any activities for which he had permission as a result of any provision of, or made under, that Schedule unless he had elected to participate in the scheme in relation to those activities at that time.

Provisions of the scheme

General.

214.—(1) The compensation scheme may, in particular, make provision—

(a) as to the circumstances in which a relevant person is to be taken (for the purposes of the scheme) to be unable, or likely to be unable, to satisfy claims made against him;

(b) for the establishment of different funds for meeting different kinds of claim;

(c) for the imposition of different levies in different cases;

(d) limiting the levy payable by a person in respect of a specified period;

(e) for repayment of the whole or part of a levy in specified circumstances;

(f) for a claim to be entertained only if it is made by a specified kind of claimant;

(g) for a claim to be entertained only if it falls within a specified kind of claim;

(h) as to the procedure to be followed in making a claim;

(i) for the making of interim payments before a claim is finally determined;

(j) limiting the amount payable on a claim to a specified maximum amount or a maximum amount calculated in a specified manner;

(k) for payment to be made, in specified circumstances, to a person other than the claimant.

[(1A) Rules by virtue of subsection (1)(h) may, in particular, allow the scheme manager to treat persons who are or may be entitled to claim under the scheme as if they had done so.

(1B) A reference in any enactment or instrument to a claim or claimant under this Part includes a reference to a deemed claim or claimant in accordance with subsection (1A).

(1C) Rules by virtue of subsection (1)(j) may, in particular, allow, or be subject to rules which allow, the scheme manager to settle a class of claim by payment of sums fixed without reference to, or by modification of, the normal rules for calculation of maximum entitlement for individual claims.]

(2) Different provision may be made with respect to different kinds of claim.

(3) The scheme may provide for the determination and regulation of matters relating to the scheme by the scheme manager.

(4) The scheme, or particular provisions of the scheme, may be made so as to apply only in relation to—
   (a) activities carried on,
   (b) claimants,
   (c) matters arising, or
   (d) events occurring,
in specified territories, areas or localities.

(5) The scheme may provide for a person who—
   (a) qualifies for authorisation under Schedule 3, and
   (b) falls within a prescribed category,
to elect to participate in the scheme in relation to some or all of the activities for which he has permission as a result of any provision of, or made under, that Schedule.

(6) The scheme may provide for the scheme manager to have power—
   (a) in specified circumstances,
   (b) but only if the scheme manager is satisfied that the claimant is entitled to receive a payment in respect of his claim—
      (i) under a scheme which is comparable to the compensation scheme, or
      (ii) as the result of a guarantee given by a government or other authority,
to make a full payment of compensation to the claimant and recover the whole or part of the amount of that payment from the other scheme or under that guarantee.

[Contingency funding]

[214A.—(1) The Treasury may make regulations ("contingency fund regulations") permitting the scheme manager to impose levies under section 213 for the purpose of maintaining contingency funds from which possible expenses may be paid.

(2) Contingency fund regulations may make provision about the establishment and management of contingency funds; in particular, the regulations may make provision about —

(a) the number and size of funds;

(b) the circumstances and timing of their establishment;

(c) the classes of person from whom contributions to the funds may be levied;

(d) the amount and timing of payments into and out of funds (which may include provision for different levies for different classes of person);

(e) refunds;

(f) the ways in which funds' contents may be invested (including (i) the extent of reliance on section 223A, and (ii) the application of investment income);

(g) the purposes for which funds may be applied, but only so as to determine whether a fund is to be used (i) for the payment of compensation, (ii) for the purposes of co-operating with a bank liquidator in accordance with section 99 of the Banking Act 2009, or (iii) for contributions under section 214B;

(h) procedures to be followed in connection with funds, including the keeping of records and the provision of information.

(3) The compensation scheme may include provision about contingency funds provided that it is not inconsistent with contingency fund regulations.]

[Contribution to costs of special resolution regime]

[**214B.**—(1) This section applies where—

(a) a stabilisation power under Part 1 of the Banking Act 2009 has been exercised in respect of a bank, building society or credit union (within the meaning of that Part), and

(b) the Treasury think that the bank, building society or credit union was, or but for the exercise of the stabilisation power would have become, unable to satisfy claims against it.

(2) Where this section applies—

(a) the Treasury may require the scheme manager to make payments in connection with the exercise of the stabilisation power, and

(b) payments shall be treated as expenditure under the scheme for all purposes (including levies, contingency funds and borrowing).

(3) The Treasury shall make regulations—

(a) specifying what expenses the scheme manager may be required to incur under subsection (2),

(b) providing for independent verification of the nature and amount of expenses incurred in connection with the exercise of the stabilisation power (which may include provision about appointment and payment of an auditor), and

(c) providing for the method by which amounts to be paid are to be determined.

(4) The regulations must ensure that payments required do not exceed the amount of compensation that would have been payable under the scheme if the stabilisation power had not been exercised and the bank had been unable to satisfy claims against it; and for that purpose the amount of compensation that would have been payable does not include —

(a) amounts that would have been likely, at the time when the stabilisation power was exercised, to be recovered by the scheme from the bank, or

(b) any compensation actually paid to an eligible depositor of the bank.

(5) The regulations must provide for the appointment of an independent valuer (who may be the person appointed as valuer under section 54 of the Banking Act 2009 in respect of the exercise of the stabilisation power) to calculate the amounts referred to in subsection (4)(a); and the regulations —

(a) must provide for the valuer to be appointed by the Treasury or by a person designated by the Treasury,

(b) must include provision enabling the valuer to reconsider a decision,

(c) must provide a right of appeal to a court or tribunal,

(d) must provide for payment of the valuer,

(e) may replicate or apply a provision of section 54 or 55, and

(f) may apply or include any provision that is or could be made under that section.

(6) Payments required to be made by the scheme by virtue of section 61 of the Banking Act 2009 (special resolution regime: compensation) shall be treated for the purposes of subsection (4) as if required to be made under this section.

(7) The regulations may include provision for payments (including payments under those provisions of the Banking Act 2009) to be made—

(a) before verification in accordance with subsection (3)(b), and

(b) before the calculation of the limit imposed by subsection (4), by reference to estimates of that limit and subject to any necessary later adjustment.

(8) The regulations may include provision—

(a) about timing;

(b) about procedures to be followed;

(c) for discretionary functions to be exercised by a specified body or by persons of a specified class;

(d) about the resolution of disputes (which may include provision conferring jurisdiction on a court or tribunal).

(9) The compensation scheme may include provision about payments under and levies in connection with this section, provided that it is not inconsistent with this section or regulations under it.]

Rights of the scheme in relevant person's insolvency.

215.—(1) The compensation scheme may, in particular, make provision—

(a) about the effect of a payment of compensation under the scheme on rights or obligations arising out of matters in connection with which the compensation was paid;

(b) giving the scheme manager a right of recovery in respect of those rights or obligations.]

(2) Such a right of recovery conferred by the scheme does not, in the event of [a person's insolvency], exceed such right (if any) as the claimant would have had in that event.

(3) If a person other than the scheme manager [makes an administration application under Schedule B1 to the 1986 Act or [Schedule B1 to] the 1989 Order] in relation to a company or partnership which is a relevant person, the scheme manager has the same rights as are conferred on the Authority by section 362.

[(3A) In subsection (3) the reference to making an administration application includes a reference to—

(a) appointing an administrator under paragraph 14 or 22 of Schedule B1 to the 1986 Act [or paragraph 15 or 23 of Schedule B1 to the 1989 Order], or

(b) filing with the court a copy of notice of intention to appoint an administrator under [any] of those paragraphs.]

(4) If a person other than the scheme manager presents a petition for the winding up of a body which is a relevant person, the scheme manager has the same rights as are conferred on the Authority by section 371.

(5) If a person other than the scheme manager presents a bankruptcy petition to the court in relation to an individual who, or an entity which, is a relevant person, the scheme manager has the same rights as are conferred on the Authority by section 374.

(6) Insolvency rules may be made for the purpose of integrating any procedure for which provision is made as a result of subsection (1) into the general procedure on the administration of a company or partnership or on a winding-up, bankruptcy or sequestration.

(7) "Bankruptcy petition" means a petition to the court—

(a) under section 264 of the 1986 Act or Article 238 of the 1989 Order for a bankruptcy order to be made against an individual;

(b) under section 5 of the 1985 Act for the sequestration of the estate of an individual; or

(c) under section 6 of the 1985 Act for the sequestration of the estate belonging to or held for or jointly by the members of an entity mentioned in subsection (1) of that section.

(8) "Insolvency rules" are—

(a) for England and Wales, rules made under sections 411 and 412 of the 1986 Act;

(b) for Scotland, rules made by order by the Treasury, after consultation with the Scottish Ministers, for the purposes of this section; and

(c) for Northern Ireland, rules made under Article 359 of the 1989 Order and section 55 of the Judicature (Northern Ireland) Act 1978.

(9) "The 1985 Act", "the 1986 Act", "the 1989 Order" and "court" have the same meaning as in Part XXIV.

Continuity of long-term insurance policies.

216.—(1) The compensation scheme may, in particular, include provision requiring the scheme manager to make arrangements for securing continuity of insurance for policyholders, or policyholders of a specified class, of relevant long-term insurers.

(2) "Relevant long-term insurers" means relevant persons who—

(a) have permission to effect or carry out contracts of long-term insurance; and

(b) are unable, or likely to be unable, to satisfy claims made against them.

(3) The scheme may provide for the scheme manager to take such measures as appear to him to be appropriate—

(a) for securing or facilitating the transfer of a relevant long-term insurer's business so far as it consists of the carrying out of contracts of long-term insurance, or of any part of that business, to another authorised person;

(b) for securing the issue by another authorised person to the policyholders concerned of policies in substitution for their existing policies.

(4) The scheme may also provide for the scheme manager to make payments to the policyholders concerned—

(a) during any period while he is seeking to make arrangements mentioned in subsection (1);

(b) if it appears to him that it is not reasonably practicable to make such arrangements.

(5) A provision of the scheme made by virtue of section 213(3)(b) may include power to impose levies for the purpose of meeting expenses of the scheme manager incurred in—

(a) taking measures as a result of any provision of the scheme made by virtue of subsection (3);

341

(b) making payments as a result of any such provision made by virtue of subsection (4).

Insurers in financial difficulties.

217.—(1) The compensation scheme may, in particular, include provision for the scheme manager to have power to take measures for safeguarding policyholders, or policyholders of a specified class, of relevant insurers.

(2) "Relevant insurers" means relevant persons who—

(a) have permission to effect or carry out contracts of insurance; and

(b) are in financial difficulties.

(3) The measures may include such measures as the scheme manager considers appropriate for—

(a) securing or facilitating the transfer of a relevant insurer's business so far as it consists of the carrying out of contracts of insurance, or of any part of that business, to another authorised person;

(b) giving assistance to the relevant insurer to enable it to continue to effect or carry out contracts of insurance.

(4) The scheme may provide—

(a) that if measures of a kind mentioned in subsection (3)(a) are to be taken, they should be on terms appearing to the scheme manager to be appropriate, including terms reducing, or deferring payment of, any of the things to which any of those who are eligible policyholders in relation to the relevant insurer are entitled in their capacity as such;

(b) that if measures of a kind mentioned in subsection (3)(b) are to be taken, they should be conditional on the reduction of, or the deferment of the payment of, the things to which any of those who are eligible policyholders in relation to the relevant insurer are entitled in their capacity as such;

(c) for ensuring that measures of a kind mentioned in subsection (3)(b) do not benefit to any material extent persons who were members of a relevant insurer when it began to be in financial difficulties or who had any responsibility for, or who may have profited from, the circumstances giving rise to its financial difficulties, except in specified circumstances;

(d) for requiring the scheme manager to be satisfied that any measures he proposes to take are likely to cost less than it would cost to pay compensation under the scheme if the relevant insurer became unable, or likely to be unable, to satisfy claims made against him.

(5) The scheme may provide for the Authority to have power —

(a) to give such assistance to the scheme manager as it considers appropriate for assisting the scheme manager to determine what measures are practicable or desirable in the case of a particular relevant insurer;

(b) to impose constraints on the taking of measures by the scheme manager in the case of a particular relevant insurer;

(c) to require the scheme manager to provide it with information about any particular measures which the scheme manager is proposing to take.

(6) The scheme may include provision for the scheme manager to have power—

(a) to make interim payments in respect of eligible policyholders of a relevant insurer;

(b) to indemnify any person making payments to eligible policyholders of a relevant insurer.

(7) A provision of the scheme made by virtue of section 213(3)(b) may include power to impose levies for the purpose of meeting expenses of the scheme manager incurred in—

(a) taking measures as a result of any provision of the scheme made by virtue of subsection (1);

(b) making payments or giving indemnities as a result of any such provision made by virtue of subsection (6).

(8) "Financial difficulties" and "eligible policyholders" have such meanings as may be specified.

Annual report

Annual report.　218.—(1) At least once a year, the scheme manager must make a report to the Authority [and the Treasury] on the discharge of its functions.

(2) The report must—

(a) include a statement setting out the value of each of the funds established by the compensation scheme; and

(b) comply with any requirements specified in rules made by the Authority [or in contingency fund regulations].

(3) The scheme manager must publish each report in the way it considers appropriate.

Information and documents

[218A Authority's power to require information]　[(1) The Authority may make rules enabling the Authority to require authorised persons to provide information, which may then be made available to the scheme manager by the Authority.

(2) A requirement may be imposed only if the Authority thinks the information is of a kind that may be of use to the scheme manager in connection with functions in respect of the scheme.

(3) A requirement under this section may apply—

(a) to authorised persons generally or only to specified persons or classes of person;

(b) to the provision of information at specified periods, in connection with specified events or in other ways.

(4) In addition to requirements under this section, a notice under section 165 may relate to information or documents which the Authority thinks are reasonably required by the scheme manager in connection with the performance of functions in respect of the scheme; and section 165(4) is subject to this subsection.

(5) Rules under subsection (1) shall be prepared, made and treated in the same way as (and may be combined with) the Authority's general rules.]

Information and documents

Scheme manager's power to require information.

219.—(1) The scheme manager may, by notice in writing [require a person]—

(a) to provide specified information or information of a specified description; or

(b) to produce specified documents or documents of a specified description.

[(1A) A requirement may be imposed only—

(a) on a person (P) against whom a claim has been made under the scheme,

(b) on a person (P) who is unable or likely to be unable to satisfy claims under the scheme against P,

(c) on a person ("the Third Party") whom the scheme manager thinks was knowingly involved in matters giving rise to a claim against another person (P) under the scheme, or

(d) on a person ("the Third Party") whom the scheme manager thinks was knowingly involved in matters giving rise to the actual or likely inability of another person (P) to satisfy claims under the scheme.

(1B) For the purposes of subsection (1A)(b) and (d) whether P is unable or likely to be unable to satisfy claims shall be determined in accordance with provision to be made by the scheme (which may, in particular —

(a) apply or replicate, with or without modifications, a provision of an enactment;

(b) confer discretion on a specified person).]

(2) The information or documents must be provided or produced —

(a) before the end of such reasonable period as may be specified; and

(b) in the case of information, in such manner or form as may be specified.

(3) This section applies only to information and documents the provision or production of which the scheme manager considers [to be necessary (or likely to be necessary) for the fair determination of claims which have been or may be made against P].

[(3A) Where a stabilisation power under Part 1 of the Banking Act 2009 has been exercised in respect of a bank, the scheme manager may by notice in writing require the bank or the Bank of England to provide information that the scheme manager requires for the purpose of applying regulations under section 214B(3) above.]

(4) If a document is produced in response to a requirement imposed under this section, the scheme manager may—
    (a) take copies or extracts from the document; or
    (b) require the person producing the document to provide an explanation of the document.

(5) If a person who is required under this section to produce a document fails to do so, the scheme manager may require the person to state, to the best of his knowledge and belief, where the document is.

(6) If [P] is insolvent, no requirement may be imposed under this section on a person to whom section 220 or 224 applies.

(7) If a person claims a lien on a document, its production under this Part does not affect the lien.

(8) ...

(9) "Specified" means specified in the notice given under subsection (1).

(10) ...

Scheme manager's power to inspect information held by liquidator etc.

220.—(1) For the purpose of assisting the scheme manager to discharge its functions in relation to a claim made in respect of an insolvent relevant person, a person to whom this section applies must permit a person authorised by the scheme manager to inspect relevant documents.

(2) A person inspecting a document under this section may take copies of, or extracts from, the document.

(3) This section applies to—
    (a) the administrative receiver, administrator, liquidator[, bank liquidator][, building society liquidator] or trustee in bankruptcy of an insolvent relevant person;
    (b) the permanent trustee, within the meaning of the Bankruptcy (Scotland) Act 1985, on the estate of an insolvent relevant person.

(4) This section does not apply to a liquidator, administrator or trustee in bankruptcy who is—
    (a) the Official Receiver;

(b) the Official Receiver for Northern Ireland; or

(c) the Accountant in Bankruptcy.

(5) "Relevant person" has the same meaning as in section 224.

Powers of court where information required.

221.—(1) If a person ("the defaulter")—

(a) fails to comply with a requirement imposed under section 219, or

(b) fails to permit documents to be inspected under section 220,

the scheme manager may certify that fact in writing to the court and the court may enquire into the case.

(2) If the court is satisfied that the defaulter failed without reasonable excuse to comply with the requirement (or to permit the documents to be inspected), it may deal with the defaulter (and, in the case of a body corporate, any director or officer) as if he were in contempt[; and "officer", in relation to a limited liability partnership, means a member of the limited liability partnership].

(3) "Court" means—

(a) the High Court;

(b) in Scotland, the Court of Session.

[Delegation of functions]

[**221A.**—(1) The scheme manager may arrange for any of its functions to be discharged on its behalf by another person (a "scheme agent").

(2) Before entering into arrangements the scheme manager must be satisfied that the scheme agent—

(a) is competent to discharge the function, and

(b) has been given sufficient directions to enable the agent to take any decisions required in the course of exercising the function in accordance with policy determined by the scheme manager.

(3) Arrangements may include provision for payments to be made by the scheme manager to the scheme agent (which payments are management expenses of the scheme manager).]

Miscellaneous

Statutory immunity.

222.—(1) Neither the scheme manager nor any person who is, or is acting as, its board member, officer[, scheme agent] or member of staff is to be liable in damages for anything done or omitted in the discharge, or purported discharge, of the scheme manager's functions.

(2) Subsection (1) does not apply—

(a) if the act or omission is shown to have been in bad faith; or

(b) so as to prevent an award of damages made in respect of an act or omission on the ground that the act or omission was unlawful as a result of section 6(1) of the Human Rights Act 1998.

Management expenses.

223.—(1) The amount which the scheme manager may recover, from the sums levied under the scheme, as management expenses attributable to a particular period may not exceed such amount as may be fixed by the scheme as the limit applicable to that period.

(2) In calculating the amount of any levy to be imposed by the scheme manager, no amount may be included to reflect management expenses unless the limit mentioned in subsection (1) has been fixed by the scheme.

(3) "Management expenses" means expenses incurred, or expected to be incurred, by the scheme manager in connection with its functions under this Act other than those incurred—

(a) in paying compensation;

(b) as a result of any provision of the scheme made by virtue of section 216(3) or (4) or 217(1) or (6)[;

(c) under section 214B].

[Investing in National Loans Fund]

[**223A.**—(1) Sums levied for the purpose of maintaining a contingency fund may be paid to the Treasury.

(2) The Treasury may receive sums under subsection (1) and may set terms and conditions of receipts.

(3) Sums received shall be treated as if raised under section 12 of the National Loans Act 1968 (and shall therefore be invested as part of the National Loans Fund).

(4) Interest accruing on the invested sums may be credited to the contingency fund (subject to any terms and conditions set under subsection (2)).

(5) The Treasury shall comply with any request of the scheme manager to arrange for the return of sums for the purpose of making payments out of a contingency fund (subject to any terms and conditions set under subsection (2)).]

[Borrowing from National Loans Fund]

[**223B.**—(1) The scheme manager may request a loan from the National Loans Fund for the purpose of funding expenses incurred or expected to be incurred under the scheme.

(2) The Treasury may arrange for money to be paid out of the National Loans Fund in pursuance of a request under subsection (1).

(3) The Treasury shall determine—

(a) the rate of interest on a loan, and

(b) other terms and conditions.

(4) The Treasury may make regulations-

(a) about the amounts that may be borrowed under this section;

(b) permitting the scheme manager to impose levies under section 213 for the purpose of meeting expenses in connection with loans under this section (and the regulations may have effect despite any provision of this Act);

(c) about the classes of person on whom those levies may be imposed;

(d) about the amounts and timing of those levies.

(5) The compensation scheme may include provision about borrowing under this section provided that it is not inconsistent with regulations under this section.]

[Payments in error]

[**223C.**—(1) Payments made by the scheme manager in error may be provided for in setting a levy by virtue of section 213, 214A, 214B or 223B.

(2) This section does not apply to payments made in bad faith.]

Scheme manager's power to inspect documents held by Official Receiver etc.

224.—(1) If, as a result of the insolvency or bankruptcy of a relevant person, any documents have come into the possession of a person to whom this section applies, he must permit any person authorised by the scheme manager to inspect the documents for the purpose of establishing —

    (a) the identity of persons to whom the scheme manager may be liable to make a payment in accordance with the compensation scheme; or

    (b) the amount of any payment which the scheme manager may be liable to make.

(2) A person inspecting a document under this section may take copies or extracts from the document.

(3) In this section "relevant person" means a person who was —

    (a) an authorised person at the time the act or omission which may give rise to the liability mentioned in subsection (1)(a) took place; or

    (b) an appointed representative at that time.

(4) But a person who, at that time—

    (a) qualified for authorisation under Schedule 3, and

    (b) fell within a prescribed category,

is not to be regarded as a relevant person for the purposes of this section in relation to any activities for which he had permission as a result of any provision of, or made under, that Schedule unless he had elected to participate in the scheme in relation to those activities at that time.

(5) This section applies to—

    (a) the Official Receiver;

    (b) the Official Receiver for Northern Ireland; and

    (c) the Accountant in Bankruptcy.

Part XVI
The Ombudsman Scheme
The scheme

The scheme and the scheme operator.

225.—(1) This Part provides for a scheme under which certain disputes may be resolved quickly and with minimum formality by an independent person.

(2) The scheme is to be administered by a body corporate ("the scheme operator").

(3) The scheme is to be operated under a name chosen by the scheme operator but is referred to in this Act as "the ombudsman scheme".

(4) Schedule 17 makes provision in connection with the ombudsman scheme and the scheme operator.

Compulsory jurisdiction.

226.—(1) A complaint which relates to an act or omission of a person ("the respondent") in carrying on an activity to which compulsory jurisdiction rules apply is to be dealt with under the ombudsman scheme if the conditions mentioned in subsection (2) are satisfied.

(2) The conditions are that—

(a) the complainant is eligible and wishes to have the complaint dealt with under the scheme;

(b) the respondent was an authorised person[, or a payment service provider within the meaning of the Payment Services Regulations 2009,] at the time of the act or omission to which the complaint relates; and

(c) the act or omission to which the complaint relates occurred at a time when compulsory jurisdiction rules were in force in relation to the activity in question.

(3) "Compulsory jurisdiction rules" means rules—

(a) made by the Authority for the purposes of this section; and

(b) specifying the activities to which they apply.

(4) Only activities which are regulated activities, or which could be made regulated activities by an order under section 22, may be specified.

(5) Activities may be specified by reference to specified categories (however described).

(6) A complainant is eligible, in relation to the compulsory jurisdiction of the ombudsman scheme, if he falls within a class of person specified in the rules as eligible.

(7) The rules—

(a) may include provision for persons other than individuals to be eligible; but

(b) may not provide for authorised persons to be eligible except in specified circumstances or in relation to complaints of a specified kind.

(8) The jurisdiction of the scheme which results from this section is referred to in this Act as the "compulsory jurisdiction".

[Consumer credit jurisdiction]

[**226A.**—(1) A complaint which relates to an act or omission of a person ("the respondent") is to be dealt with under the ombudsman scheme if the conditions mentioned in subsection (2) are satisfied.

(2) The conditions are that—

(a) the complainant is eligible and wishes to have the complaint dealt with under the scheme;

(b) the complaint falls within a description specified in consumer credit rules;

(c) at the time of the act or omission the respondent was the licensee under a standard licence or was authorised to carry on an activity by virtue of section 34A of the Consumer Credit Act 1974;

(d) the act or omission occurred in the course of a business being carried on by the respondent which was of a type mentioned in subsection (3);

(e) at the time of the act or omission that type of business was specified in an order made by the Secretary of State; and

(f) the complaint cannot be dealt with under the compulsory jurisdiction.

(3) The types of business referred to in subsection (2)(d) are—

(a) a consumer credit business;

(b) a consumer hire business;

(c) a business so far as it comprises or relates to credit brokerage;

(d) a business so far as it comprises or relates to debt-adjusting;

(e) a business so far as it comprises or relates to debt-counselling;

(f) a business so far as it comprises or relates to debt-collecting;

(g) a business so far as it comprises or relates to debt administration;

(h) a business so far as it comprises or relates to the provision of credit information services;

(i) a business so far as it comprises or relates to the operation of a credit reference agency.

(4) A complainant is eligible if—

(a) he is—

(i) an individual; or

(ii) a surety in relation to a security provided to the respondent in connection with the business mentioned in subsection (2)(d); and

(b) he falls within a class of person specified in consumer credit rules.

(5) The approval of the Treasury is required for an order under subsection (2)(e).

(6) The jurisdiction of the scheme which results from this section is referred to in this Act as the "consumer credit jurisdiction".

(7) In this Act "consumer credit rules" means rules made by the scheme operator with the approval of the Authority for the purposes of the consumer credit jurisdiction.

(8) Consumer credit rules under this section may make different provision for different cases.

(9) Expressions used in the Consumer Credit Act 1974 have the same meaning in this section as they have in that Act.]

Voluntary jurisdiction.

227.—(1) A complaint which relates to an act or omission of a person ("the respondent") in carrying on an activity to which voluntary jurisdiction rules apply is to be dealt with under the ombudsman scheme if the conditions mentioned in subsection (2) are satisfied.

(2) The conditions are that—

(a) the complainant is eligible and wishes to have the complaint dealt with under the scheme;

(b) at the time of the act or omission to which the complaint relates, the respondent was participating in the scheme;

(c) at the time when the complaint is referred under the scheme, the respondent has not withdrawn from the scheme in accordance with its provisions;

(d) the act or omission to which the complaint relates occurred at a time when voluntary jurisdiction rules were in force in relation to the activity in question; and

(e) the complaint cannot be dealt with under the compulsory jurisdiction [or the consumer credit jurisdiction].

(3) "Voluntary jurisdiction rules" means rules—

(a) made by the scheme operator for the purposes of this section; and

(b) specifying the activities to which they apply.

(4) The only activities which may be specified in the rules are activities which are, or could be, specified in compulsory jurisdiction rules.

(5) Activities may be specified by reference to specified categories (however described).

(6) The rules require the Authority's approval.

(7) A complainant is eligible, in relation to the voluntary jurisdiction of the ombudsman scheme, if he falls within a class of person specified in the rules as eligible.

(8) The rules may include provision for persons other than individuals to be eligible.

(9) A person qualifies for participation in the ombudsman scheme if he falls within a class of person specified in the rules in relation to the activity in question.

(10) Provision may be made in the rules for persons other than authorised persons to participate in the ombudsman scheme.

(11) The rules may make different provision in relation to complaints arising from different activities.

(12) The jurisdiction of the scheme which results from this section is referred to in this Act as the "voluntary jurisdiction".

(13) In such circumstances as may be specified in voluntary jurisdiction rules, a complaint—

(a) which relates to an act or omission occurring at a time before the rules came into force, and

(b) which could have been dealt with under a scheme which has to any extent been replaced by the voluntary jurisdiction,

is to be dealt with under the ombudsman scheme even though paragraph (b) or (d) of subsection (2) would otherwise prevent that.

(14) In such circumstances as may be specified in voluntary jurisdiction rules, a complaint is to be dealt with under the ombudsman scheme even though—

(a) paragraph (b) or (d) of subsection (2) would otherwise prevent that, and

(b) the complaint is not brought within the scheme as a result of subsection (13),

but only if the respondent has agreed that complaints of that kind were to be dealt with under the scheme.

Determination of complaints

Determination under the compulsory jurisdiction.

228.—(1) This section applies only in relation to the compulsory jurisdiction [and to the consumer credit jurisdiction].

(2) A complaint is to be determined by reference to what is, in the opinion of the ombudsman, fair and reasonable in all the circumstances of the case.

(3) When the ombudsman has determined a complaint he must give a written statement of his determination to the respondent and to the complainant.

(4) The statement must—

(a) give the ombudsman's reasons for his determination;

(b) be signed by him; and

(c) require the complainant to notify him in writing, before a date specified in the statement, whether he accepts or rejects the determination.

(5) If the complainant notifies the ombudsman that he accepts the determination, it is binding on the respondent and the complainant and final.

(6) If, by the specified date, the complainant has not notified the ombudsman of his acceptance or rejection of the determination he is to be treated as having rejected it.

(7) The ombudsman must notify the respondent of the outcome.

(8) A copy of the determination on which appears a certificate signed by an ombudsman is evidence (or in Scotland sufficient evidence) that the determination was made under the scheme.

(9) Such a certificate purporting to be signed by an ombudsman is to be taken to have been duly signed unless the contrary is shown.

Awards.

229.—(1) This section applies only in relation to the compulsory jurisdiction [and to the consumer credit jurisdiction].

(2) If a complaint which has been dealt with under the scheme is determined in favour of the complainant, the determination may include—

(a) an award against the respondent of such amount as the ombudsman considers fair compensation for loss or damage (of a kind falling within subsection (3)) suffered by the complainant ("a money award");

(b) a direction that the respondent take such steps in relation to the complainant as the ombudsman considers just and appropriate (whether or not a court could order those steps to be taken).

(3) A money award may compensate for—

(a) financial loss; or

(b) any other loss, or any damage, of a specified kind.

(4) The Authority may specify [for the purposes of the compulsory jurisdiction] the maximum amount which may be regarded as fair compensation for a particular kind of loss or damage specified under subsection (3)(b).

[(4A) The scheme operator may specify for the purposes of the consumer credit jurisdiction the maximum amount which may be regarded as fair compensation for a particular kind of loss or damage specified under subsection (3)(b).]

(5) A money award may not exceed the monetary limit; but the ombudsman may, if he considers that fair compensation requires payment of a larger amount, recommend that the respondent pay the complainant the balance.

(6) The monetary limit is such amount as may be specified.

(7) Different amounts may be specified in relation to different kinds of complaint.

(8) A money award—

(a) may provide for the amount payable under the award to bear interest at a rate and as from a date specified in the award; and

(b) is enforceable by the complainant in accordance with Part III of Schedule 17 [or (as the case may be) Part 3A of that Schedule].

(9) Compliance with a direction under subsection (2)(b) —

(a) is enforceable by an injunction; or

(b) in Scotland, is enforceable by an order under section 45 of the Court of Session Act 1988.

(10) Only the complainant may bring proceedings for an injunction or proceedings for an order.

(11) "Specified" means—

(a) for the purposes of the compulsory jurisdiction, specified in compulsory jurisdiction rules;

(b) for the purposes of the consumer credit jurisdiction, specified in consumer credit rules.

(12) Consumer credit rules under this section may make different provision for different cases.]

Costs.

230.—(1) The scheme operator may by rules ("costs rules") provide for an ombudsman to have power, on determining a complaint under the compulsory jurisdiction [or the consumer credit jurisdiction], to award costs in accordance with the provisions of the rules.

(2) Costs rules require the approval of the Authority.

(3) Costs rules may not provide for the making of an award against the complainant in respect of the respondent's costs.

(4) But they may provide for the making of an award against the complainant in favour of the scheme operator, for the purpose of providing a contribution to resources deployed in dealing with the complaint, if in the opinion of the ombudsman —

(a) the complainant's conduct was improper or unreasonable; or

(b) the complainant was responsible for an unreasonable delay.

(5) Costs rules may authorise an ombudsman making an award in accordance with the rules to order that the amount payable under the award bears interest at a rate and as from a date specified in the order.

(6) An amount due under an award made in favour of the scheme operator is recoverable as a debt due to the scheme operator.

(7) Any other award made against the respondent is to be treated as a money award for the purposes of paragraph 16 of Schedule 17.

Information

Ombudsman's power to require information.

231.—(1) An ombudsman may, by notice in writing given to a party to a complaint, require that party—

(a) to provide specified information or information of a specified description; or

(b) to produce specified documents or documents of a specified description.

(2) The information or documents must be provided or produced —

(a) before the end of such reasonable period as may be specified; and

(b) in the case of information, in such manner or form as may be specified.

(3) This section applies only to information and documents the production of which the ombudsman considers necessary for the determination of the complaint.

(4) If a document is produced in response to a requirement imposed under this section, the ombudsman may—

    (a) take copies or extracts from the document; or

    (b) require the person producing the document to provide an explanation of the document.

(5) If a person who is required under this section to produce a document fails to do so, the ombudsman may require him to state, to the best of his knowledge and belief, where the document is.

(6) If a person claims a lien on a document, its production under this Part does not affect the lien.

(7) "Specified" means specified in the notice given under subsection (1).

Powers of court where information required.

232.—(1) If a person ("the defaulter") fails to comply with a requirement imposed under section 231, the ombudsman may certify that fact in writing to the court and the court may enquire into the case.

(2) If the court is satisfied that the defaulter failed without reasonable excuse to comply with the requirement, it may deal with the defaulter (and, in the case of a body corporate, any director or officer) as if he were in contempt[; and "officer", in relation to a limited liability partnership, means a member of the limited liability partnership].

(3) "Court" means—

    (a) the High Court;

    (b) in Scotland, the Court of Session.

Data protection.

233. In section 31 of the Data Protection Act 1998 (regulatory activity), after subsection (4), insert—

"(4A) Personal data processed for the purpose of discharging any function which is conferred by or under Part XVI of the Financial Services and Markets Act 2000 on the body established by the Financial Services Authority for the purposes of that Part are exempt from the subject information provisions in any case to the extent to which the application of those provisions to the data would be likely to prejudice the proper discharge of the function."

Funding

Industry funding.

234.—(1) For the purpose of funding—

    (a) the establishment of the ombudsman scheme (whenever any relevant expense is incurred), and

    (b) its operation in relation to the compulsory jurisdiction,

the Authority may make rules requiring the payment to it or to the scheme operator, by authorised persons or any class of authorised person [or any payment service provider within the meaning of the Payment Services Regulations 2009] of specified amounts (or amounts calculated in a specified way).

(2) "Specified" means specified in the rules.

[Funding by consumer
credit licensees etc]

[**234A.**—(1) For the purpose of funding—

    (a) the establishment of the ombudsman scheme so far
as it relates to the consumer credit jurisdiction
(whenever any relevant expense is incurred), and

    (b) its operation in relation to the consumer credit
jurisdiction,

the scheme operator may from time to time with the approval
of the Authority determine a sum which is to be raised by way
of contributions under this section.

(2) A sum determined under subsection (1) may include
a component to cover the costs of the collection of
contributions to that sum ("collection costs") under this
section.

(3) The scheme operator must notify the OFT of every
determination under subsection (1).

(4) The OFT must give general notice of every determination so notified.

(5) The OFT may by general notice impose requirements on
—

    (a) licensees to whom this section applies, or

    (b) persons who make applications to which this section
applies,

to pay contributions to the OFT for the purpose of raising
sums determined under subsection (1).

(6) The amount of the contribution payable by a person
under such a requirement—

    (a) shall be the amount specified in or determined under
the general notice; and

    (b) shall be paid before the end of the period or at the
time so specified or determined.

(7) A general notice under subsection (5) may—

    (a) impose requirements only on descriptions of
licensees or applicants specified in the notice;

    (b) provide for exceptions from any requirement imposed
on a description of licensees or applicants;

    (c) impose different requirements on different descrip-
tions of licensees or applicants;

    (d) make provision for refunds in specified circum-
stances.

(8) Contributions received by the OFT must be paid to the
scheme operator.

(9) As soon as practicable after the end of—

    (a) each financial year of the scheme operator, or

    (b) if the OFT and the scheme operator agree that this
paragraph is to apply instead of paragraph (a) for the
time being, each period agreed by them,

the scheme operator must pay to the OFT an amount representing the extent to which collection costs are covered in
accordance with subsection (2) by the total amount of the
contributions paid by the OFT to it during the year or (as the
case may be) the agreed period.

(10) Amounts received by the OFT from the scheme operator are to be retained by it for the purpose of meeting its costs.

(11) The Secretary of State may by order provide that the functions of the OFT under this section are for the time being to be carried out by the scheme operator.

(12) An order under subsection (11) may provide that while the order is in force this section shall have effect subject to such modifications as may be set out in the order.

(13) The licensees to whom this section applies are licensees under standard licences which cover to any extent the carrying on of a type of business specified in an order under section 226A(2)(e).

(14) The applications to which this section applies are applications for—

(a) standard licences covering to any extent the carrying on of a business of such a type;

(b) the renewal of standard licences on terms covering to any extent the carrying on of a business of such a type.

(15) Expressions used in the Consumer Credit Act 1974 have the same meaning in this section as they have in that Act.]

PART XXIII
PUBLIC RECORD, DISCLOSURE OF INFORMATION AND CO-OPERATION
The public record

The record of authorised persons etc.

347.—(1) The Authority must maintain a record of every—

(a) person who appears to the Authority to be an authorised person;

(b) authorised unit trust scheme;

(c) authorised open-ended investment company;

(d) recognised scheme;

(e) recognised investment exchange;

(f) recognised clearing house;

(g) individual to whom a prohibition order relates;

(h) approved person;...

[(ha) person to whom subsection (2A) applies; and]

(i) person falling within such other class (if any) as the Authority may determine.

(2) The record must include such information as the Authority considers appropriate and at least the following information—

(a) in the case of a person appearing to the Authority to be an authorised person—

(i) information as to the services which he holds himself out as able to provide; and

(ii) any address of which the Authority is aware at which a notice or other document may be served on him;

(b) in the case of an authorised unit trust scheme, the name and address of the manager and trustee of the scheme;

(c) in the case of an authorised open-ended investment company, the name and address of—

    (i) the company;

    (ii) if it has only one director, the director; and

    (iii) its depositary (if any);

(d) in the case of a recognised scheme, the name and address of—

    (i) the operator of the scheme; and

    (ii) any representative of the operator in the United Kingdom;

(e) in the case of a recognised investment exchange or recognised clearing house, the name and address of the exchange or clearing house;

(f) in the case of an individual to whom a prohibition order relates—

    (i) his name; and

    (ii) details of the effect of the order;

(g) in the case of a person who is an approved person—

    (i) his name;

    (ii) the name of the relevant authorised person;

    (iii) if the approved person is performing a controlled function under an arrangement with a contractor of the relevant authorised person, the name of the contractor.

[(2A) This subsection applies to—

(a) an appointed representative to whom subsection (1A) of section 39 applies for whom the applicable register (as defined by subsection (1B) of that section) is the record maintained by virtue of subsection (1)(ha) above;

(b) a person mentioned in subsection (1)(a) of section 39A if—

    (i) the contract with an authorised person to which he is party complies with the applicable requirements (as defined by subsection (7) of that section), and

    (ii) the authorised person has accepted responsibility in writing for the person's activities in carrying on investment services business (as defined by subsection (8) of that section); and

(c) any person not falling within paragraph (a) or (b) in respect of whom the Authority considers that a record must be maintained for the purpose of securing compliance with Article 23.3 of the markets in financial instruments directive (registration of tied agents).]

(3) If it appears to the Authority that a person in respect of whom there is an entry in the record as a result of one of the paragraphs of subsection (1) has ceased to be a

person to whom that paragraph applies, the Authority may remove the entry from the record.

(4) But if the Authority decides not to remove the entry, it must —

(a) make a note to that effect in the record; and

(b) state why it considers that the person has ceased to be a person to whom that paragraph applies.

(5) The Authority must—

(a) make the record available for inspection by members of the public in a legible form at such times and in such place or places as the Authority may determine; and

(b) provide a certified copy of the record, or any part of it, to any person who asks for it—

(i) on payment of the fee (if any) fixed by the Authority; and

(ii) in a form (either written or electronic) in which it is legible to the person asking for it.

(6) The Authority may—

(a) publish the record, or any part of it;

(b) exploit commercially the information contained in the record, or any part of that information.

(7) "Authorised unit trust scheme", "authorised open-ended investment company" and "recognised scheme" have the same meaning as in Part XVII, and associated expressions are to be read accordingly.

(8) "Approved person" means a person in relation to whom the Authority has given its approval under section 59 and "controlled function" and "arrangement" have the same meaning as in that section.

(9) "Relevant authorised person" has the meaning given in section 66.

Disclosure of information

Restrictions on disclosure of confidential information by Authority etc.

348.—(1) Confidential information must not be disclosed by a primary recipient, or by any person obtaining the information directly or indirectly from a primary recipient, without the consent of—

(a) the person from whom the primary recipient obtained the information; and

(b) if different, the person to whom it relates.

(2) In this Part "confidential information" means information which—

(a) relates to the business or other affairs of any person;

(b) was received by the primary recipient for the purposes of, or in the discharge of, any functions of the Authority, the competent authority for the purposes of Part VI or the Secretary of State under any provision made by or under this Act; and

(c) is not prevented from being confidential information by subsection (4).

(3) It is immaterial for the purposes of subsection (2) whether or not the information was received—
   (a) by virtue of a requirement to provide it imposed by or under this Act;
   (b) for other purposes as well as purposes mentioned in that subsection.

(4) Information is not confidential information if—
   (a) it has been made available to the public by virtue of being disclosed in any circumstances in which, or for any purposes for which, disclosure is not precluded by this section; or
   (b) it is in the form of a summary or collection of information so framed that it is not possible to ascertain from it information relating to any particular person.

(5) Each of the following is a primary recipient for the purposes of this Part—
   (a) the Authority;
   (b) any person exercising functions conferred by Part VI on the competent authority;
   (c) the Secretary of State;
   (d) a person appointed to make a report under section 166;
   (e) any person who is or has been employed by a person mentioned in paragraphs (a) to (c);
   (f) any auditor or expert instructed by a person mentioned in those paragraphs.

(6) In subsection (5)(f) "expert" includes—
   (a) a competent person appointed by the competent authority under section 97;
   (b) a competent person appointed by the Authority or the Secretary of State to conduct an investigation under Part XI;
   (c) any body or person appointed under paragraph 6 of Schedule 1 to perform a function on behalf of the Authority.

Exceptions from section 348.

349.—(1) Section 348 does not prevent a disclosure of confidential information which is—
   (a) made for the purpose of facilitating the carrying out of a public function; and
   (b) permitted by regulations made by the Treasury under this section.

(2) The regulations may, in particular, make provision permitting the disclosure of confidential information or of confidential information of a prescribed kind—
   (a) by prescribed recipients, or recipients of a prescribed description, to any person for the purpose of enabling or assisting the recipient to discharge prescribed public functions;
   (b) by prescribed recipients, or recipients of a prescribed description, to prescribed persons, or persons of

prescribed descriptions, for the purpose of enabling or assisting those persons to discharge prescribed public functions;

(c) by the Authority to the Treasury or the Secretary of State for any purpose;

(d) by any recipient if the disclosure is with a view to or in connection with prescribed proceedings.

(3) The regulations may also include provision—

(a) making any permission to disclose confidential information subject to conditions (which may relate to the obtaining of consents or any other matter);

(b) restricting the uses to which confidential information disclosed under the regulations may be put.

[(3A) Section 348 does not apply to—

(a) the disclosure by a recipient to which subsection (3B) applies of confidential information disclosed to it by the Authority in reliance on subsection (1);

(b) the disclosure of such information by a person obtaining it directly or indirectly from a recipient to which subsection (3B) applies.

(3B) This subsection applies to—

(a) the Panel on Takeovers and Mergers;

(b) an authority designated as a supervisory authority for the purposes of Article 4.1 of the Takeovers Directive;

(c) any other person or body that exercises public functions, under legislation in an EEA State other than the United Kingdom, that are similar to the Authority's functions or those of the Panel on Takeovers and Mergers.]

(4) In relation to confidential information, each of the following is a "recipient"—

(a) a primary recipient;

(b) a person obtaining the information directly or indirectly from a primary recipient.

((5) "Public functions" includes—

(a) functions conferred by or in accordance with any provision contained in any enactment or subordinate legislation;

(b) functions conferred by or in accordance with any provision contained in the Community Treaties or any Community instrument;

(c) similar functions conferred on persons by or under provisions having effect as part of the law of a country or territory outside the United Kingdom;

(d) functions exercisable in relation to prescribed disciplinary proceedings.

(6) "Enactment" includes—

(a) an Act of the Scottish Parliament;

(b) Northern Ireland legislation.

(7) "Subordinate legislation" has the meaning given in the Interpretation Act 1978 and also includes an instrument made under an Act of the Scottish Parliament or under Northern Ireland legislation.

[(8)...]

Disclosure of information by the Inland Revenue.

350.—(1) No obligation as to secrecy imposed by statute or otherwise prevents the disclosure of Revenue information to—

(a) the Authority, or

(b) the Secretary of State,

if the disclosure is made for the purpose of assisting in the investigation of a matter under section 168 or with a view to the appointment of an investigator under that section.

(2) A disclosure may only be made under subsection (1) by or under the authority of the Commissioners of Inland Revenue.

(3) Section 348 does not apply to Revenue information.

(4) Information obtained as a result of subsection (1) may not be used except—

(a) for the purpose of deciding whether to appoint an investigator under section 168;

(b) in the conduct of an investigation under section 168;

(c) in criminal proceedings brought against a person under this Act or the Criminal Justice Act 1993 as a result of an investigation under section 168;

(d) for the purpose of taking action under this Act against a person as a result of an investigation under section 168;

(e) in proceedings before the Tribunal as a result of action taken as mentioned in paragraph (d).

(5) Information obtained as a result of subsection (1) may not be disclosed except—

(a) by or under the authority of the Commissioners of Inland Revenue;

(b) in proceedings mentioned in subsection (4)(c) or (e) or with a view to their institution.

(6) Subsection (5) does not prevent the disclosure of information obtained as a result of subsection (1) to a person to whom it could have been disclosed under subsection (1).

(7) "Revenue information" means information held by a person which it would be an offence under section 182 of the Finance Act 1989 for him to disclose.

Competition information.

351.—(1)...

(2) ...

(3) ...

(4) Section 348 does not apply to competition information.

(5) "Competition information" means information which —

(a) relates to the affairs of a particular individual or body;

(b) is not otherwise in the public domain; and

(c) was obtained under or by virtue of a competition provision.

(6) "Competition provision" means any provision of—

(a) an order made under section 95;

(b) Chapter III of Part X; or

(c) Chapter II of Part XVIII.

(7) ...

Offences.

352.—(1) A person who discloses information in contravention of section 348 or 350(5) is guilty of an offence.

(2) A person guilty of an offence under subsection (1) is liable —

(a) on summary conviction, to imprisonment for a term not exceeding three months or a fine not exceeding the statutory maximum, or both;

(b) on conviction on indictment, to imprisonment for a term not exceeding two years or a fine, or both.

(3) A person is guilty of an offence if, in contravention of any provision of regulations made under section 349, he uses information which has been disclosed to him in accordance with the regulations.

(4) A person is guilty of an offence if, in contravention of subsection (4) of section 350, he uses information which has been disclosed to him in accordance with that section.

(5) A person guilty of an offence under subsection (3) or (4) is liable on summary conviction to imprisonment for a term not exceeding three months [51 weeks] or a fine not exceeding level 5 on the standard scale, or both.

(6) In proceedings for an offence under this section it is a defence for the accused to prove—

(a) that he did not know and had no reason to suspect that the information was confidential information or that it had been disclosed in accordance with section 350;

(b) that he took all reasonable precautions and exercised all due diligence to avoid committing the offence.

Removal of other restrictions on disclosure

353.—(1) The Treasury may make regulations permitting the disclosure of any information, or of information of a prescribed kind—

(a) by prescribed persons for the purpose of assisting or enabling them to discharge prescribed functions under this Act or any rules or regulations made under it;

(b) by prescribed persons, or persons of a prescribed description, to the Authority for the purpose of assisting or enabling the Authority to discharge prescribed functions;

[(c) by the scheme operator to the Office of Fair Trading for the purpose of assisting or enabling that Office to discharge prescribed functions under the Consumer Credit Act 1974].

(2) Regulations under this section may not make any provision in relation to the disclosure of confidential information by primary recipients or by any person obtaining confidential information directly or indirectly from a primary recipient.

(3) If a person discloses any information as permitted by regulations under this section the disclosure is not to be taken as a contravention of any duty to which he is subject.

Co-operation

Authority's duty to co-operate with others.

354.—(1) The Authority must take such steps as it considers appropriate to co-operate with other persons (whether in the United Kingdom or elsewhere) who have functions—

(a) similar to those of the Authority; or

(b) in relation to the prevention or detection of financial crime.

[(1A) The Authority must take such steps as it considers appropriate to co—operate with—

(a) the Panel on Takeovers and Mergers;

(b) an authority designated as a supervisory authority for the purposes of Article 4.1 of the Takeovers Directive;

(c) any other person or body that exercises functions of a public nature, under legislation in any country or territory outside the United Kingdom, that appear to the Authority to be similar to those of the Panel on Takeovers and Mergers.]

(2) Co-operation may include the sharing of information which the Authority is not prevented from disclosing.

(3) "Financial crime" has the same meaning as in section 6.

PART XXIV

INSOLVENCY

Interpretation

Interpretation of this Part.

355.—(1) In this Part—

"the 1985 Act" means the Bankruptcy (Scotland) Act 1985;

"the 1986 Act" means the Insolvency Act 1986;

"the 1989 Order" means the Insolvency (Northern Ireland) Order 1989;

"body" means a body of persons—

(a) over which the court has jurisdiction under any provision of, or made under, the 1986 Act (or the 1989 Order); but

(b) which is not a building society, a friendly society or an industrial and provident society; and

"court" means—

    (a) the court having jurisdiction for the purposes of the 1985 Act or the 1986 Act; or

    (b) in Northern Ireland, the High Court.

(2) In this Part "insurer" has such meaning as may be specified in an order made by the Treasury.

Voluntary arrangements.

356.—Authority's powers to participate in proceedings: company voluntary arrangements

(1) [Where a voluntary arrangement has effect under Part I of the 1986 Act in respect of a company or insolvent partnership which is an authorised person, the Authority may apply to the court under section 6 or 7 of that Act.]

[(2) Where a voluntary arrangement has been approved under Part II of the 1989 Order in respect of a company or insolvent partnership which is an authorised person, the Authority may apply to the court under Article 19 or 20 of that Order.

(3)] If a person other than the Authority makes an application to the court in relation to the company or insolvent partnership under [any] of those provisions, the Authority is entitled to be heard at any hearing relating to the application.

Authority's powers to participate in proceedings: individual voluntary arrangements.

357.—(1) The Authority is entitled to be heard on an application by an individual who is an authorised person under section 253 of the 1986 Act (or Article 227 of the 1989 Order).

(2) Subsections (3) to (6) apply if such an order is made on the application of such a person.

(3) A person appointed for the purpose by the Authority is entitled to attend any meeting of creditors of the debtor summoned under section 257 of the 1986 Act (or Article 231 of the 1989 Order).

(4) Notice of the result of a meeting so summoned is to be given to the Authority by the chairman of the meeting.

(5) The Authority may apply to the court—

    (a) under section 262 of the 1986 Act (or Article 236 of the 1989 Order); or

    (b) under section 263 of the 1986 Act (or Article 237 of the 1989 Order).

(6) If a person other than the Authority makes an application to the court under any provision mentioned in subsection (5), the Authority is entitled to be heard at any hearing relating to the application.

Authority's powers to participate in proceedings: trust deeds for creditors in Scotland.

358.—(1) This section applies where a trust deed has been granted by or on behalf of a debtor who is an authorised person.

(2) The trustee must, as soon as practicable after he becomes aware that the debtor is an authorised person, send to the Authority—

    (a) in every case, a copy of the trust deed;

    (b) where any other document or information is sent to every creditor known to the trustee in pursuance of paragraph 5(1)(c) of Schedule 5 to the 1985 Act, a copy of such document or information.

(3) Paragraph 7 of that Schedule applies to the Authority as if it were a qualified creditor who has not been sent a copy of the notice as mentioned in paragraph 5(1)(c) of the Schedule.

(4) The Authority must be given the same notice as the creditors of any meeting of creditors held in relation to the trust deed.

(5) A person appointed for the purpose by the Authority is entitled to attend and participate in (but not to vote at) any such meeting of creditors as if the Authority were a creditor under the deed.

(6) This section does not affect any right the Authority has as a creditor of a debtor who is an authorised person.

(7) Expressions used in this section and in the 1985 Act have the same meaning in this section as in that Act.

Administration orders

[Administration order.]

[**359**.—(1) The Authority may make an administration application under Schedule B1 to the 1986 Act [or Schedule B1 to the 1989 Order] in relation to a company or insolvent partnership which—

    (a) is or has been an authorised person,

    (b) is or has been an appointed representative, or

    (c) is carrying on or has carried on a regulated activity in contravention of the general prohibition.

(2) Subsection (3) applies in relation to an administration application made (or a petition presented) by the Authority by virtue of this section.

(3) Any of the following shall be treated for the purpose of paragraph 11(a) of Schedule B1 to the 1986 Act [or paragraph 12(a) of Schedule B1 to the 1989 Order] as unable to pay its debts—

    (a) a company or partnership in default on an obligation to pay a sum due and payable under an agreement,

    ...

    (b) an authorised deposit taker in default on an obligation to pay a sum due and payable in respect of a relevant deposit[, and

    (c) an authorised reclaim fund in default on an obligation to pay a sum payable as a result of a claim made by virtue of section 1(2)(b) or 2(2)(b) of the Dormant Bank and Building Society Accounts Act 2008].

(4) In this section—

"agreement" means an agreement the making or performance of which constitutes or is part of a regulated activity carried on by the company or partnership,

"authorised deposit taker" means a person with a Part IV permission to accept deposits (but not a person who has a Part IV permission to accept deposits only for the purpose of carrying on another regulated activity in accordance with that permission),

["authorised reclaim fund" means a reclaim fund within the meaning given by section 5(1) of the Dormant Bank and Building Society Accounts Act 2008 that is authorised for the purposes of this Act,]

"company" means a company—

(a) in respect of which an administrator may be appointed under Schedule B1 to the 1986 Act, or

[(b) in respect of which an administrator may be appointed under Schedule B1 to the 1989 Order,] and

"relevant deposit" shall, ignoring any restriction on the meaning of deposit arising from the identity of the person making the deposit, be construed in accordance with—

(a) section 22,

(b) any relevant order under that section, and

(c) Schedule 2.

(5) The definition of "authorised deposit taker" in subsection (4) shall be construed in accordance with—

(a) section 22,

(b) any relevant order under that section, and

(c) Schedule 2.]

Insurers.

360.—(1) The Treasury may by order provide that such provisions of Part II of the 1986 Act (or Part III of the 1989 Order) as may be specified are to apply in relation to insurers with such modifications as may be specified.

(2) An order under this section—

(a) may provide that such provisions of this Part as may be specified are to apply in relation to the administration of insurers in accordance with the order with such modifications as may be specified; and

(b) requires the consent of the Secretary of State.

(3) "Specified" means specified in the order.

[Administrator's duty to report to Authority.]

[361.—(1) This section applies where a company or partnership is—

(a) in administration within the meaning of Schedule B1 to the 1986 Act, or

[(b) in administration within the meaning of Schedule B1 to the 1989 Order].

(2) If the administrator thinks that the company or partnership is carrying on or has carried on a regulated activity in contravention of the general prohibition, he must report to the Authority without delay.

(3) Subsection (2) does not apply where the administration arises out of an administration order made on an application made or petition presented by the Authority.]

Authority's powers to participate in proceedings.

362.—(1) This section applies if a person other than the Authority [makes an administration application under Schedule B1 to the 1986 Act] [or Schedule B1 to the 1989 Order] in relation to a company or partnership which —

(a) is, or has been, an authorised person;

(b) is, or has been, an appointed representative; or

(c) is carrying on, or has carried on, a regulated activity in contravention of the general prohibition.

[(1A) This section also applies in relation to—

(a) the appointment under paragraph 14 or 22 of Schedule B1 to the 1986 Act [or paragraph 15 or 23 of Schedule B1 to the 1989 Order] of an administrator of a company of a kind described in subsection (1)(a) to (c), or

(b) the filing with the court of a copy of notice of intention to appoint an administrator under [any] of those paragraphs.]

(2) The Authority is entitled to be heard—

(a) at the hearing of the [administration application...]; and

(b) at any other hearing of the court in relation to the company or partnership under Part II of the 1986 Act (or Part III of the 1989 Order).

(3) Any notice or other document required to be sent to a creditor of the company or partnership must also be sent to the Authority.

[(4) The Authority may apply to the court under paragraph 74 of Schedule B1 to the 1986 Act [or paragraph 75 of Schedule B1 to the 1989 Order].

(4A) In respect of an application under subsection (4)—

(a) paragraph 74(1)(a) and (b) shall have effect as if for the words "harm the interests of the applicant (whether alone or in common with some or all other members or creditors)" there were substituted the words "harm the interests of some or all members or creditors", and

[(b) paragraph 75(1)(a) and (b) of Schedule B1 to the 1989 Order shall have effect as if for the words "harm the interests of the applicant (whether alone or in common with some or all other members or creditors)" there were substituted the words "harm the interests of some or all members or creditors"].]

(5) A person appointed for the purpose by the Authority is entitled —

(a) to attend any meeting of creditors of the company or partnership summoned under any enactment;

(b) to attend any meeting of a committee established under [paragraph 57 of Schedule B1 to the 1986 Act] [or paragraph 58 of Schedule B1 to the 1989 Order]; and

(c) to make representations as to any matter for decision at such a meeting.

(6) If, during the course of the administration of a company, a compromise or arrangement is proposed between the company and its creditors, or any class of them, the Authority may apply to the court under [section 896 or 899 of the Companies Act 2006].

[Administrator appointed by company or directors.]

[**362A.** (1) This section applies in relation to a company of a kind described in section 362(1)(a) to (c).

(2) An administrator of the company may not be appointed under paragraph 22 of Schedule B1 to the 1986 Act [or paragraph 23 of Schedule B1 to the 1989 Order] without the consent of the Authority.

(3) Consent under subsection (2)—

(a) must be in writing, and

(b) must be filed with the court along with the notice of intention to appoint under paragraph 27 of [Schedule B1 to the 1986 Act or paragraph 28 of Schedule B1 to the 1989 Order].

(4) In a case where no notice of intention to appoint is required —

(a) subsection (3)(b) shall not apply, but

(b) consent under subsection (2) must accompany the notice of appointment filed under paragraph 29 of [Schedule B1 to the 1986 Act or paragraph 30 of Schedule B1 to the 1989 Order].]

Receivership

Authority's powers to participate in proceedings.

363.—(1) This section applies if a receiver has been appointed in relation to a company which—

(a) is, or has been, an authorised person;

(b) is, or has been, an appointed representative; or

(c) is carrying on, or has carried on, a regulated activity in contravention of the general prohibition.

(2) The Authority is entitled to be heard on an application made under section 35 or 63 of the 1986 Act (or Article 45 of the 1989 Order).

(3) The Authority is entitled to make an application under section 41(1)(a) or 69(1)(a) of the 1986 Act (or Article 51(1)(a) of the 1989 Order).

(4) A report under section 48(1) or 67(1) of the 1986 Act (or Article 58(1) of the 1989 Order) must be sent by the person making it to the Authority.

(5) A person appointed for the purpose by the Authority is entitled —

(a) to attend any meeting of creditors of the company summoned under any enactment;

(b) to attend any meeting of a committee established under section 49 or 68 of the 1986 Act (or Article 59 of the 1989 Order); and

(c) to make representations as to any matter for decision at such a meeting.

Receiver's duty to report to Authority.

364.—If—

(a) a receiver has been appointed in relation to a company, and

(b) it appears to the receiver that the company is carrying on, or has carried on, a regulated activity in contravention of the general prohibition,

the receiver must report the matter to the Authority without delay.

Voluntary winding up.

365.—Authority's powers to participate in proceedings

(1) This section applies in relation to a company which—

(a) is being wound up voluntarily;

(b) is an authorised person; and

(c) is not an insurer effecting or carrying out contracts of long-term insurance.

(2) The Authority may apply to the court under section 112 of the 1986 Act (or Article 98 of the 1989 Order) in respect of the company.

(3) The Authority is entitled to be heard at any hearing of the court in relation to the voluntary winding up of the company

(4) Any notice or other document required to be sent to a creditor of the company must also be sent to the Authority.

(5) A person appointed for the purpose by the Authority is entitled —

(a) to attend any meeting of creditors of the company summoned under any enactment;

(b) to attend any meeting of a committee established under section 101 of the 1986 Act (or Article 87 of the 1989 Order); and

(c) to make representations as to any matter for decision at such a meeting.

(6) The voluntary winding up of the company does not bar the right of the Authority to have it wound up by the court.

(7) If, during the course of the winding up of the company, a compromise or arrangement is proposed between the company and its creditors, or any class of them, the Authority may apply to the court under [section 896 or 899 of the Companies Act 2006].

Insurers effecting or carrying out long-term contracts or insurance.

366.—(1) An insurer effecting or carrying out contracts of long-term insurance may not be wound up voluntarily without the consent of the Authority.

(2) If notice of a general meeting of such an insurer is given, specifying the intention to propose a resolution for voluntary winding up of the insurer, a director of the insurer must notify the Authority as soon as practicable after he becomes aware of it.

(3) A person who fails to comply with subsection (2) is guilty of an offence and liable on summary conviction to a fine not exceeding level 5 on the standard scale.

[(4) A winding up resolution may not be passed—

(a) as a written resolution (in accordance with Chapter 2 of Part 13 of the Companies Act 2006), or

(b) at a meeting called in accordance with section 307(4) to (6) or 337(2) of that Act (agreement of members to calling of meeting at short notice).]

(5) A copy of a winding-up resolution forwarded to the registrar of companies in accordance with [section 30 of the Companies Act 2006] must be accompanied by a certificate issued by the Authority stating that it consents to the voluntary winding up of the insurer.

(6) If subsection (5) is complied with, the voluntary winding up is to be treated as having commenced at the time the resolution was passed.

(7) If subsection (5) is not complied with, the resolution has no effect.

(8) "Winding-up resolution" means a resolution for voluntary winding up of an insurer effecting or carrying out contracts of long-term insurance.

Winding up by the court

Winding-up petitions.

367.—(1) The Authority may present a petition to the court for the winding up of a body which—

(a) is, or has been, an authorised person;

(b) is, or has been, an appointed representative; or

(c) is carrying on, or has carried on, a regulated activity in contravention of the general prohibition.

(2) In subsection (1) "body" includes any partnership.

(3) On such a petition, the court may wind up the body if—

(a) the body is unable to pay its debts within the meaning of section 123 or 221 of the 1986 Act (or Article 103 or 185 of the 1989 Order); or

(b) the court is of the opinion that it is just and equitable that it should be wound up.

(4) If a body is in default on an obligation to pay a sum due and payable under an agreement, it is to be treated for the purpose of subsection (3)(a) as unable to pay its debts.

(5) "Agreement" means an agreement the making or performance of which constitutes or is part of a regulated activity carried on by the body concerned.

(6) Subsection (7) applies if a petition is presented under subsection (1) for the winding up of a partnership—

(a) on the ground mentioned in subsection (3)(b); or

(b) in Scotland, on a ground mentioned in subsection (3)(a) or (b).

(7) The court has jurisdiction, and the 1986 Act (or the 1989 Order) has effect, as if the partnership were an unregistered company as defined by section 220 of that Act (or Article 184 of that Order).

Winding-up petitions: EEA and Treaty firms.

368.—The Authority may not present a petition to the court under section 367 for the winding up of—

(a) an EEA firm which qualifies for authorisation under Schedule 3, or

(b) a Treaty firm which qualifies for authorisation under Schedule 4,

unless it has been asked to do so by the home state regulator of the firm concerned.

Insurers: service of petition etc on Authority.

369.—(1) If a person other than the Authority presents a petition for the winding up of an authorised person with permission to effect or carry out contracts of insurance, the petitioner must serve a copy of the petition on the Authority.

(2) If a person other than the Authority applies to have a provisional liquidator appointed under section 135 of the 1986 Act (or Article 115 of the 1989 Order) in respect of an authorised person with permission to effect or carry out contracts of insurance, the applicant must serve a copy of the application on the Authority.

[Reclaim funds: service of petition etc. on Authority.]

[**369A.**—(1) If a person other than the Authority presents a petition for the winding up of an authorised reclaim fund, the petitioner must serve a copy of the petition on the Authority.

(2) If a person other than the Authority applies to have a provisional liquidator appointed under section 135 of the 1986 Act (or Article 115 of the 1989 Order) in respect of an authorised reclaim fund, the applicant must serve a copy of the application on the Authority.

(3) In this section "authorised reclaim fund" means a reclaim fund within the meaning given by section 5(1) of the Dormant Bank and Building Society Accounts Act 2008 that is authorised for the purposes of this Act.]

Liquidator's duty to report to Authority.

370.—If—

(a) a company is being wound up voluntarily or a body is being wound up on a petition presented by a person other than the Authority, and

(b) it appears to the liquidator that the company or body is carrying on, or has carried on, a regulated activity in contravention of the general prohibition,

the liquidator must report the matter to the Authority without delay.

Authority's powers to participate in proceedings.

371.—(1) This section applies if a person other than the Authority presents a petition for the winding up of a body which—

(a) is, or has been, an authorised person;

(b) is, or has been, an appointed representative; or

(c) is carrying on, or has carried on, a regulated activity in contravention of the general prohibition.

(2) The Authority is entitled to be heard—

(a) at the hearing of the petition; and

(b) at any other hearing of the court in relation to the body under or by virtue of Part IV or V of the 1986 Act (or Part V or VI of the 1989 Order).

(3) Any notice or other document required to be sent to a creditor of the body must also be sent to the Authority.

(4) A person appointed for the purpose by the Authority is entitled—

(a) to attend any meeting of creditors of the body;

(b) to attend any meeting of a committee established for the purposes of Part IV or V of the 1986 Act under section 101 of that Act or under section 141 or 142 of that Act;

(c) to attend any meeting of a committee established for the purposes of Part V or VI of the 1989 Order under Article 87 of that Order or under Article 120 of that Order; and

(d) to make representations as to any matter for decision at such a meeting.

(5) If, during the course of the winding up of a company, a compromise or arrangement is proposed between the company and its creditors, or any class of them, the Authority may apply to the court under [section 896 or 899 of the Companies Act 2006].

Bankruptcy

Petitions.

372.—(1) The Authority may present a petition to the court —

(a) under section 264 of the 1986 Act (or Article 238 of the 1989 Order) for a bankruptcy order to be made against an individual; or

(b) under section 5 of the 1985 Act for the sequestration of the estate of an individual.

(2) But such a petition may be presented only on the ground that—

(a) the individual appears to be unable to pay a regulated activity debt; or

(b) the individual appears to have no reasonable prospect of being able to pay a regulated activity debt.

(3) An individual appears to be unable to pay a regulated activity debt if he is in default on an obligation to pay a sum due and payable under an agreement.

(4) An individual appears to have no reasonable prospect of being able to pay a regulated activity debt if—

    (a) the Authority has served on him a demand requiring him to establish to the satisfaction of the Authority that there is a reasonable prospect that he will be able to pay a sum payable under an agreement when it falls due;

    (b) at least three weeks have elapsed since the demand was served; and

    (c) the demand has been neither complied with nor set aside in accordance with rules.

(5) A demand made under subsection (4)(a) is to be treated for the purposes of the 1986 Act (or the 1989 Order) as if it were a statutory demand under section 268 of that Act (or Article 242 of that Order).

(6) For the purposes of a petition presented in accordance with subsection (1)(b)—

    (a) the Authority is to be treated as a qualified creditor; and

    (b) a ground mentioned in subsection (2) constitutes apparent insolvency.

(7) "Individual" means an individual—

    (a) who is, or has been, an authorised person; or

    (b) who is carrying on, or has carried on, a regulated activity in contravention of the general prohibition.

(8) "Agreement" means an agreement the making or performance of which constitutes or is part of a regulated activity carried on by the individual concerned.

(9) "Rules" means—

    (a) in England and Wales, rules made under section 412 of the 1986 Act;

    (b) in Scotland, rules made by order by the Treasury, after consultation with the Scottish Ministers, for the purposes of this section; and

    (c) in Northern Ireland, rules made under Article 359 of the 1989 Order.

Insolvency practitioner's duty to report to Authority.

373.—(1) If—

    (a) a bankruptcy order or sequestration award is in force in relation to an individual by virtue of a petition presented by a person other than the Authority, and

    (b) it appears to the insolvency practitioner that the individual is carrying on, or has carried on, a regulated activity in contravention of the general prohibition,

the insolvency practitioner must report the matter to the Authority without delay.

(2) "Bankruptcy order" means a bankruptcy order under Part IX of the 1986 Act (or Part IX of the 1989 Order).

(3) "Sequestration award" means an award of sequestration under section 12 of the 1985 Act.

(4) "Individual" includes an entity mentioned in section 374(1)(c).

Authority's powers to participate in proceedings.

374.—(1) This section applies if a person other than the Authority presents a petition to the court—

    (a) under section 264 of the 1986 Act (or Article 238 of the 1989 Order) for a bankruptcy order to be made against an individual;

    (b) under section 5 of the 1985 Act for the sequestration of the estate of an individual; or

    (c) under section 6 of the 1985 Act for the sequestration of the estate belonging to or held for or jointly by the members of an entity mentioned in subsection (1) of that section.

(2) The Authority is entitled to be heard—

    (a) at the hearing of the petition; and

    (b) at any other hearing in relation to the individual or entity under—

        (i) Part IX of the 1986 Act;

        (ii) Part IX of the 1989 Order; or

        (iii) the 1985 Act.

(3) A copy of the report prepared under section 274 of the 1986 Act (or Article 248 of the 1989 Order) must also be sent to the Authority.

(4) A person appointed for the purpose by the Authority is entitled—

    (a) to attend any meeting of creditors of the individual or entity;

    (b) to attend any meeting of a committee established under section 301 of the 1986 Act (or Article 274 of the 1989 Order);

    (c) to attend any meeting of commissioners held under paragraph 17 or 18 of Schedule 6 to the 1985 Act; and

    (d) to make representations as to any matter for decision at such a meeting.

(5) "Individual" means an individual who—

    (a) is, or has been, an authorised person; or

    (b) is carrying on, or has carried on, a regulated activity in contravention of the general prohibition.

(6) "Entity" means an entity which—

    (a) is, or has been, an authorised person; or

    (b) is carrying on, or has carried on, a regulated activity in contravention of the general prohibition.

Provisions against debt avoidance

Authority's right to apply for an order.

375.—(1) The Authority may apply for an order under section 423 of the 1986 Act (or Article 367 of the 1989 Order) in relation to a debtor if—

(a) at the time the transaction at an undervalue was entered into, the debtor was carrying on a regulated activity (whether or not in contravention of the general prohibition); and

(b) a victim of the transaction is or was party to an agreement entered into with the debtor, the making or performance of which constituted or was part of a regulated activity carried on by the debtor.

(2) An application made under this section is to be treated as made on behalf of every victim of the transaction to whom subsection (1)(b) applies.

(3) Expressions which are given a meaning in Part XVI of the 1986 Act (or Article 367, 368 or 369 of the 1989 Order) have the same meaning when used in this section.

Supplemental provisions concerning insurers.

376.—Continuation of contracts of long-term insurance where insurer in liquidation

(1) This section applies in relation to the winding up of an insurer which effects or carries out contracts of long-term insurance.

(2) Unless the court otherwise orders, the liquidator must carry on the insurer's business so far as it consists of carrying out the insurer's contracts of long-term insurance with a view to its being transferred as a going concern to a person who may lawfully carry out those contracts.

(3) In carrying on the business, the liquidator—

(a) may agree to the variation of any contracts of insurance in existence when the winding up order is made; but

(b) must not effect any new contracts of insurance.

(4) If the liquidator is satisfied that the interests of the creditors in respect of liabilities of the insurer attributable to contracts of long-term insurance effected by it require the appointment of a special manager, he may apply to the court.

(5) On such an application, the court may appoint a special manager to act during such time as the court may direct.

(6) The special manager is to have such powers, including any of the powers of a receiver or manager, as the court may direct.

(7) Section 177(5) of the 1986 Act (or Article 151(5) of the 1989 Order) applies to a special manager appointed under subsection (5) as it applies to a special manager appointed under section 177 of the 1986 Act (or Article 151 of the 1989 Order).

(8) If the court thinks fit, it may reduce the value of one or more of the contracts of long-term insurance effected by the insurer.

(9) Any reduction is to be on such terms and subject to such conditions (if any) as the court thinks fit.

(10) The court may, on the application of an official, appoint an independent actuary to investigate the insurer's business so far as it consists of carrying out its contracts of long-term insurance and to report to the official-

(a) on the desirability or otherwise of that part of the insurer's business being continued; and

(b) on any reduction in the contracts of long-term insurance effected by the insurer that may be necessary for successful continuation of that part of the insurer's business.

(11) "Official" means—

(a) the liquidator;

(b) a special manager appointed under subsection (5); or

(c) the Authority.

(12) The liquidator may make an application in the name of the insurer and on its behalf under Part VII without obtaining the permission that would otherwise be required by section 167 of, and Schedule 4 to, the 1986 Act (or Article 142 of, and Schedule 2 to, the 1989 Order).

Reducing the value of contracts instead of winding up.	377.—(1) This section applies in relation to an insurer which has been proved to be unable to pay its debts.

(2) If the court thinks fit, it may reduce the value of one or more of the insurer's contracts instead of making a winding up order.

(3) Any reduction is to be on such terms and subject to such conditions (if any) as the court thinks fit.

Treatment of assets on winding up.	378.—(1) The Treasury may by regulations provide for the treatment of the assets of an insurer on its winding up.

(2) The regulations may, in particular, provide for—

(a) assets representing a particular part of the insurer's business to be available only for meeting liabilities attributable to that part of the insurer's business;

(b) separate general meetings of the creditors to be held in respect of liabilities attributable to a particular part of the insurer's business.

Winding-up rules.	379.—(1) Winding-up rules may include provision

(a) for determining the amount of the liabilities of an insurer to policyholders of any class or description for the purpose of proof in a winding up; and

  (b) generally for carrying into effect the provisions of this Part with respect to the winding up of insurers.

(2) Winding-up rules may, in particular, make provision for all or any of the following matters—

  (a) the identification of assets and liabilities;

  (b) the apportionment, between assets of different classes or descriptions, of—

    (i) the costs, charges and expenses of the winding up; and

    (ii) any debts of the insurer of a specified class or description;

  (c) the determination of the amount of liabilities of a specified description;

  (d) the application of assets for meeting liabilities of a specified description;

  (e) the application of assets representing any excess of a specified description.

(3) "Specified" means specified in winding-up rules.

(4) "Winding-up rules" means rules made under section 411 of the 1986 Act (or Article 359 of the 1989 Order).

(5) Nothing in this section affects the power to make winding-up rules under the 1986 Act or the 1989 Order.

Part XXV
Injunctions And Restitution
Injunctions

Injunctions.   **380.**—(1) If, on the application of the Authority or the Secretary of State, the court is satisfied

  (a) that there is a reasonable likelihood that any person will contravene a relevant requirement, or

  (b) that any person has contravened a relevant requirement and that there is a reasonable likelihood that the contravention will continue or be repeated, the court may make an order restraining (or in Scotland an interdict prohibiting) the contravention.

(2) If on the application of the Authority or the Secretary of State the court is satisfied—

  (a) that any person has contravened a relevant requirement, and

  (b) that there are steps which could be taken for remedying the contravention, the court may make an order requiring that person, and any other person who appears to have been knowingly concerned in the contravention, to take such steps as the court may direct to remedy it.

(3) If, on the application of the Authority or the Secretary of State, the court is satisfied that any person may have-

    (a) contravened a relevant requirement, or

    (b) been knowingly concerned in the contravention of such a requirement, it may make an order restraining (or in Scotland an interdict prohibiting) him from disposing of, or otherwise dealing with, any assets of his which it is satisfied he is reasonably likely to dispose of or otherwise deal with.

(4) The jurisdiction conferred by this section is exercisable by the High Court and the Court of Session.

(5) In subsection (2), references to remedying a contravention include references to mitigating its effect.

(6) "Relevant requirement"—

    (a) in relation to an application by the Authority, means a requirement—

        (i) which is imposed by or under this Act [or by any directly applicable Community regulation made under the markets in financial instruments directive]; or

        (ii) which is imposed by or under any other Act and whose contravention constitutes an offence which the Authority has power to prosecute under this Act;

    (b) in relation to an application by the Secretary of State, means a requirement which is imposed by or under this Act and whose contravention constitutes an offence which the Secretary of State has power to prosecute under this Act.

(7) In the application of subsection (6) to Scotland—

    (a) in paragraph (a) (ii) for "which the Authority has power to prosecute under this Act" substitute "mentioned in paragraph (a) or (b) of section 402(1)"; and

    (b) in paragraph (b) omit "which the Secretary of State has power to prosecute under this Act".

Injunctions in cases of market abuse.

381.—(1) If, on the application of the Authority, the court is satisfied—

    (a) that there is a reasonable likelihood that any person will engage in market abuse, or

    (b) that any person is or has engaged in market abuse and that there is a reasonable likelihood that the market abuse will continue or be repeated, the court may make an order restraining (or in Scotland an interdict prohibiting) the market abuse.

(2) If on the application of the Authority the court is satisfied—

    (a) that any person is or has engaged in market abuse, and

(b) that there are steps which could be taken for remedying the market abuse, the court may make an order requiring him to take such steps as the court may direct to remedy it.

(3) Subsection (4) applies if, on the application of the Authority, the court is satisfied that any person—

(a) may be engaged in market abuse; or

(b) may have been engaged in market abuse.

(4) The court make an order restraining (or in Scotland an interdict prohibiting) the person concerned from disposing of, or otherwise dealing with, any assets of his which it is satisfied that he is reasonably likely to dispose of, or otherwise deal with.

(5) The jurisdiction conferred by this section is exercisable by the High Court and the Court of Session.

(6) In subsection (2), references to remedying any market abuse include references to mitigating its effect.

Restitution orders

382.—Restitution orders

(1) The court may, on the application of the Authority or the Secretary of State, make an order under subsection (2) if it is satisfied that a person has contravened a relevant requirement, or been knowingly concerned in the contravention of such a requirement, and—

(a) that profits have accrued to him as a result of the contravention; or

(b) that one or more persons have suffered loss or been otherwise adversely affected as a result of the contravention.

(2) The court may order the person concerned to pay to the Authority such sum as appears to the court to be just having regard—

(a) in a case within paragraph (a) of subsection (1), to the profits appearing to the court to have accrued;

(b) in a case within paragraph (b) of that subsection, to the extent of the loss or other adverse effect;

(c) in a case within both of those paragraphs, to the profits appearing to the court to have accrued and to the extent of the loss or other adverse effect.

(3) Any amount paid to the Authority in pursuance of an order under subsection (2) must be paid by it to such qualifying person or distributed by it among such qualifying persons as the court may direct.

(4) On an application under subsection (1) the court may require the person concerned to supply it with such accounts or other information as it may require for any one or more of the following purposes—

(a) establishing whether any and, if so, what profits have accrued to him as mentioned in paragraph (a) of that subsection;

(b) establishing whether any person or persons have suffered any loss or adverse effect as mentioned in paragraph (b) of that subsection and, if so, the extent of that loss or adverse effect; and

(c) determining how any amounts are to be paid or distributed under subsection (3).

(5) The court may require any accounts or other information supplied under subsection (4) to be verified in such manner as it may direct.

(6) The jurisdiction conferred by this section is exercisable by the High Court and the Court of Session.

(7) Nothing in this section affects the right of any person other than the Authority or the Secretary of State to bring proceedings in respect of the matters to which this section applies.

(8) "Qualifying person" means a person appearing to the court to be someone—

(a) to whom the profits mentioned in subsection (1)(a) are attributable; or

(b) who has suffered the loss or adverse effect mentioned in subsection (1)(b).

(9) "Relevant requirement"—

(a) in relation to an application by the Authority, means a requirement—

(i) which is imposed by or under this Act [or by any directly applicable Community regulation made under the markets in financial instruments directive]; or

(ii) which is imposed by or under any other Act and whose contravention constitutes an offence which the Authority has power to prosecute under this Act;

(b) in relation to an application by the Secretary of State, means a requirement which is imposed by or under this Act and whose contravention constitutes an offence which the Secretary of State has power to prosecute under this Act.

(10) In the application of subsection (9) to Scotland—

(a) in paragraph (a) (ii) for "which the Authority has power to prosecute under this Act" substitute "mentioned in paragraph (a) or (b) of section 402(1); and

(b) in paragraph (b) omit "which the Secretary of State has power to prosecute under this Act".

383.—Restitution orders in cases of market abuse

(1) The court may, on the application of the Authority, make an order under subsection (4) if it is satisfied that a person ("the person concerned")—

    (a) has engaged in market abuse, or

    (b) by taking or refraining from taking any action has required or encouraged another person or persons to engage in behaviour which, if engaged in by the person concerned, would amount to market abuse,

and the condition mentioned in subsection (2) is fulfilled.

(2) The condition is—

    (a) that profits have accrued to the person concerned as a result; or

    (b) that one or more persons have suffered loss or been otherwise adversely affected as a result.

(3) But the court may not make an order under subsection (4) if it is satisfied that—

    (a) the person concerned believed, on reasonable grounds, that his behaviour did not fall within paragraph (a) or (b) of subsection (1); or

    (b) he took all reasonable precautions and exercised all due diligence to avoid behaving in a way which fell within paragraph (a) or (b)of subsection (1).

(4) The court may order the person concerned to pay to the Authority such sum as appears to the court to be just having regard—

    (a) in a case within paragraph (a) of subsection (2), to the profits appearing to the court to have accrued;

    (b) in a case within paragraph (b) of that subsection, to the extent of the loss or other adverse effect;

    (c) in a case within both of those paragraphs, to the profits appearing to the court to have accrued and to the extent of the loss or other adverse effect.

(5) Any amount paid to the Authority in pursuance of an order under subsection (4) must be paid by it to such qualifying person or distributed by it among such qualifying persons as the court may direct.

(6) On an application under subsection (1) the court may require the person concerned to supply it with such accounts or other information as it may require for any one or more of the following purposes—

    (a) establishing whether any and, if so, what profits have accrued to him as mentioned in subsection (2)(a);

    (b) establishing whether any person or persons have suffered any loss or adverse effect as mentioned in subsection (2)(b) and, if so, the extent of that loss or adverse effect; and

    (c) determining how any amounts are to be paid or distributed under subsection (5).

(7) The court may require any accounts or other information supplied under subsection (6) to be verified in such manner as it may direct.

(8) The jurisdiction conferred by this section is exercisable by the High Court and the Court of Session.

(9) Nothing in this section affects the right of any person other than the Authority to bring proceedings in respect of the matters to which this section applies.

(10) "Qualifying person" means a person appearing to the court to be someone—

(a) to whom the profits mentioned in paragraph (a) of subsection (2) are attributable; or

(b) who has suffered the loss or adverse effect mentioned in paragraph (b) of that subsection.

Restitution required by Authority

Power of Authority to require restitution

384.—(1) The Authority may exercise the power in subsection (5) if it is satisfied that an authorised person ("the person concerned") has contravened a relevant requirement, or been knowingly concerned in the contravention of such a requirement, and—

(a) that profits have accrued to him as a result of the contravention; or

(b) that one or more persons have suffered loss or been otherwise adversely affected as a result of the contravention.

(2) The Authority may exercise the power in subsection (5) if it is satisfied that a person ("the person concerned") —

(a) has engaged in market abuse, or

(b) by taking or refraining from taking any action has required or encouraged another person or persons to engage in behaviour which, if engaged in by the person concerned, would amount to market abuse,

and the condition mentioned in subsection (3) is fulfilled,

(3) The condition is—

(a) that profits have accrued to the person concerned as a result of the market abuse; or

(b) that one or more persons have suffered loss or been otherwise adversely affected as a result of the market abuse.

(4) But the Authority may not exercise that power as a result of subsection (2) if, having considered any representations made to it in response to a warning notice, there are reasonable grounds for it to be satisfied that —

(a) the person concerned believed, on reasonable grounds, that his behaviour did not fall within paragraph (a) or (b) of that subsection; or

(b) he took all reasonable precautions and exercised all due diligence to avoid behaving in a way which fell within paragraph (a) or (b) of that subsection.

(5) The power referred to in subsections (1) and (2) is a power to require the person concerned, in accordance with such arrangements as the Authority considers appropriate, to pay to the appropriate person or distribute among the appropriate persons such amount as appears to the Authority to be just having regard—

    (a) in a case within paragraph (a) of subsection (1) or (3), to the profits appearing to the Authority to have accrued;

    (b) in a case within paragraph (b) of subsection (1) or (3), to the extent of the loss or other adverse effect;

    (c) in a case within paragraphs (a) and (b) of subsection (1) or (3), to the profits appearing to the Authority to have accrued and to the extent of the loss or other adverse effect.

(6) "Appropriate person" means a person appearing to the Authority to be someone—

    (a) to whom the profits mentioned in paragraph (a) of subsection (1) or (3) are attributable; or

    (b) who has suffered the loss or adverse effect mentioned in paragraph (b) of subsection (1) or (3).

(7) "Relevant requirement" means—

    (a) a requirement imposed by or under this Act [or by any directly applicable Community regulation made under the markets in financial instruments directive]; and

    (b) a requirement which is imposed by or under any other Act and whose contravention constitutes an offence in relation to which this Act confers power to prosecute on the Authority.

(8) In the application of subsection (7) to Scotland, in paragraph (b) for "in relation to which this Act confers power to prosecute on the Authority" substitute "mentioned in paragraph (a) or (b) of section 402(1)".

385.—Warning notices

(1) If the Authority proposes to exercise the power under section 384(5) in relation to a person, it must give him a warning notice.

(2) A warning notice under this section must specify the amount which the Authority proposes to require the person concerned to pay or distribute as mentioned in section 384(5).

386.—Decision notices

(1) If the Authority decides to exercise the power under section 384(5), it must give a decision notice to the person in relation to whom the power is exercised.

(2) The decision notice must—

    (a) state the amount that he is to pay or distribute as mentioned in section 384(5);

    (b) identify the person or persons to whom that amount is to be paid or among whom that amount is to be distributed; and

    (c) state the arrangements in accordance with which the payment or distribution is to be made.

(3) If the Authority decides to exercise the power under section 384(5), the person in relation to whom it is exercised may refer the matter to the Tribunal.

PART XXVI
NOTICES
Warning notices

387.—Warning notices

(1) A warning notice must—

    (a) state the action which the Authority proposes to take;

    (b) be in writing;

    (c) give reasons for the proposed action;

    (d) state whether section 394 applies; and

    (e) if that section applies, describe its effect and state whether any secondary material exists to which the person concerned must be allowed access under it.

(2) The warning notice must specify a reasonable period (which may not be less than 28 days) within which the person to whom it is given may make representations to the Authority.

(3) The Authority may extend the period specified in the notice.

(4) The Authority must then decide, within a reasonable period, whether to give the person concerned a decision notice.

Decision notices

388.—Decision notices

(1) A decision notice must—

    (a) be in writing;

    (b) give the Authority's reasons for the decision to take the action to which the notice relates;

    (c) state whether section 394 applies;

    (d) if that section applies, describe its effect and state whether any secondary material exists to which the person concerned must be allowed access under it; and

    (e) give an indication of—

        (i) any right to have the matter referred to the Tribunal which is given by this Act; and

        (ii) the procedure on such a reference.

(2) If the decision notice was preceded by a warning notice, the action to which the decision notice relates must be action under the same Part as the action proposed in the warning notice.

(3) The Authority may, before it takes the action to which a decision notice ("the original notice") relates, give the person concerned a further decision notice which relates to different action in respect of the same matter.

(4) The Authority may give a further decision notice as a result of subsection (3) only if the person to whom the original notice was given consents.

(5) If the person to whom a decision notice is given under subsection (3) had the right to refer the matter to which the original decision notice related to the Tribunal, he has that right as respects the decision notice under subsection (3).

Conclusion of proceedings

389.—Notices of discontinuance

(1) If the Authority decides not to take—
   (a) the action proposed in a warning notice, or
   (b) the action to which a decision notice relates, it must give a notice of discontinuance to the person to whom the warning notice or decision notice was given.

(2) But subsection (1) does not apply if the discontinuance of the proceedings concerned results in the granting of an application made by the person to whom the warning or decision notice was given.

(3) A notice of discontinuance must identify the proceedings which are being discontinued.

390.—Final notices

(1) If the Authority has given a person a decision notice and the matter was not referred to the Tribunal within the period mentioned in section 133(1), the Authority must, on taking the action to which the decision notice relates, give the person concerned and any person to whom the decision notice was copied a final notice.

(2) If the Authority has given a person a decision notice and the matter was referred to the Tribunal, the Authority must, on taking action in accordance with any directions given by—
   (a) the Tribunal, or
   (b) the court under section 137, give that person and any person to whom the decision notice was copied a final notice.

(3) A final notice about a statement must—
   (a) set out the terms of the statement;
   (b) give details of the manner in which, and the date on which, the statement will be published.

(4) A final notice about an order must—
  (a) set out the terms of the order;
  (b) state the date from which the order has effect.

(5) A final notice about a penalty must—
  (a) state the amount of the penalty;
  (b) state the manner in which, and the period within which, the penalty is to be paid;
  (c) give details of the way in which the penalty will be recovered if it is not paid by the date stated in the notice.

(6) A final notice about a requirement to make a payment or distribution in accordance with section 384(5) must state—
  (a) the persons to whom,
  (b) the manner in which, and
  (c) the period within which, it must be made.

(7) In any other case, the final notice must—
  (a) give details of the action being taken;
  (b) state the date on which the action is to be taken.

(8) The period stated under subsection (5)(b) or (6)(c) may not be less than 14 days beginning with the date on which the final notice is given.

(9) If all or any of the amount of a penalty payable under a final notice is outstanding at the end of the period stated under subsection (5)(b), the Authority may recover the outstanding amount as a debt due to it.

(10) If all or any of a required payment or distribution has not been made at the end of a period stated in a final notice under subsection (6)(c), the obligation to make the payment is enforceable, on the application of the Authority, by injunction or, in Scotland, by an order under section 45 of the Court of Session Act 1988.

Publication

391.—Publication

(1) Neither the Authority nor a person to whom a warning notice or decision notice is given or copied may publish the notice or any details concerning it.

(2) A notice of discontinuance must state that, if the person to whom the notice is given consents, the Authority may publish such information as it considers appropriate about the matter to which the discontinued proceedings related.

(3) A copy of a notice of discontinuance must be accompanied by a statement that, if the person to whom the notice is copied consents, the Authority may publish such information as it considers appropriate about the matter to which the discontinued proceedings related, so far as relevant to that person.

(4) The Authority must publish such information about the matter to which a final notice relates as it considers appropriate.

(5) When a supervisory notice takes effect, the Authority must publish such information about the matter to which the notice relates as it considers appropriate.

(6) But the Authority may not publish information under this section if publication of it would, in its opinion, be unfair to the person with respect to whom the action was taken or prejudicial to the interests of consumers.

(7) Information is to be published under this section in such manner as the Authority considers appropriate.

(8) For the purposes of determining when a supervisory notice takes effect, a matter to which the notice relates is open to review if—

(a) the period during which any person may refer the matter to the Tribunal is still running;

(b) the matter has been referred to the Tribunal but has not been dealt with;

(c) the matter has been referred to the Tribunal and dealt with but the period during which an appeal may be brought against the Tribunal's decision is still running; or

(d) such an appeal has been brought but has not been determined.

(9) "Notice of discontinuance" means a notice given under section 389.

(10) "Supervisory notice" has the same meaning as in section 395.

(11) "Consumers" means persons who are consumers for the purposes of section 138.

Third party rights and access to evidence

392.—Application of sections 393 and 394

Sections 393 and 394 apply to—

(a) a warning notice given in accordance with section 54(1), 57(1), 63(3), 67(1), 88(4)(b), 89(2), 92(1), 126(1), 207(1), 255(1), 280(1), 331(1), 345(2) (whether as a result of subsection (1) of that section or section 249(1))[, 385(1) or 412B(4) or (8)];

(b) a decision notice given in accordance with section 54(2), 57(3), 63(4), 67(4), 88(6)(b), 89(3), 92(4), 127(1), 208(1), 255(2), 280(2), 331(3), 345(3) (whether as a result of subsection (1) of that section or section 249(1))[, 386(1) or 412B(5) or (9)].

393.—Third party rights

(1) If any of the reasons contained in a warning notice to which this section applies relates to a matter which—

(a) identifies a person ("the third party") other than the person to whom the notice is given, and

(b) in the opinion of the Authority, is prejudicial to the third party, a copy of the notice must be given to the third party.

(2) Subsection (1) does not require a copy to be given to the third party if the Authority—

    (a) has given him a separate warning notice in relation to the same matter; or

    (b) gives him such a notice at the same time as it gives the warning notice which identifies him.

(3) The notice copied to a third party under subsection (1) must specify a reasonable period (which may not be less than 28 days) within which he may make representations to the Authority.

(4) If any of the reasons contained in a decision notice to which this section applies relates to a matter which—

    (a) identifies a person ("the third party") other than the person to whom the decision notice is given, and

    (b) in the opinion of the Authority, is prejudicial to the third party, a copy of the notice must be given to the third party.

(5) If the decision notice was preceded by a warning notice, a copy of the decision notice must (unless it has been given under subsection (4)) be given to each person to whom the warning notice was copied.

(6) Subsection (4) does not require a copy to be given to the third party if the Authority—

    (a) has given him a separate decision notice in relation to the same matter; or

    (b) gives him such a notice at the same time as it gives the decision notice which identifies him.

(7) Neither subsection (1) nor subsection (4) requires a copy of a notice to be given to a third party if the Authority considers it impracticable to do so.

(8) Subsections (9) to (11) apply if the person to whom a decision notice is given has a right to refer the matter to the Tribunal.

(9) A person to whom a copy of the notice is given under this section may refer to the Tribunal—

    (a) the decision in question, so far as it is based on a reason of the kind mentioned in subsection (4); or

    (b) any opinion expressed by the Authority in relation to him.

(10) The copy must be accompanied by an indication of the third party's right to make a reference under subsection (9) and of the procedure on such a reference.

(11) A person who alleges that a copy of the notice should have been given to him, but was not, may refer to the Tribunal the alleged failure and—

(a) the decision in question, so far as it is based on a reason of the kind mentioned in subsection (4); or

(b) any opinion expressed by the Authority in relation to him.

(12) Section 394 applies to a third party as it applies to the person to whom the notice to which this section applies was given, in so far as the material which the Authority must disclose under that section relates to the matter which identifies the third party.

(13) A copy of a notice given to a third party under this section must be accompanied by a description of the effect of section 394 as it applies to him.

(14) Any person to whom a warning notice or decision notice was copied under this section must be given a copy of a notice of discontinuance applicable to the proceedings to which the warning notice or decision notice related.

394.—Access to Authority material

(1) If the Authority gives a person ("A") a notice to which this section applies, it must—

(a) allow him access to the material on which it relied in taking the decision which gave rise to the obligation to give the notice;

(b) allow him access to any secondary material which, in the opinion of the Authority, might undermine that decision.

(2) But the Authority does not have to allow A access to material under subsection (1) if the material is excluded material or it—

a) relates to a case involving a person other than A; and

(b) was taken into account by the Authority in A's case only for purposes of comparison with other cases.

(3) The Authority may refuse A access to particular material which it would otherwise have to allow him access to if, in its opinion, allowing him access to the material—

(a) would not be in the public interest; or

(b) would not be fair, having regard to—

(i) the likely significance of the material to A in relation to the matter in respect of which he has been given a notice to which this section applies; and

(ii) the potential prejudice to the commercial interests of a person other than A which would be caused by the material's disclosure.

((4) If the Authority does not allow A access to material because it is excluded material consisting of a protected item, it must give A written notice of—

(a) the existence of the protected item; and

(b) the Authority's decision not to allow him access to it.

(5) If the Authority refuses under subsection (3) to allow A access to material, it must give him written notice of—
  (a) the refusal; and
  (b) the reasons for it.

(6) "Secondary material" means material, other than material falling within paragraph (a) of subsection (1) which —
  (a) was considered by the Authority in reaching the decision mentioned in that paragraph; or
  (b) was obtained by the Authority in connection with the matter to which the notice to which this section applies relates but which was not considered by it in reaching that decision.

(7) "Excluded material" means material which—
  [(a) is material the disclosure of which for the purposes of or in connection with any legal proceedings is prohibited by section 17 of the Regulation of Investigatory Powers Act 2000; or]
  (c) is a protected item (as defined in section 413).

The Authority's procedures

395.—The Authority's procedures

(1) The Authority must determine the procedure that it proposes to follow in relation to the giving of—
  (a) supervisory notices; and
  (b) warning notices and decision notices.

(2) That procedure must be designed to secure, among other things, that the decision which gives rise to the obligation to give any such notice is taken by a person not directly involved in establishing the evidence on which that decision is based.

(3) But the procedure may permit a decision which gives rise to an obligation to give a supervisory notice to be taken by a person other than a person mentioned in subsection (2) if—
  a) the Authority considers that, in the particular case, it is necessary in order to protect the interests of consumers; and
  (b) the person taking the decision is of a level of seniority laid down by the procedure.

(4) A level of seniority laid down by the procedure for the purposes of subsection (3)(b) must be appropriate to the importance of the decision.

(5) The Authority must issue a statement of the procedure.

(6) The statement must be published in the way appearing to the Authority to be best calculated to bring it to the attention of the public.

(7) The Authority may charge a reasonable fee for providing a person with a copy of the statement.

(8) The Authority must, without delay, give the Treasury a copy of any statement which it issues under this section.

(9) When giving a supervisory notice, or a warning notice or decision notice, the Authority must follow its stated procedure.

(10) If the Authority changes the procedure in a material way, it must publish a revised statement.

(11) The Authority's failure in a particular case to follow its procedure as set out in the latest published statement does not affect the validity of a notice given in that case.

(12) But subsection (11) does not prevent the Tribunal from taking into account any such failure in considering a matter referred to it.

(13) "Supervisory notice" means a notice given in accordance with section—

(a) 53(4), (7) or (8)(b);

(b) 78(2) or (5);

[(bza) 78A(2) or (8)(b);]

[(ba) 96C;]

[(bb) 87O(2) or (5);]

[(bc) 191B(1);]

(c) 197(3), (6) or (7)(b);

(d) 259(3), (8) or (9)(b);

(e) 268(3), (7)(a) or (9)(a) (as a result of subsection (8)(b));

(f) 282(3), (6) or (7)(b);

[(fa) 301J(1);]

(g) 321(2) or (5).

396.—Statements under section 395: consultation

(1) Before issuing a statement of procedure under section 395, the Authority must publish a draft of the proposed statement in the way appearing to the Authority to be best calculated to bring it to the attention of the public.

(2) The draft must be accompanied by notice that representations about the proposal may be made to the Authority within a specified time.

(3) Before issuing the proposed statement of procedure, the Authority must have regard to any representations made to it in accordance with subsection (2).

(4) If the Authority issues the proposed statement of procedure it must publish an account, in general terms, of—

(a) the representations made to it in accordance with subsection (2); and

(b) its response to them.

(5) If the statement of procedure differs from the draft published under subsection (1) in a way which is, in the opinion of the Authority, significant, the Authority must (in addition to complying with subsection (4)) publish details of the difference.

(6) The Authority may charge a reasonable fee for providing a person with a copy of a draft published under subsection (1).

(7) This section also applies to a proposal to revise a statement of policy.

PART XXVII
OFFENCES
Miscellaneous offences

397.—Misleading statements and practices

(1) This subsection applies to a person who—

    (a) makes a statement, promise or forecast which he knows to be misleading, false or deceptive in a material particular;

    (b) dishonestly conceals any material facts whether in connection with a statement, promise or forecast made by him or otherwise; or

    (c) recklessly makes (dishonestly or otherwise) a statement, promise or forecast which is misleading, false or deceptive in a material particular.

(2) A person to whom subsection (1) applies is guilty of an offence if he makes the statement, promise or

forecast or conceals the facts for the purpose of inducing, or is reckless as to whether it may induce, another person (whether or not the person to whom the statement, promise or forecast is made)—

    (a) to enter or offer to enter into, or to refrain from entering or offering to enter into, a relevant agreement; or

    (b) to exercise, or refrain from exercising, any rights conferred by a relevant investment.

(3) Any person who does any act or engages in any course of conduct which creates a false or misleading impression as to the market in or the price or value of any relevant investments is guilty of an offence if he does so for the purpose of creating that impression and of thereby inducing another person to acquire, dispose of, subscribe for or underwrite those investments or to refrain from doing so or to exercise, or refrain from exercising, any rights conferred by those investments.

(4) In proceedings for an offence under subsection (2) brought against a person to whom subsection (1) applies as a result of paragraph (a) of that subsection, it is a defence for him to show that the statement, promise or forecast was made in conformity with[—

    (a) price stabilising rules;

    (b) control of information rules; or

    (c) the relevant provisions of Commission Regulation (EC) No 2273/2003 of 22 December 2003 implementing Directive 2003/6/EC of the European Parliament and of the Council as regards exemptions for buy-back programmes and stabilisation of financial instruments].

(5) In proceedings brought against any person for an offence under subsection (3) it is a defence for him to show —

    (a) that he reasonably believed that his act or conduct would not create an impression that was false or misleading as to the matters mentioned in that subsection;

    (b) that he acted or engaged in the conduct—

        (i) for the purpose of stabilising the price of investments; and

        (ii) in conformity with price stabilising rules; ...

    (c) that he acted or engaged in the conduct in conformity with control of information rules[; or

    (d) that he acted or engaged in the conduct in conformity with the relevant provisions of Commission Regulation (EC) No 2273/2003 of 22 December 2003 implementing Directive

2003/6/EC of the European Parliament and of the Council as regards exemptions for buy-back programmes and stabilisation of financial instruments].

(6) Subsections (1) and (2) do not apply unless—

    (a) the statement, promise or forecast is made in or from, or the facts are concealed in or from, the United Kingdom or arrangements are made in or from the United Kingdom for the statement, promise or forecast to be made or the facts to be concealed;

    (b) the person on whom the inducement is intended to or may have effect is in the United Kingdom; or

    (c) the agreement is or would be entered into or the rights are or would be exercised in the United Kingdom.

(7) Subsection (3) does not apply unless—

    (a) the act is done, or the course of conduct is engaged in, in the United Kingdom; or

    (b) the false or misleading impression is created there.

(8) A person guilty of an offence under this section is liable —

    (a) on summary conviction, to imprisonment for a term not exceeding six months or a fine not exceeding the statutory maximum, or both;

    (b) on conviction on indictment, to imprisonment for a term not exceeding seven years or a fine, or both.

(9) "Relevant agreement" means an agreement—

    (a) the entering into or performance of which by either party constitutes an activity of a specified kind or one which falls within a specified class of activity; and

    (b) which relates to a relevant investment.

(10) "Relevant investment" means an investment of a specified kind or one which falls within a prescribed class of investment.

(11) Schedule 2 (except paragraphs 25 and 26) applies for the purposes of subsections (9) and (10) with references to section 22 being read as references to each of those subsections.

(12) Nothing in Schedule 2, as applied by subsection (11), limits the power conferred by subsection (9) or (10).

(13) "Investment" includes any asset, right or interest.

(14) "Specified" means specified in an order made by the Treasury.

398.—Misleading the Authority: residual cases

(1) A person who, in purported compliance with any requirement imposed by or under this Act, knowingly or recklessly gives the Authority information which is false or misleading in a material particular is guilty of an offence.

(2) Subsection (1) applies only to a requirement in relation to which no other provision of this Act creates an offence in connection with the giving of information.

(3) A person guilty of an offence under this section is liable—

    (a) on summary conviction, to a fine not exceeding the statutory maximum;

    (b) on conviction on indictment, to a fine.

399.—Misleading [the OFT]

Section 44 of the Competition Act 1998 (offences connected with the provision of false or misleading information) applies in relation to any function of [the Office of Fair Trading] under this Act as if it were a function under Part I of that Act.

Bodies corporate and partnerships

400.—Offences by bodies corporate etc.

(1) If an offence under this Act committed by a body corporate is shown—

    (a) to have been committed with the consent or connivance of an officer, or

(b) to be attributable to any neglect on his part, the officer as well as the body corporate is guilty of the offence and liable to be proceeded against and punished accordingly.

(2) If the affairs of a body corporate are managed by its members, subsection (1) applies in relation to the acts and defaults of a member in connection with his functions of management as if he were a director of the body.

(3) If an offence under this Act committed by a partnership is shown—

(a) to have been committed with the consent or connivance of a partner, or

(b) to be attributable to any neglect on his part, the partner as well as the partnership is guilty of the offence and liable to be proceeded against and punished accordingly.

(4) In subsection (3) "partner" includes a person purporting to act as a partner.

(5) "Officer", in relation to a body corporate, means—

(a) a director, member of the committee of management, chief executive, manager, secretary or other similar officer of the body, or a person purporting to act in any such capacity; and

(b) an individual who is a controller of the body.

(6) If an offence under this Act committed by an unincorporated association (other than a partnership) is shown —

(a) to have been committed with the consent or connivance of an officer of the association or a member of its governing body, or

(b) to be attributable to any neglect on the part of such an officer or member, that officer or member as well as the association is guilty of the offence and liable to be proceeded against and punished accordingly.

(7) Regulations may provide for the application of any provision of this section, with such modifications as the Treasury consider appropriate, to a body corporate or unincorporated association formed or recognised under the law of a territory outside the United Kingdom.

Institution of proceedings

401.—Proceedings for offences

(1) In this section "offence" means an offence under this Act or subordinate legislation made under this Act.

(2) Proceedings for an offence may be instituted in England and Wales only—

(a) by the Authority or the Secretary of State; or

(b) by or with the consent of the Director of Public Prosecutions.

(3) Proceedings for an offence may be instituted in Northern Ireland only—

(a) by the Authority or the Secretary of State; or

(b) by or with the consent of the Director of Public Prosecutions for Northern Ireland.

(4) Except in Scotland, proceedings for an offence under section 203 may also be instituted by [the Office of Fair Trading].

(5) In exercising its power to institute proceedings for an offence, the Authority must comply with any conditions or restrictions imposed in writing by the Treasury.

(6) Conditions or restrictions may be imposed under subsection (5) in relation to—

(a) proceedings generally; or

(b) such proceedings, or categories of proceedings, as the Treasury may direct.

402.—Power of the Authority to institute proceedings for certain other offences

(1) Except in Scotland, the Authority may institute proceedings for an offence under—

(a) Part V of the Criminal Justice Act 1993 (insider dealing); ...

(b) prescribed regulations relating to money laundering;[;] [or

(c) Schedule 7 to the Counter-Terrorism Act 2008 (terrorist financing or money laundering)].

(2) In exercising its power to institute proceedings for any such offence, the Authority must comply with any conditions or restrictions imposed in writing by the Treasury.

(3) Conditions or restrictions may be imposed under subsection (2) in relation to—

(a) proceedings generally; or

(b) such proceedings, or categories of proceedings, as the Treasury may direct.

403.—Jurisdiction and procedure in respect of offences

(1) A fine imposed on an unincorporated association on its conviction of an offence is to be paid out of the funds of the association.

(2) Proceedings for an offence alleged to have been committed by an unincorporated association must be brought in the name of the association (and not in that of any of its members).

(3) Rules of court relating to the service of documents are to have effect as if the association were a body corporate.

(4) In proceedings for an offence brought against an unincorporated association—

   (a) section 33 of the Criminal Justice Act 1925 and Schedule 3 to the Magistrates' Courts Act 1980 (procedure) apply as they do in relation to a body corporate;

   (b) section 70 of the Criminal Procedure (Scotland) Act 1995 (procedure) applies as if the association were a body corporate;

   (c) section 18 of the Criminal Justice (Northern Ireland) Act 1945 and Schedule 4 to the Magistrates' Courts (Northern Ireland) Order 1981 (procedure) apply as they do in relation to a body corporate.

(5) Summary proceedings for an offence may be taken—

   (a) against a body corporate or unincorporated association at any place at which it has a place of business;

   (b) against an individual at any place where he is for the time being.

(6) Subsection (5) does not affect any jurisdiction exercisable apart from this section.

(7) "Offence" means an offence under this Act.

PART XXVIII
MISCELLANEOUS
Schemes for reviewing past business

404.—Schemes for reviewing past business

(1) Subsection (2) applies if the Treasury are satisfied that there is evidence suggesting—

   (a) that there has been a widespread or regular failure on the part of authorised persons to comply with rules relating to a particular kind of activity; and

   (b) that, as a result, private persons have suffered (or will suffer) loss in respect of which authorised persons are (or will be) liable to make payments ("compensation payments").

(2) The Treasury may by order ("a scheme order") authorise the Authority to establish and operate a scheme for —

   (a) determining the nature and extent of the failure;

   (b) establishing the liability of authorised persons to make compensation payments; and

   (c) determining the amounts payable by way of compensation payments.

(3) An authorised scheme must be made so as to comply with specified requirements.

(4) A scheme order may be made only if—

    (a) the Authority has given the Treasury a report about the alleged failure and asked them to make a scheme order;

    (b) the report contains details of the scheme which the Authority propose to make; and

    (c) the Treasury are satisfied that the proposed scheme is an appropriate way of dealing with the failure.

(5) A scheme order may provide for specified provisions of or made under this Act to apply in relation to any provision of, or determination made under, the resulting authorised scheme subject to such modifications (if any) as may be specified.

(6) For the purposes of this Act, failure on the part of an authorised person to comply with any provision of an authorised scheme is to be treated (subject to any provision made by the scheme order concerned) as a failure on his part to comply with rules.

(7) The Treasury may prescribe circumstances in which loss suffered by a person ("A") acting in a fiduciary or other prescribed capacity is to be treated, for the purposes of an authorised scheme, as suffered by a private person in relation to whom A was acting in that capacity.

(8) This section applies whenever the failure in question occurred.

(9) "Authorised scheme" means a scheme authorised by a scheme order.

(10) "Private person" has such meaning as may be prescribed.

(11) "Specified" means specified in a scheme order.

Third countries

405.—Directions

(1) For the purpose of implementing a third country decision, the Treasury may direct the Authority to—

    (a) refuse an application for permission under Part IV made by a body incorporated in, or formed under the law of, any part of the United Kingdom;

    (b) defer its decision on such an application either indefinitely or for such period as may be specified in the direction;

    (c) give a notice of objection to a person who has served a notice of control to the effect that he proposes to acquire a 50% stake in a UK authorised person; or

    (d) give a notice of objection to a person who has acquired a 50% stake in a UK authorised person without having served the required notice of control.

(2) A direction may also be given in relation to—

   (a) any person falling within a class specified in the direction;

   (b) future applications, notices of control or acquisitions.

(3) The Treasury may revoke a direction at any time.

(4) But revocation does not affect anything done in accordance with the direction before it was revoked.

(5) "Third country decision" means a decision of the Council or the Commission under—

   [(a) Article 15(3) of the markets in financial instruments directive;]

   (b) ...

   (c) Article 29b(4) of the first non-life insurance directive; or

   [(d) Article 59(4) of the life assurance consolidation directive].

406.—Interpretation of section 405

(1) For the purposes of section 405, a person ("the acquirer") acquires a 50% stake in a UK authorised person ("A") on first falling within any of the cases set out in subsection (2).

(2) The cases are where the acquirer—

   (a) holds 50% or more of the shares in A;

   (b) holds 50% or more of the shares in a parent undertaking ("P") of A;

   (c) is entitled to exercise, or control the exercise of, 50% or more of the voting power in A; or

   (d) is entitled to exercise, or control the exercise of, 50% or more of the voting power in P.

(3) In subsection (2) "the acquirer" means—

   (a) the acquirer;

   (b) any of the acquirer's associates; or

   (c) the acquirer and any of his associates.

(4) "Associate", "shares" and "voting power" have the same meaning as in section 422.

407.—Consequences of a direction under section 405

(1) If the Authority refuses an application for permission as a result of a direction under section 405(1)(a) —

   (a) subsections (7) to (9) of section 52 do not apply in relation to the refusal; but

   (b) the Authority must notify the applicant of the refusal and the reasons for it.

(2) If the Authority defers its decision on an application for permission as a result of a direction under section 405(1)(b)—

   (a) the time limit for determining the application mentioned in section 52(1) or (2) stops running on the day of the deferral and starts running again (if at all) on the day the period specified in the direction (if any) ends or the day the direction is revoked; and

(b) the Authority must notify the applicant of the deferral and the reasons for it.

(3) If the Authority gives a notice of objection to a person as a result of a direction under section 405(1)(c) or (d) —

(a) sections 189 and 191 have effect as if the notice was a notice of objection within the meaning of Part XII; and

(b) the Authority must state in the notice the reasons for it.

408.—EFTA firms

(1) If a third country decision has been taken, the Treasury may make a determination in relation to an EFTA firm which is a subsidiary undertaking of a parent undertaking which is governed by the law of the country to which the decision relates.

(2) "Determination" means a determination that the firm concerned does not qualify for authorisation under Schedule 3 even if it satisfies the conditions in paragraph 13 or 14 of that Schedule.

(3) A determination may also be made in relation to any firm falling within a class specified in the determination.

(4) The Treasury may withdraw a determination at any time.

(5) But withdrawal does not affect anything done in accordance with the determination before it was withdrawn.

(6) If the Treasury make a determination in respect of a particular firm, or withdraw such a determination, they must give written notice to that firm.

(7) The Treasury must publish notice of any determination (or the withdrawal of any determination)—

(a) in such a way as they think most suitable for bringing the determination (or withdrawal) to the attention of those likely to be affected by it; and

(b) on, or as soon as practicable after, the date of the determination (or withdrawal).

(8) "EFTA firm" means a firm, institution or undertaking which —

(a) is an EEA firm as a result of paragraph 5(a), (b) or (d) of Schedule 3; and

(b) is incorporated in, or formed under the law of, an EEA State which is not a member State.

(9) "Third country decision" has the same meaning as in section 405.

409.—Gibraltar

(1) The Treasury may by order—

(a) modify Schedule 3 so as to provide for Gibraltar firms of a specified description to qualify for authorisation under that Schedule in specified circumstances;

(b) modify Schedule 3 so as to make provision in relation to the exercise by UK firms of rights under the law of Gibraltar which correspond to EEA rights;

(c) modify Schedule 4 so as to provide for Gibraltar firms of a specified description to qualify for authorisation under that Schedule in specified circumstances;

(d) modify section 264 so as to make provision in relation to collective investment schemes constituted under the law of Gibraltar;

(e) provide for the Authority to be able to give notice under section 264(2) on grounds relating to the law of Gibraltar;

(f) provide for this Act to apply to a Gibraltar recognised scheme as if the scheme were a scheme recognised under section 264.

(2) The fact that a firm may qualify for authorisation under Schedule 3 as a result of an order under subsection (1) does not prevent it from applying for a Part IV permission.

(3) "Gibraltar firm" means a firm which has its head office in Gibraltar or is otherwise connected with Gibraltar.

(4) "Gibraltar recognised scheme" means a collective investment scheme—

(a) constituted in an EEA State other than the United Kingdom, and

(b) recognised in Gibraltar under provisions which appear to the Treasury to give effect to the provisions of a relevant Community instrument.

(5) "Specified" means specified in the order.

(6) "UK firm" and "EEA right" have the same meaning as in Schedule 3.

International obligations

410.—International obligations

(1) If it appears to the Treasury that any action proposed to be taken by a relevant person would be incompatible with Community obligations or any other international obligations of the United Kingdom, they may direct that person not to take that action.

(2) If it appears to the Treasury that any action which a relevant person has power to take is required for the purpose of implementing any such obligations, they may direct that person to take that action.

(3) A direction under this section—

(a) may include such supplemental or incidental requirements as the Treasury consider necessary or expedient; and

(b) is enforceable, on an application made by the Treasury, by injunction or, in Scotland, by an order for specific performance under section 45 of the Court of Session Act 1988.

(4) "Relevant person" means—

    (a) the Authority;

    (b) any person exercising functions conferred by Part VI on the competent authority;

    (c) any recognised investment exchange (other than one which is an overseas investment exchange);

    (d) any recognised clearing house (other than one which is an overseas clearing house);

    (e) a person included in the list maintained under section 301; or

    (f) the scheme operator of the ombudsman scheme.

Tax treatment of levies and repayments

411.—Tax treatment of levies and repayments

(1) ...

(2) After section 76 of the 1988 Act insert—

"76A   Levies and repayments under the Financial Services and Markets Act 2000

(1) In computing the amount of the profits to be charged under Case I of Schedule D arising from a trade carried on by an authorised person (other than an investment company) —

    (a) to the extent that it would not be deductible apart from this section, any sum expended by the authorised person in paying a levy may be deducted as an allowable expense;

    (b) any payment which is made to the authorised person as a result of a repayment provision is to be treated as a trading receipt.

(2) "Levy" has the meaning given in section 76(7A).

(3) "Repayment provision" means any provision made by virtue of—

    (a) section 136(7) of the Financial Services and Markets Act 2000 ("the Act of 2000");

    (b) section 214(1)(e) of the Act of 2000.

(4) "Authorised person" has the same meaning as in the Act of 2000.

76B Levies and repayments under the Financial Services and Markets Act 2000: investment companies

(1) For the purposes of section 75 any sums paid by an investment company—

    (a) by way of a levy, or

    (b) as a result of an award of costs under costs rules, shall be treated as part of its expenses of management.

(2) If a payment is made to an investment company as a result of a repayment provision, the company shall be charged to tax under Case VI of Schedule D on the amount of that payment.

(3) "Levy" has the meaning given in section 76(7A).

(4) "Costs rules" means—

    (a) rules made under section 230 of the Financial Services and Markets Act 2000;

    (b) provision relating to costs contained in the standard terms fixed under paragraph 18 of Schedule 17 to that Act.

(5) "Repayment provision" has the meaning given in section 76A(3)."

Gaming contracts

412.—Gaming contracts

(1) No contract to which this section applies is void or unenforceable because of—

    (a) ... Article 170 of the Betting, Gaming, Lotteries and Amusements (Northern Ireland) Order 1985; or

    (b) ....

(2) This section applies to a contract if—

    (a) it is entered into by either or each party by way of business;

    (b) the entering into or performance of it by either party constitutes an activity of a specified kind or one which falls within a specified class of activity; and

    (c) it relates to an investment of a specified kind or one which falls within a specified class of investment.

(3) Part II of Schedule 2 applies for the purposes of subsection (2)(c), with the references to section 22 being read as references to that subsection.

(4) Nothing in Part II of Schedule 2, as applied by subsection (3), limits the power conferred by subsection (2)(c).

(5) "Investment" includes any asset, right or interest.

(6) "Specified" means specified in an order made by the Treasury.

[Trade-matching and reporting systems]

[412A.—Approval and monitoring of trade-matching and reporting systems]

[(1) A relevant system is an approved relevant system if it is approved by the Authority under subsection (2) for the purposes of Article 25.5 of the markets in financial instruments directive; and references in this section and section 412B to an "approved relevant system" are to be read accordingly.

(2) The Authority must approve a relevant system if, on an application by the operator of the system, it is satisfied that the arrangements established by the system for reporting transactions comply with Article 12(1) of Commission Regulation 1287/2006 of 10 August 2006 ("the Regulation").

(3) Section 51(3) and (4) applies to an application under this section as it applies to an application under Part 4.

(4) If, at any time after approving a relevant system under subsection (2), the Authority is not satisfied as mentioned in that subsection, it may suspend or withdraw the approval.

(5) The Authority must keep under review the arrangements established by an approved relevant system for reporting transactions for the purpose of ensuring that the arrangements comply with Article 12(1) of the Regulation; and for the purposes of this subsection the Authority must have regard to information provided to it under subsections (6) and (7).

(6) The operator of an approved relevant system must make reports to the Authority at specified intervals containing specified information relating to—

   (a) the system,

   (b) the reports made by the system in accordance with Article 25 of the markets in financial instruments directive and the Regulation, and

   (c) the transactions to which those reports relate.

"Specified" means specified by the Authority.

(7) The Authority may by written notice require the operator of an approved relevant system to provide such additional information as may be specified in the notice, by such reasonable time as may be so specified, about any of the matters mentioned in subsection (6).

(8) The recipient of a notice under subsection (7) must provide the information by the time specified in the notice.

(9) In this section and section 412B, "relevant system" means a trade-matching or reporting system of a kind described in Article 12 of the Regulation.]

[**412B.**—Procedure for approval and suspension or withdrawal of approval]

(1) If the Authority approves a relevant system, it must give the operator of the system written notice specifying the date from which the approval has effect.

(2) If the Authority proposes to refuse to approve a relevant system, it must give the operator of the system a warning notice.

[(3) If the Authority decides to refuse to approve a relevant system, it must give the operator of the system a decision notice.

(4) If the Authority proposes to suspend or withdraw its approval in relation to an approved relevant system, it must give the operator of the system a warning notice.

(5) If the Authority decides to suspend or withdraw its approval in relation to an approved relevant system, it must give the operator of the system a decision notice specifying the date from which the suspension or withdrawal is to take effect.

(6) Subsections (7) to (9) apply if—

    (a) the Authority has suspended its approval in relation to an approved relevant system, and

    (b) the operator of the system has applied for the suspension to be cancelled.

(7) The Authority must grant the application if it is satisfied as mentioned in section 412A(2); and in such a case the Authority must give written notice to the operator that the suspension is to be cancelled from the date specified in the notice.

(8) If the Authority proposes to refuse the application, it must give the operator a warning notice.

(9) If the Authority decides to refuse the application, it must give the operator a decision notice.

(10) A person who receives a decision notice under subsection (3), (5) or (9) may refer the matter to the Tribunal.]

Limitation on powers to require documents

413.—Protected items

(1) A person may not be required under this Act to produce, disclose or permit the inspection of protected items.

(2) "Protected items" means—

    (a) communications between a professional legal adviser and his client or any person representing his client which fall within subsection (3);

    (b) communications between a professional legal adviser, his client or any person representing his client and any other person which fall within subsection (3) (as a result of paragraph (b) of that subsection);

    (c) items which—

        (i) are enclosed with, or referred to in, such communications;

        (ii) fall within subsection (3); and

        (iii) are in the possession of a person entitled to possession of them.

(3) A communication or item falls within this subsection if it is made—

    (a) in connection with the giving of legal advice to the client; or

    (b) in connection with, or in contemplation of, legal proceedings and for the purposes of those proceedings.

(4) A communication or item is not a protected item if it is held with the intention of furthering a criminal purpose.

Service of notices

414.—Service of notices

(1) The Treasury may by regulations make provision with respect to the procedure to be followed, or rules to be applied, when a provision of or made under this Act requires a notice, direction or document of any kind to be given or authorises the imposition of a requirement.

(2) The regulations may, in particular, make provision —

    (a) as to the manner in which a document must be given;

    (b) as to the address to which a document must be sent;

    (c) requiring, or allowing, a document to be sent electronically;

    (d) for treating a document as having been given, or as having been received, on a date or at a time determined in accordance with the regulations;

    (e) as to what must, or may, be done if the person to whom a document is required to be given is not an individual;

    (f) as to what must, or may, be done if the intended recipient of a document is outside the United Kingdom.

(3) Subsection (1) applies however the obligation to give a document is expressed (and so, in particular, includes a provision which requires a document to be served or sent).

(4) Section 7 of the Interpretation Act 1978 (service of notice by post) has effect in relation to provisions made by or under this Act subject to any provision made by regulations under this section.

Jurisdiction

415.—Jurisdiction in civil proceedings

(1) Proceedings arising out of any act or omission (or proposed act or omission) of—

(a) the Authority,

(b) the competent authority for the purposes of Part VI,

(c) the scheme manager, or

(d) the scheme operator, in the discharge or purported discharge of any of its functions under this Act may be brought before the High Court or the Court of Session.

(2) The jurisdiction conferred by subsection (1) is in addition to any other jurisdiction exercisable by those courts.

Removal of certain unnecessary provisions

416.—Provisions relating to industrial assurance and certain other enactments

(1) The following enactments are to cease to have effect —

(a) the Industrial Assurance Act 1923;

(b) the Industrial Assurance and Friendly Societies Act 1948;

(c) the Insurance Brokers (Registration) Act 1977.

(2) The Industrial Assurance (Northern Ireland) Order 1979 is revoked.

(3) The following bodies are to cease to exist—

(a) the Insurance Brokers Registration Council;

(b) the Policyholders Protection Board;

(c) the Deposit Protection Board;

(d) the Board of Banking Supervision.

(4) If the Treasury consider that, as a consequence of any provision of this section, it is appropriate to do so, they may by order make any provision of a kind that they could make under this Act (and in particular any provision of a kind mentioned in section 339) with respect to anything done by or under any provision of Part XXI.

(5) Subsection (4) is not to be read as affecting in any way any other power conferred on the Treasury by this Act.

PART XXIX
INTERPRETATION

417.—Definitions

(1) In this Act—

"appointed representative" has the meaning given in section 39(2); "auditors and actuaries rules" means rules made under section 340;

"authorisation offence" has the meaning given in section 23(2);

"authorised open-ended investment company" has the meaning given in section 237(3);

"authorised person" has the meaning given in section 31(2);

"the Authority" means the Financial Services Authority;

"body corporate" includes a body corporate constituted under the law of a country or territory outside the United Kingdom;

"chief executive"—

(a) in relation to a body corporate whose principal place of business is within the United Kingdom, means an employee of that body who, alone or jointly with one or more others, is responsible under the immediate authority of the directors, for the conduct of the whole of the business of that body; and

(b) in relation to a body corporate whose principal place of business is outside the United Kingdom, means the person who, alone or jointly with one or more others, is responsible for the conduct of its business within the United Kingdom;

["claim", in relation to the Financial Services Compensation Scheme under Part XV, is to be construed in accordance with section 214(1B);]

"collective investment scheme" has the meaning given in section 235;

"the Commission" means the European Commission (except in provisions relating to the Competition Commission);

"the compensation scheme" has the meaning given in section 213(2);

"control of information rules" has the meaning given in section 147(1);

"director", in relation to a body corporate, includes—

(a) a person occupying in relation to it the position of a director (by whatever name called); and

(b) a person in accordance with whose directions or instructions (not being advice given in a professional capacity) the directors of that body are accustomed to act;

"documents" includes information recorded in any form and, in relation to information recorded otherwise than in legible form, references to its production include references to producing a copy of the information in legible form[, or in a form from which it can readily be produced in visible and legible form];

["electronic commerce directive" means Directive 2000/31/ EC of the European Parliament and the Council of 8 June 2000 on certain legal aspects of information society services, in particular electronic commerce, in the Internal Market (Directive on electronic commerce);]

"exempt person", in relation to a regulated activity, means a person who is exempt from the general prohibition in relation to that activity as a result of an exemption order made under section 38(1) or as a result of section 39(1) or 285(2) or (3);

"financial promotion rules" means rules made under section 145;

"friendly society" means an incorporated or registered friendly society;

"general prohibition" has the meaning given in section 19(2);

"general rules" has the meaning given in section 138(2);

"incorporated friendly society" means a society incorporated under the Friendly Societies Act 1992;

"industrial and provident society" means a society registered or deemed to be registered under the Industrial and Provident Societies Act 1965 or the Industrial and Provident Societies Act (Northern Ireland) 1969;

["information society service" means an information society service within the meaning of Article 2(a) of the electronic commerce directive;]

["investment services and activities" has the meaning given in Article 4.1.2 of the markets in financial instruments directive, read with—

    (a) Chapter VI of Commission Regulation 1287/2006 of 10 August 2006, and

    (b) Article 52 of Commission Directive 2006/73/EC of 10 August 2006;]

"market abuse" has the meaning given in section 118;

"Minister of the Crown" has the same meaning as in the Ministers of the Crown Act 1975;

"money laundering rules" means rules made under section 146;

"notice of control" [(except in Chapter 1A of Part 18)] has the meaning given in section 178(5);

"the ombudsman scheme" has the meaning given in section 225(3);

"open-ended investment company" has the meaning given in section 236;

"Part IV permission" has the meaning given in section 40(4);

"partnership" includes a partnership constituted under the law of a country or territory outside the United Kingdom;

"prescribed" (where not otherwise defined) means prescribed in regulations made by the Treasury;

"price stabilising rules" means rules made under section 144;

"private company" has the meaning given in section 1(3) of the Companies Act 1985 or in Article 12(3) of the Companies (Northern Ireland) Order 1986;

"prohibition order" has the meaning given in section 56(2);

"recognised clearing house" and "recognised investment exchange" have the meaning given in section 285;

"registered friendly society" means a society which is—

(a) a friendly society within the meaning of section 7(1)(a) of the Friendly Societies Act 1974; and

(b) registered within the meaning of that Act;

"regulated activity" has the meaning given in section 22;

"regulating provisions" has the meaning given in section 159(1);

"regulatory objectives" means the objectives mentioned in section 2;

"regulatory provisions" has the meaning given in section 302;

"rule" means a rule made by the Authority under this Act;

"rule-making instrument" has the meaning given in section 153;

"the scheme manager" has the meaning given in section 212(1);

"the scheme operator" has the meaning given in section 225(2);

"scheme particulars rules" has the meaning given in section 248(1);

"Seventh Company Law Directive" means the European Council Seventh Company Law Directive of 13 June 1983 on consolidated accounts (No 83/349/EEC);

["Takeovers Directive" means Directive 2004/25/EC of the European Parliament and of the Council;]

"threshold conditions", in relation to a regulated activity, has the meaning given in section 41;

"unit trust scheme" has the meaning given in section 237.

(2) In the application of this Act to Scotland, references to a matter being actionable at the suit of a person are to be read as references to the matter being actionable at the instance of that person.

(3) For the purposes of any provision of this Act [(other than a provision of Part 6)] authorising or requiring a person to do anything within a specified number of days no account is to be taken of any day which is a public holiday in any part of the United Kingdom.

[(4) For the purposes of this Act—

(a) an information society service is provided from an EEA State if it is provided from an establishment in that State;

(b) an establishment, in connection with an information society service, is the place at which the provider of the service (being a national of an EEA State or a company or firm as mentioned in Article 48 of the Treaty) effectively pursues an economic activity for an indefinite period;

(c) the presence or use in a particular place of equipment or other technical means of providing an information society service does not, of itself, constitute that place as an establishment of the kind mentioned in paragraph (b);

(d) where it cannot be determined from which of a number of establishments a given information society service is provided, that service is to be regarded as provided from the establishment where the provider has the centre of his activities relating to the service.]

418.—Carrying on regulated activities in the United Kingdom

(1) In the [five] cases described in this section, a person who —

(a) is carrying on a regulated activity, but

(b) would not otherwise be regarded as carrying it on in the United Kingdom, is, for the purposes of this Act, to be regarded as carrying it on in the United Kingdom.

(2) The first case is where—

(a) his registered office (or if he does not have a registered office his head office) is in the United Kingdom;

(b) he is entitled to exercise rights under a single market directive as a UK firm; and

(c) he is carrying on in another EEA State a regulated activity to which that directive applies.

(3) The second case is where—

(a) his registered office (or if he does not have a registered office his head office) is in the United Kingdom;

(b) he is the manager of a scheme which is entitled to enjoy the rights conferred by an instrument which is a relevant Community instrument for the purposes of section 264; and

    (c) persons in another EEA State are invited to become participants in the scheme.

(4) The third case is where—

    (a) his registered office (or if he does not have a registered office his head office) is in the United Kingdom;

    (b) the day-to-day management of the carrying on of the regulated activity is the responsibility of —

        (i) his registered office (or head office); or

        (ii) another establishment maintained by him in the United Kingdom.

(5) The fourth case is where—

    (a) his head office is not in the United Kingdom; but

    (b) the activity is carried on from an establishment maintained by him in the United Kingdom.

[(5A) The fifth case is any other case where the activity—

    (a) consists of the provision of an information society service to a person or persons in one or more EEA States; and

    (b) is carried on from an establishment in the United Kingdom.]

(6) For the purposes of subsections (2) to [(5A)] it is irrelevant where the person with whom the activity is carried on is situated.

419.—Carrying on regulated activities by way of business

(1) The Treasury may by order make provision

    (a) as to the circumstances in which a person who would otherwise not be regarded as carrying on a regulated activity by way of business is to be regarded as doing so;

    (b) as to the circumstances in which a person who would otherwise be regarded as carrying on a regulated activity by way of business is to be regarded as not doing so.

(2) An order under subsection (1) may be made so as to apply—

    (a) generally in relation to all regulated activities;

    (b) in relation to a specified category of regulated activity; or

    (c) in relation to a particular regulated activity.

(3) An order under subsection (1) may be made so as to apply—

    (a) for the purposes of all provisions;

    (b) for a specified group of provisions; or

    (c) for a specified provision.

(4) "Provision" means a provision of, or made under, this Act.

(5) Nothing in this section is to be read as affecting the provisions of section 428(3).

420.—Parent and subsidiary undertaking

(1) In this Act, except in relation to an incorporated friendly society, "parent undertaking" and "subsidiary undertaking" have the same meaning as in Part VII of the Companies Act 1985 (or Part VIII of the Companies (Northern Ireland) Order 1986) [the Companies Acts (see section 1162 of, and Schedule 7 to, the Companies Act 2006)].

(2) But—

    (a) "parent undertaking" also includes an individual who would be a parent undertaking for the purposes of those provisions if he were taken to be an undertaking (and "subsidiary undertaking" is to be read accordingly);

    (b) "subsidiary undertaking" also includes, in relation to a body incorporated in or formed under the law of an EEA State other than the United Kingdom, an undertaking which is a subsidiary undertaking within the meaning of any rule of law in force in that State for purposes connected with implementation of the Seventh Company Law Directive (and "parent undertaking" is to be read accordingly).

(3) In this Act "subsidiary undertaking", in relation to an incorporated friendly society, means a body corporate of which the society has control within the meaning of section 13(9)(a) or (aa) of the Friendly Societies Act 1992 (and "parent undertaking" is to be read accordingly).

421.—Group

(1) In this Act "group", in relation to a person ("A"), means A and any person who is—

    (a) a parent undertaking of A;

    (b) a subsidiary undertaking of A;

    (c) a subsidiary undertaking of a parent undertaking of A;

    (d) a parent undertaking of a subsidiary undertaking of A;

    (e) an undertaking in which A or an undertaking mentioned in paragraph (a), (b), (c) or (d) has a participating interest;

    (f) if A or an undertaking mentioned in paragraph (a) or (d) is a building society, an associated undertaking of the society; or

    (g) if A or an undertaking mentioned in paragraph (a) or (d) is an `incorporated friendly society, a body corporate of which the society has joint control (within the meaning of section 13(9)(c) or (cc) of the Friendly Societies Act 1992).

(2) "Participating interest" has the same meaning as in Part VII of the Companies Act 1985 or Part VIII of the Companies (Northern Ireland) Order 1986 [has the meaning given in section 421A]; but also includes an interest held by an individual which would be a participating interest for the purposes of those provisions if he were taken to be an undertaking.

(3) "Associated undertaking" has the meaning given in section 119(1) of the Building Societies Act 1986.

[421A.—Meaning of "participating interest"]

[(1) In section 421 a "participating interest" means an interest held by an undertaking in the shares of another undertaking which it holds on a long-term basis for the purpose of securing a contribution to its activities by the exercise of control or influence arising from or related to that interest.

(2) A holding of 20% or more of the shares of an undertaking is presumed to be a participating interest unless the contrary is shown.

(3) The reference in subsection (1) to an interest in shares includes —

(a) an interest which is convertible into an interest in shares, and

(b) an option to acquire shares or any such interest;

And an interest or option falls within paragraph (a)

or (b) notwithstanding that the shares to which it relates are, until the conversion or the exercise of the option, unissued.

(4) For the purposes of this section an interest held on behalf of an undertaking shall be treated as held by it.

(5) In this section "undertaking" has the same meaning as in the Companies Acts (see section 1161(1) of the Companies Act 2006).]

[422.—Controller]

[(1) In this Act "controller", in relation to an undertaking ("B"), means a person ("A") who falls within any of the cases in subsection (2).

(2) The cases are where A holds—

(a) 10% or more of the shares in B or in a parent undertaking of B ("P");

(b) 10% or more of the voting power in B or P; or

(c) shares or voting power in B or P as a result of which A is able to exercise significant influence over the management of B.

(3) For the purposes of calculations relating to this section, the holding of shares or voting power by a person ("A1") includes any shares or voting power held by another ("A2") if A1 and A2 are acting in concert.

(4) In this section "shares"—

(a) in relation to an undertaking with a share capital, means allotted shares;

(b) in relation to an undertaking with capital but no share capital, means rights to share in the capital of the undertaking;

(c) in relation to an undertaking without capital, means interests—

    (i) conferring any right to share in the profits, or liability to contribute to the losses, of the undertaking; or

    (ii) giving rise to an obligation to contribute to the debts or expenses of the undertaking in the event of a winding up.

(5) In this section "voting power"—

(a) includes, in relation to a person ("H")—

    (i) voting power held by a third party with whom H has concluded an agreement, which obliges H and the third party to adopt, by concerted exercise of the voting power they hold, a lasting common policy towards the management of the undertaking in question;

    (ii) voting power held by a third party under an agreement concluded with H providing for the temporary transfer for consideration of the voting power in question;

    (iii) voting power attaching to shares which are lodged as collateral with H, provided that H controls the voting power and declares an intention to exercise it;

    (iv) voting power attaching to shares in which H has a life interest;

    (v) voting power which is held, or may be exercised within the meaning of subparagraphs (i) to (iv), by a subsidiary undertaking of H;

    (vi) voting power attaching to shares deposited with H which H has discretion to exercise in the absence of specific instructions from the shareholders;

    (vii) voting power held in the name of a third party on behalf of H;

    (viii) voting power which H may exercise as a proxy where H has discretion about the exercise of the voting power in the absence of specific instructions from the shareholders; and

(b) in relation to an undertaking which does not have general meetings at which matters are decided by the exercise of voting rights, means the right under the constitution of the undertaking to direct the overall policy of the undertaking or alter the terms of its constitution.]

[422A.—Disregarded holdings]

[(1) For the purposes of section 422, shares and voting power that a person holds in an undertaking ("B") or in a parent undertaking of B ("P") are disregarded in the following circumstances.

(2) Shares held only for the purposes of clearing and settling within a short settlement cycle are disregarded.

(3) Shares held by a custodian or its nominee in a custodian capacity are disregarded, provided that the custodian or nominee is only able to exercise voting power attached to the shares in accordance with instructions given in writing.

(4) Shares representing no more than 5% of the total voting power in B or P held by an investment firm are disregarded, provided that it—

    (a) holds the shares in the capacity of a market maker (as defined in article 4.1(8) of the markets in financial instruments directive);

    (b) is authorised by its home state regulator under the markets in financial instruments directive; and

    (c) neither intervenes in the management of B or P nor exerts any influence on B or P to buy the shares or back the share price.

(5) Shares held by a credit institution or investment firm in its trading book are disregarded, provided that—

    (a) the shares represent no more than 5% of the total voting power in B or P; and

    (b) the credit institution or investment firm ensures that the voting power is not used to intervene in the management of B or P.

(6) Shares held by a credit institution or an investment firm are disregarded, provided that—

    (a) the shares are held as a result of performing the investment services and activities of—

        (i) underwriting shares; or

        (ii) placing shares on a firm commitment basis in accordance with Annex I, section A.6 of the markets in financial instruments directive; and

    (b) the credit institution or investment firm—

        (i) does not exercise voting power represented by the shares or otherwise intervene in the management of the issuer; and

        (ii) retains the holding for a period of less than one year.

(7) Where a management company (as defined in Article 1a.2 of the UCITS directive) and its parent undertaking both hold shares or voting power, each may disregard holdings of the other, provided that each exercises its voting power independently of the other.

(8) But subsection (7) does not apply if the management company —

    (a) manages holdings for its parent undertaking or an undertaking in respect of which the parent undertaking is a controller;

    (b) has no discretion to exercise the voting power attached to such holdings; and

    (c) may only exercise the voting power in relation to such holdings under direct or indirect instruction from —

        (i) its parent undertaking; or

        (ii) an undertaking in respect of which of the parent undertaking is a controller.

(9) Where an investment firm and its parent undertaking both hold shares or voting power, the parent undertaking may disregard holdings managed by the investment firm on a client by client basis and the investment firm may disregard holdings of the parent undertaking, provided that the investment firm—

    (a) has permission to provide portfolio management;

    (b) exercises its voting power independently from the parent undertaking; and

    (c) may only exercise the voting power under instructions given in writing, or has appropriate mechanisms in place for ensuring that individual portfolio management services are conducted independently of any other services.

(10) In this section "credit institution" means—

    (a) a credit institution authorised under the banking consolidation directive; or

    (b) an institution which would satisfy the requirements for authorisation as a credit institution under that directive if it had its registered office (or if it does not have a registered office, its head office) in an EEA State.]

423.—Manager

(1) In this Act, except in relation to a unit trust scheme or a registered friendly society, "manager" means an employee who—

    (a) under the immediate authority of his employer is responsible, either alone or jointly with one or more other persons, for the conduct of his employer's business; or

      (b) under the immediate authority of his employer or of a person who is a manager by virtue of paragraph (a) exercises managerial functions or is responsible for maintaining accounts or other records of his employer.

(2) If the employer is not an individual, references in subsection (1) to the authority of the employer are references to the authority—

      (a) in the case of a body corporate, of the directors;

      (b) in the case of a partnership, of the partners; and

      (c) in the case of an unincorporated association, of its officers or the members of its governing body.

(3) "Manager", in relation to a body corporate, means a person (other than an employee of the body) who is appointed by the body to manage any part of its business and includes an employee of the body corporate (other than the chief executive) who, under the immediate authority of a director or chief executive of the body corporate, exercises managerial functions or is responsible for maintaining accounts or other records of the body corporate.

424.—Insurance

(1) In this Act, references to—

      (a) contracts of insurance,

      (b) reinsurance,

      (c) contracts of long-term insurance,

      (d) contracts of general insurance, are to be read with section 22 and Schedule 2.

(2) In this Act "policy" and "policyholder", in relation to a contract of insurance, have such meaning as the Treasury may by order specify.

(3) The law applicable to a contract of insurance, the effecting of which constitutes the carrying on of a regulated activity, is to be determined, if it is of a prescribed description, in accordance with regulations made by the Treasury.

[424A.—Investment firm]

[(1) In this Act, "investment firm" has the meaning given in Article 4.1.1 of the markets in financial instruments directive.

(2) Subsection (1) is subject to subsections (3) to (5).

[(3) References in this Act to an "investment firm" include references to a person who would be an investment firm (within the meaning of Article 4.1.1 of the markets in financial instruments directive) if—

      (a) in the case of a body corporate, his registered office or, if he has no registered office, his head office, and

      (b) in the case of a person other than a body corporate, his head office, were in an EEA State.]

(4) But subsection (3) does not apply if the person in question is one to whom the markets in financial instruments directive would not apply by virtue of Article 2 of that directive.

(5) References in this Act to an "investment firm" do not include references to—

    (a) a person to whom the markets in financial instruments directive does not apply by virtue of Article 2 of the directive; or

    (b) a person whose home Member State (within the meaning of Article 4.1.20 of the markets in financial instruments directive) is an EEA State and to whom, by reason of the fact that the State has given effect to Article 3 of that directive, that directive does not apply by virtue of that Article.]

425.—Expressions relating to authorisation elsewhere in the single market

(1) In this Act—

    (a) ["banking consolidation directive", ["life assurance consolidation directive",] "EEA authorisation", "EEA firm", "EEA right", "EEA State",... "first non-life insurance directive", "insurance directives", ["reinsurance directive",] "insurance mediation directive",... ["markets in financial instruments directive",] "single market directives" [, "tied agent"] and "UCITS directive" have the meaning given in Schedule 3; and

    (b)] "home state regulator", in relation to an EEA firm, has the meaning given in Schedule 3.

(2) In this Act—

    (a) "home state authorisation" has the meaning given in Schedule 4;

    (b) "Treaty firm" has the meaning given in Schedule 4; and

    (c) "home state regulator", in relation to a Treaty firm, has the meaning given in Schedule 4.

APPENDIX II

European Union Directive On Insider Dealing and Market Manipulation (Market Abuse)

▼<u>B</u>   **DIRECTIVE 2003/6/EC OF THE EUROPEAN PARLIAMENT
AND OF THE COUNCIL**

of 28 January 2003

on insider dealing and market manipulation (market abuse)

(OJ L 96, 12.4.2003, p. 16)

Amended by:

	No	page	Official Journal date
	L 81	42	20.3.2008

▼<u>M1</u>   **DIRECTIVE 2008/26/EC OF THE EUROPEAN PARLIAMENT
AND OF THE COUNCIL OF 11 MARCH 2008**

▼<u>B</u>   **DIRECTIVE 2003/6/EC OF THE EUROPEAN PARLIAMENT
AND OF THE COUNCIL**

of 28 January 2003

on insider dealing and market manipulation (market abuse)

THE EUROPEAN PARLIAMENT AND THE COUNCIL OF THE
EUROPEAN UNION,

Having regard to the Treaty establishing the European Community, and in particular Article 95 thereof,

Having regard to the proposal from the Commission([1]),

Having regard to the opinion of the European Economic and Social Committee([2]),

Having regard to the opinion of the European Central Bank([3]),

---

[1] OJ C 240 E, 28.8.2001, p. 265.
[2] OJ C 80, 3.4.2002, p. 61.
[3] OJ C 24, 26.1.2002, p. 8.

Acting in accordance with the procedure laid down in Article 251(^{4}),

Whereas:

(1) A genuine Single Market for financial services is crucial for economic growth and job creation in the Community.

(2) An integrated and efficient financial market requires market integrity. The smooth functioning of securities markets and public confidence in markets are prerequisites for economic growth and wealth. Market abuse harms the integrity of financial markets and public confidence in securities and derivatives.

(3) The Commission Communication of 11 May 1999 entitled "Implementing the framework for financial markets: action plan" identifies a series of actions that are needed in order to complete the single market for financial services. The Lisbon European Council of April 2000 called for the implementation of that action plan by 2005. The action plan stresses the need to draw up a Directive against market manipulation.

(4) At its meeting on 17 July 2000, the Council set up the Committee of Wise Men on the Regulation of European Securities Markets. In its final report, the Committee of Wise Men proposed the introduction of new legislative techniques based on a four-level approach, namely framework principles, implementing measures, cooperation and enforcement. Level 1, the Directive, should confine itself to broad general "framework" principles while Level 2 should contain technical implementing measures to be adopted by the Commission with the assistance of a committee.

(5) The Resolution adopted by the Stockholm European Council of March 2001 endorsed the final report of the Committee of Wise Men and the proposed four-level approach to make the regulatory process for Community securities legislation more efficient and transparent.

(6) The Resolution of the European Parliament of 5 February 2002 on the implementation of financial services legislation also endorsed the Committee of Wise Men's report, on the basis of the solemn declaration made before Parliament the same day by the Commission and the letter of 2 October 2001 addressed by the Internal Market Commissioner to the chairman of Parliament's Committee on Economic and Monetary Affairs with regard to the safeguards for the European Parliament's role in this process.

(7) The measures necessary for the implementation of this Directive should be adopted in accordance with Council Decision 1999/468/EC of 28 June 1999 laying down the procedures for the exercise of implementing powers conferred on the Commission(^{5}).

(8) According to the Stockholm European Council, Level 2 implementing measures should be used more frequently, to ensure that technical provisions can be kept up to date with market and supervisory developments, and deadlines should be set for all stages of Level 2 work.

(9) The European Parliament should be given a period of three months from the first transmission of draft implementing measures to allow it to examine them and to give its opinion. However, in urgent and duly justified cases, this period may be shortened. If, within that period, a resolution is passed by the European Parliament, the Commission should re-examine the draft measures.

(10) New financial and technical developments enhance the incentives, means and opportunities for market abuse: through new products, new technologies, increasing cross-border activities and the Internet.

(11) The existing Community legal framework to protect market integrity is incomplete. Legal requirements vary from one Member State to another, leaving economic actors often uncertain over concepts,

---

^{4} Opinion of the European Parliament of 14 March 2002 (not yet published in the Official Journal), Council Common Position of 19 July 2002 (OJ C 228 E, 25.9.2002, p. 19) and Decision of the European Parliament of 24 October 2002 (not yet published in the Official Journal).

^{5} OJ L 184 17.7.1999, p. 23.

definitions and enforcement. In some Member States there is no legislation addressing the issues of price manipulation and the dissemination of misleading information.

(12) Market abuse consists of insider dealing and market manipulation. The objective of legislation against insider dealing is the same as that of legislation against market manipulation: to ensure the integrity of Community financial markets and to enhance investor confidence in those markets. It is therefore advisable to adopt combined rules to combat both insider dealing and market manipulation. A single Directive will ensure throughout the Community the same framework for allocation of responsibilities, enforcement and cooperation.

(13) Given the changes in financial markets and in Community legislation since the adoption of Council Directive 89/592/EEC of 13 November 1989 coordinating regulations on insider dealing([6]), that Directive should now be replaced, to ensure consistency with legislation against market manipulation. A new Directive is also needed to avoid loopholes in Community legislation which could be used for wrongful conduct and which would undermine public confidence and therefore prejudice the smooth functioning of the markets.

(14) This Directive meets the concerns expressed by the Member States following the terrorist attacks on 11 September 2001 as regards the fight against financing terrorist activities.

(15) Insider dealing and market manipulation prevent full and proper market transparency, which is a prerequisite for trading for all economic actors in integrated financial markets.

(16) Inside information is any information of a precise nature which has not been made public, relating, directly or indirectly, to one or more issuers of financial instruments or to one or more financial instruments. Information which could have a significant effect on the evolution and forming of the prices of a regulated market as such could be considered as information which indirectly relates to one or more issuers of financial instruments or to one or more related derivative financial instruments.

(17) As regards insider dealing, account should be taken of cases where inside information originates not from a profession or function but from criminal activities, the preparation or execution of which could have a significant effect on the prices of one or more financial instruments or on price formation in the regulated market as such.

(18) Use of inside information can consist in the acquisition or disposal of financial instruments by a person who knows, or ought to have known, that the information possessed is inside information. In this respect, the competent authorities should consider what a normal and reasonable person would know or should have known in the circumstances. Moreover, the mere fact that market-makers, bodies authorised to act as counterparties, or persons authorised to execute orders on behalf of third parties with inside information confine themselves, in the first two cases, to pursuing their legitimate business of buying or selling financial instruments or, in the last case, to carrying out an order dutifully, should not in itself be deemed to constitute use of such inside information.

(19) Member States should tackle the practice known as "front running", including "front running" in commodity derivatives, where it constitutes market abuse under the definitions contained in this Directive.

(20) A person who enters into transactions or issues orders to trade which are constitutive of market manipulation may be able to establish that his reasons for entering into such transactions or issuing orders to trade were legitimate and that the transactions and orders to trade were in conformity with accepted practice on the regulated market concerned. A sanction could still be imposed if the competent authority established that there was another, illegitimate, reason behind these transactions or orders to trade.

(21) The competent authority may issue guidance on matters covered by this Directive, e.g. definition of inside information in relation to derivatives on commodities or implementation of the definition of

---

[6] OJ L 334, 18.11.1989, p. 30.

accepted market practices relating to the definition of market manipulation. This guidance should be in conformity with the provisions of the Directive and the implementing measures adopted in accordance with the comitology procedure.

(22) Member States should be able to choose the most appropriate way to regulate persons producing or disseminating research concerning financial instruments or issuers of financial instruments or persons producing or disseminating other information recommending or suggesting investment strategy, including appropriate mechanisms for self-regulation, which should be notified to the Commission.

(23) Posting of inside information by issuers on their internet sites should be in accordance with the rules on transfer of personal data to third countries as laid down in Directive 95/46/EC of the European Parliament and of the Council of 24 October 1995 on the protection of individuals with regard to the processing of personal data and on the movement of such data(7).

(24) Prompt and fair disclosure of information to the public enhances market integrity, whereas selective disclosure by issuers can lead to a loss of investor confidence in the integrity of financial markets. Professional economic actors should contribute to market integrity by various means. Such measures could include, for instance, the creation of "grey lists", the application of "window trading" to sensitive categories of personnel, the application of internal codes of conduct and the establishment of "Chinese walls". Such preventive measures may contribute to combating market abuse only if they are enforced with determination and are dutifully controlled. Adequate enforcement control would imply for instance the designation of compliance officers within the bodies concerned and periodic checks conducted by independent auditors.

(25) Modern communication methods make it possible for financial market professionals and private investors to have more equal access to financial information, but also increase the risk of the spread of false or misleading information.

(26) Greater transparency of transactions conducted by persons discharging managerial responsibilities within issuers and, where applicable, persons closely associated with them, constitutes a preventive measure against market abuse. The publication of those transactions on at least an individual basis can also be a highly valuable source of information to investors.

(27) Market operators should contribute to the prevention of market abuse and adopt structural provisions aimed at preventing and detecting market manipulation practices. Such provisions may include requirements concerning transparency of transactions concluded, total disclosure of price-regularisation agreements, a fair system of order pairing, introduction of an effective atypical-order detection scheme, sufficiently robust financial instrument reference price-fixing schemes and clarity of rules on the suspension of transactions.

(28) This Directive should be interpreted, and implemented by Member States, in a manner consistent with the requirements for effective regulation in order to protect the interests of holders of transferable securities carrying voting rights in a company (or which may carry such rights as a consequence of the exercise of rights or conversion) when the company is subject to a public take-over bid or other proposed change of control. In particular, this Directive does not in any way prevent a Member State from putting or having in place such measures as it sees fit for these purposes.

(29) Having access to inside information relating to another company and using it in the context of a public take-over bid for the purpose of gaining control of that company or proposing a merger with that company should not in itself be deemed to constitute insider dealing.

(30) Since the acquisition or disposal of financial instruments necessarily involves a prior decision to acquire or dispose taken by the person who undertakes one or other of these operations, the carrying out

---

7 OJ L 281, 23.11.1995, p. 31.

of this acquisition or disposal should not be deemed in itself to constitute the use of inside information.

(31) Research and estimates developed from publicly available data should not be regarded as inside information and, therefore, any transaction carried out on the basis of such research or estimates should not be deemed in itself to constitute insider dealing within the meaning of this Directive.

(32) Member States and the European System of Central Banks, national central banks or any other officially designated body, or any person acting on their behalf, should not be restricted in carrying out monetary, exchange-rate or public debt management policy.

(33) Stabilisation of financial instruments or trading in own shares in buy-back programmes can be legitimate, in certain circumstances, for economic reasons and should not, therefore, in themselves be regarded as market abuse. Common standards should be developed to provide practical guidance.

(34) The widening scope of financial markets, the rapid change and the range of new products and developments require a wide application of this Directive to financial instruments and techniques involved, in order to guarantee the integrity of Community financial markets.

(35) Establishing a level playing field in Community financial markets requires wide geographical application of the provisions covered by this Directive. As regards derivative instruments not admitted to trading but falling within the scope of this Directive, each Member State should be competent to sanction actions carried out on its territory or abroad which concern underlying financial instruments admitted to trading on a regulated market situated or operating within its territory or for which a request for admission to trading on such a regulated market has been made. Each Member State should also be competent to sanction actions carried out on its territory which concern underlying financial instruments admitted to trading on a regulated market in a Member State or for which a request for admission to trading on such a market has been made.

(36) A variety of competent authorities in Member States, having different responsibilities, may create confusion among economic actors. A single competent authority should be designated in each Member State to assume at least final responsibility for supervising compliance with the provisions adopted pursuant to this Directive, as well as international collaboration. Such an authority should be of an administrative nature guaranteeing its independence of economic actors and avoiding conflicts of interest. In accordance with national law, Member States should ensure appropriate financing of the competent authority. That authority should have adequate arrangements for consultation concerning possible changes in national legislation such as a consultative committee composed of representatives of issuers, financial services providers and consumers, so as to be fully informed of their views and concerns.

(37) A common minimum set of effective tools and powers for the competent authority of each Member State will guarantee supervisory effectiveness. Market undertakings and all economic actors should also contribute at their level to market integrity. In this sense, the designation of a single competent authority for market abuse does not exclude collaboration links or delegation under the responsibility of the competent authority, between that authority and market undertakings with a view to guaranteeing efficient supervision of compliance with the provisions adopted pursuant to this Directive.

(38) In order to ensure that a Community framework against market abuse is sufficient, any infringement of the prohibitions or requirements laid down pursuant to this Directive will have to be promptly detected and sanctioned. To this end, sanctions should be sufficiently dissuasive and proportionate to the gravity of the infringement and to the gains realised and should be consistently applied.

(39) Member States should remain alert, in determining the administrative measures and sanctions, to the need to ensure a degree of uniformity of regulation from one Member State to another.

(40) Increasing cross-border activities require improved cooperation and a comprehensive set of provisions for the exchange of information between national competent authorities. The organisation of supervision and of investigatory powers in each Member State should not hinder cooperation between the competent national authorities.

(41) Since the objective of the proposed action, namely to prevent market abuse in the form of insider dealing and market manipulation, cannot be sufficiently achieved by the Member States and can therefore, by reason of the scale and effects of the measures, be better achieved at Community level, the Community may adopt measures, in accordance with the principle of subsidiarity as set out in Article of the Treaty. In accordance with the principle of proportionality, as set out in that Article, this Directive does not go beyond what is necessary in order to achieve that objective.

(42) Technical guidance and implementing measures for the rules laid down in this Directive may from time to time be necessary to take account of new developments on financial markets. The Commission should accordingly be empowered to adopt implementing measures, provided that these do not modify the essential elements of this Directive and the Commission acts according to the principles set out in this Directive, after consulting the European Securities Committee established by Commission Decision 2001/528/EC([8]).

(43) In exercising its implementing powers in accordance with this Directive, the Commission should respect the following principles:

— the need to ensure confidence in financial markets among investors by promoting high standards of transparency in financial markets,
— the need to provide investors with a wide range of competing investments and a level of disclosure and protection tailored to their circumstances,
— the need to ensure that independent regulatory authorities enforce the rules consistently, especially as regards the fight against economic crime,
— the need for high levels of transparency and consultation with all market participants and with the European Parliament and the Council,
— the need to encourage innovation in financial markets if they are to be dynamic and efficient,
— the need to ensure market integrity by close and reactive monitoring of financial innovation,
— the importance of reducing the cost of, and increasing access to, capital,
— the balance of costs and benefits to market participants on a long-term basis (including small and medium-sized businesses and small investors) in any implementing measures,
— the need to foster the international competitiveness of EU financial markets without prejudice to a much-needed extension of international cooperation,
— the need to achieve a level playing field for all market participants by establishing EU-wide regulations every time it is appropriate,
— the need to respect differences in national markets where these do not unduly impinge on the coherence of the single market,
— the need to ensure coherence with other Community legislation in this area, as imbalances in information and a lack of transparency may jeopardise the operation of the markets and above all harm consumers and small investors.

(44) This Directive respects the fundamental rights and observes the principles recognised in particular by the Charter of Fundamental Rights of the European Union and in particular by Article 11 thereof and Article 10 of the European Convention on Human Rights. In this regard, this Directive does not in any way prevent Member States from applying their constitutional rules relating to freedom of the press and freedom of expression in the media,

---

[8] OJ L 191, 13.7.2001, p. 45.

HAVE ADOPTED THIS DIRECTIVE:

Article 1

For the purposes of this Directive:

1. "Inside information" shall mean information of a precise nature which has not been made public, relating, directly or indirectly, to one or more issuers of financial instruments or to one or more financial instruments and which, if it were made public, would be likely to have a significant effect on the prices of those financial instruments or on the price of related derivative financial instruments.

   In relation to derivatives on commodities, "inside information" shall mean information of a precise nature which has not been made public, relating, directly or indirectly, to one or more such derivatives and which users of markets on which such derivatives are traded would expect to receive in accordance with accepted market practices on those markets.

   For persons charged with the execution of orders concerning financial instruments, "inside information" shall also mean information conveyed by a client and related to the client's pending orders, which is of a precise nature, which relates directly or indirectly to one or more issuers of financial instruments or to one or more financial instruments, and which, if it were made public, would be likely to have a significant effect on the prices of those financial instruments or on the price of related derivative financial instruments.

2. "Market manipulation" shall mean:
   (a) transactions or orders to trade:
       — which give, or are likely to give, false or misleading signals as to the supply of, demand for or price of financial instruments, or
       — which secure, by a person, or persons acting in collaboration, the price of one or several financial instruments at an abnormal or artificial level,

   unless the person who entered into the transactions or issued the orders to trade establishes that his reasons for so doing are legitimate and that these transactions or orders to trade conform to accepted market practices on the regulated market concerned;
   (b) transactions or orders to trade which employ fictitious devices or any other form of deception or contrivance;
   (c) dissemination of information through the media, including the Internet, or by any other means, which gives, or is likely to give, false or misleading signals as to financial instruments, including the dissemination of rumours and false or misleading news, where the person who made the dissemination knew, or ought to have known, that the information was false or misleading. In respect of journalists when they act in their professional capacity such dissemination of information is to be assessed, without prejudice to Article 11, taking into account the rules governing their profession, unless those persons derive, directly or indirectly, an advantage or profits from the dissemination of the information in question.

   In particular, the following instances are derived from the core definition given in points (a), (b) and (c) above:
   — conduct by a person, or persons acting in collaboration, to secure a dominant position over the supply of or demand for a financial instrument which has the effect of fixing, directly or indirectly, purchase or sale prices or creating other unfair trading conditions,
   — the buying or selling of financial instruments at the close of the market with the effect of misleading investors acting on the basis of closing prices,
   — taking advantage of occasional or regular access to the traditional or electronic media by voicing an opinion about a financial instrument (or indirectly about its issuer) while having previously taken positions on that financial instrument and profiting subsequently from the impact of the

opinions voiced on the price of that instrument, without having simultaneously disclosed that conflict of interest to the public in a proper and effective way.

The definitions of market manipulation shall be adapted so as to ensure that new patterns of activity that in practice constitute market manipulation can be included.

3. "Financial instrument" shall mean:
   — transferable securities as defined in Council Directive 93/22/EEC of 10 May 1993 on invest-ment services in the securities field([9]),
   — units in collective investment undertakings,
   — money-market instruments,
   — financial-futures contracts, including equivalent cash-settled instruments,
   — forward interest-rate agreements,
   — interest-rate, currency and equity swaps,
   — options to acquire or dispose of any instrument falling into these categories, including equiva-lent cash-settled instruments. This category includes in particular options on currency and on interest rates,
   — derivatives on commodities,
   — any other instrument admitted to trading on a regulated market in a Member State or for which a request for admission to trading on such a market has been made.
4. "Regulated market" shall mean a market as defined by Article 1(13) of Directive 93/22/EEC.
5. "Accepted market practices" shall mean practices that are reasonably expected in one or more finan-cial markets and are accepted by the competent authority in accordance with guidelines adopted by the Commission in accordance with the regulatory procedure laid down in Article 17(2a).
6. "Person" shall mean any natural or legal person.
7. "Competent authority" shall mean the competent authority designated in accordance with Article 11.

In order to take account of developments on financial markets and to ensure uniform application of this Directive in the Community, the Commission, shall adopt implementing measures concerning points 1, 2 and 3 of this Article. Those measures, designed to amend non-essential elements of this Directive by supplementing it, shall be adopted in accordance with the regulatory procedure with scrutiny referred to in Article 17(2a).

Article 2

1. Member States shall prohibit any person referred to in the second subparagraph who possesses inside information from using that information by acquiring or disposing of, or by trying to acquire or dispose of, for his own account or for the account of a third party, either directly or indirectly, financial instruments to which that information relates.

The first subparagraph shall apply to any person who possesses that information:

(a) by virtue of his membership of the administrative, management or supervisory bodies of the issuer; or
(b) by virtue of his holding in the capital of the issuer; or
(c) by virtue of his having access to the information through the exercise of his employment, profession or duties; or
(d) by virtue of his criminal activities.

2. Where the person referred to in paragraph 1 is a legal person, the prohibition laid down in that paragraph shall also apply to the natural persons who take part in the decision to carry out the transaction for the account of the legal person concerned.

---

[9] OJ l 141, 11.6.1993, p. 27. Directive as last amended by European Parliament and Council Directive 2000/64/EC (0J L 290, 17.11.2000, p. 27).

3. This Article shall not apply to transactions conducted in the discharge of an obligation that has become due to acquire or dispose of financial instruments where that obligation results from an agreement concluded before the person concerned possessed inside information.

Article 3

Member States shall prohibit any person subject to the prohibition laid down in Article 2 from:

(a) disclosing inside information to any other person unless such disclosure is made in the normal course of the exercise of his employment, profession or duties;

(b) recommending or inducing another person, on the basis of inside information, to acquire or dispose of financial instruments to which that information relates.

Article 4

Member States shall ensure that Articles 2 and 3 also apply to any person, other than the persons referred to in those Articles, who possesses inside information while that person knows, or ought to have known, that it is inside information.

Article 5

Member States shall prohibit any person from engaging in market manipulation.

Article 6

1. Member States shall ensure that issuers of financial instruments inform the public as soon as possible of inside information which directly concerns the said issuers.

Without prejudice to any measures taken to comply with the provisions of the first subparagraph, Member States shall ensure that issuers, for an appropriate period, post on their Internet sites all inside information that they are required to disclose publicly.

2. An issuer may under his own responsibility delay the public disclosure of inside information, as referred to in paragraph 1, such as not to prejudice his legitimate interests provided that such omission would not be likely to mislead the public and provided that the issuer is able to ensure the confidentiality of that information. Member States may require that an issuer shall without delay inform the competent authority of the decision to delay the public disclosure of inside information.

3. Member States shall require that, whenever an issuer, or a person acting on his behalf or for his account, discloses any inside information to any third party in the normal exercise of his employment, profession or duties, as referred to in Article 3(a), he must make complete and effective public disclosure of that information, simultaneously in the case of an intentional disclosure and promptly in the case of a non-intentional disclosure.

The provisions of the first subparagraph shall not apply if the person receiving the information owes a duty of confidentiality, regardless of whether such duty is based on a law, on regulations, on articles of association or on a contract.

Member States shall require that issuers, or persons acting on their behalf or for their account, draw up a list of those persons working for them, under a contract of employment or otherwise, who have access to inside information. Issuers and persons acting on their behalf or for their account shall regularly update this list and transmit it to the competent authority whenever the latter requests it.

4. Persons discharging managerial responsibilities within an issuer of financial instruments and, where applicable, persons closely associated with them, shall, at least, notify to the competent authority the existence of transactions conducted on their own account relating to shares of the said issuer, or to derivatives or other financial instruments linked to them. Member States shall ensure that public access to information concerning such transactions, on at least an individual basis, is readily available as soon as possible.

5. Member States shall ensure that there is appropriate regulation in place to ensure that persons who produce or disseminate research concerning financial instruments or issuers of financial instruments and persons who produce or disseminate other information recommending or suggesting investment strategy, intended for distribution channels or for the public, take reasonable care to ensure that such information is fairly presented and disclose their interests or indicate conflicts of interest concerning the financial instruments to which that information relates. Details of such regulation shall be notified to the Commission.

6. Member States shall ensure that market operators adopt structural provisions aimed at preventing and detecting market manipulation practices.

7. With a view to ensuring compliance with paragraphs 1 to 5, the competent authority may take all necessary measures to ensure that the public is correctly informed.

8. Public institutions disseminating statistics liable to have a significant effect on financial markets shall disseminate them in a fair and transparent way.

9. Member States shall require that any person professionally arranging transactions in financial instruments who reasonably suspects that a transaction might constitute insider dealing or market manipulation shall notify the competent authority without delay.

10. In order to take account of technical developments on financial markets and to ensure uniform application of this Directive, the Commission shall adopt, implementing measures concerning:

— the technical modalities for appropriate public disclosure of inside information as referred to in paragraphs 1 and 3,
— the technical modalities for delaying the public disclosure of inside information as referred to in paragraph 2,
— the technical modalities designed to favour a common approach in the implementation of the second sentence of paragraph 2,
— the conditions under which issuers, or entities acting on their behalf, are to draw up a list of those persons working for them and having access to inside information, as referred to in paragraph 3, together with the conditions under which such lists are to be updated,
— the categories of persons who are subject to a duty of disclosure as referred to in paragraph 4 and the characteristics of a transaction, including its size, which trigger that duty, and the technical arrangements for disclosure to the competent authority,
— technical arrangements, for the various categories of person referred to in paragraph 5, for fair presentation of research and other information recommending investment strategy and for disclosure of particular interests or conflicts of interest as referred to in paragraph 5. Such arrangements shall take into account the rules, including self-regulation, governing the profession of journalist,
— technical arrangements governing notification to the competent authority by the persons referred to in paragraph 9.

Those measures, designed to amend non-essential elements of this Directive by supplementing it, shall be adopted in accordance with the regulatory procedure with scrutiny referred to in Article 17(2a).

Article 7

This Directive shall not apply to transactions carried out in pursuit of monetary, exchange-rate or public debt-management policy by a Member State, by the European System of Central Banks, by a national central bank or by any other officially designated body, or by any person acting on their behalf. Member States may extend this exemption to their federated States or similar local authorities in respect of the management of their public debt.

Article 8

The prohibitions provided for in this Directive shall not apply to trading in own shares in "buy-back" programmes or to the stabilisation of a financial instrument provided such trading is carried out in accordance with implementing measures. Those measures, designed to amend non-essential elements of this Directive by supplementing it, shall be adopted in accordance with the regulatory procedure with scrutiny referred to in Article 17(2a).

Article 9

This Directive shall apply to any financial instrument admitted to trading on a regulated market in at least one Member State, or for which a request for admission to trading on such a market has been made, irrespective of whether or not the transaction itself actually takes place on that market.

Articles 2, 3 and 4 shall also apply to any financial instrument not admitted to trading on a regulated market in a Member State, but whose value depends on a financial instrument as referred to in paragraph 1.

Article 6(1) to (3) shall not apply to issuers who have not requested or approved admission of their financial instruments to trading on a regulated market in a Member State.

Article 10

Each Member State shall apply the prohibitions and requirements provided for in this Directive to:

(a) actions carried out on its territory or abroad concerning financial instruments that are admitted to trading on a regulated market situated or operating within its territory or for which a request for admission to trading on such market has been made;

(b) actions carried out on its territory concerning financial instruments that are admitted to trading on a regulated market in a Member State or for which a request for admission to trading on such market has been made.

Article 11

Without prejudice to the competences of the judicial authorities, each Member State shall designate a single administrative authority competent to ensure that the provisions adopted pursuant to this Directive are applied.

Member States shall establish effective consultative arrangements and procedures with market participants concerning possible changes in national legislation. These arrangements may include consultative committees within each competent authority, the membership of which should reflect as far as possible the diversity of market participants, be they issuers, providers of financial services or consumers.

Article 12

1. The competent authority shall be given all supervisory and investigatory powers that are necessary for the exercise of its functions. It shall exercise such powers:

    (a) directly; or
    (b) in collaboration with other authorities or with the market undertakings; or
    (c) under its responsibility by delegation to such authorities or to the market undertakings; or
    (d) by application to the competent judicial authorities.

2. Without prejudice to Article 6(7), the powers referred to in paragraph 1 of this Article shall be exercised in conformity with national law and shall include at least the right to:

    (a) have access to any document in any form whatsoever, and to receive a copy of it;
    (b) demand information from any person, including those who are successively involved in the transmission of orders or conduct of the operations concerned, as well as their principals, and if necessary, to summon and hear any such person;
    (c) carry out on-site inspections;
    (d) require existing telephone and existing data traffic records;
    (e) require the cessation of any practice that is contrary to the provisions adopted in the implementation of this Directive;
    (f) suspend trading of the financial instruments concerned;

(g) request the freezing and/or sequestration of assets;

(h) request temporary prohibition of professional activity.

3. This Article shall be without prejudice to national legal provisions on professional secrecy.

Article 13

The obligation of professional secrecy shall apply to all persons who work or who have worked for the competent authority or for any authority or market undertaking to whom the competent authority has delegated its powers, including auditors and experts instructed by the competent authority. Information covered by professional secrecy may not be disclosed to any other person or authority except by virtue of provisions laid down by law.

Article 14

1. Without prejudice to the right of Member States to impose criminal sanctions, Member States shall ensure, in conformity with their national law, that the appropriate administrative measures can be taken or administrative sanctions be imposed against the persons responsible where the provisions adopted in the implementation of this Directive have not been complied with. Member States shall ensure that these measures are effective, proportionate and dissuasive.

2. In accordance with the procedure laid down in Article 17(2), the Commission shall, for information, draw up a list of the administrative measures and sanctions referred to in paragraph 1.

3. Member States shall determine the sanctions to be applied for failure to cooperate in an investigation covered by Article 12.

4. Member States shall provide that the competent authority may disclose to the public every measure or sanction that will be imposed for infringement of the provisions adopted in the implementation of this Directive, unless such disclosure would seriously jeopardise the financial markets or cause disproportionate damage to the parties involved.

Article 15

Member States shall ensure that an appeal may be brought before a court against the decisions taken by the competent authority.

Article 16

1. Competent authorities shall cooperate with each other whenever necessary for the purpose of carrying out their duties, making use of their powers whether set out in this Directive or in national law. Competent authorities shall render assistance to competent authorities of other Member States. In particular, they shall exchange information and cooperate in investigation activities.

2. Competent authorities shall, on request, immediately supply any information required for the purpose referred to in paragraph 1. Where necessary, the competent authorities receiving any such request shall immediately take the necessary measures in order to gather the required information. If the requested competent authority is not able to supply the required information immediately, it shall notify the requesting competent authority of the reasons. Information thus supplied shall be covered by the obligation of professional secrecy to which the persons employed or formerly employed by the competent authorities receiving the information are subject.

The competent authorities may refuse to act on a request for information where:

— communication might adversely affect the sovereignty, security or public policy of the Member State addressed,

— judicial proceedings have already been initiated in respect of the same actions and against the same persons before the authorities of the Member State addressed, or

— where a final judgment has already been delivered in relation to such persons for the same actions in the Member State addressed.

In any such case, they shall notify the requesting competent authority accordingly, providing as detailed information as possible on those proceedings or the judgment.

Without prejudice to Article 226 of the Treaty, a competent authority whose request for information is not acted upon within a reasonable time or whose request for information is rejected may bring that non-compliance to the attention of the Committee of European Securities Regulators, where discussion will take place in order to reach a rapid and effective solution.

Without prejudice to the obligations to which they are subject in judicial proceedings under criminal law, the competent authorities which receive information pursuant to paragraph 1 may use it only for the exercise of their functions within the scope of this Directive and in the context of administrative or judicial proceedings specifically related to the exercise of those functions. However, where the competent authority communicating information consents thereto, the authority receiving the information may use it for other purposes or forward it to other States' competent authorities.

3. Where a competent authority is convinced that acts contrary to the provisions of this Directive are being, or have been, carried out on the territory of another Member State or that acts are affecting financial instruments traded on a regulated market situated in another

Member State, it shall give notice of that fact in as specific a manner as possible to the competent authority of the other Member State. The competent authority of the other Member

State shall take appropriate action. It shall inform the notifying competent authority of the outcome and, so far as possible, of significant interim developments. This paragraph shall not prejudice the competences of the competent authority that has forwarded the information. The competent authorities of the various Member States that are competent for the purposes of Article 10 shall consult each other on the proposed follow-up to their action.

4. A competent authority of one Member State may request that an investigation be carried out by the competent authority of another Member State, on the latter's territory.

It may further request that members of its own personnel be allowed to accompany the personnel of the competent authority of that other Member State during the course of the investigation.

The investigation shall, however, be subject throughout to the overall control of the Member State on whose territory it is conducted.

The competent authorities may refuse to act on a request for an investigation to be conducted as provided for in the first subparagraph, or on a request for its personnel to be accompanied by personnel of the competent authority of another Member State as provided for in the second subparagraph, where such an investigation might adversely affect the sovereignty, security or public policy of the State addressed, or where judicial proceedings have already been initiated in respect of the same actions and against the same persons before the authorities of the State addressed or where a final judgment has already been delivered in relation to such persons for the same actions in the State addressed. In such case, they shall notify the requesting competent authority accordingly, providing information, as detailed as possible, on those proceedings or judgment.

Without prejudice to the provisions of Article 226 of the Treaty, a competent authority whose application to open an inquiry or whose request for authorisation for its officials to accompany those of the other Member State's competent authority is not acted upon within a reasonable time or is rejected may bring that non-compliance to the attention of the Committee of European Securities Regulators, where discussion will take place in order to reach a rapid and effective solution.

5. In accordance with the regulatory procedure laid down in Article 17(2), the Commission shall adopt implementing measures on the working procedures for exchange of information and cross-border inspections as referred to in this Article.

Article 17

1. The Commission shall be assisted by the European Securities Committee instituted by Decision 2001/528/EC (hereinafter referred to as the "Committee").

2. Where reference is made to this paragraph, Articles 5 and 7 of Decision 1999/468/EC shall apply, having regard to the provisions of Article 8 thereof, provided that the implementing measures adopted according to this procedure do not modify the essential provisions of this Directive.

The period laid down in Article 5(6) of Decision 1999/468/EC shall be set at three months.

2a. Where reference is made to this paragraph, Article 5a(1) to (4) and Article 7 of Decision 1999/468/EC shall apply, having regard to the provisions of Article 8 thereof.

3. By 31 December 2010, and, thereafter, at least every three years, the Commission shall review the provisions concerning its implementing powers and present a report to the European Parliament and to the Council on the functioning of those powers. The report shall examine, in particular, the need for the Commission to propose amendments to this Directive in order to ensure the appropriate scope of the implementing powers conferred on the Commission. The conclusion as to whether or not amendment is necessary shall be accompanied by a detailed statement of reasons. If necessary, the report shall be accompanied by a legislative proposal to amend the provisions conferring implementing powers on the Commission.

Article 18

Member States shall bring into force the laws, regulations and administrative provisions necessary to comply with this Directive not later than 12 October 2004. They shall forthwith inform the Commission thereof.

When Member States adopt those measures, they shall contain a reference to this Directive or be accompanied by such a reference on the occasion of their official publication. Member States shall determine how such reference is to be made.

Article 19

Article 11 shall not prejudge the possibility for a Member State to make separate legal and administrative arrangements for overseas European territories for whose external relations that Member State is responsible.

Article 20

Directive 89/592/EEC and Article 68(1) and Article 81(1) of Directive 2001/34/EC of the European Parliament and of the Council of 28 May 2001 on the admission of securities to official stock exchange listing and on information to be published on those securities([10]) shall be repealed with effect from the date of entry into force of this Directive.

Article 21

This Directive shall enter into force on the day of its publication in the *Official Journal of the European Union*.

Article 22

This Directive is addressed to the Member States.

---

[10] OJ L 184, 6.7.20001, p. 1.

INDEX

Note 383(9) of FSMA (constitution does
order in market abuse cases) does
contemplate concurrent private claims

England price sensit & experts:
RBC Rights Issue [2015] EWHC 3433
at [50] and [30]. Good Law v Cabinet
[2021] EWHC 2091 at [31].

Misuse of non-public information:
- usually wil be breach of confid. obligation in contract:
                    Douglas v Hello! [2007] UKHL
                              21, at [275];
- where no   Racing Partnership
contract clause,   v Sports Info [2020] EWCA
breach of confid.   Civ 1300, [198]
Douglas v Hello! at [276]. ?
(or misuse of confid info?
- Racing Partnership, at [1].
- Ingredients of latter - Racing Partnership at [44-45];
Primary Group v RBS [2014] EWHC 1082,   [180(d)] + [246]
Branders; ECU v HSBC [493-495]

Fiduciary
- Lehtimaki v Cooper [2020] UKSC 33, at [46].
- not excluded: Citigroup at [278-279]
- no informed consent: Citigroup [293]; Law Common.
  Fiduciary Duties of Invest Intermed. [2014] EWLC
                                        350 [3.29]
- ownership of gains: Ensign House
                      [2023] EWHC 1563 [807-808]

Unconscionability   Yellowstone [2020] EWHC 2760,
- UK Dolare Finance v Yellowstone   at [69].
- Aust Debbie Yu 'Unconse in Eng + Oz' MULR
                                    2021 45.
        PCCC v Quantum Housing [2021] FCAFC
                               40, at [36-93]
        difference of opinion
        Pitt v Commissioner [2021] SASCA [152-67]
                            24

- ASIC v Westswift [2021] FCA 1584, at [1238]:
Ex post information may be used to check
the presumption that ex ante information
was price sensitive, similarly to A v AMF C-3...
at [54].

- two elements of Aust. defin f inside information
are broadly (i) p.ice sensitivity + (ii) non-availability

* Aust regulator is required to establish defendant's
actual or constructive knowledge of both elemen
s 1043A (1)(b) Corps Act.

- In Aust stat. prohib. on unconscion conduct
started ē s2A p Trade Practices Act in 1986. In
finance later specific prohib in s12CB ASIC Act.

- Wpac· actual on constructive knowledge relevent
+ onconsc:)2CC(i)(3)+(1) ASIC Act.   } of relrevant
                                                         in absence
- honesty + AFSL s912A (1)(a) Corps Act [COBS 2·1·1AR] also has on
- management p conflicts 912A (1)(aa) [SYSC 10·1·3 R] as fitted
- rep compliance (+ training 912A(1)(ca) + (f) [art 21L1)(b) m
- compliance ē laws 912A(1)(c) [SYSC 6·1·1 R]   org

- ESMA's Call for Er. ss 4 + 5 makes case for breaches p
insider dealing prohib + failure to manage conf
- Art 8 MAR + Art 2 in relation to general scu
(insider dealing)
Case C-302/20 A v AMF, at [43] on purpose.

- presumption without prejudice that a person in possess
of inside information uses it when transacting in relate
recital 24+25 mAR; Spector Photo C 45/08   instru
Unlike Australia, where required to est. knowledg per abo

- Exception for legit. trades p Market Maker : art 9(2)(a) MAR
- Art 7 MAR defin p inside info: 4 elements - (i) precise
- Precise not directional: Lafonta, at [38].   (ii) not public
    - But vague or general   (iii) relate to fin
        Vexcluded at [31]   or issuer
            - relevant factors: (iv) significant
                A v AMF [57] Case 628/13   effect
                          Lafonta, at [